Gábor Boros–Herman De Dijn–Martin Moors (eds)

The Concept of Love in 17th and 18th Century Philosophy

Authors: **Bartuschat, Wolfgang** University of Hamburg
Boros Gábor Eötvös University Budapest
Garrett, Aaron Boston University
James, Susan University of London
Jaquet, Chantal University of Paris I
Kambouchner, Denis Université Paris-I
Panthéon-Sorbonne
Klemme, Heiner F. Bergische Universität Wuppertal
Lemmens, Willem University of Antwerp
Moors, Martin Catholic University of Leuven
Schmal Dániel Hungarian Academy of Sciences
Schmaltz, Tad M. Duke University
Vassányi Miklós Catholic University of Leuven
Wilson, Catherine City University of New York

Editors: **Boros Gábor** Eötvös University Budapest
De Dijn, Herman Catholic University of Leuven
Moors, Martin Catholic University of Leuven

© Editors, 2007

The cover illustration is based on Giovanni Baglione's painting *"Heavenly Amor Defeats Earthly Amor"* (1602–1603).
bpk / Gemäldegalerie, Staatliche Museen zu Berlin / 381.
Photo: Jörg P. Anders

Special thanks for KVAB
(KONINKLIJKE VLAAMSE ACADEMIE VAN BELGIË VOOR WETENSCHAPPEN EN KUNSTEN;
Paleis der Academiën – Hertogsstraat 1 – B-1000 Brussel)

All rights reserved. Except in those cases expressly determined by law, no part of this publication may be multiplied, saved in an automated datafile or made public in any way whatsoever without the express prior written consent of the publishers.

Ordering information: All orders from Hungary should be sent to Eötvös University Press.
All orders from outside Hungary should be sent to Leuven University Press.

 www.eotvoskiado.hu

ISBN 978 963 463 955 8
Accountable publisher: Hunyady András, director of Eötvös University Press
Printed by Mester Nyomda

 www.kuleuven.be/upers/

Leuven University Press / Presses Universitaires de Louvain / Universitaire Pers Leuven
Minderbroedersstraat 4, B-3000 Leuven (Belgium)
ISBN 978 90 5867 651 1
D / 2007 / 1869 / 65
NUR : 736

Table of Contents

Introduction (*G. Boros, H. De Dijn, M. Moors*) 5

Cartesian Subjectivity and Love (*Denis Kambouchner*) 23

The Role of *Amicitia* in Political Life (*Susan James*) 43

L'apparition de l'amour de soi dans l'*Éthique* (*Chantal Jaquet*) 55

Spinoza über Liebe und Erkenntnis (*Wolfgang Bartuschat*) 69

Leibniz on Love (*Gábor Boros*) 79

Malebranche on Natural and Free Loves (*Tad Schmaltz*) 95

The Problem of Conscience and Order
  in the *Amour-pur* Debate (*Dániel Schmal*) 113

Love of God and Love of Creatures:
  The Masham-Astell Exchange (*Catherine Wilson*) 125

The Theory and Regulation of Love
  in 17th Century Philosophy (*Catherine Wilson*) 141

Frances Hutcheson: From Moral Sense to Spectatorial Rights (*Aaron Garrett*) .. 163

Philosophy as *medicina mentis*?
  Hume and Spinoza on Emotions and Wisdom (*Willem Lemmens*) ... 181

The Depth of the Heart – "even if a bit tumultuous". On Compassion
  and Erotic Love in Diderot's Ethics (*Miklós Vassányi*) 205

Motivational Internalism: A Kantian Perpective on Moral Motives
  and Reasons (*Heiner Klemme*) 227

Kant on: "Love God above all, and your Neighbour as yourself"
  (*Martin Moors*) 245

Introduction

Most papers collected in this volume owe their origins, at least partly, to the two "ContactFora" organized within the framework of the research project *Actuality of the Enlightenment: the Moral Science of Emotions* by the members of the research group supported generously by Koninklijke Vlaamse Academie van Belgie voor Wetenschappen en Kunsten. The research project was centred on the problem of the interplay between descriptive and normative elements and aspects of Enlightenment emotion theories, a problem that had never been examined in its full range.

The philosophico-scientific inquiry into emotions (passions or affects, as they were called) in early modern and Enlightenment philosophy pushed the study of man in a new direction: what was formerly a descriptive discipline came to be called (philosophical) anthropology. However, philosophers' interest in emotions also influenced the way they looked at specific fields such as moral philosophy, religion, and politics. The research project aimed to undertake the reconstruction of these developments. This is not just a task for the historian of philosophy; it also raises problems for the contemporary systematic philosopher who critically examines the role emotions play in laying the groundwork for morality, religion, and political authority.

What is new in our research is the historical inquiry of a twofold process. On the one hand, we investigated the way the new scientific-naturalistic philosophy of passions and emotions penetrated into the different complementary systems of evaluation – morality, religion, and politics – jeopardizing, at the same time, their very evaluative character. On the other hand, we also examined the ways these systems of evaluation made a determinative impact on the scientific project itself. No scientific philosopher could get rid of his pre-theoretical convictions even (or, precisely) when confronting the scientific understanding of passions and emotions with the systems of evaluation. Descartes, for example, wanted to investigate the nature of emotions *en physicien*, as a natural scientist. Nevertheless, he based his system of passions on the concept of a created nature directed to the realization of *the good* construed almost in the medieval manner of having interchangeable transcendental concepts like being, beauty, and truth. In Descartes' case, as well as in cases of his fellow seventeenth century philosophers, this points to a *desideratum* of the research: one has to follow the traces of concealed evaluative positions in the new scientific systems of the emotional man.

The research project (which, for all intents and purposes, has not really 'ended' after its six-month period) will be of immediate interest to all those who focus their research on the origins of modern philosophical anthropology. And, since historical research is not to be separated from the systematic issues, the results of the project are also of considerable importance for those who investigate the relations between emotions and modern anthropology, political, ethical, and aesthetical theories.

Workshops ("ContactFora") around specific topics with specialists in the field were part and parcel of the research project itself. We organized two such workshops for analyzing love, the most appropriate emotion to open up and deepen the discussion. Love was regarded as one of the most important emotions by the seventeenth and eighteenth century authors. Descartes placed love among the primary passions, and later thinkers certainly followed him as far as the distinctive role of love was concerned. Spinoza, for example, considered love to be the first affect after the primary ones. Malebranche took love and aversion to be the primary passions that succeeded admiration. When Leibniz defined justice as the charity of the wise he also had a certain kind of love in mind.

These few examples clearly show how love provides us with a paradigm case for the investigation of the changes in the treatment of emotions effectuated by the intrusion of the descriptive-mechanical methods in a field previously characterized by predominantly normative approaches.

What are the most intriguing aspects brought to light in the analyses of love, specifically in view of the fact that in the period under investigation philosophy was given a new character? The original *élan*, present, e.g., in Hobbes' philosophy, of the renewal of thinking in the form of a mechanical philosophy neutral to religious-theological and political issues soon ceased. As a result, mainstream philosophy began searching for a compromise between the "old" and the "new" philosophy, which was more than just a superficial juxtaposition of an old metaphysics and a new physics. This *philosophia novantiqua* attributed to systematic philosophical thinking an important role in answering the great religious and/or theological-political questions of the age. In Spinoza's *Ethics*, the cognitive aspect dominated the treatment of love, whereas his *Theological-Political Treatise* considered *amor erga proximum* as part and parcel of the divine verb ("reason" in Spinoza's vocabulary) imprinted in everybody's heart. In Leibniz, "the charity of the wise" was a combination of juristically rationalized Christianity and Platonic philosophy aimed at the emendation of the life-standards of humankind. Malebranche tried to find the middle course between a sort of egoistic *amour-propre* and a pure love without any consideration of the lover's own interest.

One of the general morals to be drawn from these findings is that, regardless of all the differences between these thinkers with respect to the accents put on different aspects of their respective theories of emotions, the late seventeenth century philosophical study of man cannot, in reality, be separated from the study of emotions regarded usually as reason's main antagonists. We can even find early-modern evidences in favour of various views endorsed by today's theoreticians of emotion, for example, that emotions have a salient role in decision-making. Contemporary theories maintain that emotions cut the potentially infinite series of arguments and counter-arguments in the process of decision-making on the basis of an underlying value not necessarily accessible to reason. According to the seventeenth century theories, it is precisely through the emotions, and especially love, that the explicitly or implicitly made assumptions concerning basic values enter the field of both our everyday concerns and the principally value-free scientific-philosophical investigation. Love is what directs the steps of the Spinozean philosopher to real wisdom; love of a God who creates and maintains order and harmony in the world is the cornerstone of the philosophy of Malebranche and Leibniz.

Given love's paramount importance on a general level, a number of questions dominate the theory of love in the seventeenth and eighteenth centuries. To name but a few:
- Is love an emotion in which the will plays a role?
- Can we love only human beings or can we also love beings above and below human?
- Can we speak of a hierarchy within the concept of love?
- Can love play a role in providing an historical or systematic explanation of how political or other human societies and/or communities have come about and continue functioning?
- Which roles do the two extremities – *amour propre* and *amour pur* – play in late seventeenth century concepts of love?

These questions are treated in the papers of the present volume, and are also briefly discussed here by way of introduction.

Let us begin with Descartes. In the last decade, it has become more and more evident that Descartes was not the rigid rationalist that earlier interpretations have made him out to be. This is partly due to the fact that his *Passions of the Soul* is considered to be the *chef-d'œuvre* of the early modern theory of emotion, and also because his concept of love became indisputably the main starting point of subsequent treatments of love. For these reasons, we will dwell on his concept of love more than that of other authors. What are the main elements of Descartes' concept of love?

Descartes' general definition of love is given in Article 79 of the *Passions of the Soul*:

> Love is an emotion of the soul caused by a movement of the spirits, which impels the soul to join itself willingly to objects that appear to be agreeable to it (CSMK I, 356.).

We do not need to dwell now on the famous problem of how the bodily "spirits" can cause emotions in the thinking soul. Instead, I want to stress first the will's quite unique role in this account of love. As stated in Article 80:

> [I]n using the word 'willingly' I am not speaking of desire, which is a completely separate passion relating to the future. I mean rather the assent by which we consider ourselves henceforth as joined with what we love in such a manner that we imagine a whole, of which we take ourselves to be only one part, and the thing loved to be the other (Ibid.).

"Will" is meant here in the technical sense of 'assenting to' (or, 'withdrawing from') what has been presented to us by the intellect or the imagination. However, the result of the assent of love is not a proposition in which an idea or a bit of knowledge articulates itself, as in Descartes' basic analysis of the will in the Fourth Meditation. What we are given here is rather a kind of motivation for action: the assent produces a new state of affairs, namely, our being involved in a whole of which we willingly acknowledge ourselves to be only one part. This means that the ego acknowledges and assents to its essential limitations with respect to the other that presents a claim upon it and invites it to act somehow in relation to the other's challenge. But the way the ego reacts depends a great deal on which part of the whole gets acknowledged to be the "greater" or the "lesser" part. Descartes, the natural philosopher, cannot help applying in the theory of love the same consideration applied when determining the main laws of movement: it matters a lot which of any two colliding bodies outweighs or is stronger than the other. The stronger or the bigger body will determine the joint movement of the new unit. Likewise, the interests of the stronger part of the whole will determine the actions that will be permitted or tolerated by the weaker part. Descartes assigns special names for the three main possible combinations of this love-relation:

> We may, I think [...] distinguish kinds of love according to the esteem which we have for the object we love, as compared with ourselves. For when we have less esteem for it than for ourselves, we have only a simple affection for it; when we esteem it equally with ourselves, that is called 'friendship'; and when we have more esteem for it, our passion may be called 'devotion' (Art. 83; CSMK I, 357.).

The love construed along these lines is not a static end of one's strivings: there is a considerable action-readiness resulting from the love-relation. When transposed in the world of real human beings who love each other, what is a simple physical (i.e., descriptive) law on the level of pure bodily movements becomes a normative law that lets moral values enter the scene, allegedly issuing from pure physical considerations about the relation of magnitudes. In all of the above kinds of love-relation,

> we consider ourselves as joined and united to the thing loved, and so we are always ready to abandon the lesser part of the whole that we compose with it so as to preserve the other part (Ibid.).

This statement is only a disguised version of the following general law: for all wholes made up of a lover and a beloved object, the greater or stronger part can legitimately achieve its own interest through the lesser part (i.e., the interest of the greater part is to be valued more than the interest of the lesser part). In this way, moral evaluation enters the scene of the putatively pure physical theory. The first step, i.e., the first kind of love, seems innocent in this regard:

> In the case of simple affection this results in our always preferring ourselves to the object of our love (Ibid.).

The case of devotion, however, is more suspicious:

> In the case of devotion... we prefer the thing loved so strongly that we are not afraid to die in order to preserve it (Ibid.).

There are thinkers who would identify the sphere in which some are entitled to command people to die for a cause and people are willing to obey to this command with the sphere of "the political." The same thinkers would certainly also endorse at least one aspect of the so-called secularization theorem: the main political concepts of our modern age are but secularized theological concepts of the Middle Ages. They would also maintain that the seventeenth century is the period where these two sets of concepts existed simultaneously and began to be transposed into or intermingled with each other. These people would appreciate Descartes embedding the third kind of love in a theological-political context. For him, the most appropriate object of love *qua* devotion is God *or our prince*, and the main effect of such a love is that the lesser part of the whole, i.e., man, as either a creature or a subject, feels obliged to sacrifice himself to the whole, i.e., the greater part – God or the sovereign.

> As for devotion, its principal object is undoubtedly the supreme Deity, for whom we cannot fail to have devotion when we know him as we ought. But we may also have devotion for our sovereign, our country, our town, and even for a particular person when we have much more esteem for him than for ourselves... We have often seen examples of such devotion in those who have exposed themselves to certain death in defense of their sovereign or their city, or sometimes even for particular persons to whom they were devoted (Ibid.).

This Article does not connect the theological to the political in a haphazard way. There are passages both in the *Discourse on Method* and in the letters to Princess Elisabeth of Bohemia on Machiavelli that attest to Descartes' willingness to submit himself to the sovereign on the basis of his God-given power – political-military as well as moral. Without going into the details of Descartes' political commitment, we can simply draw the obvious consequence based on what the *Passions* says about the kinds of love. For Descartes, love does have a role in politics, specifically in the explanation of how cohesion can be achieved in a political community. Although he had a preference for monarchic government, he probably did not have any difficulty, in principal, in theoretically accepting other forms of government, for example, in the case of a town. When, in Article 194, he characterizes gratitude as a passion which is "always a virtue and one of the principal bonds of human society" (reference) we can certainly infer from this that gratitude must have a place in the Cartesian good man and good "citizen": we must feel gratitude towards the beloved God or sovereign to whom we must devote ourselves. But we can perhaps also argue in favor of the presence of the idea of another kind of society in Descartes, rather than just a political community: namely, a society constituted by the kind of gratitude the generous human being feels towards the other (human being). But this is an idea that leads to the concept of the society of "free men" in Spinoza, the philosopher whose analyses of love cannot be left out in this introductory survey.

At the surprising end of Book 5 of *The Ethics* remarkable passages crop up on the intellectual love of God. We are first confronted with the Cartesian issue of the fear of death. As we have seen, for Descartes, the best medicine against this fear is devotion, i.e., love of God or the sovereign, which provides the groundwork for an (underdeveloped) political theology. In contrast, although Spinoza's therapy against the fear of death is based upon a kind of love of God, it is not politically motivated but belongs to a metaphysic of knowledge.

> Because human Bodies are capable of a great many things, there is no doubt but that they can be of such a nature that they are related to Minds which have a great knowledge of themselves and of God, and of which the greatest, or chief, part is eternal. So they hardly fear death (E 5P39 S; Curley, 614).

Even if we can find passages in Descartes connecting love of God to the knowledge of certain truths, the political-theological layer is undeniably much more accentuated in his writings than in those of Spinoza. At the same time, we have also a passage in Spinoza where he connects political-theology to the love of God. In the Preface to *Theologico-political Treatise* he speaks of the "precious name of religion" that can be misused in despotic regimes to make "men... fight as bravely for slavery as for safety, and count it not shame but highest honor to risk their blood and their lives for the vainglory of a tyrant" (Elwes, 5.).

It seems that for Spinoza, the counterpart of a politically exploited superstitious religion in favor of a tyrant would not be the political use of the true religion in favor of a God-given prince. The politico-theological use of love could not be a viable option – which certainly does not mean that patriotic love itself could not have an *uncontaminated* political *and* religious role according to Spinoza. This view is supported by Susan James in the present volume. James demonstrates that Spinoza was one of those political thinkers of early modernity who opted for love instead of fear when dealing with the question of whether love or fear is more apt to render the coherence between members of a particular state as stable as possible. Unlike other patriarchal thinkers, Spinoza did not construe political societies as coherent unities bound up by the same kind of natural love emotion that bind members of natural families together. But, like Jean Bodin and other (almost) contemporary thinkers, he did reckon with the benevolent effects of a sort of artificial love aroused by the realization of similarities and resemblances "in some significant respects" such as shared "occupation or civic duty," coming from the same village, being "united by a particular vocation," or being "students and teachers, or adherents of a single religion" (page 50). These are quotations from James' description of Bodin's views since, as she puts it, "Spinoza does not say a great deal about devotional practices [i.e., about the appropriate means to arouse and maintain the artificial love between adherents of a particular group of people], and mainly focuses on their role in arousing patriotism and love of the moral law" (page 52).

Notwithstanding this lack of interest in elaborating on the practical means, we can refer to an interesting chain of propositions in *The Ethics*, Book 3 where Spinoza connects the ideas of similitude, love, and a social class or nation. (Wolfgang Bartuschat also refers to these propositions in his paper in the present volume, although from a different perspective.)

> If we imagine a thing like us, toward which we have had no affect, to be affected with some affect, we are thereby affected with a like affect (Prop. 27, Curley, 508).

In other words, pure similarity – certainly "in some significant respect" – suffices to let the "mechanism," or, what today biologists would call "emotional contagion," function. And although Spinoza does not say this explicitly, we are entitled to think that, according to him (just like Bodin), with the realization of some significant similarity comes the likelihood of feeling the kind of artificial love needed for the establishment of "class-consciousness." According to Proposition 21, this love can multiply the force of the "emotional contagion":

> He who imagines what he loves to be affected with Joy or Sadness will also be affected with Joy or Sadness; and each of those affects will be greater or lesser in the lover as they are greater or lesser in the thing loved (Curley, 506).

Proposition 22 says essentially the same thing from a different angle:

> If we imagine someone to affect with Joy a thing we love, we shall be affected with Love toward him (Ibid.).

The first corollary to this proposition shows us clearly how love arises out of that "imitation of affects" Spinoza is describing here:

> If we imagine that someone toward whom we have had no affect affects a thing like us with Joy, we shall be affected with Love toward him (Ibid.).

Not only does love multiply the efficacy of emotional contagion but one of love's essential aspects is its striving to be multiplied, as Proposition 33 reminds us:

> When we love a thing like ourselves, we strive, as far as we can, to bring it about that it loves us in return (Curley, 513).

Note that Spinoza is perfectly aware of the awkward fact that hatred in a particular group of people against another group of people can considerably enhance cohesion among the members of both groups: Love – an affect of joy – is able to unite people internally, whereas hate – an affect of sadness – is able to create group-cohesion in an external way. What Spinoza says in Proposition 46 can be interpreted along these lines:

> If someone has been affected with Joy or Sadness by someone of a class, or nation, different from his own, and this Joy or Sadness is accompanied by the idea of that person as its cause, under the universal name of the class or nation, he will love or hate, not only that person, but everyone of the same class or nation (Curley, 520).

But, going back to the concept of love in *The Ethics*, the main definition is the following:

> VI. Love is a Joy, accompanied by the idea of an external cause. Explication: This definition explains the essence of Love clearly enough. But the definition of those authors who define Love as a will of the lover to join himself to the thing loved expresses a property of Love, not its essence. And because these Authors did not see clearly enough the essence of Love, they could not have any clear concept of this property. Hence everyone has judged their definition quite obscure (E 3AD6, Curley, 533).

There are a number of open questions concerning this definition, and also the way Spinoza makes use of it. Wolfgang Bartuschat addresses and settles these questions through a thorough analysis of the systematic links between the ontological groundwork of the doctrine of affects in the three "cardinal affects" – desire, joy, sadness – and the emerging of the intellectual love of God itself.

But, however troublesome the interpretation of the peculiar facets of Spinoza's concept of love might be, one thing is clear enough: the thinker whom Spinoza criticizes for his obscure concept of will's role in love is Descartes. Spinoza thinks that the laws that regulate the arousal of the affects presented in Book 3 of *The Ethics* have the status of the geometrical laws he promises to imitate when treating the affects. From this point of view will can, at best, be seen as a concept of folk-psychology, which is not given any explanatory role in a really – not only nominally – *more geometrico* philosophical treatise.

It is in the light of Tad Schmaltz's paper on Malebranche and Daniel Schmal's paper on the *amour-pur* debate at the end of the seventeenth century that the question posed by Chantal Jaquet gains considerable significance. This question concerns the Spinozean concept of self-love, *amor sui*, which appears in *The Ethics* only rarely, interestingly enough. Furthermore, the concept of self-love seems to dissolve in another concept, that of self-esteem, *acquiescentia in se ipso*. Jaquet argues that self-love is a positive affect since it expresses our joy arising from the contemplation of our power of acting. And, since Spinoza did not consider the power of acting as something essential to human beings before writing *The Ethics*, it is no wonder that the concept of self-love is missing in his earlier works. A "passage from the anthropology of weakness to the anthropology of the power" takes place between the early works and *The Ethics*, and this implies a positive assessment of self-love (Bartuschat calls our attention to another concept of the early *Short Treatise* that is missing in *The Ethics*: union). This self cannot, however be simply given: the process of the constitution of the self goes *via* the ideas of those objects affecting our bodies. This entails that self-love cannot be the primary expression of our striving for the enhancement of the power of acting of the *self*. However, once the self is constituted, this self is both the lover and the beloved object of self-love; consequently, it is in the *acquiescentia in se ipso* that self-love attains its purest form.

We turn to Leibniz on the issue of the ties between love and political theology touched upon above. In the seventeenth century, questions of political theology addressed the appropriate relation between a particular human being and his princely sovereign, who was associated with the divine sovereign. One of the conceptual means employed to answer these questions was love. Leibniz's approach to love originates from the treatment of some complex issues in political theology and is clearly bifurcated: on one hand, a considerable role is attributed to love in metaphysics; on the other hand, his natural law theory is also connected to the concept of love.

In general, Leibniz refuses to treat love within a quasi-mechanical theory like that of Descartes. His view on love is not independent of his stance against the atomists' view of the world, which implies that he is not willing to identify the corporeal world analyzable in mechanico-philosophical terms with our own, proper world. The souls that render even bodies living can in no way be analyzed in those mechanical terms: their proper being cannot be understood without constant reference to God. If they succeed in establishing an adequate relation to God, their own life is thereby already adequately ordered without further efforts: "...God alone operates on me, and God alone can do good or evil to me" (DM §32).

Leibniz's God is therefore the only source of a creature's well-being or misery. The mechanistic approach that implies the postulate of a value-free Nature is therefore excluded from his metaphysics of morals – and of love in particular – from the very beginning. And since the only appropriate starting-point for the metaphysical consideration of what happens to us can only be the goodness of God, the only appropriate relation of souls to him is love that manifests itself in human beings as the will and readiness to satisfy and be satisfied in the divine volition. This true love of God results from appropriate philosophical investigations:

> But the more someone loves God, the more she can give reasons for her love. And to find pleasure in someone's perfection means already to love him. Therefore the supreme function of our mind is the cognition or – which is in that object the same

> – the love of the most perfect being, which necessarily entails the highest and most durable pleasure, that is felicity (reference).

We can also raise the question about what role love has, for Leibniz, in establishing political communities. Given that his concept of love is highly intellectualistic we would not expect this love to enter the field of real politics. In my view, a society of human beings loving each other in the Leibnizean way would resemble neither a religious community nor the reality of a body politic. Rather, we should search for parallels to such societies in the projected philosophical community we find in both Descartes and Spinoza. For Leibniz, this is the systematic place of the *cité de Dieu*: the almost utopian concept of a future state of humankind projected in the final sentence of the *New Essays*.

The scope of the theories of love at the turn of the eighteenth century was not exhaustively determined by the deliberations of pros and cons of the mechanical approach to the world. St. Augustine's influence was felt throughout the seventeenth century in the writings of religious authors like St. Francis of Sales and those pertaining to the Jansenist movement. This alternative approach to love becomes important for us through the work of the oratorian father, Nicolas Malebranche. As Tad Schmaltz convincingly argues in his paper, Malebranche's treatment of love was characterized by the bifurcation of natural love on the one hand and free love on the other. This had harmful consequences to Malebranche's occasionalist doctrine he had to struggle with throughout his life.

In any case, it is clear that Malebranche follows Descartes' at least partial anchoring of the concept of love in the will. He defines the will in terms of love saying that the will is the "capacity the soul has of loving different goods." The capacity for love is defined as "the impression or natural motion that carries us toward the undetermined good in general" (see 99). Given this general characterization of love based on will and vice versa, he goes on to differentiate natural love and free love. Roughly speaking, and according to the *Research on Truth*, we have an "irresistible natural love of the good in general and a resistible free love of particular goods" (page 104). The natural love of the good in general is irresistible simply because the meaning of this love is nothing but our elementary striving to happiness. But, "Malebranche's considered position is" that not only this general movement of the will has been impressed in us by God. There is some sort of guidance even for our free will attracted to particular goods that makes it impossible for that free will to be indifferent. This means that we are not independent from God's control over us even when we "freely execute all that He wills" (see 104). Obviously, there is a problem here: although this view fits the occasionalist position well, it seems to involve God's participation even in our actions when we freely choose the bad, when we are captured by a "disordered love of our self." Or, if we emphasize the independence of our choice, then we are attributing a proper causal efficiency to ourselves, if not when consenting to divine guidance at least when we are resisting it, which clearly runs against the occasionalist position that recognizes only God as a real cause in the universe.

Tad Schmaltz's paper examines thoroughly the different attempts to solve this double problem in the Malebranchean *œuvre*. His conclusion seems to relieve that part of the difficulty that concerns our contribution to the decision: "Malebranche's most considered position seems to be that the acts themselves are *rien de physic* since far from involving the turning of our natural or free love, they consist merely in the cessation or continuation of the search for the good" (page 111). Notwithstanding this solution, the other part of the dilemma seems to have become even more pressing: How to account for God's role in our becoming disordered if our own contribution shrinks to nothing?

Though we may not be able to fully answer this question, we can at least clarify the problem further if we take into account what Dániel Schmal writes regarding "the problem of conscience and order in the *amour-pur* debate." Our question concerns nothing less than Malebranche's theodicy and the concept of order that plays an eminent role in it. Schmal maintains that at least "all physical disorder in the world can be explained by the fact that God, who is the only agent in nature, mostly acts in accordance with general rules" (page 118). A dangerous consequence of the application of general rules is that it is difficult to avoid the unintended side effects or collateral damages brought about by these rules, which affect severely the view finite human beings have of the order. To be sure, Malebranche's 'Order', which the general rules must obey, is not the order accessible to humans living in the everyday world. This Order is "the immutable order of the divine perfections," "a matter of the inner perfection in the divine nature with no reference to any external being" (page 118). Regardless of how many collateral damages might be let in by the generality of the operational rules, those who really love God in an unselfish manner must not complain even if they are afflicted by those effects in their own persons.

All this belongs to the Augustine tradition, including the role the will is given to play. Malebranche binds the will by the bonds of divine justice; therefore it is not an indifferent agent: "the essential rule of the will of God is the immutable order of justice."

From this it follows that those aspects of love for which the motion of the will is impressed in us by God – natural love and the ordered love of our self – must comply with the basic, double rule of God's acting, i.e., fecundity and simplicity, which necessitates the application of general rules. When Fénelon defends the idea of a pure and disinterested love against all efforts to prove that it cannot be realized, one of his main points is that we must not give up the absolute indifference of the divine will. According to Fénelon's view developed in his *Réfutation du système du père Malebranche*, the divine will's indifference is not cancelled by any pre-given order. God's original choice was not carried out on the basis of an "objective" insight into one of the possible worlds being the best from among an infinity of other possible worlds. There is no best choice predetermining God's decision. On the contrary: "He cannot do anything that is not good, and, consequently, everything possible – if it is really so – ...is good and conforms to Order" (page 121). Contrary to Malebranche's Order, the Order of Fénelon to be loved disinterestedly "is consequent upon and is not presupposed by God's decisions" (page 121). In fact, when Leibniz informed Pierre Coste of his own view on love (although he did not publish books contributing to the *amour-pur* debate), he developed the ideas of the Preface to the *Codex Juris Gentium Diplomaticus* further in order to assess to the question of whether a perfectly disinterested love is possible. His answer can be taken as favoring Malebranche's view.

> I explained there the problem of how one can love God above all things with a non mercenary love, and at the same time how one can relate everything to his own well-being following his propitious nature. The solution is that loving is nothing else than being attracted to find our pleasure in the happiness or perfection of the other, and this definition shows us that separating the love of others from our own well-being is just to create a chimera.

The British developments in the third quarter of the seventeenth century attracted Catherine Wilson's attention as expressed in her papers, "The theory and regulation of love in 17th century philosophy" and "Love of God and Love of Creatures: The Masham-Astell Exchange."

In the first half of the seventeenth century Augustinianism meant more than just what we have seen in the *amour-pur* debate. The main tenor of religious writers is echoed in the title of Jean Senault's *Man become guilty; or The corruption of nature by sinne, according to St Augustines sense*. Love of creatures is "an imperious passion." Those affected by love become slaves of the objects of their loves. On the other hand, we have poets of the same century like Dryden or Shakespeare in whose plays women – the main objects of that "imperious passions" – "appear kind, noble, intelligent, brave and resourceful."

Wilson's main thesis is that there were two developments in the philosophy of the period to be praised or blamed for the emergence of some more favorable views on love that characterize early eighteenth century French and English letters. One was the rediscovery of Platonism; the other was the Cartesian naturalization of ethics. One of the first books written in the "Platonizing spirit" was Robert Waring's, *Amoris Effigies, sive, Quid sit amor?* (1650) or, in the English translation by John Norris, *The Picture of Love Unveiled*. This work "legitimizes the pursuit of love," so much so that in an ironic way it elevates love to an even higher status than that of the gods: the Epicureans could do without gods but not without love. The translator of this work, John Norris, was an important philosopher in his own right. His own major work, the title of which has been borrowed by Wilson, is an apology of love. Love is what "makes men images of God": it is "as much the Glory of man to be an Amorous, as to be a Rational Being."

I would like to pay some attention to two more points in Wilson's paper, which will remind us of what was elaborated on in earlier parts of this introduction. The first point has to do with the analogy of love Norris employs to make the coherence of societies explicable. He says, "Tis Love that begets and Keeps up the great Circulation and Mutual Dependence of Society…" Concerning Society itself, he endorses the view that because Society is a harmonious system like a "Musical Instrument" it provides us with the norm of the Public Interest. It is difficult to find underlying this a more elementary norm, "a presocial notion of moral purity," which Henry More tries to defend in his letters to Norris as the ideal of "Moral Perfection of human nature antecedent to all Society."

The second point to be mentioned is Cartesianism's role in mitigating the rigid theological views of the early seventeenth century. Wilson notes that Antoine Le Grand, who introduced Cartesian Ethics into English philosophy, "composed a treatise in defense of pleasure," "and the same mixture of Cartesianism and Epicureanism is present in Walter Charletons's *Epicurus' morals*" (1670). In her second paper she highlights also the merits of Descartes' own appeasing approach to the dichotomy 'love of God–love of the creatures' from a contemporary perspective. There is no simple way to decide which of the alternatives is to be preferred: the ascetic ideal of Mary Astell or Damaris Masham's view recommending the delightful involvement in various forms of relations with creatures, finite beings. Wilson interprets Descartes' famous letter to Chanut on the natural way of loving God as a middle course: God can be loved in a natural way but primarily for the providential manner he ordered the created universe.

The concept of love is a bit disguised in Aaron Garrett's paper on Hutcheson's moral theory. In the same way benevolence is, in Leibniz, a clue to the ethics of love, so it is for Hutcheson, who builds his moral sense theory on the concept of benevolence involving the affection for rational beings instead of a "love of God tempered with reverence" as in Carmichael. It is within the concept of love *qua* benevolence that the principal differences make themselves seen between such influential ethical options as the Hobbes-Mandeville theory of a morality based on self-interest, the natural right theories of Carmichael's type based on a superior's will, and Hutcheson's own Shaftesburyan theory of a morality based on the concept of the moral sense informed by benevolence, love for rational beings. "Not only is benevolence paradigmatic for the moral sense theory, but it is the ultimate basis for all moral approval in the moral sense theory" (page 168). This type of theory entails at least a moderate acceptance of a disinterested love, although in a perfectly different, much more secularized context than the one we saw in the *amour-pur* debate. When we perceive pleasure in the contemplation of our or someone else's morally praiseworthy actions, no expectation of personal advantage comes into play. Our love towards the actor of a morally good action is disinterested.

Wim Lemmens' paper displays the interesting gap between the seventeenth century high-rationality of the ethics of love in the form of Spinoza's overwhelmingly cognitivistic account of emotions (affects) and the moderate sceptical account of the passions in Hume's *Treatise*. Spinoza's concept of an intellectual love of God "transcends, in a way, the finiteness of the self" in moving towards the classical idea of a *bios philosophicos*. It is "in participating in the Divine thinking" that the highest activity of the mind is achieved, which appears as the *Amor Dei intellectualis*, i.e., an active emotion. In contrast with this theory of the ideally achievable perfectly active state of mind of the philosopher, Hume turns back his attention to the life of the common man to be analyzed "experimentally" via the thorough observation of many of the situations "everyman" gets in: the *more geometrico* philosophical ideals are contrasted with the presuppositions of the then emerging new science of philosophical anthropology. It is not so much the systematic place of love in the theory of passions strictly speaking that attracts the attention; it is rather the concept of sympathy that stands for love now, something prefigured in the contagious character of the emotions in Spinoza. "Hume stresses the 'contagious' character of the emotions and passions, and considers the mechanism of sympathy to be one of the chief regulating principles of human nature" (page 200). However, whereas Spinoza will not ignore the ambiguous character of the imitation of affects (it can be both a hindrance and a promoter of the aspirations of the sage), "Hume welcomes the fact that minds are 'like mirrors for each other', sympathetically responding to one another's emotions," which is for him "directly constitutive for the identity of the self." In line with this development, reason loses its capacity to transcend human finitude via participation in divine thinking and providing human beings with the ideal possibility of acquiring the status of the sage.

With Martin Moors' paper we arrive at the final part of our investigations, namely, the Kantian perspective on the problem of love. We have two papers and two different points of view regarding Kant's arguments. Moors considers Kant a thinker for whom the bulk of his philosophical explorations on love is to be found in his autonomy-seized ethics of pure practical reason. As a major theme in his metaphysical *Doctrine of Virtue*, Kant's idea of practical love is loaded with the imperative weight of being a duty, primarily to others and to myself, and subsequently *seen as* a divine command. As a consequence of this duty-bound definition of practical love, Kant, in his anthropology, is vehemently reluctant to make any room whatsoever for a possible positive energetic momentum of emotions and passions in the practice of love. There is even an interesting link, a noteworthy harmony between Catherine Wilson's last paragraph and Martin Moors' final view on Kant elaborated in his paper on the biblical command of love quoted by Kant. Wilson's Kant is "a notable reaction" where matters of love are concerned, "a swing of the pendulum back to other-worldliness and the devaluation of women and amorous passion" (page 161). Moors confesses, after a careful study of the merits and demerits of the Kantian approach, that his philosophy of (the duty of) love fails to seduce.

Heiner F. Klemme's paper is a plea for a Kantian standpoint in the debate between contemporary internalists and externalists. He argues that besides the Descartes-Spinoza-Leibniz line another sort of ethical rationalism of the seventeenth-eighteenth century is of great importance to the understanding of later developments: those British thinkers – Cudworth, Clarke, Balguy – who sided with Spinoza rather than Hume concerning the main moral motivational force are to be taken into account if we are to understand today's philosophical debates on internalism and externalism. Klemme maintains that modern Kantians are motivational internalists and normative externalists: the persuasion that "we have no reason at all to believe that one person has more value than another person" is, in fact, the modern descendant of what was called in the seventeenth and eighteenth centuries love, generosity, charity, sympathy, and benevolence that issued in the Kantian categorical prohibition of taking the other person as only a means. This is a formally evaluative statement that does not imply any materially evaluative stance, i.e., the Kantian will not decide which life is more worth living than another: "We do not have insight into anything that would make our lives or our persons more important than the life or existence of another person," Klemme argues, formulating the basic formal presupposition of being a member of the above-listed conceptual family of love. "Persons have value," he continues, "but they do not have this value because of their subjective ends. Rather, they have value because they are human beings who must lead their own lives." They must be attributed and granted the ability to choose their ways of life independently of the particular subjective ends they strive to attain.

The editors wish to express their indebtedness to the Koninklijke Vlaamse Academie van Belgie voor Wetenschappen en Kunsten for supporting their research activity and the permission for publishing the papers read at the ContactFora. We are grateful to those whose personal engagement helped us overcome the difficulties, Professor Niceas Schamp, permanent secretary of the Academy, and his collaborators Inez Dua and Sophie Dejaegher.

Abbreviations

CSMK: The Philosophical Writings of Descartes. Translated by J. Cottingham, R. Stoothoff, D. Murdoch. Cambridge: Cambridge University Press, 1985.

Curley: The Collected Works of Spinoza Translated by E. M. Curley. Princeton: Princeton University Press, 1985.

DM: Leibniz: Discourse on Metaphysics

Elwes: Spinoza: A Theologio-political Treatise. A Political Treatise. Translated by R. H. M. Elwes, New York: Dover Publications, 1951.

LO: Malebranche: The Search after Truth. Translated by T. M. Lennon and P. J. Olscamp. Cambridge: Cambridge University Press, 1997.

OCM: Œuvres completes de Malebranche, 20 volumes. Edited by A. Robinet. Paris: J. Vrin, 1958–84.

Riley: Leibniz: Political Writings. Translated by P. Riley. Cambridge: Cambridge University Press, 1988 (1972).

Wiener: Leibniz: Selections. Philip Wiener. Scribner, 1982.

Affiliations of the Contributors

Bartuschat, Wolfgang; University of Hamburg

Boros, Gábor; Eötvös University Budapest

De Dijn, Herman; Catholic University of Leuven

Garrett, Aaron; Boston University

James, Susan; University of London

Jaquet, Chantal; University of Paris I

Kambouchner, Denis; University of Paris I

Klemme, Heiner; University of Wuppertal

Lemmens, Wim; University of Antwerp

Moors, Martin; Catholic University of Leuven

Schmal, Daniel; Institute for Philosophical Research, Hungarian Academy of Sciences

Schmaltz, Tad; Duke University

Vassányi, Miklós; Catholic University of Leuven

Wilson, Catherine; City University of New York, The Graduate Center

Cartesian Subjectivity and Love[1]
Denis Kambouchner,
Université Paris-I Panthéon-Sorbonne

The title given to this paper might appear, at first, problematic. Everyone knows the extent to which Descartes' century was concerned with reflections upon love. Descartes was twenty years old and about to finish his studies when Francis de Sales published his *Treatise on the Love of God* (1616). He was thirty-two and working on the layout of the *Regulae* when Balthazar Baro, former secretary of Honoré d'Urfé, published the *Conclusion and the Last Part* of *Astrée* (1628), the novel which remained the seventeenth century's most popular. At the age of forty-one, Descartes published the *Discourse on the Method* at the very moment when Corneille made the *extravagant lover* of his comedy *La Place Royale* (1637) say:

> Il ne faut point servir d'objet qui nous possède;
> Il ne faut point nourrir d'amour qui ne nous cède;
> Je le hais s'il me force: et quand j'aime, je veux
> Que de ma volonté dépendent tous mes voeux.[2]

Certainly, Descartes himself devoted a considerable number of pages to this passion, love. Yet the claim that the author of the *Meditations* was also a theorist of love seems paradoxical and requires clarification.

This air of paradox results partly from the fact that the theme of love appears significantly only in Descartes' later writings. The noun *love* does not appear in the *Discourse*, in which the verbs *love* and *to be in love with* have only three minor occurrences (e.g., "I... was in love with poetry..."). Neither the noun nor the verb can be found in the Latin text of the *Meditations*. At the end of the *Third Meditation*, Descartes' only concern, described eloquently but perhaps conven-

---

[1] Another version of this paper was published as "La subjectivité cartésienne et l'amour", *Les passions à l'âge classique,* edited by P.-F. Moreau, (Paris: PUF, 2006): 77–97. An earlier version of this study has been translated in Portuguese by Adelino Cardoso: "A subjectividade cartesiana e o amor", *Amor e subjectividade. Textos sobre a Paixao,* edited by Adelino Cardoso, (Lisboa: Sociedade Portuguesa de Psicossomatica, 1999): 17–34, and into Hungarian by Gábor Boros: "A szeretet fogalma Descartes-nál", *Ész és Szenvedély* (Reason and Passions), edited by Gábor Boros (Budapest: Áron Kiadó, 2002): 77–93. Special thanks go to the present editor, Gábor Boros, to the translator, Bálint Kékedi, and to Jonathan David Cottrell who revised the English text.

[2] Pierre Corneille, *La Place Royale ou l'Amoureux extravagant*, First act, scene IV, l.

tionally – and rather ambiguously – is to pause and "behold, admire, and adore" the dazzling and incomparable beauty of divine perfections, as much as is possible for the mind.[3] Only in the French version (translated by the Duke of Luynes in 1647) are *love* and *hatred* included amongst the properties of the thinking thing enumerated at the beginning of the *Third Meditation* ("I am a thing that thinks: that is, a thing that doubts, affirms, denies, understands a few things, is ignorant of many things, loves, hates, is willing, is unwilling, and also which imagines and has sensory perceptions").[4]

Certainly, this is not just the rectification of an omission, that of the *affectus*, which is not yet included by the *Third* and *Sixth Meditations* among the "modes of thinking" (*cogitandi modi*). This addition is contemporary with the two letters on love to Chanut (of February 1 and June 6 1647), and follows shortly upon the first writing of the *Treatise on Passions*. It is an evident sign of Descartes' progress in reflecting upon the place of the passions within human nature. Nevertheless, it is important to note that until then – and even in his first letters to Elisabeth (up to that of 15 September 1645) – the *ego* (the Cartesian subject) is never depicted as the subject of any kind of love in an essential and constitutive manner. This *ego* is defined firstly as understanding (mind, understanding, reason), and, secondly, as will (if understanding and will are the two main faculties of the human mind or soul); but the *Principles* of 1644, in which the question whether one can conceive a thinking thing without the faculty of will is set (I, 53), makes no mention of love in its classification among the *modes of willing* (*modi volendi*), the operations or dispositions of desire, aversion, assertion, denial, and doubt (I, 32).

Nevertheless, one may speculate about the philosophical import of the later Cartesian texts, which present love as a chief and prime element of affective life. Here, one would think primarily of the *Passions of the Soul* (1649), from which the following three considerations arise.

First, among the six primitive passions that Descartes identifies as so many "genera, while all others are species of them" (Art. 69), love is found in a notable spot: right after wonder, and before hatred, desire, joy and sadness. We therefore must acknowledge that love is not, according to the Cartesian classification, the first in the series of passions (as it is according to the Thomistic classification of the *concupiscible* passions, which come before the *irascible* ones). However, the first passion – wonder – is a very specific one, whose object is merely the knowledge of things (not their convenience or harmfulness with respect to us), and whose physiological place is limited to the brain (instead of being spread to the heart and the rest of the body). Since the passion of wonder is confined to this particular status, love preserves a certain form of primacy in the Cartesian classification. Being the passion we feel towards things that seem agreeable to us (in

---

[3] From the standard *Oeuvres de Descartes*, edited by Adam and Tannery (Paris: Vrin, 1974). (Abbreviated 'AT'.) AT VII, 52, 15–16; IX, 41.

[4] AT IX, 27.

general), love is the first of the literally vital passions of the composite human body. Indeed, among the first passions of our life (those felt even in the womb before birth, according to the internal disposition of the body and the more or less satisfying sustainment of cardiac warmth), it is love that is identified and analyzed here in the first place, as a particularly appropriate nourishment for this warmth (Art. 107).

Two other considerations are raised: on the one hand, love which aims at real goods (and this is possible only in the adult constitution of the conscience) is called *extremely good*. That is to say that this kind of love "can never be too great ...because by joining real goods to us it makes us to that extent more perfect" (Art. 139). On the other hand, in his long letter to Chanut of 1 February 1647, devoted entirely to the subject of love, with a particular explanation of the love of God, Descartes admits that "to treat fully of this passion would take a large volume."[5]

So the problem is the following: do these texts, which appear to concede to love a fundamental role in one's affective and, consequently, one's moral life, state (in terms of Cartesian subjectivity) a truth that the earlier texts, with their carefully delineated issues, had not had occasion to emphasize? Or, do they uphold (partially or completely) the initial reservation which makes the relation or the passion of love inessential to this subjectivity? Moreover, is love, as defined in these texts, really a prominent passion that, for better or worse, leads the subject beyond himself, towards the beloved thing or into union with this thing? Or is it just a relation immediately tempered by the self-presence and self-interest of the Cartesian *ego*?

In this context, we must refer to a particularly important study in the recent Cartesian bibliography entitled "Does the Ego Alter the Other?" which is the sixth chapter of *Cartesian Questions* by Jean-Luc Marion.[6]

Marion enters into the Cartesian theory of love as the last concern of a broader study, whose aim is to show the manner in which the Cartesian ego restricts all possible otherness, apart from that of God. Marion emphasizes, first, the extent to which the depiction of love in the *Treatise on Passions* reestablishes love as a part of the sphere of the ego's own activity, defined as *representation*. To love an object – in other words, "to be joined with what we love in volition" – is (according to Art. 80) to consider or to represent ourselves as forming a whole with it. Marion explains:

---

5 AT IV, 606, 27–30.

6 Jean-Luc Marion, *Questions cartésiennes*, (Paris: PUF, 1991): 189–219. First published under the title: "L'unique *ego* et l'altération de l'autre," *Archivio di Filosofia*, (1986): 1–3. For the English translation, see: *Cartesian Questions: Method and Metaphysics*, (Chicago: University of Chicago Press, 1999): 118–138. For a more general approach to the problem, see: *Prolégomènes à la charité*, (Paris: La Différence, 1986): 91–120 ("L'intentionnalité de l'amour"), and *Le Phénomène érotique*, (Paris: Grasset, 2003): 16–19 and 25–37.

Hence, it becomes impossible to distinguish between a concupiscent love and a benevolent love, for given that the essence of love implies the representation of its "object" by an anterior, prior *ego*, it seems illusory or contradictory to demand the disappearance of the self, as is the case, for instance, in the Augustinian position of *uti* to *frui*.[7]

Moreover, insofar as the *ego* starts from itself to represent another self, this other self – an *alter ego* – cannot possibly be grasped or aimed at in its otherness. It always remains an "altered ego and thus objectified."[8]

These remarks suggest that it is the Cartesian form of love which is condemned by Pascal in the name of charity by his famous words: "the self is hateful."[9] To encourage this thought, Marion has only to draw attention to the fact that charity is not an unknown disposition for Descartes: it is the subject matter of a long development in his polemical *Letter to Voet* of 1643.[10] But, with this text in hand, we must conceive a *totally different form* of one's relation to another self, mediated by God and by the love of God: "the *ego* loves God and knows that God loves other men; thus, imitating God, the *ego* loves these other men."[11] This form of love, which passes "indirectly through the unobjectifiable par excellence" (God), implies a sort of renunciation of the representation and thus a transgression of the initial problem. "To represent or to love – one must choose," concludes Marion.[12] And it is possible that Descartes did choose. But in that case he did it rather covertly, for apparently the ambiguity still remains; as Marion puts it, "an essential part of Descartes' moral doctrine has yet to be examined and understood."

---

7 Ibid., p. 212/134. We must understand that in this opposition between *using* something and *enjoying* it, the self appears only in enjoyment.

8 Ibid, p. 215/136.

9 Fr. 597 Lafuma, cited and commented by Marion on p. 189–193. On this Pascalian theme, see J. Mesnard, "Pascal et le 'moi haïssable", *La Culture du XVIIème siècle*, (Paris: PUF, 1992): 405–413; V. Carraud, *Pascal et la philosophie*, (Paris, PUF, 1992): 327–345, and the recently published and important discussion by L. Thirouin, "Le moi haïssable, une formule équivoque", *Croisements d'anthropologies. Pascals Pensées im Geflecht der Anthropologien*, hsg. von R. Behrens, A. Gipper, V. Mellinghoff-Bourgerie (Heidelberg: 2005): 217–247.

10 See AT VIII-B, 107–135; particularly 112–113.

11 Ibid, 138.

12 Marion, *Questions cartésiennes:* 219. See also *Le phénomène érotique, op. cit.*: "L'*ego cogito* ne s'établit lui-même qu'à l'encontre de l'instance érotique et qu'en la refoulant", p. 17; "l'ego exclut l'amour (et la haine) de ses modalités d'origine (pour le soumettre ensuite, arbitrairement et non sans danger, à la volonté)", p. 19; "l'amant s'oppose donc au cogitant", p. 50.

If we consider this in more detail, Marion's thesis will appear even more entrenched and refined. First, we have to consider the fact that for Descartes all love whose object is not God remains fundamentally "egoist": it is granted by the ego, but with an eye to the ego itself. Indeed, according to Marion, Descartes thinks "love first as a love of oneself, and then as a foundation,"[13] a proof of which can be found in the letter to Chanut, 1 February, 1647: "Anger... borrows its strength from the love of self, which is always its foundation, and not from the hatred which is merely an accompaniment."[14] Consequently, Marion writes: "...any experience of otherness by love should deploy itself without altering the *ego*-ness (*égoïté*) that transcendentally determines it entirely."[15]

Yet, the manner in which the ego views itself here does not seem to be open to any kind of empirical definition. Marion, for instance, does not assert – like A. Matheron in another important study on the matter[16] – that, in Cartesian subjectivity, love always corresponds to the representation of a gain in terms of power. Most likely, the will of love by and for the ego is meant to be understood here in a solely *transcendental* way, as an exercise of the representative faculty and absolute "primacy" of this representation.[17] This representation appears in the form of a pure seizure of possession, a pure intentional appropriation. Since the ego always has a part there, the *res cogitans* is "self-referential by virtue of its very intentionality."[18]

But this is exactly why natural or human love (i.e., love not aiming at or mediated by God) seems to have only a relatively secondary status in the life of the ego or within its functions, and this is the third important feature of this interpretation. It is under the mode of love that the power of representation brings itself to completion (love "completes the emergence" of the *cogitatio*[19]) by representatively constituting union with things that were unfamiliar to it. But here again, it is the *cogitatio* that continues expanding its sphere without encountering any authentic otherness (and Marion at this point cites Merleau-Ponty: "pour une philosophie qui s'installe dans la vision pure, il ne peut y avoir de rencontre d'autrui"[20]). Without encountering any authentic otherness – or perhaps before the *cogitatio* encounters the non-object –, the non-representable who will make it

---

13 Marion, *Questions cartésiennes*: 133.
14 AT IV, 616, 1–5.
15 Marion, *Questions cartésiennes*: 211/133.
16 "Amour, digestion et puissance selon Descartes", *Revue philosophique de la France et de l'Etranger*, (1988–4): 433–445.
17 Marion, *Questions cartésiennes*: 212/134.
18 Ibid, 210/133.
19 Ibid, 211/133.
20 "In a philosophy which settles into the pure vision, there is no encounter of the other." Maurice Merleau-Ponty, *Le Visible et l'invisible*, (Paris: Gallimard, 1964): 109; quoted by Marion, *Questions cartésiennes* p. 216.

pass into a totally different order (in the Pascalian sense). This non-object *par excellence* is God. Undoubtedly, His grace will be necessary for this encounter by which the *cogitatio* ultimately transgresses itself.

It is nevertheless possible to imagine three sorts of objections to this vigorous and brilliant interpretation, in which many crucial questions of contemporary philosophy can be recognized. The exposition of these objections will provide three modes by which we can exhibit the question of the Cartesian status of love. The first objection will be directed towards the form of the emotion, the second towards the act of the representation, and the last one towards the nature of the intention or the interest presiding over the distribution and the experience of love.

1. The problem of the emotion

Marion immediately cites[21] the definition from Art. 79, according to which love is: "an emotion of the soul caused by a movement of the spirits [the animal spirits, the 'parts of the blood which are the most agitated and penetrating'] which impels the soul to join itself in volition to objects that appear to be agreeable to it."

And even before recalling this definition, Marion cites those Cartesian statements (taken from the letter to Chanut of 1 February, 1647) that present passions in general as being "sensations or very confused thoughts" that are "aroused in the soul by some motion of the nerves."[22] However, as Marion interprets it, this bodily action does not seem to play any decisive role in the reality of Cartesian love. Rather, it is purposely withdrawn from that reality by means of several remarks, like the one which asserts that taking into consideration its own passions as "confused thoughts" the ego "still determines that which it nonetheless bears."[23] Or again, passions are distinguished from other sorts of perceptions which are caused by the nerves in so far as we refer passions "only to the soul", because "we do not normally know any proximate cause to which we can refer them" (Art. 25). From this fact, it is concluded that "passions, since they occur in the soul, never leave it and are entirely absorbed in it."[24] Following the same line of interpretation, the very fact that the ego, in the passion of love, represents things to itself as being united with itself means that the *cogitatio* reaches here "the last dependence with regard to the ego"; that is to say, the last degree of this dependence.[25]

---

21 Marion, *Questions cartésiennes*: 209/132.
22 See AT IV, 602, 23; 603, 1.
23 Marion, *Questions cartésiennes*: 208/131.
24 Marion, *Questions cartésiennes*: 209/132.
25 Ibid.

From a certain phenomenological perspective, passion does not appear as an effect of a cause (the body) that is external to the thought, but rather as a lived-experience resulting from a certain transcendental constitution. Nevertheless, even without mentioning the difficulties of a phenomenology of the affectivity (as found in the second volume of the *Ideen* of Husserl, along with the works of Merleau-Ponty and Michel Henry), it seems that, in this case, one must choose between two alternatives: either we undertake a phenomenological reduction or we take seriously the guidelines given by Descartes – taking into consideration the fact that in the Cartesian formulations, the principle of a physiological causality of the passions remains much less problematic than the way we can say that the passion of love resides in the soul.

Indeed, Article 79 does not only provide us with a definition of love in general ("and hatred is an emotion caused by the spirits, which impels the soul to want to be separated from objects which are presented to it as harmful"), it also defines more precisely the *passions* of love and hatred, distinguishing them from other kinds of thoughts falling under the same denominations:

> I say – adds Descartes – that these emotions are caused by the spirits in order to distinguish Love and Hatred, which are passions and depend on the body, both from judgements which also incline the soul to join itself in volition with the things it deems good… and from emotions which these judgements excite by themselves in the soul.

This text can be put directly together with the letter to Chanut of 1 February 1647, in which Descartes begins by distinguishing two kinds of love: the "intellectual or rational" love and the love that is a passion and that one would call "sensual or sensuous."[26] Articles 91 and 92 of the *Passions* make a similar distinction between an intellectual and a sensuous enjoyment, or sadness, respectively. Now, this distinction of the two forms of emotion is at the basis of a singular problem.

Let us set aside for the moment the difficulty of the expression "to join itself in volition" in the definition of Article 79. The fact that the soul is inclined to "join itself in volition" to an object through the emotion of love means, strictly speaking, that the soul, in so far as it is subject to the passion of love, *does not yet join itself "in volition"* to the object in question. On the contrary, it seems that the soul can experience this passion as an impulse or emotion that imposes itself on it (by means of a certain physiological causality) *without the soul being involved entirely*. This feeling of foreignness, which is the same feeling that the *Sixth Meditation* highlighted about the simple sensations,[27] is what Marion's interpretation seemingly fails to admit, insofar as he emphasizes the sole agency of the ego. Yet, if it is *not exactly* because the soul is subject to the passion of love that it "joins itself

---

26 AT IV, 601, 13; 603, 20.
27 See AT VII, 75; IX, 59.

in volition" to an object, what does the soul require to join itself to that object? It requires a judgement of the soul, according to which the object aimed by this passion becomes actually loveable – and *intellectual* or *rational love* is precisely what follows right from this judgement.

What, then, is this intellectual love? Is it really another form of emotion which we feel in a different way than the emotion of passion? If this is the case, it seems necessary that the soul be animated by two different emotions simultaneously. But if this is not the case, in what does their distinction really consist? The of Article 79 – and, incidentally, all of the *Treatise on Passions* – with respect to this question shows in itself a real difficulty. Insofar as this difficulty is not resolved, we can easily find ourselves confronting the paradox that *the soul is not the subject of any emotion of love at all*, because the passion of love which is excited in the soul by the body *is, strictly speaking, not the soul's own movement*; and as far as its own movement of love which is the consequence of its judgement is concerned, *it is, to be precise, not an emotion* (but, at best, the *idea* of a certain emotion, as advocated by Herbert Spencer, William James, and Bergson two or two and a half centuries later).

Certainly this difficulty in specifying what would be the features of a love that is located *only in the soul* is one of the reasons for the discretion Descartes maintained over that question before 1645. We shall return to this question later.

However, in reality the two kinds of love can scarcely be separate: "commonly," writes Descartes in his letter to Chanut, "these two loves occur together."[28] The two follow each other very closely: either the thought of love, conceived only by the soul, makes an impression in the brain which triggers the physiological process corresponding to the passion of love, or this passion, this "confused thought aroused in the soul by some motion of the nerves... disposes it [i.e., the soul] to the other, clearer, thought which constitutes rational love."[29] This connection or succession is remarkable from several points of view: it means in particular that despite an occasional reference to the "good affections" (*eupatheiai*) that the Stoics distinguished from passions in general,[30] the "intellectual love" is not necessarily *rational in the strictest sense of the term*. In fact, for Descartes, there are only *accidental* exceptions to the connection of the two kinds of love: we could feel a certain warmth in our heart without relating it to any determined object, or we could esteem an object to be most loveable while not having our body disposed "in the required manner" for the passion of love to be excited in us.

---

28 AT IV, 603, 21–22.
29 AT IV, 602, l. 26; 603, l. 3.
30 "In the same way, when we hear good news, it is first of all the mind which makes a judgement about it and rejoices with that intellectual joy which occurs without any bodily disturbance and which, for that reason, the Stoics allowed that the man of wisdom could experience {although they required him to be free of all passion}": *Principles of Philosophy*, IV, art. 190. CSMK 1, 280.

Nor does it seem to be the case that love could give rise to the sort of difference of phase or ambivalence in the soul that we can observe in the case of other passions. For instance, a certain sadness "in the outer parts of the soul" may be compatible with a certain joy in its "inner parts" (Art. 147), or a false joy can leave a certain bitterness in the soul (*to Elisabeth*, 6 October, 1645). On the contrary, it does not seem possible that loving an object can be accompanied by hating or intellectually rejecting that object, or in other words, that an intellectual love is compatible with a passion of hate towards the same object. This is because love (and hatred) cannot have a *merely occasional or apparent* object, unlike pleasure, pain, joy or sadness. Not only do we experience intellectual love only towards things that *seem* agreeable to us, but moreover, we feel the passion of love only for objects whose benefits and pleasantness can be experienced repeatedly.[31] Thus, if there is an ambivalence, it will not generate a competition between *a passion and an intellectual emotion* – nor, of course, between two intellectual emotions, considered as rational affections – but only between *two differently founded passions*.

All this leads us to the following conclusion: if love, mentioned without further specification, is not just the passion of love as confused thought, nor just the *movement of the will* which is the definition of the intellectual love, but the *synthesis or the unity* of these two affections, then we must say that in "this life", the soul *never loves alone*, but rather loves *with the body it is joined to*. In other words, it is only insofar as the soul is united with its body and feels the effects of certain movements of that body that it feels love at its highest degree of effectiveness. This does not mean, of course, that *the subject* of all kinds of love *is the body* and that the soul does not have its own relation to objects. On the one hand, even the relation it has to its own objects seems to require a sort of reinforcement through

---

31 Apparently, there is a counter-example in which one feels a violent attraction to someone of the opposite sex. According to Art. 90 of the *Passions* this "inclination or desire... arises from attraction" and "the name 'love' is applied more often to it... than to the passion of love described previously," which, by the way "provides writers of romances and poets with their principal subject-matter." Even if we reckon that this passion is transferred here from the genus of love to that of desire, the "attraction" which gives its basis still remains a kind of love. That is to say, it is not exactly the kind of love "we have for good things" but rather "the love we have for beautiful things" that are represented to the soul "by the external senses" and not "by the internal ones and by its reason" (Art. 85). But this attraction, even if aroused only once and and by the simple appearance of the object, gives rise to a very strong relation, intensively consumed by thought. And if this case appears to provoke a difference of phase between passion and intellectual emotion, we shall wonder if an incidental, intellectual rejection of passion should be about the attraction itself or rather about the desire that arises from it. On these texts, see our study: *L'Homme des passions*, (Paris: Albin Michel, 1995): vol. I, 268–281.

the process of the passions. Descartes' efforts prove this when, in his letter to Chanut of 1 February 1647, he explains how even God (whose nature is entirely unimaginable to us and only makes itself known to the pure understanding) can become the object of "a most violent passion" in us. On the other hand, love in its most general physiological reality appears to be a passion or an affection that the rational soul as such must submit to a kind of surveillance. That means that love, generally speaking, *is obviously not a thing that originates from the ego, considered as purely cogitative agency.* One would rather tend to say that the ego *happens to love*, or happens to be subject to love. It is even less appropriate to consider it as purely cogitative agency than to think about it as the substantial being (the compound of soul and body) that constitutes the primary and permanent object. We must stress that it is also the object, and not just the subject – of the *cogitatio*.

2. Love and representation

The *second objection* we can raise to Marion's interpretation is based on the definition of the relation between love and representation (Art. 80). Descartes comments on the very curious and obscure expression: *to join itself in volition*,

> I am not speaking of desire, which is a completely separate passion relating to the future. I mean rather the assent by which we consider ourselves henceforth as joined with what we love in such a manner that we imagine a whole, of which we take ourselves to be only one part, and the thing loved to be the other.

Can we speak here – as Marion suggests – of a *pure act of representation*? At least the assent in question remains, categorically speaking, an act or a *movement of the will*. Similarly, the union with the beloved thing remains an object of the will (at the same time as an object of representation). Moreover, insofar as there is representation here, the substance and the status are far from clear.

Given this, consider first: *under what relation* does the subject (which here is no longer the soul, exactly) consider itself as being joined to the beloved thing? As a man, as a compound of body and soul, or simply as a soul? Is it the nature of the beloved thing that determines the answer to this question? But then, doesn't this define different forms of union which should have been distinguished?

What is more, this representation of the *union* seems to be a representation of the *distinction* as well. In the whole that I form with the thing I love, I represent myself *as being only one part and the thing as another*. Even in the whole that I represent to myself, the thing's part and my own part are, speaking in terms of proportions, subject to variation according to "the *esteem* which we have for the object we love, as compared with ourselves" (Art. 83). This will serve as a principle to the most consistent distinctions one could possibly make concerning love: the distinction of simple *affection*, *friendship* and *devotion*. We shall touch upon the moral implications of these distinctions soon. For the moment, our question is the following: is this representation of the whole (one part of which is the thing I love, the other part of which is myself) always conceivable?

There are at least three difficult cases. First, there is "the love we have especially for ourselves," of which there is no mention before Art. 139. What shall we represent to ourselves as *union with ourselves?*

There is also the distinction introduced by Art. 82 between the pure and simple love for objects (or for persons) and the love for one's own *possession of those objects*. Descartes claims that a miser does not have love for money, nor a drunkard for wine, nor a brutish man for a woman he wants to violate, in the same way that an honourable man has love for his friend or a good father for his children. The former love only the *possession* of objects and not "the objects themselves: for these objects they have merely desire mingled with other particular passions." However, (and this question has already been asked by F. Alquié in his notes to his edition[32]) what exactly does it mean "to join itself in volition to the possession of an object"? Do we have to imagine ourselves as being a part of a whole whose other part is our *possession* of the object? Moreover, if "to join itself in volition" to something does not only mean "wanting to be joined" to that very thing, but also – as a consequence of this union – "to be in a certain volitional community with what we love," what would we wish *to* the possession of an object (when we love this possession)?

Finally, there is the problem of the love of God, as Descartes puts it, after Chanut, in the middle section of his long letter. If in fact "nothing about God can be visualized by the imagination,"[33] how could we imagine ourselves adding up to a whole with him? And provided that such a representation were possible, how would it be legitimate, given the immense disproportion between "the infinity of His power" and our "smallness"?[34]

With similar difficulties ahead, it is useful to keep some distance from the Cartesian manner of expressing things. If we consider the *status* of the above-mentioned representation of the union with the object, it seems that we necessarily come to this point: if Descartes has to appeal to a certain representation (Art. 81) to explain the expression "to join itself in volition", it is because this representation (of the whole we form with the object) constitutes a sort of schema (in the Kantian sense of the term) for a relation of love which can be scarcely understood *outside of this schema*.

However, the point is not simply that there is a certain movement of the will with which this representation is associated. Rather, it is that in all possible respects, the representation is secondary to the primary reality or realization of

---

32 See Descartes, *Œuvres Philosophiques*, Classiques Garnier, vol. III, p. 1015, n. 2 (hereafter, 'O. Ph').
33 AT IV, 607, 14.
34 Ibid., 608, l. 24; 609, l. 1.

the union, which is its object. Undoubtedly, it is only by means of such a representation that the reality of love is consummated in the mind and that the union as simple "union of the will" is brought to completion. However, a prior joining with or adherence to the object is always necessary for this to happen. Of course, the representation need not properly display the loveable character of the object in question. And naturally, the assent which is realized *through* this representation (rather than this representation's object, i.e., "the assent *by which* we consider ourselves henceforth as joined with what we love in such a manner that we imagine a whole...") originates prior to the representation.

But if it is appropriate here to speak about a 'schema' as the unique form of the intuitive representation of the relation of love, then this representation will have a constitutively vague character. This is not the place to require a mathematical exactitude in describing the ratio of the parts within the whole. Mentioning the composition of a whole out of parts was, of course, inevitable once we talked about the *union* of the soul with the object. Indeed, for Descartes, no union is to be understood without a *real distinction* of the things that are united. And certainly, the word *union* is more relevant here than *unity*, because neither the ego, nor the mind or the soul, or even the man, constitute (or are said to constitute) an indivisible unity with other things. However, each of us is really a part of one or more wholes, outside of which we could not subsist[35] (as is said in Descartes' most important and famous letter to Elisabeth, 15 September 1645). It is surely in a certain *unity* with its objects that Cartesian love finds its greatest reality. That is why in Art. 139, cited at the beginning of our present inquiry, Descartes writes more exactly of love whose objects are real goods that: "...it cannot be too great, since the only thing that the most immoderate [love] can do is join us so perfectly to those goods that the love we have for ourselves in particular makes no distinction between us and them, which I believe can never be bad." Furthermore, according to Descartes' description of the relation between friends or the relation of a good father to his children as a relation to "another self" or to "other selves," it seems that we should not understand here that one friend represents the other, or that the father thinks of his children, originally *from himself*. Rather, we should understand rather that he happens to be *so united to them*, that the ordinary representation of the distinction of persons is, in some respects, eliminated from his mind.

Thus, we must understand in the broadest possible manner the rule that when I love a thing, I consider myself and that thing as forming a whole, of which the thing is one part and I am another. For the verification of this rule, it is not necessary that I consider the beloved thing as something that is truly distinct from me. It is enough that the thing constitute a *particular object of thought* for me and that its usefulness to me or its connection to me is available for me to know or to feel. But I could also refer to a thing which belongs to me, such as a quality which I

---

35 See AT IV, 293, 3 sq.

recognize as mine, or a thing which exists only in my experience (like a certain pleasure) or in my imagination (like a certain glory). In this respect, love is *the most general relation possible. A priori*, all the things that have a distinctive place in my empirical or mental universe are possible objects of love, insofar as I recognize this universe as mine – that is, insofar as I consider myself, even in the most indirect manner, as connected to them. In this respect, the privilege of persons, however real they are, is only relative. As far as the infinite being is concerned, if it cannot enter as a simple part in any whole of which I would be the other part, I can have at least a certain thought relating to this being, and considering it as such. I can experience that this thought constitutes a whole with me and that it is in the highest degree accessible to me.

3. The problem of the interest

Is it not the case that claiming the *ego cogitans* as such presides over love, and that the experience of being in love is determined from top to bottom by "egoness" designates in this love a passion which is impure and related to a frantic ambition? It is quite clear that Marion transposes all the elements of the traditional condemnation of self-love as opposed to the love of God or to charity, into the transcendental register on which he wants to build. In the final analysis, representation proves to be an appropriation. *The other* is attained only in an altered form, reduced to an *alter ego*, and therefore adapted to the ego itself, in a somewhat paradoxical mode. In presenting the distinction between a benevolent love and a concupiscent love as one of secondary importance (Art. 81), Descartes, in sum, seals their unity. Marion's ultimate expression ("To represent or to love – one must choose") shows the inauthenticity of this love, which would be representation through and through. What is more, even if he reduces the moral egoism to an extra-moral – in other words, metaphysical[36] – determination, the initial development, concerning the Pascalian notion of the ego, marks the rest of the analysis as bearing the imprint of what one could call Augustinianism.

However, Descartes' language remains very different, and not of the Augustinian kind at all. While he disapproves of the effects of a disordered love (such as Paris's passion for Helen of Sparta, which is his example in the letter to Chanut[37]), Descartes does not have a bad word to say about the ordinary forms of human love. On the contrary, Descartes relates to this natural love – and not to the love of God or to a particular grace – many heroic and praiseworthy actions, as, for example, in the case of "those who have exposed themselves to cer-

---

36 Marion, *Questions cartésiennes*: 191.
37 See AT IV, 617, 1–12.

tain death in defence of their sovereign or their city,"[38] or those who risk their life or "suffer some other evil to bring good to others."[39] For, says the letter to Chanut: "It is the nature of love to make one consider oneself and the loved one as a single whole of which one is a part; and to transfer the care one previously took of oneself to the preservation of this whole."[40] And Article 83 of the *Treatise* says: "...inasmuch as in all of them [in the three kinds of love: affection, friendship and devotion] we consider ourselves as joined and united to the thing loved, we are always ready to abandon the lesser part of the whole we compose with it in order to preserve the other."

As F. Alquié has also observed,[41] the nature of this rule and the forms of its application can raise some important difficulties, which essentially concern the relation between the representation and the action. In a critical situation – in other words, in a situation where the preservation of the whole and of its parts is at stake – it seems that the action is determined by the esteem in which one holds the beloved thing compared to that in which one holds oneself. Or, to put it another way, the action is determined by the importance the thing has within the whole. This principle raises at least two questions. First, what happens in the case of a friendship, when "we esteem the object of our love equally with ourselves" (Art. 83)? Second, in other cases (just as in this one), how shall we determine exactly what we owe to the object of our love? In this respect, will things change according to our representation of ourselves (within this whole that we constitute with the object) as a relatively lesser part than the object, or as a far lesser or even insignificant part? According to the letter to Chanut, it seems that we have to go quite far with the weighing. In Descartes' own words:

> It is the nature of love to make one consider oneself and the loved one as a single whole of which one is only a part; and to transfer the care one previously took of oneself to the preservation of this whole, so that one keeps for oneself only a part of one's care, a part which is great or little in proportion to whether one thinks oneself a larger or smaller part of the whole to which one has given one's affection.[42]

A certain expectation of exactitude renders the French formulation rather indigestible – more so than its English translation. The question is whether this expectation intervenes here in an inappropriate manner, insofar as its application would raise more problems than it would resolve. Furthermore, it would present an operation of an eminently reflected and calculating conscience, instead of the movement of passion that one would expect.

---

38 *Passions*, Art. 83; *to Chanut*, 1 Feb. 1647, AT: IV, 612.
39 *To Elisabeth*, 15 September 1645, AT: IV, 293–294.
40 AT IV, 611, 25–29; n.s.
41 *O. Ph.* III, p. 720, note 1.
42 AT IV, 611, 25; 612, 2; n.s.

However, these confusions can be resolved in exactly the same style as was the aforementioned problem of the representation of the whole and its parts. The Cartesian formulations are not about something which is phenomenologically given. Rather, they provide a certain mathematical form for a mental reality – which reality, Descartes himself is well aware, appears in a far more informal way to the ordinary consciousness.

This is confirmed by the letter to Elisabeth of 15 September 1645, which contains Descartes' most important remarks on those "heroic actions" in which we risk our lives for our children, for our friend, for our country or for our sovereign. Such actions can easily agree with the rule stated just before them, according to which "the interest of the whole, of which each of us is a part, must always be preferred to those of our individual personality."[43] In a certain way, they are always performed *according to this rule*. But, as the letter attests, it is not necessary that this rule should be clearly in the mind of the person who performs such an action at the very moment of his acting. It is sufficient, says Descartes, that "the thought may be only confusedly in his mind."[44] This rule is therefore *the most general reason* for which the subject of the heroic action performs his action, and this rule provides him with all the reasons for his action. Nevertheless, the disposition to perform the action does not result from any definite *reasoning*.

We should make connection here with another Cartesian theory; namely, that of the evaluation of the distance, the shape and magnitude of objects of vision. We know, of this evaluation, that it must be obtained "as if by a natural geometry", from a certain consciousness of the angular relation of the directions of the eyes and of the line which connects the rear side of the two eyes to one another (or the same eye in different positions). The triangle thus described will be reconstructed in its characteristic proportions so quickly that Descartes is able to invoke "an action of thought which, although it is only a simple act of imagination, nevertheless implicitly contains a reasoning quite similar to that used by surveyors, when, by means of two different stations, they measure inaccessible places."[45]

As Malebranche and Berkeley later emphasized, it is extremely difficult to determine exactly how this reconstruction is carried out. Now, it may well seem that we are dealing here with the same kind of accomplishment, that it is somehow immediately, and not by thinking of it, that the person in love knows what

---

43 AT IV, 293, 12–14.; CSMK 3, 172.

44 "[W]hen a man risks death because he believes it to be his duty, or when he suffers some other evil to bring good to others, then he acts in virtue of the consideration that he owes more to the community of which he is a part than to himself as an individual, though this thought may be only confusedly in his mind without his reflecting upon it." AT: IV, 294.

45 *Dioptrique*, VI, AT VI, 138, 8–12 translated by Paul J. Olscamp, (Indianapolis: Hackett Publishing Company, 2001): 106.

he has to do when the one he loves is in danger. The true proportion which defines his duty is nothing but a certain practical scenario which offers itself to his mind and to which he immediately agrees, rather than to another.

The problem raised by one's equality with the object of friendship (what would be the reason to sacrifice myself for a being that I esteem as much as myself, *but not more?*) is rather easily resolved. That my friend, who is another self, is equal to me, means exactly that I do not prefer myself to him and that there is between us a particular form of recognition, of identification or of assimilation. Precisely in these conditions, if I see my friend in danger, *it will be impossible for me not to try everything I can to save him.* Far from being obligated to take into account what I owe to myself independently of what I owe to him, it is him, as it happens, who will be *entirely myself*, and if I fail to do what is not even a duty but a natural act, it is me who, in a certain sense, will not survive.

It is important to understand that the point is not that Cartesian love is essentially pure and disinterested – such a claim would properly be nonsense from the Cartesian perspective. The point is only that, by definition, no love aimed at objects (this is to be distinguished from the love of their simple possession) is purely egoist, for this sort of love is only the manifestation of a union and of a connection, which only needs to be preserved or to be deepened in terms of its kind. The subject of a certain love can also be the subject of desires which are extraneous to the love in question, and what is inconceivable here is rather a total affective exclusiveness. Some of his desires can be related to this love or to its object without, properly speaking, originating from this love. But the desire which proceeds from love has only one object; namely, the good of the whole that we form with the object, and that is the only thing to be noted here.

From all this, we should be able to draw some conclusions. Marion's interpretation, in general outline, consists in reconstructing an entirely metaphysical concept of love within the Cartesian corpus (determined by the "primacy" of the ego and the realms of representation), in order to oppose this rather inauthentic love to a charity which Descartes would have approached without placing it in the foreground of his problems. The preceding remarks suggest to us a slightly different and perhaps more economical approach: that (a) love, for Descartes, is simply absent from the sphere of pure metaphysics (that of the *Meditations*), but this being – rightly – admitted, (b) its proper place is in the theory of man, without a necessary appeal to a transcendent principle, though with a somehow secondary metaphysical significance.

Foremost is the fact that once we consider only the mind, or even the mind in its relation to God, we will hardly find there any relation of love to any object. The opening passage of the letter to Chanut concerning the soul which – *not being united to a body* – perceives "that there are many very fine things to be known about Nature" to such a degree that "its will would be infallibly impelled to love the knowledge of those things"[46] may appear strange and tacked on. It is only

---

46 AT IV, 602, 10–12.

when we descend in the order of the union of soul and body – or, in the terminology of the 1643 letters to Elisabeth, when we pass from the consideration of the first primitive notion to the third – that we cannot avoid encountering love and the other passions in their own right. This fact was indicated by the First part of the *Principles*, in the passage about the simple notions which can be found in ourselves.[47]

Does the fact that love does not have an assured place in Descartes' metaphysics ground the conclusion that love is not essential to Cartesian subjectivity? Can it constitute merely a mode of extension or of moral or practical translation of the metaphysical domination of the ego? This conclusion would be highly dubious.

First, insofar as it suffices to indicate the division of the three primitive notions, the plane of reality to which we gain access at the moment of the metaphysical protocol when the *mens* again finds its body is absolutely irreducible to the preceding plane – namely, the plane of the pure exercise of the *cogitatio*. However, even if it cannot be reduced to this exercise of the *cogitatio*, that plane of reality is evidently no less constitutive of the life of the soul in its present condition. Of course, even in this metaphysical protocol, the return of the *mens* into the body with which it is united has never been seriously jeopardized nor has it been let out of sight. As Marion himself seems to have suggested elsewhere,[48] in the Cartesian framework the complete view over the subjective life (and consequently a complete egology, so to say) is possible only with the re-descent of the ego into the union with its body, and not into its metaphysical reduction to a pure mind.

In fact, when we reach the plane of the union of the soul and the body, we rediscover certain conditions which belong to the body, namely its need for a huge amount of things to subsist or (as Spinoza would put it) to be "regenerated."[49] These are precisely those relations of dependence, of need and of objective utility that are established before our birth by the nourishment of cardiac warmth, and that are expressed by the inner movements of love, hate, joy and

---

47 See *Principles* I, Art. 48. Once he recalled that "perception, volition and all the modes both of perceiving and of willing are referred to thinking substance" and gave details of the properties of the body, Descartes adds: "But we also experience within ourselves certain other things which must not be referred either to the mind alone or to the body alone. These arise, as will be made clear later on, in the appropriate place, from the close and intimate union of our mind with the body. This list includes, first, appetites like hunger and thirst; secondly, the emotions or passions of the mind which do not consist of thought alone, such as the emotions of anger, joy, sadness and love; and finally, all the sensations, such as those of pain, pleasure, light, colours, sounds, smells, tastes, heat, hardness and the other tactile qualities." CSMK 1, 208.

48 Jean-Luc Marion, *Sur le prisme métaphysique de Descartes*, (Paris: PUF, 1986): §15, 214–216.

49 See *Ethics*, Part II, Postulate IV (after proposition 13).

sadness. We could say (taking a further step towards Spinoza) that the reality of human body is – if not a simple mode – that of a substance in the weaker sense of the word, for it certainly does not depend on any other substance immediately and exclusively, but nevertheless it preserves its form only through an ordered system of relations with other substances.

This does not mean that the relations of love are limited to relations between bodies, or that the sole subject of love is the body. For both the *Treatise* and the letter to Chanut make the following point very clear: in the body, there are internal movements which correspond to the passion of love, but love, properly speaking, *is only in the soul*, although perhaps it appears there only in relation to those bodily movements. Love is thus *the way in which the soul lives, notices and recognizes the relation that the body manifests*. Moreover, *if the body needs nourishment, so does the soul,* and knowledge is *par excellence* such a nourishment. It is true that in the metaphysical protocol this knowledge appears to be generated by the self-thinking of an agency (the ego) which, at first, reduces to itself and discovers any truth in itself or by reflection upon itself. At the same time, it is also clear that this agency could not be assured of this knowledge had its elements and faculties not been given to it by a Creator to whom it can and must feel gratitude. And, beyond all doubt, the reestablishment of metaphysics could have been conceived only from a certain communication between minds, whose reality is eliminated from the *Meditations*, but which Descartes never wished to deny altogether.

Under these conditions, everything happens as if the way that the body recognizes those things that are agreeable to it and the way it reacts on their occasion would support the mind in its recognition and consolidation of *its own relations*. The letter to Chanut offers, as an example, the love of God which, in certain conditions, can become "the most delightful and useful passion possible and can even be the strongest."[50] And if – in the metaphysical experiment – the ego can experience all of its force and its independence, this cannot be dissociated from the recognition of certain forms of dependence, which relate the ego particularly to its Creator, but not just to Him. It is undoubtedly an essential act of the Cartesian subject *to distinguish itself from all the other beings*. But then we must add that this distinction is based on a more *original non-distinction* of the subject and its various objects. *In a certain way,* this non-distinction must remain effective and present to the mind.

There will not, of course, be too much hope that the love which arises from and gives evidence of this non-distinction always appears to be clear in respect of its distribution or its motives. The object of love is what gives, or seems to give, some good to the subject. This aspect is constitutive, not just occasional or accidental. However – as can be gleaned from Descartes' own explications – there is so much room for resemblance or analogy in the excitation of this passion that the ways of this excitation cannot easily be reconstructed. In this regard, the "secret incli-

---

50 AT IV, 608, 4–6.

nations" mentioned in the second letter to Chanut of 6 June 1647[51] are certainly not the general rule, but their status is not that of a mere exception.

At the same time, does this residual obscurity of the phenomenon of love with respect to the subject in love possess a great importance? Of course, we have to make an effort to love only deliberately and to seek – as far as the objects are concerned – the real and not just apparent perfections. But, in reading Descartes correctly, it does not seem to be the case that, from an ethical point of view, love is the place of the ultimate decisions. Not only is the Cartesian will not love in its reality (rather, the will always has to find the good to which it should attach itself), but even a disordered love will not be directly guilty, once we admit – as indicated by the first letter to Chanut – that "love, however disordered, has always goodness for its object", unlike hatred "whose only object is evil."[52] Indeed, insofar as love unites us "in volition" to certain objects, it can only cause harm indirectly. As far as self-love is concerned – whose definition would need further specification – it seems to be a constant in the life of the soul rather than a variable. Rather, we have to relate the great ethical bifurcations to the way in which we consider ourselves – in other words, to self-esteem. For this esteem ("an inclination the soul has to represent to itself the worth of the thing esteemed", Art. 149) has functions other than love. This is undoubtedly one of the most insistent lessons of the *Treatise on Passions*: the moral problem, insofar as it is related to passions, must be transposed from the passion of love towards the passions which depend on wonder, of which esteem is the first. It is thus not the way of loving ourselves, but the way of admiring ourselves – that is to say, of knowing ourselves – that can cause problems. And this amounts to saying also that, provided this wonder is duly ordered, we can love as we please.

---

51 AT V, 58, 9.
52 AT IV, 614, 1–4.

The Role of *Amicitia* in Political Life
Susan James, University of London

The ancient idea that love consists in an urge to unite oneself to another reverberates throughout the literature of the early-modern period. It is explicated, for example, by Descartes, who explains that, when one is in love, one considers oneself and the object of one's affection as part of a whole, and cares for this union in the way that one previously cared for oneself.[1] For the most part, however, the unity of lovers is compatible with their distinctness. While Descartes does not rule out the possibility of states in which the boundary between lover and beloved is entirely dissolved, he maintains that the character of the bond between them is usually shaped by the lover's perception of his relation to the object of his passion. In particular, the nature of his love depends on whether he perceives himself as the lesser element in the whole, or as its greater and nobler part. For example, if he loves a flower, a bird, or a building:

> [T]he highest perfection which this love can properly reach cannot make us put our life at any risk for the preservation of such things. For they are not among the nobler parts of the whole which we and they constitute, any more than our nails or our hair are among the nobler parts of our body; and it would be preposterous to risk the whole body for the preservation of our hair.[2]

The lover therefore needs to retain a robust sense of his own worth, as compared with that of his beloved, and this in turn presupposes that he remains an individual with distinct interests and qualities. The same applies, moreover, when an individual perceives the object of his affection as greater than himself, as when a man loves his ruler or his country. "If his love is perfect," Descartes warns, "he should regard himself as only a tiny part of the whole which he and they constitute, [and] should be no more afraid to go to certain death for their service than one is afraid to draw a little blood from one's arm to improve the health of the rest of the body."[3] Even where self-sacrifice may be required, the

---

1 "Letter to Chanut, 1 February 1647," C. Adam et P. Tannery, *Oeuvres de Descartes. Nouvelle présentation* (12 vols., Paris, Vrin, 1964–76), iv, 600–617, translated in J. Cottingham, R. Stoothoff, D. Murdoch and A. Kenny, *The Philosophical Writings of Descartes* (3 vols., Cambridge: Cambridge University Press, 1985–91), iii, 305–14.

2 J. Cottingham, R. Stoothoff, D. Murdoch and A. Kenny, *The Philosophical Writings of Descartes* (3 vols., Cambridge: Cambridge University Press, 1985–91), iii, 311.

3 Ibid.

union that constitutes love is not a complete merging. While it alters the lover's conception of his interests, and thus changes his sense of what it is rational for him to do, he continues to identify certain qualities as his own, and conceives of himself as a distinct part of the whole, whose actions can promote or undermine its wellbeing.

This account is organised around an underlying conception of love as a way of overcoming neediness or lack. While some early-modern writers trace this interpretation back to Adam's longing for a companion, to the soul's yearning for the world of forms, or to a nostalgia for our prenatal experience in the womb, Descartes argues that our adult loves hark back to the time when the soul was first joined to the body and recognised its dependence on the matter that nourished it. "The soul, uniting itself willingly to that new matter, felt love for it; and later, if the food happened to be lacking, it felt sadness. And if its place was taken by some other matter unsuitable as food for the body, it felt hatred."[4] Thus, human love originates when the soul willingly joins itself to the body and begins to be concerned for the body's needs, at which point its emotions begin to be organised around bodily satisfactions; but so-called real union does not destroy the distinctness of body and soul any more than subsequent loves destroy the distinctness of self and other.

The view that love is grounded in the relationship between body and soul is consonant with Descartes' view that our passions answer to the needs we possess as embodied creatures. The soul's original love for the matter that fed the body is reiterated in our everyday loves for things that preserve or enhance our embodied existence, which include objects such as birds, flowers and buildings, as well as other humans.[5] However, while such loves may answer to our needs and wants, we can nevertheless survive their loss, just as we are able to survive the cutting of our nails or hair. These physical parts regenerate; and in a similar fashion, so Descartes seems to imply, our disposition to maintain the unity of body and soul inclines us to replace lost loves with new ones.

Such a cool analysis suggests that humans whose yearning for unity with the beloved causes them to lose touch with their existence as individuals succumb to passions that are excessive and inappropriate. A lover like Shakespeare's Orlando, who pins verses to his mistress on every forest tree,[6] becomes faintly ridiculous, much in the manner of the lovesick crane described by Descartes' contemporary, Osier Ghislen de Busbecq, in his *Turkish Letters*:

> This Balearic crane showed the most obvious signs of affection for a Spanish soldier... So devoted was it to him that it would walk for hours at his side, and stop when he stopped, and stand at his side while he sat down, and allow itself to be

---

4 Ibid.
5 Ibid.
6 William Shakespeare, *As you Like It*, Act 3, Scene 2.

patted and stroked... When he was away from home it would go to his room and peck at the door with its beak... If it was opened it would look about everywhere trying to discover him; finding this to be in vain it would go all over the house with such loud and piercing cries as to be quite intolerable... When its friend returned, it would spread its wings and rush to meet him with such absurd and ungainly movements that it seemed to be practising the figures of some outlandish dance or preparing to skirmish with a pygmy. As though this were not enough, it finally made a habit of sleeping under his bed, where it actually laid an egg for him.[7]

There are nevertheless cases where love and individuality come into direct and serious conflict. According to Descartes, a good citizen who conceives of himself both as a distinct individual and as a part of a nation should ideally be prepared to sacrifice himself for this greater whole. His love for his country should include a desire for its survival and wellbeing that is stronger than his own desire to be united to it, and thus stronger than his desire to survive as one of its parts. The theoretical difficulty posed by this transition is reflected in Descartes' awkward analogy between dying for one's country and losing blood for the sake of one's health. Like cutting one's hair, losing a little blood does not threaten one's life and, according to seventeenth-century medical opinion, may even improve it. However, Descartes is not talking here about such minor palliative measures as cupping, but rather about the political equivalent of bleeding to death. The perfect, patriotic love that he extols may require the sacrifice of one's life, and the self-obliterating passion that prompts a citizen to yield it willingly sits uncomfortably with the idea that love feeds or strengthens the embodied self. To sacrifice himself for his country, a citizen must believe that he is distinct from it, and that the country will survive without him; but in order to view its wellbeing as more valuable than his own survival, his love for it must extend beyond any care for his individual needs. So the sense of insufficiency by which love is aroused can be social as well as individual, and sometimes transcends concern for the body.

The idea that love is a response to lack carries with it the implication that one loves what one is not. If we were perfect we might not experience love at all; but, finite as we are, our loves are for the most part an attempt to make ourselves more complete, and their variety is a reminder of the numerous kinds of insufficiency that human beings suffer. In our yearning for completion there is very little that we are incapable of loving, and a mark of the strength and versatility of the imagination is its capacity to represent so many different objects and states of affairs as lovable. In contrast to this focus on difference, however, stands the no less influential Aristotelian contention that we love objects which resemble us. This provides a way to account for the fact that humans tend to love other mem-

---

7 Ogier Ghislen de Busbecq, *Turkish Letters*, 1656–60, trans. Edward Seymour Foster, (Oxford: Oxford University Press 1927). Republished by Sickle Moon Books, 2001, p. 68.

bers of their own species, and, as Descartes, among others, points out, offers to explain why people find it easier to love an incarnate as opposed to an immaterial deity. In addition, though, it underlies the long-established belief that individuals tend to be drawn to those who share with them some significant feature, such as their profession, language, temperament, nationality or class. This ancient and deeply-entrenched view had been pithily expressed by Augustine, who pessimistically remarks that diversity of languages makes a man better pleased with his dog than with his equal,[8] and is taken up by a string of early-modern authors who hold that our loves are directed and limited by perceptions of similarity which incline us to favour neighbours over strangers, and the familiar over the exotic. Because similarity and difference are perceived by the imagination, and therefore vary with our individual as well as our collective histories and temperaments, the disposition to love those who resemble us does not impose a very strong constraint. Shared interests can easily overcome differences of language and nationality, and the associative mechanisms that guide the passions give each person's affections an individual twist. For example, as Descartes recounts, a childhood affection left him with a fondness for people with squints.[9]

Nevertheless, there remains a discrepancy between the view that we are inclined to love objects that resemble us and the claim that we love what we perceive ourselves as lacking. One of the ways that early-modern theorists aim to lessen this tension is by producing typologies of types of love that are broad enough to encompass both dispositions. To take a standard, if relatively obscure, example of this approach, the English author Haworth explains that love for an object that one esteems less than oneself is benevolence; love for an equal is friendship or charity; and love for 'higher' objects such as one's parents, a city, a country, or a prince is devotion.[10] Here, benevolence and devotion are directed to objects that differ from oneself, and contribute to the organisation and maintenance of social and political hierarchy. Friendship, by contrast, is what one feels for an equal, and it is often discussed in the context of the individual friendships between men, so celebrated in the literature of the Renaissance and the seventeenth century. A famous example of this trope is to be found in Montaigne's lament for his 'equitable and equable' relationship with Étienne La Boétie, in which similarities of age, status, and intellectual interests precipitated a love so exceptional that nature could only be expected to achieve such a thing about once in every three centuries.[11] Their two souls 'mingled and blended so completely that they effaced the seam between them' and they became 'one soul in two bodies'. As Montaigne acknowledges, his own account echoes Aristotle's and

---

8 Augustine, *De Civitate Dei*, I, xix. vii.
9 Letter to Chanut, 6 June 1647, cf. AT V, 57.
10 S. Haworth, *Anthropologia* (London, 1680).
11 Montaigne, *Essays*, trans. D. Frame (Hamish Hamilton: London, 1958), "Of Friendship," 139–42.

Cicero's assertion that true *amicitia* can only exist between virtuous men, a claim that had already been taken up a generation earlier by Sir Thomas Elyot in his *The Book Named the Governor*. While Cicero is right, Elyot comments, virtue is not sufficient for friendship, because men bound by *amicitia* need to have something else in common, namely "semblable or much like manners." This explains why it is unusual for a sour-faced and inflexible man to be friends with a sweet-faced and tractable one, and why *amicitia* seldom springs up between individuals of different ranks. Moreover, it also accounts for the fact that the greatest friendships arise between people who resemble one another not only in tastes and manner, but physically as well.[12] Here Elyot retells the much-cited history of Titus, a young Roman, and Gisippus, a young Athenian, who "seemed to be one in form and personage", and whose mutual affection made each willing to give his life for the other, as well as enabling them to love the same woman without suffering from mutual jealousy.

Although writers distinguish the types of love which unite us to objects that resemble us from those which prompt us to join with objects unlike ourselves, it remains to consider how these two dispositions are thought to manifest themselves in political life, and whether they are held to conflict. I shall suggest that both models are used to describe and legitimate the role of love in sustaining political communities, and that some theorists explicitly address the points at which they are in tension with each other. The role played by love in creating and sustaining political communities is often discussed in terms of the Ciceronian conundrum, 'Is it better to rule by love or by fear?' Despite Machiavelli's and Hobbes's insistence that the most powerful tool available to sovereigns is fear, it remained widely agreed that the best way to generate stable and productive communities is to rule as far as possible by love. Among absolutist writers, this conclusion is often defended with the help of an analogy between the state and the family. The family, it is assumed, is a natural institution, held together by the heterosexual love of men and women and the natural affection between parents and their children. Furthermore, it is hierarchically organised; love should properly incline a wife to obey her husband, who possesses a right to command her as well as a responsibility for her welfare; and the reverence due to parents should incline children to do what they are told. Since the state is a re-creation of these family relationships, the love it generates should be guided by the principle of proportionality we have already encountered. Citizens should be devoted to their country, to the patriarchal sovereign who symbolises it, and to the laws he commands, and should value all of these above themselves. The sovereign should feel appropriate degrees of paternal benevolence for the citizens collectively and for individuals according to rank; and citizens of a given rank should feel a fundamentally fraternal devotion, friendship, or benevolence for one another.

---

12 Sir Thomas Elyot, *The Book Named the Governor*, 1531 (London: Dent, 1962), 132–4.

This image of political society emphasises its hierarchical character, and principally represents political relationships as bonds of love for people who differ from oneself. However, just as there are within the family brothers who possess the same status, so the state contains citizens whose love for one another ought to be a love between equals. It is therefore important to consider what role is played in the maintenance of the state by this love between people who are, socially speaking, the same. Does love grounded on similarity strengthen or undermine the hierarchical loves on which, according to this analysis, absolutist societies depend? Or is it so overshadowed as to be politically invisible?

Among the principal defenders of early-modern absolutism, this question is perhaps most explicitly addressed by Jean Bodin, although, as I shall go on to show, his argument is not confined to advocates of monarchy and is taken up in other quarters. Bodin, however, provides an exceptionally clear analysis, which occurs in both the Latin and French editions of his *Six Livres de la République*, and is also included in the English translation of 1606 from which my quotations are drawn.

Invoking the analogy we have already considered, Bodin begins by comparing state and family: "a family, well and wisely ordered, is the true image of a city; so also is the manner of the government of a family the true model for the government of a commonwealth."[13] Societies arise when individual families, made up of some combination of wives, children, and servants under the authority of a father, join together, motivated by considerations of security and a desire for company and conversation. Gradually, the love that unites spouses and their children modulates into friendship between extended families or kinsmen, and goodwill between those who share some common interest or purpose. By degrees, families create a civil society in imitation of the natural society with which they are familiar. Houses combine into hamlets, villages, and towns, and their inhabitants unite into what Bodin variously describes as fraternities, corporations, and colleges. Finally, a commonwealth is formed when people who have created these pre-political institutions unite under a single sovereign, possessed of the power to make and enforce the law.[14] It is perfectly possible for a sovereign to rule directly over a group of families without any intermediate colleges or corporations, just as it is perfectly possible for a people to unite into colleges or corporations and live, like the tribes of Israel, without a sovereign. In most commonwealths, however, the sovereign rules over both families and colleges, and this arrangement brings with it a number of benefits.

The primary task of a sovereign is to guarantee justice by making and enforcing law. But while the law is a good way of resolving disputes, so Bodin explains, it is also a source of conflict. The fact that justice is inflexible and always keeps

---

13 Jean Bodin, *Six books of a Commonweale*, translated into English 1606. Facsimile edition ed. Kenneth Douglas McRae (Cambridge: Harvard University Press, 1962), 8.
14 Op. cit., pp. 361, 363.

the "uprightness of itself" may enable it to put an end to law suits; but because it creates winners and losers it does not put an end to hatred, and can often inflame anger and turn friends into enemies.[15] A prince who wants to be loved must therefore take care not to administer justice himself, since doing so will inevitably attract the disdain and hatred of those whom he punishes. He should therefore delegate this risky task to his magistrates, and confine himself to distributing benefits.[16] As a result, his subjects will love him, and will "discharge their choler upon the magistrates and judges." (This, Bodin remarks in an aside, "even nature hath figured out to us in the king of the bees, who never hath sting, lest he should hurt any."[17])

While a prince may be able to deflect hatred away from himself, the fact that the rule of law generates hostility as well as satisfaction remains a problem. Even when animosity is not directed at the sovereign, hatred between citizens and the representatives of the law poses a danger to the state, and can, in principle, undermine its stability. Here Bodin appeals to the colleges and corporations which, as we have seen, mediate between families and the state. These, he argues, can hold society together by maintaining love and friendship among citizens, thus offsetting the destructive effects of justice. For unlike either the family or the state, corporations, colleges, and fraternities are relatively non-hierarchical institutions, in which friendship between equals can flourish.

Echoing Aristotle's view that good legislators have had more care for friendship than for justice, Bodin cites the achievements of the greatest of the ancient lawmakers. When Numa made the Roman law, he followed the example of Solon and established guilds or fraternities for each occupation or profession, giving each the power to govern their own affairs. In Sparta, Lycurgus ordered his subjects to eat together in groups bound by friendship, and in most of the towns of Greece there were fraternities and companies bound by "unity, company and friendship, eating and drinking together for the most part, and having no judges but themselves."[18] The reason for creating these associations was that amity and friendship are the only foundation of all human and civil society, and are more effective as a means of maintaining a polity than justice itself. They enforce natural as opposed to legislative justice, and "pluck up all controversies by the root, with great quietness and love reconciling subjects among themselves, together with the commonweale."[19]

Bodin therefore takes the role of colleges and corporations extremely seriously, both as a historical phenomenon and as a feature of the type of commonwealth he wants to defend. Historically, he argues, they existed in pagan societies, and

---

15 Op. cit., p. 364.
16 Op. cit., p. 512.
17 Op. cit., pp. 378, 512.
18 Op. cit., p. 363.
19 Op. cit., pp. 363–4.

also in the early Church, where Christians held regular feasts at which they gave one another "devout kissing and charitable embraces." These ceremonies survive in the feasts and banquets still celebrated in Venice, and above all in Switzerland, where "the fraternities and companies in every town have their common houses or halls, where they makes feasts and banquets. If any strife or contention arises among them that be of the fellowship or company, it is by common consent there ended, and the definite sentence there written on the table, and that not in ink, but chalk."[20] Turning more earnestly to his own day, Bodin examines the legal issues surrounding the constitutions and discipline of colleges, technical issues that are of paramount importance precisely because properly governed colleges and corporations are in his view essential to the survival of a state. So much so, that to ask whether it could endure without them "is as much as to demand whether a commonwealth can be maintained without love and amity; without which the world itself cannot long stand."[21]

One of the defining features of a college is the fact that it brings together individuals who resemble one another in some significant respect. They may, for example, share an occupation or civic duty, come from the same village, or be united by a particular vocation. They may be students and teachers, or adherents of a single religion. (Colleges made and ordained for religion or public devotion, Bodin remarks, "are grown into number almost infinite, differing as we see in laws, manners, life, attire, orders, fashions and apparel"[22]). The love that binds the members of such an institution together, and enables them to avoid the conflicts born of civil justice, arises principally out of this similarity and the common interests it generates. So while natural love can successfully unite the members of a family into a hierarchically ordered whole, its civil counterpart cannot, in Bodin's view, hold a commonwealth together. The devotion that citizens feel towards their prince, and his benevolence for them, are not as powerful as familial love, and because they cannot efface the divisive effects of justice, they need to be supplemented by amity and friendship among the nearly equal members of corporations. To put the point in more general terms, the body politic can only be secure and peaceful when love for those who differ from oneself exists alongside love for those who resemble one. Moreover, the latter kind of love, fostered in colleges and fraternities, is the stronger and less fragile of these two bonds. Thus, the kind of sovereignty that Bodin advocates is absolute, but not too absolute. As well as defending the need for a sovereign monarch, he recognises the value of allowing people to combine around their similarities, and settle their disagreements among themselves, and views this as a vital condition of political harmony. It is true, of course, as he acknowledges, that corporations may rule themselves badly and become seditious and rebellious; and also true that they

---

20 Op. cit., p. 364.
21 Op. cit., p. 379.
22 Op. cit., p. 365.

may do this under the cover of religion, like the Anabaptists of Munster.[23] So this route to security is far from foolproof. But its dangers are less grave than those that attend more authoritarian forms of monarchy, in which the unadulterated rule of justice is more likely to destroy the love on which the commonwealth depends.[24]

Bodin's analysis of the means by which corporations sustain friendship and amity lays considerable emphasis on the ceremonies that hold them together. God, he reminds his readers, commanded the Jews to celebrate Passover and the feast of tabernacles in an appropriately solemn manner.[25] When Numa first created fraternities in ancient Rome, he gave each one its own patrons, priests, and sacrifices, ordering that the sacrifices should take place on certain fixed days of the year. The early Christians likewise had their feasts and kissings, while advocates of different religions express their beliefs through laws and fashions. The conviction that love and loyalty can be most effectively aroused through ceremonies that appeal to the senses and imagination, and that these resources can be used to strengthen collective identity, is a commonplace of early-modern culture, appreciated by supporters of a wide range of political and theological positions. Thus, defenders of monarchy tend to dwell on the benign consequences of displays of royal grandeur, while Christian writers chart the forms of reverence aroused by styles of preaching, liturgy, or church architecture. There is therefore no intrinsic link between Bodin's view that corporations need ceremonies to arouse and maintain amity and the political significance with which he endows them. What gives them their special role is not so much the fact that they rely on rituals, which might in principle be used to generate various passions for various purposes, as the fact that, within corporations, ritual is used to encourage love among equals. Ceremonies, costumes, and traditions may all help to give a corporation a distinctive identity, and serve to define a sense of belonging that both unites its members and separates them from others. The fact that a particular group of people are all students, for example, will breed a certain sympathy among them; but the fact that they hold regular meetings and exchanges of news, undertake common projects, and eat together, will, so Bodin claims, consolidate their friendship.

It is also possible to separate Bodin's central claim that a successful state depends on a division of political and psychic labour between sovereign and corporations from his defence of absolute monarchy. What seems paramount in this part of his argument is that the sovereign, whether an individual or a collectivity, should possess enough power to make and dispense justice, and that a range of corporations should indirectly strengthen it by building solidarity among their members and censoring them when necessary. Detached from a monarchical

---

23 Op. cit., p. 389.
24 Op. cit., p. 383.
25 Op. cit., pp. 363–4.

form of sovereignty, Bodin's analysis of corporations can, in principle, be incorporated into defences of other kinds of political constitution, and, perhaps, it is therefore unsurprising that comparable arguments are deployed by opponents of kingship. A full-scale discussion of this topic would need to examine the various contexts in which amity is regarded as a goal of political institutions, a project too large to undertake here. However, we can begin to get a sense of the range of types of position that acknowledge the need for states to foster this kind of civic love between equals if we consider how a strand of argument comparable to Bodin's is used by Spinoza in his *Tractatus Theologico-Politicus* to defend a broadly republican stance.

Spinoza is keen to consider how passionate citizens can be prevented from sliding into superstition, and thus into faction and conflict. As long as citizens are passionate, a simple appeal to the rationality of obeying the sovereign law will probably fail to move them. And because passionate people are different from one another, their responses to measures designed to make them comply with the law will be diverse and to some extent unpredictable. However, the very fact of these differences provides a partial way out. As Spinoza presents the matter, citizens will co-operate with one another when they feel devotion – a combination of love and wonder which easily changes into love as its objects become familiar[26] – for some aspect of their common way of life. The problem is that different people are devoted to different things. For example, some are attached to sectarian religions and others to the state, and the feelings of each group are reinforced by distinctive traditions and ceremonies. To cater for this variety, a state will have to make room for many devotional practices, as I shall call them, each with its own ways of fostering reverence for, or identification with, the values or way of life on which the state depends.[27] These practices, as Spinoza conceives them, are organised around narratives, images, and ceremonies, and their truth status is relatively unimportant. It is immaterial, for example, whether the religious believe that God is a fire or a spirit, whether he is just or merciful, or whether he acts from free will or from the necessity of his nature;[28] what matters is just that some belief or other should be incorporated into practices that strengthen the ability to live co-operatively by generating the devotion on which this depends.[29]

While Spinoza does not say a great deal about devotional practices, and mainly focuses on their role in arousing patriotism and love of the moral law, one can perhaps envisage them on the model laid out by Bodin in his account of corporations and colleges. Both authors agree that these institutions of civil society serve to create friendships between individuals by enabling them to combine

---

26 Spinoza, *Ethics,* III.52s; III. Definitions of the Affects, X.
27 Spinoza, *Tractatus Theologico-Politicus*, Ch. 19.
28 *TTP,* ed. Gebhardt, p. 178.
29 Spinoza explains how this might work in an aristocracy in *Tractatus Politicus*, VIII. 46.

with others who share their tastes, interests and experience; both agree that a state needs to permit the existence of a range of such institutions, so that people of many different types can benefit from them; both agree that rituals and ceremonies are an important means of generating and sustaining the relevant kind of love; and both agree that this passion is not simply love for other individuals, but love for institutions, and thus for some aspect of the political order. By describing the passion that grows up in this way as devotion, Spinoza also offers a further way of resolving the tension from which we began, the tension between love understood as a yearning for the other and love understood as an attraction to an object that resembles oneself. Where Bodin concentrates on friendship, the love between equals that colleges and corporations foster, Spinoza instead highlights devotion, the love for an institution or way of life larger than oneself. Each, however, is an element of the love that an institution can arouse and sustain, and it will often be difficult to achieve the one without the other.

The view that civil institutions are needed to create a kind of love without which the state cannot function is congenial both to defenders of republican forms of sovereignty such as Spinoza, and defenders of monarchical constitutions such as Bodin. Moreover, as the work of these authors suggests, the defence of the kind of institutions that Bodin calls colleges can provide the basis of an argument for religious pluralism, which also attracted advocates across a broad political spectrum. In his *Six Livres*, Bodin uses the view that people need to be able to combine with those who resemble them in order to explain the existence of a plurality of religions. It follows from this need that people are liable to form themselves into different sects, and a wise sovereign will not put his power at risk by trying to stop them. Nor will he worry too much about the existence of superstition, as long as this does not threaten the state. Writing somewhat later in his *Heptaplomeres*, a set of dialogues that was complete by 1588 though never published, Bodin reiterates this view and places it alongside a further set of arguments for religious toleration. One only has to look at earlier societies, he claims, whether these are Greek, Latin, or pagan, to see that it is perfectly possible for states to accommodate a great number of religions. Moreover, their existence may strengthen the power of the sovereign, which is why the Turks and Persians have always allowed them. But there is also a philosophical case for regarding different religions as diverse expressions of the harmony of the universe, and as a just reflection of the diversity of nature itself.[30] Spinoza is a less enthusiastic exponent of religious pluralism than some of the participants in Bodin's dialogue who take a thoroughly modern-seeming delight in diversity. Nevertheless, he confronts the need to permit groups of citizens to find their own forms of worship and their own ways of conceiving and following the moral law, and emphatically recommends devotional practices as the means to achieve this end. He

---

30 Jean Bodin, *Colloquium of the Seven about Secrets of the Sublime*, trans. Marion Leathers Daniels Kuntz (Princeton: Princeton University Press, 1975).

even remarks at one point that individuals have an obligation to discover some form of practice that will indirectly strengthen their ability to conform to the law by arousing a love capable of binding them to the political order.

Among early-modern writers, only Machiavelli is sure that fear is a stronger bond than love for maintaining the state. Across a wide spectrum of opinion about the best form of government, practically everyone else agreed that love is an essential ingredient of political society. A rational understanding of the role of law may persuade a few individuals to adhere to its commands. But for most people, the bonds of civil society need to be more compelling. If they are to be compelling, however, they must be responsive to the ways in which groups identify themselves and are able to live together successfully in peace and concord. Few doubted the Biblical contention that the strongest bond of concord is the bond of love.

L'apparition de l'amour de soi dans l'*Éthique*
Chantal Jaquet, University of Paris I

Souvent présenté comme un philosophe de la joie, Spinoza devrait plus justement être défini comme un philosophe de l'amour. Toute l'*Éthique*, en effet, tend à conduire l'homme vers la béatitude ou liberté qui consiste, d'après le scolie de la proposition XXVI de la partie V, «dans un amour constant et éternel envers Dieu, autrement dit dans l'amour de Dieu pour les hommes.» Le caractère fondamental et déterminant de l'amour, que Spinoza assimile, comme chacun sait, à une joie qu'accompagne l'idée d'une cause extérieure[1] est avéré dès les premiers écrits. Dans le *Traité de la réforme de l'entendement*, Spinoza affirme déjà que «toute notre félicité et notre misère ne résident qu'en un seul point: à quelle sorte d'objet sommes-nous attachés par l'amour?»[2]. Toute la réflexion éthique chez Spinoza s'ordonne ainsi autour de la nature de nos attachements et de la détermination de nos objets d'amour.

Pourtant, paradoxalement, cette philosophie de l'amour semble accorder peu de place à l'amour-propre ou à l'amour de soi, à tel point que le prologue du *Traité de la réforme de l'entendement* qui s'ouvre sur le recensement des objets d'amour omet de les mentionner. Chez Spinoza, il est question de l'amour des richesses, de l'amour des honneurs, ou du plaisir,[3] il est question de l'amour du corps,[4] du prochain,[5] de la patrie, de Dieu, et plus généralement de l'amour des choses périssables ou des choses éternelles, mais guère de l'amour de soi. Est-ce à dire que cet amour de soi soit hors de question? On peut en tout cas se le demander si l'on en juge par l'absence totale de ce concept dans les écrits de jeunesse, et par sa rareté dans l'*Éthique*. En effet, les concepts d'amour de soi ou d'amour-propre ne figurent ni dans le *Court Traité* ni dans le *Traité de la réforme de l'entendement* ni même dans le *Traité théologico-politique*. Les termes «*liefde*», ou «*amor*» sont certes bien présents dans le corpus antérieur à l'*Éthique*, mais jamais l'amour n'est rapporté à soi.

L'apparition des concepts d'amour-propre et d'amour de soi est non seulement tardive, mais fugitive, si l'on en croit la rareté de leurs occurrences. Le terme d'amour-propre (*philautia*) apparaît pour la première fois dans la partie III de l'*Éthique* et n'est utilisé qu'à deux reprises, dans le scolie de la proposition LV,

---

1 Cf. *Éthique* III, définitions des affects VI.
2 Cf. § 3, Appuhn.
3 Cf. *Traité de la réforme de l'entendement*, § 1–4.
4 Cf. *Court Traité*, II, XIX, § 14.
5 *Ibid.*, XVIII, § 4. Cf. également *Traité théologico-politique*, XIV, § 3.

puis dans l'appendice final au cours de la définition XXVIII. Dans le scolie de la proposition LV, la *philautia* est présentée comme un affect joyeux lié à la contemplation de soi et opposé à l'humilité.

> «Cette tristesse qu'accompagne l'idée de notre faiblesse s'appelle humilité; et la joie qui naît de la contemplation de nous-même, amour-propre, (*philautia*) ou bien satisfaction de soi-même.»

Quant au concept d'amour de soi (*amor sui*), il n'est pas vraiment distingué de celui d'amour-propre et il figure uniquement dans l'énoncé et l'explication de la définition XXVIII consacrée à l'orgueil.

> «L'orgueil est de faire de soi par amour de soi plus d'état qu'il n'est juste (*superbia est de se præ amor sui plus justo sentire*)».

Spinoza précise alors au cours de l'explication de la définition que «de même que l'estime est un effet ou propriété de l'amour, de même l'orgueil l'est de l'amour-propre (*philautiæ*), lequel pour cette raison peut également se définir comme l'amour de soi (*amor sui*), autrement dit la satisfaction de soi-même, en tant qu'elle affecte un homme de telle sorte qu'il fait de soi plus d'état qu'il n'est juste.»

Curieusement toutefois, à peine la *philautia* et l'*amor sui* sont-ils mentionnés qu'ils sombrent aussitôt dans l'oubli. Les deux substantifs vont disparaître totalement du vocabulaire de Spinoza et ne figurent plus ultérieurement ni dans l'*Éthique* ni dans le *Traité politique*. Tout au plus, retrouve-t-on quelques occurrences du verbe «s'aimer soi-même», appliqué aux modes dans la partie IV, au scolie de la proposition XVIII,[6] et à Dieu dans la partie V.[7] Néanmoins, les deux substantifs de *philautia* et d'*amor sui* que l'on s'attendrait à rencontrer dans la partie V de l'*Éthique* pour exprimer la joie liée à la contemplation de la puissance éternelle de l'esprit saisissant les choses par le troisième genre de connaissance sont totalement absents. Ils sont supplantés par celui de satisfaction de soi-même (*acquiescentia in se ipso*) auquel ils sont assimilés, comme en témoignent les formules, «*philautia vel acquiescentia in se ipso*, et *amor sui sive acquiescentia in se ipso* qui figurent respectivement dans le scolie de la proposition LV de l'*Éthique* III et dans la définition XXVIII des affects.

Ce constat au sujet de l'absence des concepts d'amour-propre et d'amour de soi dans les œuvres de jeunesse, d'une part, et de leur rareté dans l'*Éthique*, d'autre

---

[6] «Comme la raison ne demande rien contre la nature, c'est donc elle-même qui demande que chacun s'aime lui-même (*seipsum amet*)».

[7] Cf. *Éthique*, V, XXXV: Dieu s'aime lui-même d'un amour intellectuel infini: V, XXXI, proposition, démonstration, corollaire.

part, pose un double problème. Comment expliquer premièrement que ni l'amour-propre ni l'amour de soi ni même la satisfaction de soi-même auxquels ils renvoient ne figurent dans les premiers écrits de Spinoza, et notamment dans le *Court Traité* qui traite pourtant des affects de manière détaillée? Comment expliquer deuxièmement qu'ils apparaissent dans l'*Éthique* de manière tardive pour disparaître aussitôt au profit de la satisfaction de soi-même? En somme, la question est de savoir quelles sont les raisons de leur absence première, puis de leur émergence et enfin de leur éclipse finale. Dans cette optique, il s'agira d'abord d'examiner la nature et les fondements de l'amour-propre et de l'amour de soi dans l'*Éthique*, puis de prendre appui sur leur définition pour déterminer les causes de leur absence dans le *Court Traité* et le *Traité de la réforme de l'entendement* et de mettre au jour enfin les changements doctrinaux qui rendent possibles leur apparition dans l'*Éthique*.

Nature et fondement de l'amour-propre ou de l'amour de soi

Il faut remarquer d'abord que l'amour-propre tel qu'il apparaît pour la première fois dans le scolie d'*Éthique* III, XLV, ne se définit pas comme une simple tendance à la conservation de soi, comme un attachement à soi-même qui pousse chacun à prendre soin de soi et à chercher les moyens nécessaires à cet effet, mais il implique une certaine forme de réflexivité, car il naît d'une contemplation de soi et présuppose donc une idée de soi. À ce titre, il requiert non seulement une idée du corps, mais une idée de l'esprit, autrement dit une idée de l'idée puisque l'esprit chez Spinoza n'est rien d'autre que l'idée du corps. L'amour-propre est donc non seulement un affect composé à partir d'un affect primaire, en tant qu'il est une «joie qui naît de la contemplation de nous-même», mais il est un affect complexe en tant qu'il nous renvoie à la sphère de l'idée de l'idée. La contemplation de soi implique un recul réflexif, un regard de soi sur soi qui ne va pas de soi. La question se pose donc de savoir ce que signifie au juste se contempler soi-même, et de quelle nature doit être ce soi pour qu'on puisse en tirer de la joie. Il est clair que la condition de possibilité d'une contemplation joyeuse est l'existence réelle ou imaginaire d'un soi fort, doté de vertu et d'une puissance d'agir. Se contempler soi-même n'est donc rien d'autre que contempler sa puissance d'agir. L'idée de sa propre faiblesse, en effet, s'accompagne de tristesse et ne saurait donner naissance à l'amour-propre, mais seulement au sentiment d'humilité. C'est ce qui ressort clairement du scolie de la proposition LV de l'*Éthique* III, l'affect de joie qu'implique l'amour-propre «se répète toutes les fois que l'homme contemple ses vertus, autrement dit sa puissance d'agir.» C'est ce qui apparaît également de façon très nette au cours de la définition non plus de l'amour-propre, mais de la satisfaction de soi-même auquel la *philautia* est assimilée.

> «La satisfaction de soi-même est une joie qui naît de ce qu'un homme se contemple lui-même, lui et sa puissance d'agir (*homo seipsum, suamque agendi potentiam contemplatur*)».[8]

Cette formule, «lui et sa puissance d'agir», qui explicite ce qu'il faut entendre derrière le fait qu'un homme se contemple lui-même n'apparaît pas par hasard, car elle figure également dans la proposition LIII de la partie III.[9] En réalité, se contempler soi-même et contempler sa puissance d'agir constituent une seule et même chose. La puissance d'agir, n'est rien d'autre que l'essence actuelle donnée de l'homme, c'est-à-dire l'aptitude à produire des effets qui dépendent des lois de sa nature. Spinoza assimile en effet la *potentia agendi* d'une chose à son *conatus*, à son effort pour persévérer dans l'être, ou ce qui revient au même à son essence actuelle. C'est ce qui ressort notamment de la démonstration de la proposition VII de l'*Éthique* III:

> «La puissance ou effort, par lequel elle (une chose) s'efforce de persévérer dans son être n'est rien à part l'essence donnée, autrement dit actuelle de cette chose».

La puissance d'agir d'une chose désigne la réalité ou la perfection qu'elle s'efforce d'affirmer en vertu de sa nature propre. Il est donc bien clair que se contempler soi-même, équivaut à contempler sa puissance d'agir et qu'il n'y a pas de distinction fondamentale entre les deux. Cette joie liée à la contemplation de la puissance d'agir est de nature psychophysique; elle concerne aussi bien les forces corporelles que mentales, puisque Spinoza explique dans le scolie de la proposition LV que l'amour-propre «peut conduire à faire étalage de ses forces tant spirituelles que corporelles» et il observe à ce propos que «les hommes pour cette raison sont pénibles les uns aux autres».

Cette remarque nous conduit à comprendre que l'amour-propre peut très vite dégénérer en orgueil et donner lieu à des passions comme l'envie et son cortège de haine. L'amour-propre n'est pas mauvais en lui-même, mais il peut tout aussi bien être une action qu'une passion. En soi, la contemplation de soi n'a rien de haïssable, mais l'amour-propre qui en naît peut reposer aussi bien sur une vraie qu'une fausse joie. Ainsi, selon que la contemplation repose sur une idée adéquate ou inadéquate de soi, l'amour-propre sera un affect actif, une vertu, ou au contraire un affect passif. Il faut se rappeler en effet qu'un affect est une action lorsque nous en sommes cause adéquate, c'est-à-dire lorsque nous produisons des effets qui s'expliquent par notre seule nature; il est une passion lorsque nous en sommes cause inadéquate, autrement dit partielle, de sorte que l'effet ne peut se

---

8 Cf. *Éthique* III, définitions des affects, XXV.
9 «Quand l'esprit se contemple lui-même, lui et sa puissance d'agir, il est joyeux, et d'autant plus qu'il s'imagine plus distinctement, lui et sa puissance d'agir.»

comprendre par elle seule.¹⁰ De ce point de vue, si la première occurrence de ce concept laisse entièrement ouverte la possibilité d'une contemplation adéquate ou non et englobe aussi bien la *philautia* active que passive, la seconde occurrence du terme dans la définition XXVIII met en jeu l'amour-propre en tant que passion qui donne lieu à l'orgueil où l'homme fait de soi par amour de soi plus d'état qu'il n'est juste. Ainsi l'amour-propre est un affect passif si la joie liée à la contemplation de la puissance d'agir repose sur une évaluation erronée qui surestime cette puissance. Il est au contraire une action si la joie liée à la contemplation de la puissance d'agir se fonde sur une connaissance adéquate et une juste évaluation de la perfection de cette puissance.

Il faut noter, cependant, que dans la définition XXVIII où il intervient pour la première et la dernière fois, le concept d'amour de soi, à la différence de celui d'amour-propre, est rattaché uniquement à une passion. Spinoza, il est vrai, ne semble pas distinguer *philautia* et *amor sui*, puisqu'il les assimile tous deux à la satisfaction de soi-même et présente l'orgueil comme un effet «de **l'amour-propre** et qui peut se définir pour cette raison comme **amour de soi**, autrement dit la satisfaction de soi-même en tant qu'elle affecte un homme de telle sorte qu'il fait plus d'état qu'il n'est juste». Ne pourrait-on pas toutefois conclure en s'en tenant à la lettre même du texte que l'amour-propre a une acception plus large et englobe aussi bien une action qu'une passion tandis que l'amour de soi n'est qu'une passion? Il y aurait ainsi une différence entre les deux concepts, bien que Spinoza les ait assimilés. Cette hypothèse est d'autant plus séduisante qu'elle va à l'encontre des distinctions couramment admises selon lesquelles l'amour de soi est vertueux et l'amour-propre vicieux et que Spinoza renverserait la hiérarchie des valeurs en plaçant la *philautie* plus haut que l'*amor sui*. Elle doit néanmoins être écartée pour plusieurs raisons. D'une part, si l'*amor sui* ne figure qu'à l'occasion de la définition d'une passion, à savoir l'orgueil qui en dérive, il n'est pas légitime d'en inférer qu'il est lui aussi toujours de nature passionnelle. Ce n'est pas parce que l'effet dérivé dans un cas donné est une passion, que la cause en est systématiquement une. L'amour de soi peut très bien avoir des effets actifs ou passifs et être une action comme une passion.

Deuxièmement, l'hypothèse selon laquelle l'amour de soi serait exclusivement une passion tandis que l'amour-propre engloberait aussi bien les affects actifs que passifs est infirmée par la prescription de la raison énoncée dans le scolie de la proposition XVIII de l'*Éthique* IV qui «demande que chacun s'aime lui-même». Il est clair dans ce cas que l'affect d'amour de soi est une action en tant qu'il naît de la raison. Cette conclusion s'impose à plus forte raison, lorsque Spinoza fait valoir que «Dieu s'aime lui-même d'un amour intellectuel infini»¹¹ et qu'il explique que cet amour vient de ce que «la nature de Dieu tire

---

10 Cf. *Éthique* III, définitions I, II, III.
11 *Éthique* V, XXXV.

contentement d'une infinie perfection, et ce (...) accompagné de l'idée de soi».[12] Enfin l'assimilation de l'amour-propre et de l'amour de soi à la satisfaction de soi-même ne laisse plus planer aucun doute: ils sont tous les deux des affects susceptibles d'être des actions ou des passions à l'instar de l'*acquiescentia in se ipso*. Si Spinoza ne dit jamais expressément de l'amour-propre qu'il peut être une action et naître d'une connaissance adéquate de sa puissance d'agir, mais le sous-entend simplement, s'il n'évoque l'amour de soi que dans le cadre passionnel de l'orgueil, en revanche, il distingue clairement deux satisfactions de soi, la passionnelle, qui figure notamment au cours de la définition de l'orgueil, et la rationnelle qui repose sur la vraie puissance d'agir. C'est ce qui ressort de la proposition LII de l'*Éthique* IV où Spinoza affirme que «la satisfaction de soi-même peut naître de la raison, et seule la satisfaction qui naît de la raison est la plus haute qui puisse exister.» Ainsi, si l'amour-propre et l'amour de soi ne sont autres que la satisfaction de soi-même, il est clair qu'ils peuvent être des affects actifs ou passifs. Mais qu'ils soient fondés sur ce que Spinoza appelle dans cette proposition la vraie puissance d'agir de l'homme (*vera hominis agendi potentia*), c'est-à-dire sur la contemplation de sa puissance de comprendre ou qu'ils reposent sur la puissance d'agir simple, laquelle n'est rien d'autre que l'effort pour persévérer dans l'être, il n'en reste pas moins que dans tous les cas de figure, il ne saurait y avoir d'amour-propre ou d'amour de soi sans puissance d'agir.

À partir de cette conclusion il devient possible, dans un deuxième temps, de comprendre pourquoi le concept d'amour de soi ne figure pas dans les premiers écrits.

L'absence d'amour-propre dans le *Court Traité* et le *Traité de la réforme de l'entendement*

En effet, si la condition pour que l'homme puisse éprouver de l'amour-propre est l'existence d'une *potentia agendi* que l'homme contemple comme la sienne, de manière soit adéquate soit inadéquate, il est clair que ces affects ne sauraient trouver droit de cité ni dans le *Court Traité* ni dans le *Traité de la réforme de l'entendement*.

Dans le *Court Traité*, l'homme ne dispose pas d'une puissance d'agir; il est pensé comme un être faible qui n'a pas d'existence par lui-même et qui a besoin de s'unir à autre chose que lui-même pour se conserver et atteindre sa perfection. Le point de départ de la réflexion anthropologique et de la théorie de l'amour dans cet ouvrage est le constat de la faiblesse humaine et de l'impuissance.

---

12 *Ibid.*, démonstration.

> «En raison de la faiblesse de notre nature, sans quelque chose dont nous jouissons, à quoi nous sommes unis, et par quoi nous soyons fortifiés, nous ne pourrions exister.»[13]

Seul l'amour d'un objet peut nous arracher à l'impuissance, nous permettre d'exister et de persévérer dans notre être. Spinoza insiste sur ce point:

> «Il est nécessaire, avons-nous dit, à cause de la faiblesse de notre nature, que nous aimions quelque objet et que nous nous unissions à lui pour exister.»[14]

Sans un objet d'amour nous cessons d'être. C'est d'ailleurs la raison pour laquelle nous ne pouvons nous affranchir de l'amour. Cesser d'aimer, c'est cesser de vivre. Mais cet amour vital ne saurait être un amour de soi, car l'homme n'a pas de pouvoir propre d'exister. Il est impensable de s'aimer soi-même, car pour exister, il faut pour ainsi dire sortir de soi. Il n'y a de salut que dans l'amour d'une autre chose que soi. C'est pourquoi d'ailleurs le seul véritable amour est l'amour de Dieu. En effet, «il est certain que par l'amour des choses périssables et notre union avec elles, nous ne serons nullement fortifiés dans notre nature, considérant qu'elles sont faibles elles-mêmes, et qu'un invalide ne peut en porter un autre.»[15] Dieu seul a l'existence et possède l'être. Par conséquent, seule l'union avec Dieu confère à l'homme l'être et la puissance.

> «Puisque l'essence de Dieu est infinie, il y a en lui une activité infinie et une négation infinie de toute passivité (...) et conséquemment dans la mesure où ayant plus d'essence, elles sont plus étroitement unies à Dieu, les choses ont aussi plus d'activité et moins de passivité, et sont aussi plus affranchies du changement et de la corruption».[16]

Par conséquent, si l'amour de soi présuppose la puissance d'agir, il ne saurait exister dans le *Court Traité*.

C'est le même phénomène qui se produit dans le *Traité de la réforme de l'entendement*, où la nature humaine se définit par sa faiblesse native,[17] de sorte qu'il faut à tout prix la renforcer par l'institution d'une vie nouvelle et la recherche d'un souverain bien. Spinoza met l'accent sur le caractère tragique de l'existence qui est sans cesse menacée et exposée à périr si nul remède n'est trouvé.

---

13 *Court Traité*, II, V, § 5.
14 *Ibid.* § 6.
15 *Ibid.*
16 *Ibid.* II, XXVI, § 8.
17 Cf. § 5 où Spinoza fait allusion à l'homme dans sa faiblesse qui «conçoit une nature humaine de beaucoup supérieure à la sienne» et s'efforce de l'acquérir.

> «Je me voyais, en effet, dans un extrême péril et contraint de chercher un remède fût-il incertain: de même un malade atteint d'une affection mortelle, qui voit la mort imminente, s'il n'applique un remède, est contraint de le chercher, fût-il incertain, de toutes ses forces, puisque tout son espoir est dans ce remède.»

La maladie de l'existence ne se soigne qu'à l'aide d'amour et d'union. Mais pour que le remède soit efficace, cet amour et cette union doivent porter sur une chose éternelle, comme la Nature ou Dieu et non sur les biens périssables recherchés par la foule.

> «Les objets que poursuit le vulgaire non seulement ne fournissent aucun remède propre à la conservation de notre être, mais ils l'empêchent, et fréquemment cause de perte pour ceux qui les possèdent, ils sont toujours cause de perte pour ceux qu'ils possèdent».[18]

Il en irait alors de l'amour de soi comme de l'amour des choses périssables. Loin de permettre à l'homme de se conserver, il le conduirait à sa perte. Ainsi, pour reprendre l'analogie entre l'existence et la maladie, s'aimer soi-même, équivaudrait pour un malade à aimer sa maladie au lieu de la fuir. L'amour de soi serait alors la mort de soi et s'apparenterait à une forme de suicide. S'aimer soi-même, c'est pour ainsi dire mourir.

C'est pourquoi un tel affect ne saurait raisonnablement avoir de place dans une ontologie marquée par l'impossibilité de subsister par soi seul. L'existence sans union à Dieu n'est rien d'autre que l'antichambre de la mort et se ramène à une forme de dépérissement et de dégénérescence. La preuve en est que l'union avec Dieu dans le *Court Traité* est présentée non seulement comme une fortification de l'existence, mais comme une seconde naissance, voire comme une régénération.[19] En tant qu'il est indissociable de l'existence d'une puissance d'agir et d'une

---

18 *Traité de la réforme de l'entendement*, § 2.

19 *Court Traité*, II, XXII, § 6: «Si notre connaissance et notre amour viennent à tomber sur cet être sans lequel nous ne pouvons ni exister, ni être conçus, et qui n'est aucunement corporel, les effets qu'aura aussi en nous une telle union seront et devront être incomparablement plus grands et plus magnifiques, puisqu'ils doivent s'accorder toujours avec la nature des choses auxquelles nous sommes unis.

§ 7: Et quand nous percevons de tels effets, nous pouvons dire en vérité que nous naissons encore une fois; car notre première naissance a lieu alors que nous nous sommes unis au corps, par où tels effets et mouvements des esprits animaux se sont produits, mais cette autre et seconde naissance aura lieu quand nous percevrons en nous de tout autres effets de l'amour, grâce à la connaissance de cet objet immatériel; effets qui diffèrent des premiers autant que diffère le corporel de l'incorporel, l'esprit de la chair. Cela peut d'autant mieux être appelé une régénération que de cet amour et de cette union seulement peut suivre une stabilité éternelle et inaltérable, ainsi que nous le montrerons.»

aptitude à se conserver, l'amour de soi n'a donc pas lieu d'être dans des écrits où l'homme se voit refuser une force propre pour subsister.

Il est possible toutefois de formuler une objection à cette thèse, car un point aveugle subsiste. S'il est clair que les hommes ne peuvent s'aimer eux-mêmes car ils n'ont pas vraiment d'être avant leur union à Dieu, il n'est pas évident que ce raisonnement puisse toujours tenir après leur union à Dieu. On pourrait en effet se demander pourquoi les hommes n'en viendraient pas à s'aimer eux-mêmes après cette union avec Dieu et cette régénération qui les renforce au point de les rendre éternels par leur entendement. Cette seconde naissance confère à l'homme une puissance que la première lui avait déniée. De ce point de vue, les conditions requises pour l'émergence d'un véritable amour de soi semblent réunies puisque l'homme pourrait à bon droit contempler sa puissance à travers son union avec Dieu. Il serait alors possible de concevoir un amour de soi qui découlerait de l'union avec Dieu, un amour de soi qui ne serait pas premier, mais second et consécutif à l'amour pour Dieu. L'amour de Dieu pourrait ainsi fonder un amour de soi en retour.

Mais tel n'est pas le cas dans le *Court Traité*. L'amour de Dieu confère la félicité et la liberté, mais Spinoza ne va pas jusqu'à dire qu'il s'accompagne d'amour ou de satisfaction de soi. On peut alors se demander pourquoi il en est ainsi. À cela il est possible d'avancer deux raisons:

Premièrement, l'union avec Dieu se présente sous la forme d'une fusion qui abolit toute identité personnelle, toute distinction entre l'amant et l'aimé, entre le soi et l'autre, pour promouvoir une unité telle qu'ils ne forment plus qu'un seul être et une seule essence. C'est notamment le type d'explication avancée par Léon l'hébreu dans ses *Dialogues d'amour* publiés en 1535, que Spinoza avait lus et dont il aurait pu s'inspirer dans le *Court Traité*. Le philosophe espagnol, marqué par l'école néo-platonicienne de Florence, soutient en effet que la contemplation de Dieu n'est pas contemplation de soi, mais elle implique la perte ou l'abolition de soi dans l'autre ainsi que la transformation de l'essence de l'amant en celle de l'aimé.[20]

---

20 *Dialogues d'amour*, III, 11. «Mais celui qui est transporté en contemplation perd non seulement les sens avec le sentiment du froid et du chaud: ains encore demeure vide de toute cogitation et fantaisie, excepté de celle chose qui contemple. Et encore que celle seule méditation qui reste à l'amant pensif et contemplant le fait être tant hors de tout autre souvenir, qu'il ne pense aucunement en soi, ainsi en celle qu'il contemple et désire. Qu'ainsi soit pendant qu'en cet extatique amour il contemple ce qu'il aime, aucune sollicitude ou mémoire de soi ne lui vient en pensée; et en faveur de soi ou de son bien ne fait aucune œuvre naturelle, sensitive, motive ou raisonnable: demeurant (ant il est hors et aliéné de soi) propre et totalement transformé en celle qu'il aime. Car l'essence de l'âme n'est autre que son propre acte, tellement que si elle se unit pour contempler un objet, son essence se transporte en icelui, et celui est sa propre essence: ce n'est plus âme ou essence de celui qui aime, mais seulement une actuelle espèce de la personne aimée».

Il n'est pas certain, toutefois, que Spinoza souscrive à cette thèse, car il n'aborde pas directement la question de savoir si la contemplation de Dieu est d'une nature telle que l'homme ne pense plus à lui-même et voit son essence transformée en celle de la chose aimée. Néanmoins, il laisse entendre que l'union des hommes à Dieu produit une seule et même nature. C'est ce qui ressort du chapitre XXVI où sont analysés les effets du partage avec le prochain de l'union à Dieu:

> «Nous pouvons tous avoir part également à ce salut, comme il arrive quand il excite en eux le même désir qu'en moi et fait ainsi que leur volonté se confonde avec la mienne, et que nous formions une seule et même nature s'accordant en tout».[21]

Il n'est pas question ici toutefois d'abolition de soi, mais d'accord entre les entendements.

En réalité, la véritable raison qui explique qu'il n'existe pas d'amour de soi consécutif à l'union à Dieu tient à l'absence d'un soi. L'amour de soi implique l'existence d'un sujet constitué comme tel. Pas plus qu'il n'y a de «soi» constitué au départ en vertu de la faiblesse humaine, il ne saurait y en avoir à l'arrivée. L'existence d'un soi est corrélative d'une puissance propre d'agir. Or si l'union avec Dieu confère à l'homme une force qu'il n'avait pas et le régénère, cette force d'exister n'est pas une force propre et ne permet pas l'émergence d'un soi distinct. Par conséquent, à travers l'union à Dieu il ne saurait y avoir de contemplation de soi, et partant pas d'amour de soi. La philautie est impossible, là où il n'y a ni soi ni puissance d'agir. Et pourtant elle finit par émerger dans l'œuvre de la maturité. Il importe alors comprendre pourquoi ce qui était impossible dans le *Court Traité* devient possible dans l'*Éthique*.

L'émergence de l'amour-propre et de l'amour de soi dans l'*Éthique*

La présence des concepts d'amour-propre et d'amour de soi dans l'*Éthique* soulève principalement trois questions: *Primo*, quels sont les changements théoriques qui président à leur apparition? *Secundo*, pourquoi cette apparition est-elle si tardive et n'intervient-elle qu'à la fin de la partie III? *Tertio*, pourquoi est-elle aussi rare et fugitive?

Il est clair tout d'abord que l'émergence de l'amour-propre ou de l'amour de soi est liée à une évolution de la pensée de Spinoza et à une modification radicale de sa conception de la puissance humaine. Du *Court Traité* à l'*Éthique* s'opère le

---

21 *Court Traité*, II, XXVI, § 5, point 4.

passage d'une anthropologie de la faiblesse à une anthropologie de la puissance. Certes, l'homme dans l'*Éthique* naît dans la servitude et y passe probablement le plus clair de son temps, néanmoins, il est doté d'une puissance d'agir dont il était dépourvu dans le *Court Traité*. Dans l'*Éthique*, Spinoza s'oriente vers une conception plus dynamique de la puissance et de l'activité humaine. La clé de voûte de ce changement réside dans la théorie du *conatus* qui est formulée pour la première fois dans la proposition VI de l'*Éthique* III:

> «Chaque chose, autant qu'il est en elle (*quantum in se est*) s'efforce de persévérer dans son être».

Chaque chose possède une force d'exister qui est fonction de son essence. C'est ce *quantum* de puissance inhérent à sa nature qui rend possible chez l'homme la contemplation de sa propre force d'exister et la naissance d'un affect d'amour de soi. Spinoza justifie cette attribution d'un *conatus*, d'une *vis existendi* aux choses, en faisant valoir qu'elles ne sont rien d'autre que des modes «qui expriment de manière précise et déterminée la puissance de Dieu, par laquelle Dieu est et agit».[22] Ainsi la puissance d'agir de chaque chose est une partie de la puissance de Dieu et prend la forme d'un effort pour persévérer dans l'être, c'est-à-dire pour affirmer son existence et s'opposer à tout ce qui peut la détruire. La condition *sine qua non* de l'amour-propre est l'existence d'une puissance d'agir qui s'exprime à travers l'effort pour persévérer dans l'être. C'est pourquoi la théorie du *conatus* joue un rôle déterminant. Dans le *Court Traité* cette théorie ne figure pas. Chaque chose possède, certes, une tendance à se maintenir dans le même état et à s'élever à un meilleur,[23] mais ce phénomène n'implique nullement une force propre d'exister, car il relève de ce que Spinoza appelle la providence divine. Cette providence, qui est un propre de Dieu, désigne la tendance se trouvant dans la nature en général et dans chaque chose en particulier à se conserver dans le même état. Elle s'apparente plutôt à une loi d'inertie et disparaît dans l'*Éthique* où elle est relayée par une conception plus dynamique de la puissance. Le *Court Traité* en reste à une conception intermédiaire entre la thèse des *Pensées métaphysiques* selon laquelle les choses n'ont pas de force propre pour exister et agir[24] et l'*Éthique* où elles disposent d'un pouvoir de persévérer dans leur être proportionnel à leur essence.

Une fois mis au jour les changements théoriques qui rendent raison de l'apparition de l'amour-propre dans l'*Éthique*, il reste à comprendre pourquoi ce concept surgit seulement à la fin de la partie III. En effet, si l'homme dispose originairement d'une puissance d'agir, il paraît logique qu'il s'aime d'emblée lui-

---

22 *Éthique*, III, VII, démonstration.
23 Cf. *Court Traité*, I, V, § 1.
24 Cf. *Pensées métaphysiques*, I, XI: Les choses n'ont jamais d'elles-mêmes aucune puissance pour produire quoi que ce soit, ni pour se déterminer à aucune action.

même. La question se pose alors de savoir pourquoi l'amour de soi n'est pas un affect primaire, consubstantiel au *conatus* et pourquoi il n'apparaît que tardivement dans l'*Éthique*. Alors que le *conatus* est établi dès la proposition VI de la partie III, que le désir est défini dans le scolie de la proposition IX, l'amour-propre n'est mentionné pour la première fois que dans la proposition LV. Comment comprendre son apparition à la toute fin de la partie III?

En réalité, l'amour-propre ou l'amour de soi n'implique pas seulement l'existence d'une puissance d'agir, mais un acte de contemplation de soi. Or l'existence d'un soi ne va pas de soi. Elle suppose en effet que l'homme puisse ramener toutes ses affections à l'unité d'une conscience à laquelle il se réfère. Mais l'homme ballotté et tiraillé en tous sens par ses affections n'a pas au départ la conscience de soi. Il ne se définit pas d'emblée comme un sujet conscient, mais plutôt comme un être assujetti aux causes extérieures. Le soi, par conséquent, n'est pas donné, il est à constituer. Il faut donc rendre raison de sa constitution. L'homme ne se saisit jamais directement lui-même chez Spinoza, mais il ne se connaît qu'à travers ses affections.[25] C'est pourquoi l'amour de soi ne peut pas être premier et constituer un principe anthropologique de conservation. C'est seulement à travers son effort pour persévérer dans l'être et les rencontres qui l'affectent que l'homme s'appréhende lui-même et devient conscient de soi. Il est d'abord conscient de soi comme effort ou appétit. C'est pourquoi le premier affect qui le définit est le désir entendu comme appétit conscient et non l'amour de soi. C'est seulement par réflexion sur cette force d'agir, cette *potentia agendi* qui se manifeste comme effort, puis comme désir que l'homme peut en venir à se contempler lui-même comme un être conscient de soi, à en éprouver de la joie et de l'amour-propre. L'émergence de l'amour-propre est donc tardive, car elle est le produit d'une idée de soi qu'il faut former à travers les affections du corps.

Reste enfin à comprendre pourquoi les concepts d'amour-propre et d'amour de soi disparaissent de l'horizon. Comment se fait-il que Spinoza les définisse sans en faire un usage massif? Est-ce à dire qu'ils sont simplement mentionnés pour mémoire au cours de la genèse des affects et qu'ils retombent dans l'oubli sans avoir vraiment d'incidence particulière? Une telle conclusion ne serait guère légitime, car l'amour-propre et l'amour de soi, nous l'avons vu, sont ramenés à la satisfaction de soi-même et sont présentés comme des équivalents ou des synonymes. Or la satisfaction de soi-même (*acquiescentia in se ipso*) est un concept central puisque Spinoza dira dans le scolie de la proposition LII de l'*Éthique* IV que lorsqu'elle naît de la raison, elle «est ce que nous pouvons espérer de plus haut». Le concept de satisfaction de soi-même fait non seulement l'objet d'une définition en bonne et due forme, mais il ne connaît pas le même sort que l'amour-propre ou l'amour de soi puisque Spinoza continue à en faire un usage ultérieurement. Le problème ne réside donc pas dans la minimisation des concepts d'amour-propre et d'amour de soi, vu qu'il est possible de leur appliquer à

---

25 Cf. *Éthique* II, XIX et XXII.

bon droit, en tant que synonymes, tout ce qui vaut pour la satisfaction de soi-même et de considérer, par exemple, qu'ils constituent ce que l'homme peut espérer de plus haut, lorsqu'ils sont des affects actifs, mais dans leur éclipse au profit de l'*acquiescentia in se ipso*.

Le primat du terme de satisfaction de soi-même n'obéit pas à un simple choix lexical gratuit, il correspond au souci de choisir le langage le plus adéquat pour exprimer la joie liée à la contemplation de soi-même. En effet, en toute rigueur, les termes d'amour-propre et d'amour de soi sont impropres, car l'amour par définition est une joie accompagnée de l'idée d'une cause extérieure. Or, dans le cas qui nous occupe, la joie éprouvée à la contemplation de sa propre puissance est rattachée à une cause intérieure et ne peut donc pas vraiment s'appeler de l'amour. C'est ce que Spinoza fait valoir dans le scolie de la proposition XXX de la partie III, où il examine, entre autres, les noms à donner aux affects de joie et de tristesse, liés à la contemplation de soi.

> «Puisque l'amour est une joie qu'accompagne l'idée d'une cause extérieure, et la haine une tristesse qu'accompagne également l'idée d'une cause extérieure, les affects dont je viens de parler seront donc des espèces d'amour et de haine. Mais comme amour et haine se rapportent à des objets extérieurs, nous signifierons donc ces affects par d'autres noms, à savoir [...] la joie qu'accompagne l'idée d'une cause intérieure, je l'appellerai satisfaction de soi-même, et la tristesse qui lui est contraire repentir.»

Il n'est donc pas faux de parler d'amour-propre ou d'amour de soi, car la joie liée à la contemplation de soi-même est bien une espèce d'amour, mais il est plus juste de parler de satisfaction de soi-même. Ce terme pris à la lettre manifeste davantage l'intériorité puisqu'il signifie en réalité une satisfaction en soi-même, *in se ipso*, ce que la traduction ne rend pas suffisamment.

Par ailleurs, il y a une nécessité du passage de l'amour de soi à la satisfaction de soi qui outrepasse le cadre d'un simple choix sémantique et le souci d'un langage aussi adéquat que possible. En effet, le concept d'amour implique la satisfaction, de sorte que s'aimer soi-même, c'est nécessairement se satisfaire de soi. La satisfaction est une propriété nécessaire de l'amour, comme le fait valoir l'explication de la définition VI de l'*Éthique* III. L'amour a pour propriété et non pour essence d'inciter l'amant à se joindre de volonté à la chose aimée selon Spinoza. Qu'est-ce à dire?

> «Quand je dis que c'est une propriété dans l'amant de se joindre de volonté à la chose aimée, je n'entends, moi, par volonté, ni un consentement, ni une délibération de l'âme, autrement dit un libre décret, [...] par volonté, j'entends la satisfaction (*acquiescentiam*) qui est dans l'amant à cause de la présence de la chose aimée qui renforce la joie de l'amant, ou du moins l'alimente.»

Comme tout amour, l'amour de soi implique donc, en tant que l'amant et l'aimé sont une seule et même personne, une satisfaction liée à la présence de soi à soi qui n'est autre que la contemplation de sa propre puissance. Il s'agit donc bien d'une satisfaction en soi-même, car l'amant ne saurait sortir de soi pour contempler l'aimé. C'est pourquoi l'*acquiescentia in se ipso* est l'expression véritable de ce qui se joue dans l'amour de soi.

En définitive, bien que rare, l'amour de soi est ce qu'il y a de plus cher, lorsqu'il naît d'une contemplation rationnelle de soi. Miroir de la puissance d'agir, son apparition est aussi le reflet de la mutation profonde de la conception de l'existence humaine dont la faiblesse se commue en force du *Court Traité* à l'*Éthique*. L'amour devient donc moins le signe de la finitude que de la plénitude. Rapporté à soi, à juste titre, il témoigne de l'existence d'une «*acquiescentia*», d'une quiétude en soi-même, et peut ainsi permettre de conjurer tout ce malheur de l'homme qui consiste pour Pascal «à ne pas savoir demeurer en repos dans une chambre.»

Spinoza über Liebe und Erkenntnis
Wolfgang Bartuschat, University of Hamburg

Dem Affekt der Liebe kommt in Spinozas Theorie der Affekte eine besondere Bedeutung zu. Er ist der einzige Affekt, der sich in den Teilen III bis V der „Ethik" durchhält, also durch das Ganze der Darlegung zur Theorie der Affekte, und er ist der einzige Affekt, mit dem Spinoza das Merkmal vernünftigen Einsehens (intelligere) so eng verknüpft, dass dieser Affekt durch Einsicht selbst definiert werden kann: amor intellectualis. Ich habe diesen Terminus ins Deutsche mit „geistige Liebe" übersetzt. Denn in „geistig" geht ein, dass die Liebe allein dem Geist (mens humana) angehört, nicht nur ein Affekt des Geistes ist (das sind für Spinoza alle Affekte, die er im 3. Teil seiner „Ethik" vorstellt), sondern ein Affekt, der durch den Geist allein bestimmt ist. Ich möchte heute nicht das schwierige Problem des amor intellectualis erörtern, aber zeigen, inwiefern Spinozas Theorie durch die enge Verknüpfung von Liebe und Verstand zu dieser Art von Liebe hinführt.

Ich beginne mit einer Erörterung der Stellung des Affekts der Liebe im Gefüge der Affekte, beginne also mit dem 3. Teil der „Ethik", der überschrieben ist „De Origine et Natura Affectuum" (Von dem Ursprung und der Natur der Affekte). In aller Kürze zusammengefasst, sieht Spinozas Theorie so aus: der Ursprung der Affekte ist der conatus perseverandi, das Streben nach Selbsterhaltung; die Natur der Affekte ergibt sich daraus, wie dieser conatus sich vollzieht. Aus dem conatus gewinnt Spinoza drei Kardinalaffekte und zwei aus ihnen direkt abgeleitete, die darin ebenfalls grundlegend sind; aus dem Vollzug des conatus gewinnt er alle übrigen Affekte. Das ist ein klares Deduktionsprogramm, das Spinoza ermöglicht, eine wissenschaftliche Theorie der Affekte zu geben, in der jeder Affekte einen bestimmten Ort hat, der es erlaubt, einen Affekt, in dem, was er ist, zu begreifen.

Die Kardinalaffekte, die dem conatus perseverandi unmittelbar entspringen, sind cupiditas (Begierde), laetitia (Freude) und tristitia (Trauer). Begierde ist nichts als das Streben selbst, sofern es durch etwas Äußeres bestimmt wird, gegen das ein Individuum sich selbst zu erhalten strebt; sie ist weitgehend blind, ein natürlicher Trieb (appetitus), der jedem Seienden zukommt, der beim Menschen allerdings von einem Bewusstsein begleitet ist, das ihn das Streben in einer bestimmten Weise erfahren lässt. Wenn das Individuum in seinem Streben das, was zu ihm selbst gehört und was Spinoza die eigene Macht (potentia) nennt, gegenüber Einflüssen, die von Äußerem ausgehen, vergrößern kann, dann ist mit dieser Vergrößerung der Affekt der Freude verbunden; gelingt ihm dies nicht und wird die Macht verringert, dann ist damit der Affekt der Trauer verbunden. So ist es das Streben eines Individuums und die mit diesem Streben verbundene

Steigerung oder Hemmung, die zu drei elementaren Affekten führen. Darin ist gelegen: 1. Affekte resultieren aus einer Spannung zwischen dem Streben, sich selbst zu erhalten, und einem Äußeren, gegen das die Selbsterhaltung zu realisieren ist. 2. Das Individuum hat eine natürliche Tendenz zu dem Affekt der Freude, weil Freude Steigerung bedeutet und Streben nach Selbsterhaltung bedeutet, die eigene Macht angesichts von Äußerem, das ein Individuum bedroht, zu steigern.

Aus diesen beiden Momenten folgt: 1. Affekte sind abhängig von einem Äußerem, das die Wirkungsmacht eines Individuums entweder befördert oder behindert, indem es das Streben nach Selbsterhaltung steigert oder hemmt. Die das Streben eines Individuums charakterisierenden emotionalen Zustände Freude und Trauer haben somit zwangsläufig eine äußere Ursache. Daraus gewinnt Spinoza die beiden Affekte von Liebe und Haß: das Äußere, das Ursache der eigenen Machtsteigerung ist, wird geliebt, und konsequenterweise streben wir, dieses Äußere zu erhalten, dasjenige, das Ursache einer Machtminderung ist, wird gehasst, und konsequenterweise streben wir, dieses Äußere zu vernichten. Da Freude und Trauer ursprünglich im conatus gründen, dieser aber notwendigerweise in einer Relation zu Äußerem steht, gegen das er angeht, sind mit Freude und Trauer notwendigerweise die Affekte von Liebe und Hass verbunden. Liebe, so definiert Spinoza, ist Freude unter Begleitung der Idee einer äußeren Ursache (amor est laetitia concomitante idea causae externae, III, aff. def. 6). 2. Da der Mensch natürlicherweise auf Steigerung der eigenen Macht aus ist und damit auf Freude als emotionaler Ausdruck einer solchen Steigerung, wird er nicht nur das, was er liebt, zu erhalten suchen, sondern auch, generell, der Trauer zu entgehen suchen. Also wird er, so könnte man meinen, den Hass zu vermeiden suchen und an seine Stelle die Liebe setzen.

Doch hier zeigt sich eine entscheidende Differenz zwischen Freude und Liebe, die Freude einen ursprünglichen Affekt sein lässt, Liebe aber zu einem abgeleiteten macht. Freude ist eine Emotion, die ein das Individuum förderndes Begehren einfach begleitet, während Liebe eine Emotion ist, die wiederum die Freude begleitet, aber mit einer Idee, nämlich der Vorstellung eines Objekts, das als Ursache von Freude geliebt wird. Auf Freude ist der Mensch immer schon aus, sofern er nur begehrt; sie signalisiert lediglich den Erfolg des Begehrens, ohne dass sie enthielte, was der Mensch unternehmen muss, damit sein Begehren erfolgreich ist. Der Affekt der Liebe hat demgegenüber die Objekte im Blick, die als Grund eines solchen Gelingens angesehen werden. Objekte werden geliebt, *weil* sie einen Beitrag zur subjektiven Steigerung der Macht geleistet haben. Daher ist in der Liebe der Begehrende nicht nur auf Objekte gerichtet; er weiß auch um sie; er muss sie *als* etwas wissen, nämlich als eine Ursache, damit er sie überhaupt lieben kann. Dieses Wissen ist aber alles andere als eine adäquate Erkenntnis, und genau das ist der Grund menschlicher Knechtschaft, dessen, dass der Mensch in seinen Affekten, auch in der Liebe etwas erleidet (patitur).

Das Medium, in dem der Mensch eine Idee des Objekts als Ursache hat, das Medium also, das den Status der Idee der äußeren Ursache charakterisiert, ist,

Spinoza sagt es ausdrücklich, die Erkenntnisart der imaginatio. Es ist wichtig zu sehen, dass Spinoza im Rückgriff auf sie die Affekte von Liebe und Hass herleitet. Die ursprünglichen Affekte, Begierde, Freude und Trauer, werden nicht durch eine subjektive Form des Erkennens charakterisiert; sie sind Momente einer Ontologie des conatus perseverandi, und Spinoza gewinnt sie auch aus dieser Ontologie. Die ein Individuum essentiell bestimmende Wirkungsmacht (potentia agendi) ist schlicht Begierde (III, prop. 9), und mit dem Tatbestand einer Mehrung dieser Wirkungsmacht ist Freude, mit dem einer Minderung Trauer verbunden (III, prop. 11). Mit Lehrsatz 12 beginnt dann die Theorie derjenigen Affekte, die sich aus den ursprünglichen herleiten lassen, indem Spinoza die spezifische Weise erläutert, in welcher der Mensch nach Selbsterhaltung strebt. Er tut es nämlich als Geist. Der Lehrsatz lautet: „Der Geist strebt, soviel er kann, sich das vorzustellen, was die Wirkungsmacht seines Körpers vermehrt oder fördert" (Mens, quantum potest, ea imaginari conatur, quae corporis agendi potentiam augent vel juvant). Der menschliche Geist strebt nicht nur, wie jedes andere Seiende auch, sondern er strebt sich etwas *vorzustellen* (imaginari conatur). Der conatus des Geistes wird als ein conatus imaginandi verstanden, und aus dem imaginari erklärt Spinoza, in Lehrsatz 13, was Liebe und Hass sind. D.h.: der Mensch liebt nicht das, was tatsächlich die äußere Ursache der Steigerung seiner eigenen potentia agendi ist, sondern das, was er dafür hält, von dem er also lediglich meint, dass sie es ist. Und daraus folgert Spinoza, dass nicht nur Hass, sondern auch Liebe zu den Passionen zählt. Das imaginari führt zu einer Instabilität des menschlichen Lebens, zu einer Schwankung des Gemüts (fluctuatio animi), generell zu einem Umschlagen von Liebe in Hass. Und daraus gewinnt Spinoza auch das Umschlagen von Freude in Trauer, die Gefährdung der Freude durch die Trauer. Sie leitet Spinoza nicht aus den elementaren Affekten selbst her, sondern aus der Struktur der mit dem imaginari verbundenen Liebe, dass der Mensch nämlich Objekte liebt, die sich nicht als das erweisen, deretwegen er sie geliebt hat und die deshalb bei ihm Hass auf sie provozieren. Aus dieser durch die imaginatio bedingten internen Spannung zwischen Liebe und Hass gewinnt Spinoza dann alle übrigen Affekte, die er im 3. Teil der „Ethik" auflistet und im Rückgriff auf Liebe und Hass als Affekte von Freude und Trauer bezeichnet.

Eine wichtige Rolle spielt dabei das die imaginatio kennzeichnende Merkmal, auf die Unmittelbarkeit des Gegenwärtigen bezogen zu sein. Dies lässt uns etwas als für uns gut begehren, das sich in einem größeren Kontext als für uns schlecht erweist, das unsere potentia agendi also nur momentan befördert, im Anschluss daran, in anderen Zusammenhängen, aber tatsächlich mindert, so dass wir das, was wir geliebt haben, nunmehr hassen, ein Hass, der umso größer ist, weil wir in unserer Einschätzung, generell in unserer Erwartung, getäuscht worden sind. Eine andere wichtige Rolle spielt der Mechanismus assoziativer Verknüpfungen von Vorstellungen, den Spinoza bei der Beschreibung des inadäquaten Erkennens im 2. Teil der „Ethik" geschildert hat und den er bei der Beschreibung des Gefüges der einzelnen Affekte aufgreift: Erinnerung und Nachahmung auf der Basis bloßer Ähnlichkeitsbeziehungen bringen den Menschen dazu, sich Kontexte auszudenken, die das, was er liebt, nach Möglichkeit stabilisieren. Dies ist aber einerseits nicht mehr als ein Verdrängen der tatsächlichen Realität und andererseits, und das ist gravierender, Ausdruck einer rein privaten Einschätzung dessen, was als nützlich für den Einzelnen und deshalb als Objekt der Liebe anzusehen ist.

In Lehrsatz 51 des 3. Teils der „Ethik" sagt Spinoza, dass ein Mensch von ein und demselben Gegenstand zu verschiedenen Zeiten verschiedenartig affiziert werden kann und dass er deshalb im Laufe der Zeit gegenüber einem und demselben Gegenstand in verschiedenartige Affekte geraten kann, d.h. dass er ihn jetzt lieben und später hassen kann, ohne dass sich am Gegenstand etwas geändert hätte. Geändert hat sich nur etwas an der Verfassung des Individuums, das aufgrund anderer Erfahrungen einen Gegenstand später anders erfährt als jetzt. Den Grund hierfür hat Spinoza im 2. Teil der „Ethik" entwickelt, dass wir nämlich Kenntnis von äußeren Gegenständen nur über die Affektionen unseres Körpers erlangen und dass die Weise, in der unser Körper Eindrücke von außen empfängt, ganz zufällig ist, nämlich abhängig von seiner individuellen Disposition und von der Lebenswelt, in der ein Mensch agiert, die ihn die Eindrücke in je subjektiver Weise assoziieren lassen. Infolgedessen beurteilt der Mensch das, was er wahrnimmt, auch unter einem rein subjektiven Aspekt, ohne dabei um seine Privatheit zu wissen. Der Sache nach ist aber nicht nur ein Individuum von ein und demselben Gegenstand verschiedenartig affiziert, sondern auch verschiedene Menschen sind es (Spinoza sagt es in demselben Lehrsatz), so dass verschiedene Individuen jeweils anderes als für sich gut und damit erstrebenswert ansehen. Weil der Einzelne diese Verschiedenartigkeit nicht im Blick hat, sondern aufgrund seines individuellen conatus ganz auf sich selbst bezogen ist, wird er die Anderen nur in seiner Perspektive sehen und ihre Lebensführung von dem her beurteilen, was er selbst verfolgt. Er erwartet von ihnen, dass sie so leben wie er selbst, d.h. nach seiner eigenen, bloß privaten Sinnesart („ex suo ingenio"). Und genau das führt zu intersubjektiven Konflikten – es ist nicht die Knappheit von Gütern, um die sich die Menschen streiten, nicht einmal der Tatbestand, dass die Menschen ein und dasselbe Objekt haben wollen, das nicht alle besitzen können (mit Ehre und Reputation verbundene Positionen etwa), obschon dies in der Tat ein Quell von Konflikten ist, sondern dass sie sich zu den Objekten in einer bestimmten Weise verhalten und die anderen Menschen in den Dienst eines solchen Verhaltens nehmen.

Insofern ist das Äußere, das der Mensch als Ursache seiner eigenen Machtsteigerung ansieht und deshalb liebt, immer schon gebrochen durch das Verhalten anderer Menschen zu den Objekten. Das Äußere, das wir für unsere Selbsterhaltung bedürfen und das wir lieben, wenn es dieser Selbsterhaltung dienlich ist, sind deshalb nicht einfach natürliche Gegenstände, sondern in erster Linie die anderen Menschen, deren Verhalten es macht, dass wir sie, wenn sie uns im Wege stehen, nicht lieben, sondern hassen. Was Spinoza eingangs der Erörterung seiner Affektenlehre so allgemein formuliert mit der Wendung „Idee einer äußeren Ursache" und „Affekte gegenüber einem als förderlich oder hinderlich anzusehenden Ding (res)", das hat seine eigentliche Bedeutung nicht in einem Verhältnis des Subjekts zu äußeren Dingen der Natur, sondern in dem Verhältnis des Subjekts zu anderen Menschen, also in der intersubjektiven Sphäre. Das ist ja von der Sache her klar. Der Fluss, der mir bei meinem Drang zur Wanderung im Wege steht, das Auto, das meinem Drang nach schneller Fortbewegung aufgrund eines Defekts im Wege steht, werde ich nicht hassen, es sei denn ich bin kindisch. Über diese intuitive Plausibilität hinaus will Spinoza zeigen, dass die Selbsterhaltung des Menschen nicht in erster Linie durch Naturereignisse gefährdet ist, sondern durch das durch Affektivität gekennzeichnete Verhalten der Mitmenschen. Gerade diese Form von Bedrohung ist aber zugleich eine Chance für den Menschen, die Gefährdungen, die von außen kommen, auch zu meistern. Und hierbei spielt die Liebe eine besondere Rolle.

Spinoza hat den Affekt der Liebe so eingeführt, dass er Ausdruck eines inadäquaten Erkennens ist. Solange er dies ist, ist er eine Passion, die Gefahr läuft, in Hass umzuschlagen. Aber Spinoza zeigt auch, dass sie die Kraft hat, den Hass zu überwinden, eine Kraft, die sich aus dem adäquaten Erkennen speist, in der die Liebe aber immer noch eine Passion bleibt, denn sie bleibt solange dem inadäquaten Erkennen verhaftet, wie sie sich *gegen* es wendet, solange sie also im Kampf gegen den Hass steht. In seiner frühen Abhandlung, dem sogenannten „Kurzen Traktat über Gott, dem Menschen und dessen Glück", hat Spinoza die Liebe noch nicht unter diesem Aspekt differenziert, sondern allein von der Beschaffenheit ihres Objekts her beurteilt (Teil II, Kap. 5) und war dabei zu einer simplen Gegenüberstellung gekommen. In der Unterscheidung zwischen vergänglichen Dingen und ewigen Dingen vertritt Spinoza dort die Auffassung, dass endliche und darin vergängliche Dinge nicht nur nicht adäquat erkannt werden können und deshalb keine Gewißheit hinsichtlich ihrer tatsächlichen Nützlichkeit für uns gestatten, dass sie vielmehr in sich schädlich für uns sind und wir sie deshalb zu vermeiden haben.

Diese Position wird Spinoza in der „Ethik" aufgeben, weil sie mit einem obskuren Begriff operiert, den Spinoza später aus guten Gründen aufgibt, dem der Vereinigung. Liebe, so definiert Spinoza im „Kurzen Traktat", sei nichts anderes, als ein Ding in der Weise zu genießen, dass man mit ihm vereinigt ist. Weil nun die Vereinigung mit einem vergänglichen Ding uns nicht zu stärken vermag, sei die Liebe zu Dingen dieser Art schädlich für uns. In der „Ethik" ist aber keine Rede mehr davon, dass Liebe etwas mit Vereinigung zu tun hätte. Liebe ist dadurch definiert, auf ein Äußeres bezogen zu sein, dessen Äußerlichkeit gar nicht aufgehoben werden kann, auf die der Mensch vielmehr stets angewiesen bleibt. Es kommt nicht darauf an, dass der Mensch sich mit ihnen vereinigt, was in der Tat auch völlig sinnlos wäre, sondern dass er sich zu ihnen so verhält, dass sie ihn selbst in seinen natürlichen Streben nach Selbsterhaltung befördern. Niemals können wir es dahin bringen, schreibt Spinoza in der Anmerkung zu Lehrsatz 18 des 4. Teils, „zur Erhaltung unseres Seins nichts außerhalb unserer selbst zu bedürfen". Vielmehr gibt es viele Dinge außerhalb von uns, die nützlich für uns sind und deshalb aufgesucht werden sollten. Keine Flucht in eine unio mystica. Lieben können wir nur Dinge, die von uns getrennt sind und getrennt bleiben, und ist unser Zugang zu den Dingen niemals direkt, sondern stets vermittelt über das Verhalten anderer Menschen, dann muss sich unsere Liebe auf andere Menschen erstrecken, die uns äußerlich sind und bleiben müssen. Nicht dass sich Menschen vereinigen, ist das an Liebe orientierte Programm, sondern dass sie übereinstimmen (convenire). Und es ist eine Grundthese Spinozas, dass Übereinstimmung eine positive Bestimmung ist, die über das, was Menschen haben, zu erklären ist und nicht über das, was sie nicht haben (vgl. IV, prop. 32). Sie setzt voraus, dass Menschen etwas von sich aus tun, d.h. dass sie aktiv sind. Liebe zu anderen Menschen heißt deshalb nichts anderes, als sie in ihrer Aktivität zu befördern.

Ich möchte dies an Lehrsatz 46 des 4. Teils der „Ethik" erläutern. Er lautet: „Wer nach der Leitung der Vernunft lebt, strebt, so viel er kann, des anderen gegen ihn gerichteten Hass [...] mit Liebe [...] zu vergelten". Und in der Anmerkung dazu schreibt Spinoza: „Wer Schlechtigkeiten rächen will, indem er ihnen Hass entgegenbringt, führt sicherlich ein armseliges Leben. Wer andererseits darauf aus ist, Hass mit Liebe zu vergelten, kämpft gewiss freudig und zuversichtlich; gleich leicht hält er einem wie vielen stand und bedarf am wenigsten der Hilfe des Schicksals. Die er aber besiegt, die fallen freudig, nicht aus einem Mangel an Kraft, sondern aus einem Zuwachs ihrer Kräfte. Das alles folgt so klar aus der bloßen Definition von Liebe und Verstand, dass es nicht nötig ist, es im einzelnen zu beweisen". Auffallend ist an dieser Stelle die enge Verbindung von Liebe und Verstand (intellectus), aus deren beider Definition das hier Behauptete ohne weiteres folge, des weiteren die Betonung eines freudigen Tuns (laetus) und zwar auf beiden Seiten, bei dem Sieger wie dem Besiegten. Etwas aus Liebe tun, gibt einem Sicherheit und Zuversicht im Hinblick auf das, was erreicht werden soll. Denn der Liebende unterdrückt nicht den, den er liebt, aus dem Bewusstsein heraus, dass der Andere dem eigenen Sein nur förderlich ist, wenn seine Affektivität geläutert wird, also von der verworrenen Erkenntnis der imaginatio befreit wird. Zu einer solchen Einstellung kann nur derjenige gelangen, der schon weiß, dass der Gebrauch der Vernunft im höchsten Maße der Erhaltung des eigenen Seins dienlich ist (dass das der Fall ist, hat Spinoza zuvor gezeigt, Lehrsätze 23-28) und dass deshalb die anderen Menschen einem selbst nur dann wirklich förderlich sind, wenn auch sie die Vernunft gebrauchen. Das setzt aber voraus, dass der Einzelne die Anderen nicht unterdrückt, sondern deren Sein zu fördern sucht. Und genau deshalb sind die, deren Hass durch Liebe besiegt wird, freudig gestimmt, denn sie erfahren in der Liebe, die ihnen entgegengebracht wird, dass ihre eigene Aktivität befördert wird, und darin werden sie nicht gehemmt, sondern erfahren einen Zuwachs ihrer Kräfte, also eine Steigerung ihrer eigenen Macht. Und insofern ist Liebe eng mit dem Verstand verknüpft. Jemanden zu lieben, heißt, dessen Aktivität zu befördern, und das heißt ihn als einen Partner anzuerkennen, der die gleichen Ansprüche hat, sein Leben aus sich heraus zu führen und zu gestalten.

Darin wird die Liebe zu einer Haltung, die die Freiheit des Geistes (libertas animi) zu ihrer Ursache hat, und dies in einer Wechselseitigkeit, sowohl bei dem, der liebt, wie bei dem, der geliebt wird. Der Liebende liebt das und nur das, was die Aktivität seines Geistes fördert, und hierfür hat er die Aktivität des Anderen, den er liebt, zu befördern, ihn also als einen gleichberechtigten Partner anzuerkennen. Und diese Gleichheit zeigt sich allein in der freien Betätigung der eigenen Kräfte eines jeden und nicht in dem, was mit ihnen, im Vergleich mit anderen, erreicht worden ist. Die energeia ist mehr wert als das ergon, um einen Satz des Aristoteles zu variieren. In intersubjektiver Perspektive ist die Liebe auf das gerichtet, was eine Person kann, nicht auf das, was sie faktisch getan hat. Spinoza hat dies auch für die eheliche Liebe gelten lassen und diese von einer bloß sinnlichen Liebe unterschieden. In Caput XX des 4. Teils der „Ethik" heißt es: „Was die Ehe anbelangt, in Einklang mit der Vernunft ist sie sicherlich, wenn die Begierde nach körperlicher Vereinigung nicht nur von der äußeren Erscheinung hervorgerufen wird, sondern auch [...] und insbesondere, wenn beider Liebe, die des Mannes wie der Frau, nicht bloß die äußere Erscheinung, sondern vor allem Geistesfreiheit zu ihrer Ursache hat".

Bei der ehelichen Liebe, die natürlich auch sinnlich ausgerichtet ist, hatte Spinoza gesagt, dass sie, wenn sie bloß sinnlich ist, leicht in Hass übergeht („facile in odium transit", IV, Caput XIX). Nun stellt die Liebe zwischen Mann und Frau eine Sonderform dar, die sich gewiss nicht auf die Liebe der Menschen zu einander in einem größeren Raum der Fernbeziehungen übertragen lässt. Ist die eheliche Liebe natürlich immer auch eine sinnliche Liebe und deshalb, nach Ansicht Spinozas, intern gefährdet, so sind die weiter gefassten zwischenmenschlichen Beziehungen ebenfalls durch Sinnlichkeit gekennzeichnet, nämlich durch die Orientierung der Menschen an sinnlichen Objekten, also vergänglichen Gegenständen. Sinnliche Objekte sind Gegenstand einer in sich gefährdeten Liebe, nicht weil sie vergänglich sind, sondern weil Menschen keine adäquate Erkenntnis von deren Nützlichkeit haben und sie deshalb häufig lieben, ohne dass sie ihnen tatsächlich förderlich sind. Nicht vergängliche Objekte sind schädlich, sondern deren Vorstellung in Form der imaginatio, schon für ein Individuum allein, besonders aber in der intersubjektiven Sphäre. Begehren Subjekte, die nicht von der Vernunft geleitet sind, etwas Äußeres lediglich für sich und nicht zugleich auch für andere, so durchbricht die Vernunft die Unmittelbarkeit des Begehrens und schafft jene Distanz, die es möglich macht, das Begehrte in einen größeren Kontext zu stellen, der auch die Mitmenschen in deren Begehren berücksichtigt.

Gleichwohl, eine solche Berücksichtigung muss es sich versagen, den Unvernünftigen durch die Vernunft zwingen zu wollen. Im 4. Teil beschreibt Spinoza, was in Bezug auf seine Mitmenschen der Vernünftige alles tun kann, der einerseits weiß, dass es auf die adäquate Erkenntnis ankommt, andererseits aber auch weiß, dass ihre Kraft beschränkt ist. Das gilt besonders im Hinblick auf die anderen Menschen, die dem Vernünftigen nur nützlich sind, wenn sie selbst die Vernunft gebrauchen, und dazu kann er sie nicht durch seine eigene

Vernunft zwingen. Gerade weil sie als selbständige Personen zu respektieren sind, ist ihnen zuzugestehen, dass sie sich unter den Bedingungen ihrer Besonderheit selbst entfalten und das heißt dass sie nach ihrer Sinnesart („ex suo ingenio") leben, zu der auch die irrende Erkenntnis gehört. Spinoza zeigt, dass die Tendenz, nach der eigenen Sinnesart zu leben, die Tendenz enthält, auch andere mögen nach dieser Art leben, also die Tendenz, andere mögen die eigene Einstellung übernehmen. Das bringt notwendigerweise eine Unterdrückung und Fremdbestimmung der anderen mit sich und einen daraus resultierenden Hass. Aber Spinoza weiß auch, dass nicht nur der Versuch, eine bloß private Auffassung von Lebensführung zu universalisieren, bei denen zu Hass führt, denen eine solche Auffassung aufgedrängt wird, sondern auch der Versuch, eine an der Vernunft orientierte Haltung anderen aufzudrängen. Deshalb ist mit der Liebe zu anderen Menschen, die sich allein auf den Verstand stützt, eine Vorsicht und besondere Achtsamkeit verbunden, die Menschenkenntnis verlangt, insbesondere Kenntnis menschlicher Schwächen, alles Sachverhalte, bei denen sich der Mensch gerade nicht auf seinen Verstand allein stützen kann. Und deshalb behandelt Spinoza all dies in dem Teil der „Ethik", der von der menschlichen Knechtschaft handelt, d.h. von der menschlichen Unfreiheit angesichts der Kraft der Affekte.

Der Vernünftige ist zwar seiner selbst sicher, und seine Liebe ist nicht durch Hass gefährdet, aber er wird in der Liebe zu anderen Menschen Zugeständnisse machen müssen. Sie können ihn unsicher machen, ob die Liebe zu anderen Menschen sich tatsächlich in der Beförderung der Verstandesaktivität erfüllt und nicht in etwas anderem. Spinoza muss also zeigen, dass derjenige, der Liebe und Gebrauch des Verstandes eng miteinander verknüpft, bei allen Hindernissen zumindest auf dem richtigen Weg ist. Hierfür muss er zeigen, dass die Liebe ihre Höchstform im Gebrauch des Verstandes erreicht, darin nämlich, dass sie sich auf das richtet, was die Ursache dafür ist, dass der Mensch ihn in richtiger Weise gebrauchen kann.

Dieser Gegenstand ist Gott, der für Spinoza bekanntlich für die Menschen allein eine Bedeutung hat als das Prinzip, das ihnen eine adäquate Erkenntnis ermöglicht. Wenn der Mensch eine Idee von Gott hat, die adäquat ist, dann kann er all seine anderen Ideen, die seiner Körpers, der Affektionen seines Körpers und damit korrespondierend das emotional Bestimmtsein durch diese Affektionen, auf diese Idee beziehen und darin einen klaren und deutlichen Begriff von ihnen haben. Ein solches Beziehen von Ideen auf die Idee Gottes ist ein Bilden von Begriffen, und in diesem Bilden sind wir aktiv. Und wir können das immer mehr, weil alles, was ist, in Gott ist und deshalb aus Gott begriffen werden kann. Wir können also im Akt zunehmender Erkenntnis unsere Tätigkeit steigern. Diese Steigerung ist, wie jede Form von Steigerung, mit Freude verbunden, und sie ist begleitet von der Idee eines Objekts, das wir als Ursache dieser Freude lieben und das in diesem Fall Gott ist.

Diese Liebe zu Gott unterscheidet sich von der Liebe zu irgendeinem innerweltlichen Ding der Qualität nach, obwohl sie mit ihr gemeinsam hat, ein Affekt zu sein, d.h. bezogen zu sein auf ein Äußeres, das als Ursache der eigenen Machtsteigerung begriffen und deshalb geliebt wird. Der Unterschied besteht darin, dass es sich jetzt um eine adäquat erkannte Ursache handelt und nicht um eine bloß vorgestellte. Daraus folgert Spinoza das wesentliche Merkmal der Liebe zu Gott, dass nämlich diese Liebe ein in sich stabiler Affekt ist. Sie kann sich nicht in Hass kehren (V, prop. 18, coroll.). Denn wenn wir Gott betrachten, sind wir aktiv und nichts als aktiv; weil wir nichts erleiden, sind wir von keiner Trauer betroffen und damit auch von keinem Affekt des Hasses.

Diesem Argument, das ganz auf die Aktivität des Erkennens setzt, fügt Spinoza zwei weitere Argumente hinzu. Das eine bezieht sich auf den Gegenstand der Liebe, das andere auf die anderen Menschen, die lieben. Der Gegenstand der Liebe, Gott, hat, anders als der Mensch, keine Emotionen, denn er ist nicht unterwegs zur Vollkommenheit, sondern selbst die höchste Vollkommenheit, die keiner Steigerung fähig ist. Also kann der Mensch von dem Gegenstand seiner Liebe keine Emotionen erwarten, insbesondere nicht, dass Gott ihn seinerseits liebt (V, prop. 19). D.h., in der Liebe zu Gott kann der Mensch nicht strategisch verfahren, nicht jemanden lieben, um von ihm etwas zurückzubekommen. Seine Erwartung kann also nicht enttäuscht werden, und damit entfällt ein wesentlicher Grund dafür, dass Liebe in Hass umschlägt. Was die anderen Menschen angeht, sie können Gott lieben, ohne dass sie damit den Anderen etwas wegnehmen. Alle innerweltlichen Gegenstände können nicht allen gehören. In Bezug auf sie gibt es deshalb eine natürliche Konkurrenz der Menschen untereinander. Eine solche Konkurrenz gibt es in Bezug auf Gott nicht. Die Liebe zu Gott kann deshalb nicht von einem Affekt des Neides oder der Eifersucht getrübt werden (V, prop. 20). Die Erkenntnis Gottes gehört allen gleichermaßen. Die Liebe zu den Menschen erfüllt sich dann konsequenterweise darin, sie so zu fördern, dass sie zu einer Erkenntnis Gottes gelangen. Die Verbindung zwischen Liebe und adäquater Erkenntnis ist gerechtfertigt.

All dies ist richtig, *wenn* der Mensch sein Leben an der Erkenntnis Gottes ausrichtet. Die Frage ist aber, ob er das wirklich kann, d.h. ob sich das Ganze seines Lebens daran ausrichten lässt und ob der Einzelne den anderen Menschen dies zumuten kann, d.h. die Liebe zu ihnen als eine Beförderung des reinen Erkennens verstehen darf. Hier bleibt eine Unsicherheit, und deshalb tritt am Ende der Darlegungen zur Liebe Gottes als eines Aktes des Verstandes noch einmal und zum letzten Mal das „imaginari" auf. Die Liebe zu Gott, sagt Spinoza, wird um so mehr genährt, von je mehr Menschen wir uns vorstellen (imaginamur), dass auch sie diese intellektuelle Haltung einnehmen (V, prop. 20, demonstr.). Der Einzelne ist so unsicher, dass er der Bestätigung durch möglichst viele andere Menschen bedarf, unabhängig davon, ob sie selbst es wirklich tun. Es reicht, dass er sich dies vorstellt.

Die imaginatio feiert ihren letzten Triumph, der noch einmal zu überwinden ist. Ein weiterer Schritt ist erforderlich, der dann zur Theorie der geistigen Liebe Gottes führt, eine Theorie, die ich hier nicht diskutieren kann. Ich möchte nur darauf verweisen, dass Spinoza in diesem Zusammenhang darzulegen sucht, dass die wahre Natur des Menschen dessen Verstand ist, die Instanz nämlich, die es ihm ermöglicht, sich selbst als ewig zu begreifen, d.h. als ein Modus Gottes, der nicht vergeht, solange der Mensch denkt. Und Denken, Spinoza hebt dies energisch hervor, das nicht den ganzen Menschen ausmacht, sondern nur einen Teil von ihm, kann ausgedehnt werden im Hinblick auf den anderen Teil, weil der Mensch dazu motiviert wird von der Liebe zu einem Gegenstand, aus dem er seine wahre Natur begreifen kann. Aber unabhängig von dem Ausmaß einer solchen Vergrößerung kann der, der durch die geistige Gottesliebe bestimmt ist, Spinoza zufolge wissen, dass der Teil von ihm, den der Verstand ausmacht, von einer solchen Natur ist, dass der andere Teil, der auf die imaginatio bezogen ist, relativ darauf kaum von Bedeutung ist (V, prop. 39).

Vielleicht ist diese Theorie des Menschen falsch. Aber Spinoza selbst sagt ausdrücklich (V, prop. 41), dass unabhängig von seiner Theorie reiner Einsicht wir immer noch das als das Wichtigste anzusehen haben, was zuvor entwickelt worden ist. Es ist der Tatbestand, in diese Richtung möchte ich interpretieren, dass unsere Affekte ein Ausdruck unserer Aktivität sind, die zu vergrößern die einzige Rechtfertigung ist, sie als in jeder Hinsicht gut zu bezeichnen. Bezogen auf unseren Gegenstand, den Affekt der Liebe, bedeutet dies, dass dieser Affekt dann gut ist, wenn derjenige, der von ihm affiziert ist, die Gegenstände seiner Liebe (generell natürliche Dinge, insbesondere aber andere Menschen und schließlich Gott) als Gegenstände versteht, die etwas an sich selbst sind, und nicht als Gegenstände, wie er sie sich in bloß subjektiver Perspektive vorstellt.

Leibniz on Love
Gábor Boros, Eötvös University Budapest

We rarely think of Leibniz as a philosopher whose thinking primarily revolved around the passionate relationship we call love. Nevertheless, if we read his works on natural law or practical philosophy, we find the frequency with which he speaks about love (or, say, charity) startling. When imagining the mutually involved, intense relationship between Leibniz and the Prussian Queen Sophie Charlotte, who is not tempted to think about love? In what follows, I shall try to connect the threads running through Leibniz's remarks on love into an integrated theory of the passions. I shall begin with an investigation into how Leibniz understood passion and action in general. I will proceed then to explore the metaphysical sense of love in his work. Finally, I will turn to love's role in Leibniz's natural law theory.

1.1. Passions, Passivity

The word "passion" stems from the Latin *patior*, which means that something undergoes something. This means that something becomes the object of an action involuntarily. When analyzing a particular theory of passions, it is important to see who or what undergoes what sort of action and who or what is the agent, according to the theory in question. In Descartes, for example, we find that "we are not aware of any subject which acts more directly upon our soul than the body to which it is joined. Consequently we should recognize that what is a passion in the soul is usually an action in the body."[1] But what is the agent and what undergoes the action in Leibniz's theory? Is it the body that acts upon the soul, as in Descartes? Or is it that the soul – itself having a bodily nature – suffers agitation from other parts of the body, as in Hobbes? Or is it like Spinoza's theory, where the soul and the body, being one and the same thing, act and suffer together, not really suffering at all except from the active power of the rest of nature?

We can only answer such questions by looking at the metaphysical foundations of Leibniz's thinking. A permanent element within his metaphysics is the idea

---

[1] CSMK 1, 328. "[N]ous ne remarquons point qu'il y ait aucun sujet qui agisse plus immediatement contre nostre ame, que le corps auquel elle est jointe; et que par consequent nous devons penser que ce qui est en elle une Passion, est communement en luy une Action" (*Les Passions de l'âme*, Art. 2).

that, far from being able to act on something on its own, the body in itself is incapable of forming a real unity, i.e., a real entity. Bodies cannot form substances on the basis of what constitutes their bodily nature; they need something else that is non-corporeal. This thesis turned Leibniz against the corpuscular thinkers, who held that there is something substantial in matter made up of small, perfectly rigid globes. Leibniz offers the counter-hypothesis that primary matter is perfectly fluid and has no internal limits or interconnections whatsoever.

> It is indeed rather hard to explain cohesion. But this cohesion of parts appears not to be necessary to make an extended whole, since perfectly rarefied and fluid matter may be said to make up an extended thing, without its parts being joined to one another. In fact, though, I think that perfect fluidity is appropriate only to primary matter – i.e., matter in the abstract, considered as an original quality like motionlessness. But it does not fit secondary matter – i.e., matter as it actually occurs, invested with its derivative qualities – for I believe that no mass is ultimately rarefied and that there is some degree of bonding everywhere. This is produced by motions, when they all run the same way so that any division would have to set up cross-currents, which cannot happen without some turbulence and resistance... On this, however, I believe that the doctrine of substantial unities – monads – will throw a good deal of light.[2]

According to Leibniz (and here he agrees with Spinoza), the body alone is incapable of performing any action "upon" (*contre*) its soul. What makes the body subsist is, paradoxically, something that has no bodily character, something that has the nature of a soul. Consequently, even if nothing prevents us from speaking about a body making the soul undergo its action, we must not forget that it is always in the soul (i.e., in the individual substance or monad) that the passivity of a passion and the activity of an action originates.

---

2 *Nouveaux essais* 2, 23, 23. "Il y a assez de difficulté dans l'explication de la *cohésion*; mais cette *cohésion* des parties ne paroit pas nécéssaire pour faire un tout étendû, puisqu'on peut dire que la matiére parfaitement subtile et fluide compose un étendû, sans que les parties soyent attachées les unes aux autres. Mais pour dire la vérité, je crois que la fluidité parfaite ne convient qu'à la *matiere premiere*, c'est à dire en abstraction, et comme une qualité originale, de même que le repos; mais non pas à la *matiére seconde*, telle qu'elle se trouve effectivement, revêtue de ses qualités derivatives, car je crois qu'il n'y a point de masse, qui soit de la dernière subtilité, et qu'il y a plus ou moins de liaison par tout, laquelle vient des mouvemens, en tant qu'ils sont conspirans et doivent estre troublé par la separation ce qui ne se peut faire sans quelque violence et resistence... je crois que la doctrine des unités substantielles ou Monades l'eclaircira beaucoup" (A VI/6, 222–23).

> [I]t must be said that, on a rigorous definition, the soul has within it the principles of all its actions, and even of all its passions, and that the same is true in all the simple substances scattered throughout Nature, although there be freedom only in those that are intelligent. In the popular sense notwithstanding, speaking in accordance with appearances, we must say that the soul depends in some way upon the body and upon the impressions of the senses: much as we speak with Ptolemy and Tycho in everyday converse, and think with Copernicus, when it is a question of the rising and the setting of the sun.[3]

Having excluded the possibility that the essence of a substance is constituted by, at the very least, its primary qualities, no alternative remains for Leibniz except that in which the internal life of a monad consists: activity and passivity, distinct and confused perception.

> If there is some reality, we cannot search for it but in the power of performing or undergoing an action, and this is what constitutes the substance of the body like matter and form... The substance has metaphysical matter or passive force as far as it expresses something confusedly, and it has active force as far as it expresses something distinctly.[4]

But are activity and passivity nothing more than two sorts of perception? Did Leibniz not achieve anything more than a simple renewal of a Stoic theory of passions? The expressions "passive force" and "active force" suggest, indeed, that he did. But to fully answer this question, we need to look at what Leibniz took over from the seventeenth-century theory, something variously termed *conatus*, *appetitus*, "endeavour," tendency, or effort.

---

3 G. W. Leibniz, *Theodicy*, trans. E. M. Huggard, (Ontario: J. M. Dent & Sons, 1966). "[I]l faut dire que, prenant les choses à la rigeur, l'âme a en elle le principe de toutes ces actions, et même de toutes ces passions; et que le même est vrai dans toutes les substance simple répandues par toute la nature... Cependant, dans le sens populaire, en parlant suivant les apparences, nous devons dire que l'âme dépend en quelque manière du corps et des impressions des sens, à peu prés comme nous parlons avec Ptolémée et Tycho dans l'usage ordinaire, et pensons avec Copernic, quand il s'agit de lever ou du coucher du soleil" (Théodicée, I/65).

4 "Et si quid est reale, id solum esse vim agendi et patiendi adeoque in hoc (tanquam materia et forma) substantiam corporis consistere, [...] Substantiae habent materiam Metaphysicam seu potentiam passivam quatenus aliquid confuse exprimunt, activam quatenus distincte." (De modo distinguendi... A VI/4/B, 1504).

1.2. The Conatus

It was Hobbes who imparted the concept of conatus to Leibniz.[5] Hobbes developed a reductionist analysis of cognition and the formation of affects on the basis of the fundamental role of conatus in the physics of *De corpore*[6] and *Leviathan*.

> The cause of sense, is the externall body, or object, which presseth the organ proper to each sense, either immediately [...] or mediately [...] which pressure, by the mediation of nerves, and other strings, and membranes of the body, continued inwards to the brain, and heart, causeth there a resistance, or counter-pressure, or endeavour of the heart, to deliver itself: which endeavour because outward, seemeth to be some matter without. And this seeming, or fancy, is that which men call sense.[7]

Thus, Hobbes replaces the functions traditionally attributed to the soul with the newly discovered functions of the body. Hobbes accomplishes this task by means of a return to the concept of conatus or endeavour. This concept originally belonged to the realm of the soul, but was transferred to the realm of the physical by Descartes. In Chapter 6 of *Leviathan*, Hobbes applies the same device to our present subject matter, the theory of affects.

> And because going, speaking, and the like voluntary motions depend always upon a precedent thought of whither, which way, and what, it is evident that the imagination is the first internal beginning of all voluntary motion [...] These small beginnings of Motion within the body of Man, before they appear in walking, speaking, striking, and other visible actions, are commonly called Endeavour [...] This Endeavour, when it is toward something which causes it, is called Appetite or Desire [...] And when the Endeavour is fromward something, it is generally called Aversion.[8]

We can see how the term conatus, which originally signified more or less conscious efforts, was first applied to pure bodily phenomena, then reinstated in its original meaning one sentence later, although – and this is Hobbes' point – deprived of any characteristics inherited from the former metaphysics based on the conception of a substantial soul.

Returning to Leibniz, we can state, first of all, that his conception of conatus is diametrically opposed to that of Hobbes. He reproaches Hobbes for having failed

---

5 As is witnessed by the only letter Leibniz wrote to Hobbes (13/23 July, 1670).
6 "Primo definiemus *conatum esse motum per spatium et tempus minus quam quod datur, id est, determinatur, sive expositione vel numero assignatur*, id est, *per punctum*" Ch. 15, *OL* I, 177.
7 *Leviathan* ed. Molesworth, p. 1.
8 *Leviathan* ed. Molesworth, p. 38.

to see the proper significance of the conatus for a true theory of the soul.[9] For Leibniz, it is the conatus that helps us identify the real difference between the body and the soul, construed as the only real substance. In a letter to Arnauld at the beginning of November 1671, Leibniz elaborates on the role of the conatus in both the body and the soul:

> All bodies can be understood as momentary minds, but lacking memory. No endeavor in bodies can be destroyed with regard to its determination; in the mind, it cannot be destroyed with regard to its degree of speed either. As the body consists in the course of motions, the mind consists in the harmony of endeavors. The present motion of the body originates in the composition of the preceding endeavors, whereas the present endeavor of the mind, that is, the will, is from the composition of the preceding harmonies in a new harmony, that is, by way of pleasure; yet if the harmony of this pleasure gets disturbed by the intrusion of another endeavor, we'll have pain.[10]

That is, the conatus is the most important conceptual means to both connect and separate body and soul at the same time. The soul's ability to retain its past conatus is, for Leibniz, the feature that distinguishes it from the body; an ability which must be anchored in the substantial character of the soul.

1.3. Passions and Actions Reconsidered

Now we can return to our question concerning the proper character of Leibniz's theory of passions and actions. First, I propose we consider the now relevant aspect of another debate in which Leibniz was involved, namely, the debate with Locke. Locke writes in his *Essay Concerning Human Understanding*, 2,21,5:

> We find in our selves a power to begin or forbear, continue or end several actions of our [soul], and motions of our bodies, barely by a thought or preference of the mind ordering, or as it were commanding the doing or not doing such and such a

---

9 "De natura Mentis untinam etiam aliquid distinctius dixisses" A II/I, 58.
10 "Omne corpus intelligi posse mentem momentaneam, sed carentem recordatione; conatum omnem in corporibus quoad determinationem esse indestruibilem, in mente etiam quoad gradum velocitatis; ut corpus in motuum tractu, ita mentem in conatuum harmonia consistere; motum corporis praesentem oriri ex praecedentium conatuum compositione; conatum mentis praesentem, id est voluntatem ex compositione harmoniarum praecedentium in unam novam seu voluptate, cuius harmonium si quid aliud conatu impresso turbat, facit dolorem" A II/I, 173.

particular action. This power which the mind has is that which we call the will. The actual exercise of that power [is called] volition."[11]

The most interesting feature of Leibniz's answer is precisely the fact that, and the way in which, he introduces the concept of conatus.

> I shall say that volition is the effort or endeavor (conatus) to move towards what one finds good and away from what one finds bad, the endeavor arising immediately out of one's awareness of those things. This definition has as a corollary the famous axiom that from will and power together, action follows; since any endeavour results in action unless it is prevented. So it is not only the voluntary inner acts of our minds which follow from this conatus, but outer ones as well, i.e., voluntary movements of our bodies, thanks to the union of body and soul which I have explained elsewhere [e.g., 'New system of the nature and communication of substances']. There are other efforts, arising from insensible perceptions, which we are not aware of; I prefer to call these 'appetitions' rather than volitions, for one describes as 'voluntary' only actions one can be aware of and can reflect upon when they arise from some consideration of good and bad; though there are also appetitions of which one can be aware.[12]

So if we take a passion (or affect or emotion) to be a state of mind immediately preceding an act, the conatus constitutes an integral part of all passions. (This is the case in Hobbes and Spinoza as well.) Here, we have reached the point where we are able to explain the presence of "force" in both passive and active states of mind, according to Leibniz. However important the cognitive component in Leibniz's theory of the passions might be, the hidden basis of the mind's affective states is the conatus. In this respect, it would be a big mistake to consider this theory of passions to be Stoic in an unqualified way. His explicit definition of passion in § 9, ch. 20, book 2 of the *New Essays* stresses the element that distinguishes his theory from Stoic ones, according to which passions are merely opinions. This element is precisely the conatus.

> The Stoics took the passions to be beliefs: thus for them hope was the belief in a future good, and fear the belief in a future evil. But I would rather say that the passions are not contentments or displeasures or beliefs, but endeavours – or rather modifications of endeavour – which arise from beliefs or opinions and are accompanied by pleasure or displeasure.[13]

---

11 Nidditch: 236.
12 *NEH*. 172.
13 *NEH*. 167. "Mais j'aime mieux dire que les passions ne sont ny des contentemens, ou des déplaisirs, ny des opinions, mais des tendences, ou plustost des modifications de la tendence, qui viennent de l'opinion ou du sentiment, et qui sont accompagnées de plaisir ou de déplaisir" (A VI/6, 167).

The passions are therefore not beliefs, and not even simple perceptions. They are first of all endeavors modified by confused perceptions that the soul possesses before everything else. This is the way we can best interpret the famous 'uneasiness' (*inquiétude/Unruhe*) in the same chapter of the *New Essays*. Leibniz certainly agrees with Locke concerning the thesis that, "[t]he chief if not the only spur to human industry and action is uneasiness."[14] But he dismisses as mistaken the way in which Locke continues his argument, namely, that it is through the absence of a thing that carries with it displeasure or pain that uneasiness urges us to acquire that thing. Contrary to this Lockean view, Leibniz suggests that uneasiness is nothing but a small, inapperceptible pain, which is, at worst, a matter of indifference for us. We "enjoy the advantage of evil without enduring its inconveniences" and:

> [O]ur continual victory over these semi-sufferings – a victory we feel when we follow our desires and somehow satisfy this or that appetite or itch – provides us with many semi-pleasures; and the continuation and accumulation of these (as with the continuing thrust of a heavy body gaining impetus as it falls) eventually becomes a whole, genuine pleasure. In fact, without these semi-sufferings there would be no pleasure at all, nor any way of being aware that something is helping and relieving us by removing obstacles which stand between us and our ease. This also exhibits that affinity of pleasure with suffering which Socrates comments on in Plato's *Phaedo* [606c], when his feet are itching.[15]

Therefore, the fundamental structure of the Leibnizean soul consists in an infinity of small, confused perceptions directing an infinity of inapperceptible endeavours, which, on the one hand, become condensed into various desires, and, on the other hand, accumulate to become apperceptible pains and pleasures.

The quality of the cognition that directs the omnipresent conatus plays a fundamental role in the formation of the passions. Given that, in Leibniz's thought, the dominant aspect of reality is the mental, it will hardly surprise us that it is cognition or perception that determines the basic quality of our affects. The only factor responsible for the passivity of passions is the confusion in our perceptions. If we could ever achieve a state devoid of confused perceptions, we would become divine beings living without passions.

> Moreover, since all that passes in the soul depends, according to this system, only upon the soul, and its subsequent state is derived only from it and from its present state, how can one give it a greater independence? It is true that there still remains some imperfection in the constitution of the soul. All that happens to the soul

---

14 Nidditch: 230.
15 2,20,6, *NEH* 165.

depends upon it, but depends not always upon its will; that were too much. Nor are such happenings even recognized always by its understandings or perceived with distinctness. For there is in the soul not only an order of distinct perceptions, forming its dominion, but also a series of confused perceptions or passions, forming its bondage: and there is no need for astonishment at that; the soul would be a Divinity if it had none but distinct perceptions.[16]

Passions are merely confused perceptions. Therefore, if we had no confused perceptions, we would have no more passions. Beyond the cognitive basis of our whole mental life – passions included – there emerges an aspect of Leibniz's theory of passions that can rightly be termed Stoic in character. Terms like "Divinity" or "bondage" are also reminiscent of the Stoics. Leibniz certainly did not think of the Christian God as dispassionate. Rather, what he had in mind was the then commonplace concept of the Stoic sage who rivals his gods. He certainly shared much of Spinoza's conatus-based Stoic view of the passions: both construe passions as bondage, as human slavery.

There is, however, another feature of Leibniz's theory that is worth considering. At first glance, it would seem that Leibniz – contrary to Spinoza – does not admit the possibility of active affects, i.e., affective states in which the basic conatus is directed by distinct, not confused perceptions. We shall come back to this feature later.

2. Leibnizean Love

Given that Leibniz comments on Locke's views on love in relation to the passions in general, and uneasiness in particular, the transition to the concept of love can be stated briefly. Locke first defines love in the following manner: "One has love for something which can produce pleasure."[17] If Locke had stopped here, it would be difficult to understand why Leibniz begins his commentary expressing his agreement: "That definition of love is almost the same as the one I gave, when expounding the principles of justice in the Preface to my *Codex juris gentium*, where I said that to love is to be disposed to take pleasure in the perfection, well-being or happiness of the object of one's love."[18] But Locke supplements his first definition with the following statement: "[B]ut hatred or love, to beings capable of happiness or misery, is often [a displeasure or a contentment] which we find in our selves arising from a consideration of their very being, or of the happiness

---

16 *Theodicy*, I, 64; op. cit. p. 56.
17 Nidditch: 230.
18 *NEH* 163.

which they enjoy."[19] Leibniz limits the extension of love to the second case. Thus, the two philosophers are in virtual agreement regarding the question of love. However, this is the scene set by Locke, and not the way Leibniz himself proceeds in his interpretation.

Leibniz's approach is also rather independent of the way in which we have presented Leibniz's analysis, as building on typical, seventeenth-century affect-theoretical foundations. At the same time, Leibniz himself starts from the equally typical seventeenth-century issue of political theology, in a broad sense. One set of questions in political theology addressed the proper relationship between a particular human being and his sovereign. And since the political sovereign was readily associated with the divine sovereign, it is perfectly understandable that the concept of love was at least one of the conceptual means applied to answer this question. Leibniz's approach to love originates from the treatment of complex issues in political theology and is clearly bifurcated: on the one hand, love is given a prominent role in metaphysics, and, on the other hand, his natural law theory is also connected to the concept of love.

2.1. The Metaphysical Concept of Love

In the first part of this paper, I touched upon Leibniz's fundamental metaphysical position against the atomists. Leibniz's refusal to treat love within a quasi-mechanical theory like that of Descartes is not independent of this position. Leibniz refuses to regard the corporeal world as being analyzable in mechanico-philosophical terms. The souls that render bodies living, the beings for which the world was created, cannot principally be analyzed in those terms. They are, mutatis mutandis, in the same situation as the eternal modes of thinking of the Scholium to Prop. 40 of Book 5 of Spinoza's *Ethics*: their being cannot but be understood with constant reference to God. Their being is primarily about their proper relation to God, rather than being taken on its own terms. If they succeed in establishing an adequate relation to God, their own being is thereby adequately ordered, without any further effort.

> For one sees clearly that all other substances depend on God, in the same way as thoughts emanate from our substance, that God is all in all, and that he is intimately united with all creatures, in proportion to their perfection, that it is he alone who determines them from the outside by his influence, and, if to act is to determine immediately, it can be said in this sense, in the language of metaphysics, that God alone operates on me, and God alone can do good or evil to me.[20]

---

19 Nidditch: 230.
20 *PES* 63; Discourse on Metaphysics § 32.

Leibniz's God is therefore the only source of its creature's well-being or misery. The mechanistic approach, which implies the postulate of a value-free Nature, is excluded from this kind of metaphysics of morals, from the outset. And given that the only appropriate starting point for the metaphysical consideration of everything that happens to us cannot but be the goodness of God, the only proper metaphysical relation of souls to Him is love: "THE GENERAL KNOWLEDGE of this great truth, that God acts always in the most perfect and desirable way possible, is, in my judgment, the foundation of the love that we owe God in all things."[21]

The justification for this claim is the interpretation of love reminiscent of what we found in the *New Essays* to be the true definition of love: "[S]ince he who loves seeks his satisfaction in the happiness or perfection of the object loved and in his actions."[22] Or, as it is defined in the "Principles of Nature and Grace, Based on Reason:" "[G]enuinely pure love consists in the state that allows one to take pleasure in the perfections and felicity of the beloved."[23]

This definition clearly shows that, with the rejection of the mechanical approach to love, Leibniz also dismisses those Cartesian kinds of love that involve an asymmetry between lover and beloved, affection and devotion. But obviously, for any account of love, it makes a great deal of difference whether or not "the object loved" is God or a human being of limited perfection. We shall come back to this question later.

Leibniz's love toward God manifests itself in the will to satisfy divine volition:

> I hold, therefore, that, according to these principles, in order to act in accordance with the love of God, it is not sufficient to force ourselves to be patient; rather, we must truly be satisfied with everything that has come to us according to his will. I mean this acquiescence with respect to the past. As for the future, we must not be quietists and stand ridiculously with arms folded, awaiting that which God will do, according to the sophism that the ancients called logon aergon, the lazy reason. But we must act in accordance with what we presume to be the will of God, insofar as we can judge it, trying with all our might to contribute to the general good and especially to the embellishment and perfection of that which affects us or that which is near us, that which is, so to speak, in our grasp.[24]

---

21 *PES* 37; Discourse on Metaphysics § 4.
22 Ibid.
23 *PES* 212.
24 *PES* 37; Discourse on Metaphysics § 4. See also: "Pour l'aimer, il faut applaudir à sa volonté certaine qui paroist à l'égard du passé, et tacher de satisfaire à sa volonté presomtive à l'égard de l'avenir" (Leibniz à la Kurfürstin Sophie).

This is the manifestation of true love toward God in us. But how can we be instrumental to its coming into being? To Leibniz, it is evident that this true love of God results from appropriate philosophical investigations:

> The first and most important advantage of science is that we understand God's highest perfection and the nature of our mind, from which it follows that God is to be loved above all things (and this is extremely difficult for those who do not know him in the right way).[25]

> But the more someone loves God, the more she can give reason for her love. And to find pleasure in someone's perfection means already to love him. Therefore the supreme function of our mind is the cognition or – which is in that object the same – the love of the most perfect being, which necessarily entails the highest and most durable pleasure, that is felicity [...] But to show these things in further details belongs to another science: still we had to call your attention to them in order not to let the best advantages of rational Physics be neglected – as is almost always the case.[26]

There is a further lesson to be drawn from this passage, which takes up a question we provisionally set aside earlier. The question is whether or not Leibniz acknowledges something parallel to Spinoza's active affects (i.e., "actions"), the most prominent examples of which are strength of character, (divided into Tenacity and Generosity) and the intellectual love of God. Clearly, if Leibniz can state that *cognitio* and *amor perfectissimae rei* are the same, or, in other words, that knowing and loving are identical in the case of the most perfect thing, then there must be a kind of love presupposed that increases and diminishes with the increase and diminishing of knowledge, i.e., clear and (perhaps) distinct perception.

The notion of love emerging from these passages is highly intellectual. There is one stock question that can be posed to the author of any intellectualistic ethics who at the same time claims to be a Christian: Is it not the case that these two

---

25 Initia scientiae generalis. Praefatio. "Primum ergo summumque scientiae beneficium est ut summam Dei perfectionem Mentisque nostrae naturam intelligamus, ex quo sequitur nos Deum super omnia amaturos (quod eum minus recte cognoscentibus utique difficillimum est) [...] fore" (A VI/4/B 368).

26 Praefatio ad libellum elementorum physicae. "Sed et tanto quisque magis Deum amat, quanto magis amoris sui rationem reddere potest. Et voluptatem ex perfectione alicujus capere, hoc ipsum amare est. Itaque summa mentis nostrae functio est cognitio sive (quod in hoc objecto idem est) amor, perfectissimae rei, unde voluptatem nasci necesse est maximam, maximeque duraturam, hoc est felicitatem. [...] Sed haec fusius ostendere ad aliam pertinet scientiam: Admonenda tamen fuerunt, ne potissima Physicae rationalis utilitas, ut fere fit, negligeretur" (A VI/4/C 1995).

stances exclude each other? However this question might be answered in general, Leibniz, himself, was not at all ambiguous about the utility of his approach to Christian religion:

> FOR THE REST, it seems that the thoughts we have just explained, particularly the great principle of the perfection of the operations of God and the principle that the notion of a substance contains all its events with all their circumstances, far from harming, serve to confirm religion, to dispel enormous difficulties, to enflame souls with a divine love."[27]

Another question worth asking concerns the relationship between this intellectualistic love and the traditional concept of charity – with regard to the love of finite human beings. According to my interpretation, a society made up of human beings loving each other in the Leibnizean way would resemble neither a religious community nor a body politic. Rather, we should search for parallels to such a society in the projected philosophical community we come across in both Descartes and Spinoza. In Leibniz, this is the systematic place of the "cité de Dieu." One way in which he introduces this concept, in the "Principles of Nature and Grace, Based on Reason" § 15, is the following:

> That is why all minds, whether of men or genies, entering into a kind of society with God by virtue of reason and eternal truths, are members of the City of God, that is, members of the perfect state, formed and governed by the greatest and best of monarchs. Here there is no crime without punishment, no good action without proportionate reward, and finally, as much virtue and happiness as is possible.[28]

However, since in this state there are vices and punishments, the Leibnizean society I have in mind is, rather, the nearly utopian concept of a future state of humankind mentioned in the final sentence of *New Essays*:

> If the principles of all these professions, arts and even trades were taught in a practical way by the philosophers – or it might be in some other faculty of learned men – the latter would truly be the teachers of mankind. But this would require many changes in the present state of things in literature, in the education of the young, and thus in public policies. When I reflect on how greatly human knowledge has increased in the past century or two, and how easy it would be for men to go incomparably further along the road to happiness, I am not in despair of the achievement of considerable improvements, in a more peaceful time under some great Prince whom God may raise up for the good of mankind.[29]

---

27 *PES* 63; Discourse on Metaphysics § 32.
28 *PES* 212.
29 *NES* 522.

Again, due to the general access to the sources of knowledge, this society would be permeated by the love that grows with the increase of knowledge. And as we have seen, this love cannot be a passion in Leibniz's sense. Passion has been defined as an endeavor directed by a confused perception, and it is precisely this confusion that is to be blamed for the passivity of the passion. An omniscient divine sage would be necessarily exempt from all passions. At the same time, he or she would be filled with intellectual love, constituting the basis of the only 'city of God' worthy of the name.

So, although I cannot recall explicit statements of the distinction by Leibniz, I would insist on a twofold Leibnizean concept of love: one is a passion, defined by lack of knowledge; the other is an "action," defined by the increase and plenitude of knowledge. But of course, the term "action" is not meant in the Aristotelian sense, as opposed to habit or potential. For example, when Leibniz writes in a letter to Nicaise in 1697 that, "Love is this act or active state of the soul which makes us find our pleasure in the happiness or satisfaction of others,"[30] this "act of the soul" is not what I have in mind, for this act is defined by its opposition to benevolence as a habit, disposition, or inclination to love. Instead, what I mean is the above-mentioned Spinozistic sense of an active affect originating from an adequate idea.

Aided by a short text from the 1690's entitled "Felicity," we can even formulate the difference between the two kinds of love in Leibniz's own terms, on two different levels. To begin with, Leibniz tells us that pleasure is to be taken to be "a knowledge or feeling of perfection" either in ourselves or in others. "To love is," Leibniz continues, "to find pleasure in the perfection of another."[31] What needs to be done to achieve our end is first to introduce two kinds of perfection – one merely apparent, the other real – and then to connect these to two different kinds of knowledge. This is exactly what Leibniz does in § 6a of this text:

> Now it is necessary to explain the feeling or the knowledge of perfection. The confused perception of some perfection constitutes the pleasure of sense, but this pleasure can be [productive] of greater imperfections which are born of it, as a fruit with a good taste and a good odor can conceal a poison. This is why one must shun the pleasures of sense, as one shuns a stranger, or, sooner, a flattering enemy.[32]

When the perfection (either in ourselves or in others) is perceived confusedly, we feel only a pleasure of sense. Yet this is hopelessly uncertain due to its defective nature: we can never know if there is some great imperfection concealed within it. Although Leibniz does not draw out this consequence explicitly, we can say that the love the pleasure of sense might arouse in us on the basis of some

---

30 Wiener 565.
31 Riley 83.
32 Ibid.

confusedly perceived perfection of another would be a passionate love. The pleasures lurking behind this love are those pleasures of § 3 that are "good to abandon or moderate" because they "can be injurious, by causing misfortunes or by blocking [the attainment of] better and more lasting pleasures."[33] Against this, the pleasures we need to have are those conducive to "a lasting state of pleasure" – which is the very definition of felicity, the most important feature of the society considered in the final lines of the *New Essays*, referred to above. These pleasures are called the "pleasures of the mind." They are based on the (non-confused) knowledge of facts and reasons, which Leibniz calls perception and intelligence respectively. "Pleasures of the mind" can only be produced by the non-confused perception of some perfection. If, in this way, we find pleasure in the perfection of another, we can consider the love aroused as active, i.e., an action rather than a passion.

Perhaps the reason why Leibniz resolves, in a way, this dichotomy of confused and non-confused perception of action and passion – a well-known dichotomy to the reader of seventeenth-century philosophy – has something to do with his principle of continuity. In this way, he introduces an intermediary level of pleasure. Furthermore, it is certainly not by chance that the domain he opens up with this move is that of art and the aesthetic (a topic rather neglected by seventeenth-century philosophers). There are "pleasures of sense," Leibniz says, "which most closely approach pleasures of the mind." These are said to be "the most pure and the most certain."[34] Leibniz mentions two kinds of harmony as examples, that of music and symmetry. These harmonies are perceived by the ears and the eyes respectively. Given his numerous references to Raphael, we can suppose that it was this artist's painting that Leibniz had in mind when speaking of symmetry as a kind of harmony. Literature is also a source of intermediary pleasure. Leibniz makes many references to literary works, and in a German version of the same text, Leibniz refers to literature in a similar context. However, it is not silently read literature that he has in mind, but verses that sound like music to the ear when they set our animal spirits in motion.[35] However, my point is that between passions and actions, Leibniz recognizes an intermediary level of (let us anachronistically say) aesthetic affects, where the respective kinds of love may vary considerably according to the proportion of confusion and distinctness in the perception from which they originate.

---

33 Ibid.
34 Ibid.
35 Holz 392.

3. Love in Natural Law

With this tripartite scheme in hand, we can now approach the main text to which Leibniz refers whenever he gives an "intelligible definition of love."[36] In the Preface to the *Codex Juris Gentium Diplomaticus*,[37] we can distinguish three kinds of love. First, we have "mercenary love," the overcoming of which Leibniz considers "the difficult knot, which is also of great moment in theology." It is difficult, because the standard theories, reflecting ordinary life, mostly deal with some sort of egoistic love. This love can correctly be considered a passion, since it involves confused perceptions, not only of the perfection of (improperly) loved objects, but also of what is actually useful for us. The second kind of love is divided into two parts. The first part (although mercenary love is already overcome) is called a "symbol of love" (*simulacrum amoris*). The reason for this is the same that we have seen in Leibniz's reply to Locke: the proper objects of love can only be beings capable of feeling felicity. What induces love in this case is a non-sentient being, a work of art: "a painting by Raphael affects him who understands it, even if it brings no riches." In this way, we have a much better conception of both the perfection of the object and of our own real needs than on the first level, but the object itself cannot properly become an object of love. The second part of the second kind of love is "true love," "when the beautiful object is at the same time also capable of happiness." I would propose that this love is a state of the soul in which the distinct perceptions are in a clear majority among the perceptions of the beloved object. The third kind of love is *divinus amor*, divine love. As is to be expected, this love excels all other kinds of love. But the reason for this may be somewhat surprising.

> [This love] surpasses other loves because God can be loved with the greatest result, since nothing is at once happier than God, and nothing more beautiful and more worthy of happiness can be known than he. And since he also possesses the highest power and wisdom, his happiness not only enters into ours (if we are wise, that is love him) but it also constitutes it.[38]

I think the best explanation of this position can be found in a feature we have highlighted before: the double character of the object of our perceptions involved in love. In addition to the perception of the perfections of the object, the perception of our own perfection (or rather, of our real need) also plays a significant role.

Needless to say, this divine love is the archetype of all our love toward human beings, not only in the sense of being *amour de bienveillance*, but also in the sense

---

36 Letter to Coste.
37 Cf.: Riley 171 ff.
38 Wiener 560.

of being a totally active affect originating in distinct perceptions. Now, of course, the whole Preface revolves around the famous definition of justice offered by Leibniz in the following terms: *"justitiam... definiemus caritatem sapientis,"* or, "Justice... will be defined... as the charity of the wise man."[39] I believe that a consequence of the above account is as follows: Justice is both the habit (*benevolentia*) and the act of universal, active love toward all human beings seeking (i.e., directing) our endeavors to make them happier based on distinct perceptions of the perfections of God, of the nature of the lasting pleasures, and of our own real needs.

Abbreviations

A: Leibniz: Sämtliche Schriften und Briefe. Berlin: Akademie-Verlag

CSMK: The Philosophical Writings of Descartes. Translated by J. Cottingham, R. Stoothoff, D. Murdoch. Cambridge: Cambridge University Press, 1985.

Holz: Leibniz: Kleine Schriften zur Metaphysik. Translated by H. H. Holz. Frankfurt am Main: Suhrkamp, 1996.

NEH: Leibniz: New Essays on Human Understanding. Translated by J. Bennett, P. Remnant. Cambridge: Cambridge University Press, 1981.

Nidditch: The Works of John Locke. Edited by P. H. Nidditch. Oxford: Clarendon Press, 1975.

OL: Hobbes: Opera philosophica quae latine scripsit omnia. Edited by G. Molesworth. Aalen: Scientia Verlag, ²1966.

PES: Leibniz: Philosophical Essays. Edited and Translated by R. Ariew and D. Garber. Indianapolis & Cambridge: Hackett, 1989.

Riley: Leibniz: Political Writings. Translated by P. Riley. Cambridge: Cambridge University Press, 1988 (1972).

Wiener: Leibniz: Selections. Philip Wiener. Scribner, 1982.

---

39 Riley 171.

Malebranche on Natural and Free Loves
Tad M. Schmaltz, Duke University

Love would not seem, initially, to be a promising candidate for a central principle of Cartesian psychology. After all, Descartes portrayed love not as a single phenomenon, but rather as something that can be conceived either as a non-volitional feeling that derives from the body, or as a movement of the will that derives from the mind itself. Even so, there is a unitary conception of love that is at the center of what we could call – somewhat inelegantly – Malebranche's "Augustinized" version of Cartesian psychology. Malebranche was inspired by Augustine to hold not only that all love pertains to the will, but also that love is identical to the will as manifested in a mental motion toward the good. What is most important for Malebranche is not Descartes' distinction between passionate and rational love, but rather the distinction between the "natural love" produced in us by God, which occurs "in us without us," and the "free love" that derives from our own undetermined consent to love of a particular good. In opposition to commentators who see Malebranche as adhering to a consistent account of the will and its freedom,[1] I emphasize developments in his views of natural and free loves over the course of his philosophical career. Whereas he suggested initially that we can convert natural love into free love by "turning" the former toward a particular good, Malebranche later distinguished more sharply between a natural love for particular goods that is outside of our direct control and a free love for such goods that we determine by means of "acts" that produce "nothing physical."

I begin here with the bifurcated account of love that emerges from Descartes' later writings. Then I turn to Malebranche's attempt to provide a unified treatment of love that identifies it with a motion directed toward the good. Though he sometimes spoke as if the natural love that God produces in us is directed primarily toward "the good in general", his considered position is that our freedom requires that this natural love be directed toward particular goods. Moreover, he suggested in his mature writings that free action involves the direct determination not of our natural love, but rather a parallel form of free love. I argue in closing that a proper understanding of Malebranche's final account of the distinction between the two loves allows us to make some progress in addressing the notorious problem of reconciling his insistence on our undetermined freedom with his occasionalist doctrine that God is the only real cause.

---

1 See, e.g., E. J. Kremer, "Malebranche on Human Freedom," in *The Cambridge Companion to Malebranche*, ed. S. Nadler (Cambridge: Cambridge University Press, 2000): 190–219.

1. Descartes on Passionate and Rational Love

1.1. Passionate love in the Passions

Descartes offered his official account of love in his final work, the *Passions de l'âme* (1649).[2] There he listed love as one of six "principal passions" (the others being wonder, hatred, desire, joy, and sadness), and he defined it as "an emotion of the soul caused by a motion of the spirits, which impels the soul to join itself willingly to objects that appear to be agreeable to it" (*PA* II.79, AT 11:387/CSMK 1:356).[3] He explained that the willful joining to which this passion impels is not a desire, but rather "the assent by which we consider ourselves henceforth as joined with what we love in such a manner that we imagine a whole, of which we take ourselves to be only one part, and the thing loved to be the other" (*PA* II.80, AT 11:387/CSM 1:356). In terms of his account of judgment in the *Fourth Meditation*, this assent is an act of will directed to the perception of the understanding that we form a whole with the loved object. Since the love merely impels this assent, and since it is a perception rather than a volition, it must be distinguished from this act of will. The love must further be distinguished from the perception that we form a whole with the loved object, given Descartes' claim that passions in the strict sense are perceptions referred particularly to the soul and not to external objects or our own body (*PA* I.29, AT 11:350/CSM 1:339). For surely the perception that we form a whole with something else is not referred just to our soul. The claim that love is an emotion suggests that it is a feeling that is normally coupled with, though is distinct from, the soul's judgment that an object is agreeable to it. I say 'normally' because Descartes noted in his (as we will see) important 1647 letter to Chanut that we can have a feeling of love prompted by the heat of the heart "without our will being impelled to love anything, because we do not come across any object we think worthy of it" (*To Chanut*, 1 Feb. 1647, AT 4:603/CSMK 307). Stripped to its essentials, then, the passion of love seems to be a mere feeling – most akin, perhaps, to a feeling of comfortable warmth.

According to Descartes, the passion of love is merely one among other primitive passions. There is even a sense for him in which it is not the most important of these passions. Rather, it is the primitive passion of desire that is the central focus of the *Passions*. For a central claim in this text is that our pursuit of happi-

---

[2] Abbreviated as "*PA*".

[3] *Oeuvres de Descartes*, edited by Adam and Tannery (Paris: Vrin, 1974), abbreviated as "*AT*". *The Philosophical Writings of Descartes*, 3 volumes, translated by John Cottingham, Robert Stoothoff, Dugald Murdoch and Anthony Kenny (Cambridge: Cambridge University Press), 1984–91, abbreviated as "*CSMK*".

ness depends on our limiting our desires to those things that depend on our free will. Descartes noted that the control of desire is most crucial since "passions cannot lead us to perform any action except by means of the desire they produce" (*PA* II.144, AT 11:436/CSM 1:379). Whereas in the earlier *Principia Philosophiae* (1644), Descartes had listed desire as a "mode of willing" along with aversion, assertion, denial and doubt (*PP* I.32, AT 8-1:17/CSM 1:204), he settled in the *Passions* on the view that it is a passion rather than a volition and that it is the passion most directly connected to action.[4]

Although love does not have a particularly central role in Descartes's system when conceived as a passion, such a conception does not exhaust its nature. We can see how this is so by considering an ambiguity in Descartes' claim that love is an emotion. In the *Passions* itself, he distinguished the passions from what he called the "internal emotions" of the soul. In contrast to the passions, which are "caused, maintained and strengthened by some motion of the spirits" (*PA* I.27, AT 11:349/CSM 1:339), internal emotions are "produced in the soul only by the soul itself" (*PA* II.147, AT 11:440/CSM 1:381). At the start of this text, he had mentioned only two kinds of states that can be produced in the soul, namely, volitions (or acts of will), and "perceptions of our volitions and of all the imaginings or other thoughts that depend on them" (*PA* I.18–19, AT 11:343/CSM 1:335). The claim in the *Passions* that internal emotions "are often joined with passions that are similar to them" would seem to suggest that these emotions are internally produced perceptions rather than volitions, insofar as they are similar to a non-volitional state of the soul. On this suggestion, the internal emotion of love would be an internally produced feeling that is similar to the feeling that the heat of the heart produces in us. However, a consideration of Descartes's 1647 letter to Chanut yields a very different account of love as an internal emotion, or what is called in that letter "purely intellectual or rational" love.

1.2. Rational love in the letter to Chanut

The portion of the letter to Chanut that is relevant for our purposes contains Descartes' response to his correspondent's request for an explanation of his views on the nature of love. In this response, Descartes started with the distinction between "the love that is purely intellectual or rational and the love that is a passion." He then noted his view that rational love consists "simply in the fact that when our soul perceives some present or absent good, which it judges to be fitting for itself, it joints itself to it willingly [*de volonté*], that is to say, it considers

---

[4] In further contrast with this passage from the *Principia*, Descartes denied in the *Passions* that there is any passion of aversion distinct from the passion of desire: *PA* II.87, AT 11:393/CSM 1:359.

itself and the good in question as a whole of which it is one part, the good another" (*To Chanut*, 1 Feb. 1647, AT 4:601/CSMK 306). Thus, at this point, we seem to have something very similar to the passion of love as defined in the *Passions*. As in the case of the passion of love, rational love is connected to the judgment of the soul that it forms a whole with the object judged to be beneficial to it. I have argued, however, that the passion of love must be distinguished from both the perception that the soul and the beneficial object form a whole and from the assent to that perception. In contrast, Descartes' remarks to Chanut suggest that rational love is identical to the act of will by which the soul considers itself and the beneficial object to form a whole. In particular, this form of love is said to be the "motion of the will" by which the soul so considers itself. But then rational love cannot be a mere feeling – even a mere intellectual feeling – that straddles the judgment that an object is beneficial and the judgment that the soul forms a whole with this object. Unlike the passion of love, rational love in fact is the volitional element of the latter judgment.

As I have noted, the implication in the *Passions* is that the passion of love is simply one among many, and even in a sense subordinated to the passion of desire. But in the letter to Chanut, rational love seems to play the most important role of all of the intellectual emotions mentioned there. Descartes told Chanut that when the judgment constituted by love is joined with knowledge that the soul possesses the beneficial object, the motion is transformed into joy; when joined with the knowledge that this object is absent, the motion is transformed into sadness; and when joined with the knowledge that an absent object is good to acquire, the motion is transformed into desire. Joy, sadness and desire therefore would seem to be simply different manifestations of the master emotion of love. It certainly cannot be said that the account of rational love in this letter is entirely satisfactory. For instance, there is no consideration there of how exactly we are to understand the metaphor of the "motion of the will" used to explicate the nature of this love. Moreover, his off-hand remarks in this letter concerning the rational emotions certainly do not match the comprehensiveness of his enumeration of the passions in his final work. Even so, the letter to Chanut anticipates, as the *Passions* does not, a view in Malebranche on which love is a foundational feature of the will.

2. Malebranche on Love and the Will

2.1. Descartes and Augustine

Malebranche's psychology was of course profoundly influenced by Descartes' views. Most notably, he adopted Descartes' substance dualism, with its real distinction between mind as thinking substance and body as extended substance. He also accepted the position in Descartes that our mind possesses the two basic faculties of understanding and will, and he followed Descartes in breaking with the scholastic tradition by holding that judgment does not pertain solely to the understanding but is constituted also by an act of the will.

Even so, Malebranche's view of the relation of the will to love is informed not by Descartes's account of love, but rather by the views of his other great intellectual mentor, St. Augustine. In *De civitate Dei*, Augustine had emphasized that there are two different cities that are founded on two basic kinds of love. The first, a love of self, provides the foundation a secular city dominated by a desire for personal enjoyment of goods of the body and mind, whereas the second, a love of God, provides the foundation a celestial city dominated by a desire for conformity to the divine will (*De civ. Dei*, XIV.28). Here, love is not (as in Descartes) merely a particular passion or emotion among others, but rather is the very basis of the will.[5] The interchangeability of *amor* and *voluntas* in Augustine is reflected in Malebranche's definition of the will in his *Recherche de la vérité* as the "capacity the soul has of loving different goods." The capacity for love is defined in turn in terms of "the impression or natural motion that carries us toward the undetermined good in general" (*RV* I.1, *OCM* 1:46/LO 5).[6] The love of the good in general is simply the desire for happiness, which Malebranche took to be beyond our power to forego. He insisted, however, that our motion toward particular goods other than God is in our power to resist, and so our love of such goods is, in contrast to our love of the good in general, not invincible.

I do not want to suggest that Descartes' account of love, even as found in the *Passions*, had no influence on Malebranche. After all, Malebranche did allow in the *Recherche* that there is the passion of love, and that this passion is directed to objects judged to be beneficial. However, he differed from Descartes in taking this passion to be the particular motion of the will that is so directed (*RV* V.9, *OCM* 2:213/LO 390).[7] In this respect, Malebranche's passionate love is more similar to the rational love of the letter to Chanut than it is to the passionate love of the *Passions*.

---

5 On the historical importance of Augustine's conception of the will, see C. H. Kahn, "Discovering the Will: From Aristotle to Augustine," in *The Question of "Eclecticism": Studies in Later Greek Philosophy*, ed. J. M. Dillon and A. A. Long (Berkeley: University of California Press, 1988): 234–59.
6 *RV* = *De la Recherche de la vérité*, 1674–1675; *OCM* = *Œuvres complètes de Malebranche*, 20 vols., ed. A. Robinet (Paris: J. Vrin, 1958–84), cited by volume and page.
7 For a helpful discussion of the differences between the views of Descartes and Malebranche on this point, see P. Hoffman, "Three Dualist Theories of the Passions," *Philosophical Topics* 19 (1991): 153–200, esp. 182f.

2.2. Three characteristics of the will

There are three distinctive characteristics of Malebranche's account of the will that I want to pause to consider: the first, his description of the will in terms of motion; the second, his view that this motion is directed toward the good in general; and the third, his identification of the love of this good with the desire for happiness.

2.2.1. Will as motion

Malebranche's talk of the will as an impression or motion is anticipated by Descartes claim to Chanut that rational love consists in a certain "motion of the will." Though Descartes was not explicit on this point, it is clear that he conceived of this love on analogy to features of body. After all, in his view, the mind cannot literally move in the way a body does, but only possesses something analogous to the motion of body in a certain direction insofar as it has volitions directed toward an object that is judged to be good.

Malebranche recognized more explicitly that a characterization of the will in terms of motion is merely analogical. In general, he offered a conception of the difference between the mental faculties of understanding and will in terms of the difference between two kinds of bodily faculties. Malebranche noted at the start of the *Recherche* that the distinction between the mental faculties is rendered "more distinct and more familiar" when the understanding is conceived as a faculty of receiving ideas (or, more accurately, perceptual modifications distinct from ideas in God) that is akin to the bodily faculty receiving various shapes, and when the will is conceived as a faculty of receiving inclinations that is akin to the bodily faculty of receiving various motions. Malebranche himself emphasized that this analogy is severely restricted insofar as the soul is an indivisible and unextended substance, and so cannot possess anything that presupposes divisible extension in the way that shape and motion do. The analogy is further restricted in the case of the will. Whereas the body, as a mere extended thing, "is entirely passive" and "has no force to assist its motion or to direct it or turn it in one direction rather than another," the mind "in a sense can be said to be active, because our soul can direct in various ways the inclination or impression that God gives it" (*RV* I.1, *OCM* 1:46/LO 4). However, Malebranche held not only that the analogy to body cannot yield a clear understanding of the activity of the will, but also that we have no clear understanding of this activity at all, but only a confused "inner sensation" of its existence. As he later insisted in his *Réponse à la Dissertation* (1685),[8] the fact that we can conceive of this activity only in terms of

---

[8] *Réponse à une dissertation de Mr Arnaud contre un éclaircissement du Traité de la nature et de la grâce.*

a comparison to bodily motion that does not capture its true nature serves to reveal that "we do not have a clear idea of the soul" (*RD* XII.13, *OCM* 7:568). This fact, as Malebranche noted repeatedly, undermines Descartes' official doctrine that mind is better known than body. Whereas Descartes wrote to Chanut that there is nothing in the motions of the will that constitute its various rational emotions that would be obscure to the soul "provided it reflected on its own thoughts" (AT 4:602/CSMK 306), Malebranche emphasized that the very conception of love as a motion reveals our lack of access to a clear idea of the nature of the soul.[9]

2.2.2. Will as directed to the good

Malebranche's claim that the will is a motion directed toward the good seems to distinguish his conception of the will from Descartes'. In the *Meditations*, Descartes explicitly bracketed the relation of the will to the good and focused on its role in judgments concerning the truth. But the differences here are not as great as they first appear. For one thing, Descartes never denied that the will has a role in the pursuit of the good. Furthermore, his remarks in the *Passions* suggest that there is a sense in which such a pursuit is primary. In his discussion there of *générosité*, Descartes made the point that the resolution to use the will well – that is, to judge in accord with evident perception – is motivated by the desire for happiness. Arguably, the implication in this text is that the search for truth is instrumental to the attainment of this practical end.[10]

I have also noted that Malebranche accepted the anti-scholastic view in Descartes that an act of will is a constituent of judgment concerning truth. In the *Recherche*, he explicitly distinguished between consent to the good, which affects us insofar as it concerns the agreement objects have with us, and consent to the truth, which does not so affect us insofar as it concerns merely relations among objects (*RV* I.2, *OCM* 1:53/LO 9). This distinction may seem to conflict with Malebranche's characterization of the will in general as love of the good, insofar as it allows for an act of will directed toward the true rather than the good. However, in a way similar to Descartes, we could say that consent to the truth is itself motivated by consent to the good, and so even the former involves some sort of motion toward the good. Indeed, this move is suggested in a note to the passage just cited concerning the two kinds of consent, in which Malebranche

---

9 For a study focusing on Malebranche's various arguments for the view that we lack access to a clear idea of the soul, see my *Malebranche's Theory of the Soul: A Cartesian Interpretation* (New York: Oxford, 1996).

10 In *Freedom of the Will, Passion, and Virtue in Descartes's Theory of Judgment* (Ph.D. diss., Duke University, 2005), Joel Schickel offers a detailed and plausible defense of this reading of Descartes.

claimed that "Geometers do not love the truth, but knowledge of the truth, whatever might otherwise be said." Bare truth does not move the geometer to consider geometrical propositions, but rather the good of knowing the truth. Malebranche indicated that it is the love of this good that yields the desire for the truth, and that this desire can be fully satisfied only when the understanding presents a perfectly evident representation of its object. In this way, the love of the good is central to the psychological explanation in Malebranche of Descartes' view that we are led inevitably to assent to clear and distinct perceptions since "a great light in the intellect is followed by a great inclination of the will" (AT 7:59/CSM 2:41).

2.2.3. Will as the desire for happiness

Jean-Christophe Bardout has argued in a recent study that there is a transition in Malebranche's thought from a "metaphysical morality", that stresses a conception of our moral end in terms of abstract "relations of perfection", to a "sensible morality", that stresses a conception of this end in terms of the cause of our pleasure.[11] Bardout links this transition to the emergence in Malebranche during the mid-1690s of a theory of "efficacious ideas," in which ideas in God are the source of our sensations as well as our purely intellectual perceptions.[12] He finds a related emphasis on God's causation of pleasure in Malebranche's dispute during the late-1690s with his admirer and fellow Oratorian, François Lamy. In his *Connaissance de soi-même* (1697), Lamy cited passages from Malebranche's writings that he took to be favorable to "quietism," the view that one can attain through proper mystical practice a "pure love" of God wholly untainted by self-interest. The most prominent statement of quietism in the *Maximes des saintes* (1697) of the French Archbishop Fénélon holds the view (which Lamy endorsed) that such a love would, free of a concern for the self, lead one to welcome even eternal damnation should God will it. Fénélon and Lamy took Augustine's own contrast between selfish love and love of God to imply that any self-concern is incompatible with the true love of God.

For his part, Malebranche countered that he had never meant to endorse a quietist conception of love of God. Thus, in his *Traité de l'amour de Dieu* (1697),[13]

---

11 J.-C. Bardout, *La vertu de la philosophie. Essai sur la morale de Malebranche* (Hidesheim: G. Olms, 2000): 111–62. In ibid., 119, n.3, Bardout cites as complementary the accounts of the evolution of Malebranche's moral theory in A. Robinet, *Système et existence dans l'œuvre de Malebranche* (Paris: Vrin, 1965): 367–412 and 449–80, and G. Dreyfus, *La volonté selon Malebranche* (Paris: Vrin, 1958): 300–51.
12 For the classic discussion of Malebranche's theory of efficacious ideas, see Robinet, *Système et existence*, 259–84.
13 Abbreviated as *TAD*.

later editions of which included *Trois letters ... au Lamy*, he accused Lamy of misreading the passages which he had cited. In this text, Malebranche insisted on the principle that "the desire for formal happiness or pleasure in general is the foundation or the essence of the will" (*TAD, OCM* 14:10). He concluded that in his system, as well as in Augustine's, "the love of God, even the most pure, is interested in this sense, that it is excited by the natural impression that we have for the perfection and felicity of our being, in a word for pleasure taken in general, or for agreeable perceptions that relate to the true cause that produces that and that make us love it" (*TAD, OCM* 14:23). Love of God is to be contrasted not with love of self *per se* (*amour propre*), but rather with a "disordered" love of self (*amour propre déréglé*), which takes created goods to be more important than the Creator who makes such goods possible.[14]

There is something to Bardout's claim that the emphasis in Malebranche's response to Lamy on the importance of pleasure marks some sort of shift in his moral theory. However, it seems to me that this shift is in some respects not as dramatic as the changes marked by his theory of efficacious ideas, or – more to the point – the changes in his conception of freedom.[15] The view that God is our true good insofar as He is the sole cause of pleasure is present already in the first edition of the first volume of the *Recherche* (see *RV* I.17, *OCM* 1:172f/LO 76f). Although it is true that Malebranche did not initially define the will in terms of pleasure, there is from the beginning a stress on the fact that our will is directed essentially to our happiness. This is reflected particularly in Malebranche's claim, again from the first edition of the *Recherche*, that we do not love the good in general freely since "it is not in the power of our will not to wish to be happy" (*RV* I.1, *OCM* 1:47/LO 5).

So, while Malebranche held that we have an invincible love of the good in general, or desire for happiness, he also emphasized that our disordered love of particular goods is not invincible, but is instead due to the misuse of our free will. In order to address this position, I begin with a brief discussion of invincible natural love, which, on Malebranche's considered view, can be directed toward particular goods as well as the good in general. Then I consider in more detail his treatment of our free love of particular goods.

---

14 It must be said on Lamy's behalf that, in his earlier writings, Malebranche tended to contrast love of God with *amour propre* and that the qualification that the latter must be conceived as *déréglé* is on the whole a later addition, dating from after the time of his exchange with Lamy. For more on Malebranche's engagement with quietism, see Y. de Montcheuil, *Malebranche et le quiétisme* (Paris: Aubier, 1947). But cf. the critical evaluation of Montcheuil's decidedly pro-Malebranche view of the exchange with Lamy in Dreyfus, *La volonté*, 302–08, 318–322.

15 I indicate the profound changes linked to the theory of efficacious ideas in my "Malebranche on Ideas and the Vision in God," in *The Cambridge Companion to Malebranche*, 59–86, esp. 76–81. I discuss the changes in his conception of freedom in § 4 below.

3. Malebranche on Natural Love

The distinction in the *Recherche* between the irresistible natural love of the good in general and the resistible free love of particular goods may seem to suggest that only the good in general, and not particular goods, can serve as the object of natural love. Indeed, Malebranche did claim later in his *Réponse* that "the natural motion of the soul is an indeterminate motion." Whereas Malebranche was sometimes careless in suggesting that natural love is directed only to the good in general and not to particular goods, by the time of the *Réponse* he was clear that the indeterminate nature of this motion does not preclude its determination to such goods. He indicated in this later text that in order for this motion to be determined to particular objects, "it suffices to represent them to the soul" (*RD* XII.14, *OCM* 7:569). By its nature, the motion is not restricted to a particular object, but is directed to whatever is represented to the will as good – that is, as pleasurable or conducive to happiness.[16]

Indeed, Malebranche's considered position is that natural motion must be directed to objects represented as conducive to happiness, prior to any act of free will. From the start, in the 1674 edition of the first volume of the *Recherche*, he noted that, in the case where a person loves some particular honor, his natural impression is directed to that honor prior to any act of consent on his part (*RV* I.1, *OCM* 1:48/LO 5). And in the 1678 *Eclaircissement I*,[17] which is devoted to his discussion of the will (in the aforementioned volume of the *Recherche*), Malebranche emphasized that God leads us initially to all particular goods, for since "God leads us to all that is good, it is a necessary consequence that He lead us toward particular goods when he produces the perception or sensation of them in our soul" (*Ecl. I*, *OCM* 3:18/LO 547f). Thus, in this text, he affirmed that when we sense our freedom, we do not sense a "pure indifference [or] a power determining us to will something without any physical motive [*motif physique*]." Since it is always the case that a natural love for objects we perceive to be good precedes any free love we may have for those objects, it is impossible that our free will render us independent "of God's control over us or of the physical motives that He produces in us, by which He knows and can make us will and freely execute all that He wills" (*Ecl. I*, *OCM* 3:29/LO 553).[18] The difference

---

16 A related point in Malebranche is that since only an infinite good can fully satisfy our natural love, finite particular goods cannot hold it permanently, and thus it is constantly driven to other goods; see, e.g., *RV* IV.2, *OCM* 2:16f/LO 269f.

17 In: *De la Recherche de la Vérité, où l'on traite de la nature de l'Esprit de l'homme, & de l'usage qu'il en doit faire pour éviter l'erreur dans les Sciences. Quatrième édition, revuë, & augmentée de plusieurs Eclaircissemens,* Paris, 1678.

18 Here, Malebranche in effect rejected Descartes' own suggestion in the *Fourth Meditation* that there is a possible, albeit imperfect, case of free action in which inclinations for and against action are perfectly balanced, and thus in which we will with complete indifference; see AT 7:57f/CSM 2:40.

between natural and free love therefore cannot hinge on the fact that free love is directed toward particular goods, since Malebranche required that natural love can also be so directed. Rather, the main difference is whether it is God or our own free will that is responsible for the determination of the motion.

But there is an obvious problem here. Malebranche would seem to be committed (by his occasionalist doctrine that God is the only real cause) to the conclusion that He is also the cause of all features of our love. However, it would seem to follow from this doctrine that all love is natural, including the disordered love of the self. Alternatively, if the determination of our disordered love comes from our free will rather than from God, then it seems that not only God but also our will can be a real cause. Malebranche himself recognized the problem (which he expressed in *Eclaircissement I*) as the demand of his critics that he explain "what God does in us and what we ourselves do when we sin, because in their opinion, I would be obliged, by my explanation, either to agree that man is capable of giving himself some new modification, or to recognize that God is the true cause of sin" (*Ecl. I, OCM* 3:17f/LO 547). It is left to us now to consider Malebranche's attempt – or rather, his different and not wholly compatible attempts – to address this problem.[19]

4. Malebranche on Free Love

In the *Recherche*, Malebranche defined freedom as "the force that the mind has of turning this impression [i.e., the impression toward general and indeterminate good] toward objects that please us so that our natural inclinations are made to settle upon some particular object" (*RV* I.1, *OCM* 1:46/LO 5). Given this definition, free love would seem to be a natural impression that the mind has turned toward a particular object. However, this suggestion is problematic for reasons I have already indicated. Furthermore, Malebranche later transformed his view here that freedom involves a power to turn an impression, first, into the view that this turning involves a mere rest on our part, and, then, into the view that it involves an act of will that determines our free love by producing something that is itself "nothing physical."

4.1. The turning of natural love

I have noted Malebranche's claim toward the start of Book One of the *Recherche* that our will is "in a sense" active. He explained there that this activity consists

---

19 My discussion here draws on the treatment of Malebranche's account of freedom in my *Malebranche's Theory of the Soul*, 220–28. See also the distinction indicated in note 26.

in the fact that "our soul determines [*déterminer*] in various ways the inclination or impression that God gives it." Although the soul cannot stop the motion that God creates in it, "it can in a sense turn [*détourner*] it toward that which pleases it, and thus cause all the disorder in its inclinations, all the miseries that are the certain and necessary results of sin" (*RV* I.1, *OCM* 1:46/LO 4f). In Malebranche's view here, then, there is a fundamental difference between God's control over bodily motion and His control over our inclinations. God is the sole cause of any motion of body. He creates in such a way as to completely determine the direction not only of motion that proceeds in a straight line, but also of motion that deviates from this path. Though God is also the sole cause of our inclinations, insofar as they proceed toward goodness or truth, our soul determines the direction of those inclinations created by God that deviate from this path when it consents to the love of some object not clearly perceived to be wholly good or assents to some proposition not clearly conceived to be wholly true (*OCM* 1:45/LO 4).

Malebranche's initial account of our freedom is reminiscent of the account in a 1660 letter from Claude Clerselier to Louis de la Forge, which Clerselier placed at the end of the third and last volume of his edition of the *Lettres de Descartes*. In this letter, Clerselier argued that though God alone can create any new motion in a body, finite minds "could have the power to change the direction of motion that is in bodies" and so "determine the motion" (*determiner le mouvement*) that God has created, since such a determination "adds nothing real to nature."[20] The resemblance here to the account in the *Recherche* of our freedom to "determine" the impression that God creates in us by "turning" it toward particular objects may be not merely coincidental, since Malebranche owned the volume that includes Clerselier's letter.[21] In any event, it is clear that his first attempt to reconcile God's creation of our inclination and our freedom to act on this inclination is similar to Clerselier's attempt to reconcile God's creation of motion with our power to cause voluntary motion.

---

20 From "Observations de Monsieur Clerselier, touchant l'action de l'Ame sur le Corps," in *Lettres de Mr Descartes*, vol. III, *Lettre de Mr Descartes oû il répond à plusieurs difficultez sur la dioptrique, la geometrie, et sur plusieuers autres sujets* (Paris: Ch. Angot, 1667): 642f. This is a possible source for Leibniz's (mistaken) claim in his *Théodicée* that Descartes held that though the law of the conservation of motion precludes any production of new motion by our mind, it nonetheless is the case that we "could have the power to change the direction of the motions that are in bodies" (*Die Philosophischen Schriften von Gottfried Wilhelm Leibniz*, ed. C. I. Gerhardt (Hildesheim: G. Olms, 1960–61): 6:135f). For a defense of the view that this claim concerning Descartes is mistaken, see D. Garber, "Mind, Body, and the Laws of Nature in Descartes and Leibniz," *Midwest Studies in Philosophy*, 8 (1983): 105–33.

21 Lelong's inventory of Malebranche's library lists Clerselier's three-volume edition of Descartes's letters as items 142–44 (*OCM* 20:237, 261).

One problem with Malebranche's attempt in Book One of the *Recherche*, however, is that it conflicts with the claim in the very same section of this text that it is God (rather than our will) that directs our natural impression toward particular objects. In the considered position in the *Recherche*, our free love of a particular object cannot involve a turning of our natural love, since we already have a natural love of that object that God produced when, immediately after our perception of the object as beneficial or pleasing, He directed our inclination toward it.

As I have indicated, Malebranche emphasized in *Eclaircissement I* that God's determination of our natural love must precede our free love of an object. But there seems to be no way to avoid the conclusion that this commentary on the *Recherche* involves a rejection of the view in that text (suggested by the reference there to our turning of inclinations that God directs to the good in general) that we, rather than God, initially determine our inclinations toward a particular object.

4.2. The rest of consent

It is to be expected, then, that Malebranche's explanation of free love in *Eclaircissement I* will differ from an explanation in the *Recherche* that appeals to the activity involved in the turning of our inclinations. In fact, the difference is dramatic. Far from invoking this sort of activity, Malebranche emphasized precisely the *inactivity* involved in our free love of a particular good. More specifically, he held that such love involves a consent to the love of a particular good that is nothing more than resting in the enjoyment of that good, and that this "rest [*repos*] upon viewing a particular good is nothing real or positive on our part" (*Ecl. I, OCM* 3:20/LO 548).

The claim that consent is merely rest, that it is nothing real or positive in us, is problematic. In particular, it seems that rest itself involves a real change in us that we bring about. Malebranche himself seems to have realized the difficulty here, for in a passage added to the 1712 edition of *Eclaircissement I*, he claimed that consent is accomplished:

> ...by an act without doubt, but by an immanent act that produces nothing physical [*rien de physic*] in our substance; by an act that in this case does not even require a true cause of some physical effect [*effet physic*] in us, neither ideas nor new sensations; ... for the rest of the soul as that of the body has no force or physical efficacy [*force ou efficace physique*] (Ecl. I, OCM 3:25/LO 551).

One might object that even if it is granted that no force is required for the *continuation* of rest in the body and soul, some force is nonetheless required for the *onset* of this state in both kinds of substance. Malebranche did indicate an important difference between the two states of rest when he wrote in *Eclaircissement I* that, while the rest of the body requires the destruction of motion, the rest of the soul does not require the destruction of inclination, since God creates us with the same amount of inclination, whether or not we consent to love of a particular good (*Ecl. I*, *OCM* 3:22/LO 549). So one might respond, on Malebranche's behalf, that although force is needed to bring about destruction of motion involved in bodily rest, this same consideration does not reveal that force is required to bring about mental rest. Nevertheless, Malebranche's admission that consent is an immanent act seems to entail that it involves some change in us, and thus his insistence that we bring about consent seems to entail that there is some kind of force in us that produces this change.

Certain passages from the first edition of *Eclaircissement I* encourage the view that no such force is required, since our consent is merely the continuation of the natural love of particular objects that God produces in us. The suggestion here is that in the case of consent, our free love consists of merely the combination of this natural love and our inactivity. Yet Malebranche insisted that we also use our freedom when we "suspend" our consent to natural love of a particular good. Since it is opposed to consent, this act of suspense would seem to bring about a change in our natural love of particular objects. It is difficult to see how such an act could nonetheless be similar to consent in being a mere inactivity.

Malebranche in fact granted in *Eclaircissement I* that when we suspend consent to love particular goods, "we give ourselves a new modification in this sense, that we actually and freely will to think of other things than the false goods that tempt us." He attempted to mitigate the tension with occasionalism by noting that we produce no real change here, since, in suspending consent, "we will to be happy only by the motion toward the good in general that God constantly impresses on us" (*Ecl. I*, *OCM* 3:25/LO 551). But now it seems even more difficult to conceive the opposition between consent and its suspense, since both would appear to be simply the continuation of natural love.

We can make some progress, however, by focusing on the claim in this same text that acts of consent are to be characterized not as the mere continuation of natural love, but rather as the "free cessations of search and examination" (*Ecl. I*, *OCM* 3:25/LO 551). The contrast here would be with a suspense that involves a continuation of such a search and examination. In order to conceive of this contrast, however, we need to distinguish the search that is continued or discontinued from the natural love that God impresses on us. Malebranche provided some assistance when he emphasized in his later writings that this natural love differs from a free love that our various acts of consent and suspense "determine."

4.3. The determination of free love

Malebranche provided his most careful account of natural and free loves in the *Traité de Morale* (1684),[22] the first edition of which appeared ten years after the

---

[22] Abbreviated as *TM*.

initial publication of the first volume of the *Recherche* and six years after the initial publication of *Eclaircissement I*. In the *Traité*, he held that the love that "justifies us before God must be a habitual, free and dominant love of immutable order" (*TM* I.3, *OCM* 11:50). Malebranche insisted that even though we have certain acts and habits of "natural, necessary and purely voluntary" love that are contrary to order, our moral worth depends only on the nature of the habits that derive from our free acts. In contrast to his earlier suggestion that free love involves either a turning of natural love or an inactivity coupled with such love, Malebranche's view here is that the habits and acts of our free love are distinct from the corresponding features of our natural love.

Malebranche further distinguished – in the case of free love – between the *force* involved in the search for truth and the *liberté* that directs this search (*TM* I.6, *OCM* 11:70). In his discussion here, *liberté* involves the free acts of consent and suspense that depend on us, whereas *force* involves the dispositions that God produces in us on the occasion of these acts.[23] In the previous chapter, Malebranche had defined an "occasional cause" as that "which infallibly determines the efficacy of the general law" by which God produces effects in nature (*TM* I.5, *OCM* 11:59).[24] In light of this definition, we could take our free acts of consent and suspense to be occasional causes that determine the efficacy of the general law, so as to produce the free dispositional *force* that we have to either desist from or continue with in the search for the ultimate good.[25]

---

23 In *Eclaircissement VII*, Malebranche suggested the possibility that our facility for thought and action consists solely in the manner in which God causes certain occurrent thoughts in the soul. In this case there would be nothing in the soul itself corresponding to dispositional habits. However, he claimed that certain "proofs from Theology" lead him to believe that "after the soul's action there remain in its substance certain changes that really dispose it to the same action" (*OCM* 3:67f/LO 577f). The nature of these proofs is indicated by the thesis in the *Traité de Morale* that we are justified not by our temporary thoughts but rather by the stable dispositions in us that underlie these thoughts (*TM* I.3, *OCM* 11:48).

24 There is some controversy in the literature over whether occasional causes determine the efficacy of the general laws themselves, or whether they merely determine God to act by volitions to produce particular effects that are in accord with general laws. For an argument that Malebranche had only the latter sort of determination in mind, see S. Nadler, "Occasionalism and the General Will in Malebranche," *Journal of the History of Philosophy*, 31 (1993): 31–47. In "Cartesian causation: body-body interaction, motion, and eternal truths," *Studies in History and Philosophy of Science*, 34 (2003): 737–62, esp. 747f, I defend the view that Malebranche in fact was thinking of the former sort of determination.

25 In earlier work, I had taken Malebranche's talk of the determination of free love to indicate that consent involves the turning of this love; see *Malebranche's Theory of the Soul*, 224–28. I now think that this interpretation depends on a mistaken understanding of what Malebranche meant by "determination".

We have a reasonably clear sense here of how free acts of consent and suspense themselves produce *rien de physic* in us. Just as bodily collisions are mere occasions that determine the efficacy of God's general laws governing motion to produce certain changes in bodies, so acts of *liberté* are mere occasions that determine the efficacy of God's general laws governing our free love to produce certain changes in the *force* of that love. There is, however, still the problem that the acts themselves seem to be, like the collisions, something real, and thus that we are the causes of *quelque chose de physic* in producing these acts.[26]

It must be admitted that Malebranche was not always careful to distinguish the claim that our free acts produce nothing real from the claim that the acts themselves are nothing real. Even in his final work, *Réflexions sur la prémotion physique* (1715),[27] one finds the argument that free acts are *rien de physic* simply on the grounds that "they produce nothing physical by their own efficacy" (*RPP* X, OCM 42). Yet I think we can construct an argument for the claim that the acts themselves involve no real or physical change by drawing on the suggestion in *Eclaircissement I* that consent is a mere cessation of a search or examination and suspense is the mere continuation of that search. Both consent and suspense determine God to produce certain effects: in the case of consent, it is a change in *force* that reinforces the natural love of a particular object, and in the case of suspense, it is a change in *force* that itself serves as an occasional cause of the extinguishing of such a natural love.[28] In themselves, neither consent nor suspense involve a real change: not consent, because it consists merely in the privation of a search, and thus does not itself involve the production of a new being, and not suspense, because it consists merely in the continuation of a search, and thus does not itself involve any change, real or otherwise.[29] It is in light

---

26 For a clear statement of this objection, see Kremer, "Malebranche on Human Freedom," 210–14.
27 Abbreviated as *RPP*.
28 Andrew Pyle has argued recently that Malebranche is committed by his claim that free acts are occasional causes of changes in habits to the conclusion that the acts "are as 'physically real' as any of the other modifications of our souls" [A. Pyle, *Malebranche* (London: Routledge, 2003): 232]. However, it is not clear why mere cessations or continuations that do not consist in the production of a new being could not serve as occasional causes. Cf. the response in note 21 to Kremer's objection to Malebranche (which Pyle cites with approval in ibid., 277, n. 46).
29 Kremer argues that Malebranche's reconciliation of our freedom with occasionalism fails given the acceptability of the principle: "Any change in a thing that is not a real change in that thing is a real change in something else" ("Malebranche on Human Freedom," 213). According to the view I attribute to Malebranche, this principle would not come into play in the case of suspense, since there is no change in that case. And in the case of consent, the principle would not hold because there can be a change involving a mere cessation, or the privation of a previous search, that does not involve a real change, that is, the production of a real being, in anything.

of this line of argument, I believe, that we can best understand Malebranche's claim in his *Réponse* that the "determination of our will" does not involve any "real power" since consent "is on our part only a simple rest," whereas in suspending consent, we simply continue to "follow the natural impression that God gives me for all good" (*RD* XII.13, *OCM* 7: 567).[30]

I have argued, then, that Malebranche did not have a stable view throughout his career of the relation between natural and free loves. While he began by speaking of free love as consisting in our "turning" a natural love of the good in general toward particular goods, it becomes increasingly clear in his writings both that natural love is directed to particular goods by God, and that our free acts involve the determination of a distinct sort of free love. The reference to "determination" signals the fact that these acts do not directly produce any real being, but serve as mere occasions that determine the efficacy of God's action. But Malebranche's most considered position seems to be that the acts themselves are *rien de physic*, since far from involving the turning of our natural or free love, they consist merely in the cessation or continuation of the search for the good.

---

30 It may appear to be problematic for my interpretation that Malebranche spoke in this passage of consent as the following of a natural impression. One might expect that a free, rather than a natural, impression is involved in suspense. However, given that the *Traité de Morale* that introduces the distinction between natural and free acts and habits dates from around the same time as the *Réponse*, it seems that we can understand the *following* of the natural impression to which Malebranche referred in the latter text as involving the persistence of a free habit that corresponds to this natural impression.

The Problem of Conscience and Order in the *Amour-pur* Debate
Dániel Schmal, Hungarian Academy of Sciences

The famous '*amour-pur*' debate – opposing Bossuet to his former protégé, Fénelon, and Nicolas Malebranche to his one-time follower, François Lamy in the last decade of the seventeenth century – can be seen as polarizing the interpretations of the same corpus of traditional texts. Almost all participants in the debate refer to very similar theological formulations of love and call the same authors to witness to bolster their positions. The multiple meanings of the texts and the polysemantic character of the terms gave rise to solutions that pretended to provide the public with authoritative interpretations of the tradition. Inspecting the texts, one can easily discern a common language and vocabulary used indiscriminately by the antagonists during the debate. I will identify two common features that, I will argue, should be related to each other: the theme of illusions and the repeated reference to the idea of order.

1.

Thinkers in the second half of the seventeenth century are surprisingly obsessed with the problem of illusion. One's support for the moral order can be a mask for the imposition of one's interest and ambition to succeed, veiled by virtue and piety. The problem grows worse once selfish interest starts to dissimulate the real motivations of acts even from the consciousness of their subject. In this case, the most honest and most sincere love (pretended to be in accordance with the highest moral values) can easily prove to be an illusion that stems from pure egoism. Moral rules, piety, and devotion can conceal the quest for one's own reputation as a man of virtue or as a saint. As Henry Gouhier notes,[1] the Cartesian principle of error, formulated in Descartes's *Meditations*, also holds in the matter of virtue: it is difficult to recognize falsity since "*in hoc ipso error consistat, quod a nobis sub specie erroris non advertatur.*"[2] Beyond the overall suspicion about socially sanc-

---

1 Vö. Henri Gouhier, *Fénelon philosophe* (Paris: Librairie Philosophique Jacques Vrin, 1977), 79.
2 "[E]rror consists in the fact that we are unable to recognize it as such." René Descartes, *Oeuvres* vols. I–XI.; publ. by Charles Adam and Paul Tannery (Paris: Librairie Philosophique Jacques Vrin, 1897–1913), vol. VII, 354.

tioned institutions and moral values – present in La Rochefoucauld, Nicolas Malebranche, and almost all other moralists of the century – this theory has far-reaching theological consequences and complications as well. Applying the general schema to the love of God, the upshot will be an essential uncertainty with regard to one's future destiny: salvation or damnation. If the love of God is indispensable to future happiness, one may feel strong affections toward one's Creator as a condition *sine qua non* of one's well-being and pursue, meanwhile, one's own well-conceived interest. Due to the possibility that even the most convincing form of piety may well be hypocritical, a specious act of the Augustinian *amor sui*, no one can be sure about his or her present or future status.[3] In this case the object of suspicion is the human self, and the problem of love, true or imaginary, opens up, so to speak, an infinite abyss where humans cannot find a foothold against fear and anxiety. Given this perspective the central question seems to be: how can we detect the illusions of self-love under the veil of a devout spirituality, or – to put it in the terms of Nicolas Malebranche – how can we escape "the suppleness of self-love who especially are its fools, who think themselves to be experts in it?"[4]

One of the most characteristic responses of the age is given in the works of Madame Guyon, the principal exponent of the quietist or semi-quietist cause in late seventeenth-century France, whose spiritual writings continued to gain adherents (especially in Protestant pietist circles) even long after her death in 1717.

Madame Guyon's solution is not without elegance. Her writings offer simple and easy-to-learn precepts to get rid of all fear and illusion. In contrast with the overall method of the Tridentine reform that required relentless concern with one's future destiny and demanded a permanent effort from the believer to persist in grace, Madame Guyon emphasized the "facility of the way" she proposed. "I use the term facility," she adds "meaning that perfection is easy, because it is easy to find God once we seek Him in our interior (*au-dedans de nous*)."[5] Even the

---

3 Cf. John M. Rist, *Augustine* (Cambridge: Cambridge UP, 1994), 190 and 129.
4 "Les souplesses de l'amour-propre dont ceux-là mêmes sont la duppe qui paroissent les mieux connoître." Cf. *Réponse générale aux lettres du R. P. Lami*, in *Œuvres complètes de Malebranche*, 20 vols., dir. André Robinet (Paris: Librairie Philosophique Jacques Vrin, 1958–1967), vol. XIV (published by André Robinet in 1978), 150.
5 Jean Marie Guyon, *Moyen court et très facile de faire oraison que tous peuvent pratiquer très aisément et arriver par là dans peu de temps à une haute perfection,* Lyon: Briasson, 1686. préface (without pagination) Modern edition: Madame Guyon, *Le Moyen court et autres écrits spirituels* 1685, texte établi, présenté et annoté par Marie-Louise Gondal, Grenoble: Jérôme Millon, 1995. (The present pagination refers to the original.) For further readings on Madame Guyon and the 'amour-pur' debate see: Louis Cognet, *Crépuscule des mystiques, Bossuet, Fénelon*, new edition by J. R. Armogathe, Paris: Desclée, 1991, and Michel Terestchenko, *Amour et désespoir de François de Sales à Fénelon,* Paris: Seuil, 2000. For a 2005 online bibliography see website: http://www.age-classique.fr/article.php3?id_article=4.

title of one of her most popular books offers a way to arrive at the highest degree of perfection in prayer in a short time.[6] Prayer defined "as an inner exercise of love" is at the same time the most efficacious means to get out of bad habits and acquire all virtues.[7] God, "communicative of Himself," desires to give us Himself, and since He exists in us "there is nothing so easy as to possess and to taste Him."[8] The author tries to guide all believers to the cores of their being and invites them to enter the "*Sancta sanctorum*," the center of their selves where the soul begins to find "the experimental taste of the presence of God."

What is striking here is not so much the sensuality of the metaphors, which is in line with the mystical tradition, but the absence of the institutional context of the history of salvation. Madame Guyon's manual bypasses the practical forms of Tridentine Catholicism to take a short cut on the road. She criticizes, for example, the catechetical praxis of the parish priests all over the country who prefer a school-bookish instruction in doctrinal terms to an introduction to prayer and spiritual life. Here the use of the cathecism – typical of post-Tridentine religiosity – is clearly secondary to the real experience of the faith that is easy enough to acquire by a serious attention to the heart. Likewise, sacramental praxis is clearly relegated to second class. In contrast with the spiritual manuals of her age, Madame Guyon did not support a thoroughgoing self-examination before confession. Her claims that a painstaking scrutiny may risk mistaking one's own conscience, and that "self-love deceives us easily," fit well into the above-mentioned scheme of late seventeenth-century moral thinking.[9] Instead of combatting the illusions of *amour-propre*, or (to put it otherwise), instead of making the center of the discussion the presence of one's real self, Madame Guyon focuses on the presence of God in the soul. The feeling of this presence is the sole religious act that matters. This act of internal feeling – which amounts to the love of God – contains all perfections, including contrition, since true love is "an eminent act which comprises all other acts even though not in a multiple and distinct form."[10]

Accordingly, the facility-claim does not only mean the absence or the secondary role of the external praxis of the Christian life, but it also helps the author to focus the agenda on the lack of activity, on the silence and the rest on the part of the believer. After having entered the inner sanctuary of the soul, the contemplative has "nothing to do but to persist in being returned to God in a continuous adherence."[11] It is not so much ourselves who are in the middle of our

---

6 Ibid.
7 Ibid., pp. 4–5.
8 *Ibid.* p. 6. Cf. François de Salignac da La Mothe-Fénelon, *Explication des maximes des saints sur la vie intérieure;* in: Fénelon, *Œuvres;* éd. Jacques le Brun; vol. II. Paris: Gallimard, 1983. p. 1037.
9 Jean Marie Guyon, *Moyen court,* p. 62.
10 Ibid., p. 64.
11 Ibid., p. 43.

being but God who, as a center of gravity, attracts us to Himself. "And in this moment – Madame Guyon says – it is of the highest consequence to stop all activity and operations in order to permit God to act in us."[12] In this last phase of prayer the believer ceases to make efforts and the remnants of his activity are eclipsed by the presence of the Almighty. The exact formulation of this situation is worth noting. The end of the process does not involve the destruction of the self, as the rise of the Sun, strictly speaking, does not annihilate the light of the stars.[13] However, the self becomes indistinguishable from the activity of God at this point. There is no return to the self; "we can hardly feel what we are."[14] It is apparent therefore that in the method of Madame Guyon it is the final absence of the reflection and the "annihilation" or the quasi-destruction of the self that solves the problem of illusion and anxiety. Being resigned to the will of the Creator the soul does not refuse what Madame Guyon calls, in accordance with the tradition, "the nothingness of the creature":[15] the soul submits herself even to "her own destruction and to her annihilation to honour the sovereignty of God."[16] The interpretation of this last point is a delicate matter. I take the author not to state the destruction and the annihilation of the self as a real possibility, partly because she expressly denies this in her *Commentary on the Canticle of Canticles*,[17] and partly because she repeatedly speaks about the joy and the happiness of Saints in the presence of God.[18] The resignation to one's damnation seems to me, on the contrary, a dramatic representation of a conceptual limit in the analysis of love, portraying "a supple heart without resistance" through an excessive act of love.[19] The suppleness of the *amour-propre* is to be met by an extreme suppleness of the heart.

In any case, it is clear that the writings of Madame Guyon, with their strong emphasis on the internal experience of the soul, echo the voice of Catholic reform in general and that of some devout circles of late seventeenth-century France in particular. However, in stark contrast with other movements – Jansenism for instance – the *via interna* of Madame Guyon is not accompanied by reflections about original sin nor by the need of any external means to overcome the obstacles to the pure love of God. The problem does not lie so much with the absurdity of the damnation of the saints, as with the fact that Madame Guyon's

---

12 Ibid., p. 48.
13 Ibid., p. 49. Cf. Jeanne Marie Guyon, *Le cantique des cantiques de Salomon interprété selon le sens mystique et la vraie représentation des états intérieurs* (Lyon: Antoine Briasson, 1688), 8–9.
14 *Moyen court*, p. 70.
15 "Le néant de la Créature." Ibid., p. 77.
16 *Ibid.* p. 75.
17 *Le cantique des cantiques*, loc. cit.
18 Ibid., p. 5., Cf. *Moyen court*, p. 2.
19 "Un cœur souple et sans résistance." *Le cantique des cantiques*, Préface (without pagination).

book, the *Moyen court* seems like a concise manual that promises immediate success in different fields of life. Though stressing the nothingness of humankind, it does not seem to attach much importance to the grace operating in the sacraments. The author speaks of an ordinary grace common and available to all Christians, and she takes this divine gift to be enough for the highest degree of the love.

According to the official criticism of Bossuet, Harlay de Champvallon (Archbishop of Paris) and some other divines, the interior experiences of Madam Guyon derive from a vivid and enthusiastic imagination. It was especially Jacques-Bénigne Bossuet who, in his writings against Madame Guyon, and in his pastorals issued in connection with the quietist affair, emphasized the political connotations of Madame Guyon's mysticism. According to him the spiritual experience of the via interna, which can only be judged by those who had it,[20] serves the quietists as a pretext to get rid of all ecclesiastical control. They have the intention, he says, "to render these new doctors independent of the censorship and the judgement of the Church."[21] Consequently, Bossuet deems the ideal of Madam Guyon *"une perfection imaginaire"*[22] that lacks institutionalized order and knowledge, and he opposes to this *"insania amantium"* the official teaching and praxis of the Church: *"scientiam et regulam,"* as he says.[23] He deems the quietist attempt to avert the threat of the illusions of the *amour-propre* an eminent case of illusion. In his view the suppleness of self-love is to be met by the infallibility of the Church.

The obvious shortcomings of Madam Guyon's works (some of them placed on the Index in 1688) and the ecclesiastical reponse that underlined the importance of the theological and sacramental institutions of the Church, set the agenda for those who engaged in the debate later. The events made it clear that the core of the mystical experience is to be defended or to be opposed by a systematic theology that rests on the traditional concept of order. As is well known, it was especially Fénelon who undertook to give an impeccable formulation of the mysticism of *"amour-pur et désinteressé"* in his *Maximes des saints*. He carefully and relentlessly emphasized that the doctrine in question was by no means contrary to the official statements of the Church. Fénelon's book clearly illustrates the use of the term 'order' and related ideas.

In what follows first I will talk about the Malebranchean conception of this notion, then I will turn to the Fénelonian interpretation of the idea of order.

---

20 Cf. Ibid., "On prie ceux qui ne sont pas experimentés dans ces voies du saint amour de ne pas en juger par la seule lumiere de la raison."
21 Jacques Bénigne Bossuet, *Instruction sur les états d'oraison: ordonance et instruction pastorale*, in *Œuvres complètes de Bossuet évêque de Meaux*, publ. by Jacques-Paul Migne (Petit-Montrougue (Paris): J-P. Migne, 1856), tom. IV. App., 25.
22 Ibid., p. 16.
23 Ibid., pp. 26–27. (with a slight modification of the original text).

2.

The Malebranchean understanding of love reflects the concept of *amor ordinis*, the Augustinian "love of order." In his *Traité morale*, the French philosopher defines virtue as "an exact obedience to the divine law… a constant and dominant disposition to regulate all the movements of one's heart and all the manners of one's conduct in accordance with the order known, in a word: the love of Order."[24] And in his *Traité de l'amour de Dieu*, he identifies virtue (so defined) with the love of God, "the love of Order is the love of God."[25]

These are very traditional formulations. Closer scrutiny will, however, reveal substantial differences between the Malebranchean conception of order and its Augustinian ancestry. Though order is often explained by Malebranche (as well as by Augustine) as the hierarchy of values attached to all beings, this is neither the primary nor the most important meaning of the word in his writings. In spite of numerous texts where he refers to the differences of value between, for example, a man and an animal,[26] order is, above all, the rational system of the perfections in God, or more precisely, it is the economy of the divine attributes: "the immutable order of the divine perfections."[27] Thus, Malebranchean order, transcending the created universe, is, so to speak, a matter of the inner perfection in the divine nature with no reference to any external being.

The importance of this position (the core of which is still traditional) can be measured by the fact that this conception of order is one of the basic principles on which Malebranchean theodicy rests. According to Malebranche, all physical disorder in the world can be explained by the fact that God, who is the only agent in nature, mostly acts in accordance with general rules. To be sure, general rules have unintended consequences in the world, since the overall goal of the rule cannot take into account all particular needs. Thus, anomalies are due to the fact that God does not suspend the laws in accordance with which he acts even in the case of some disorder in the effect.[28] But why does an omnipotent being prefer to act in accordance with general laws instead of simply doing the best? This is

---

24 "Une obéissance exacte à la loi divine… une disposition stable et dominante de régler sur l'ordre connu tous les mouvements de son cœur, et toutes les démarches de sa conduite, en un mot l'amour de l'Ordre." *Traité de morale* I. 7. 2, in *Œuvres de Malebranche*, 2 vols., ed. Geneviève Rodis-Lewis (Paris: Gallimard, vol. I: 1979), vol. II: 1992, II, 481.

25 "L'amour de l'ordre n'est que l'amour de Dieu." *Traité de l'amour de Dieu*, in *Œuvres complètes de Malebranche*, 20 vols., dir. André Robinet (Paris: Librairie Philosophique Jacques Vrin, 1958–1967), vol. XIV (published by André Robinet in 1978), 8.

26 Cf. for example *Traité de morale* I. 1. 13., p. 429.

27 "C'est l'ordre immuable des perfections divines." *Traité de l'amour de Dieu*, p. 8.

28 Cf. *Traité de la nature et de la grâce*, I. 1. 22., in *Œuvres complètes de Malebranche*, 20 vols., dir. André Robinet (Paris: Librairie Philosophique Jacques Vrin, 1958–1967), vol. V (published by Ginette Dreyfus in 1976), 35.

because his will, Malebranche explains, conforms to the prescriptions of Order, that is to say, to the demands of the divine attributes, one of which – namely, infinite wisdom – requires simplicity in the acts of a perfect being. "An excellent craftsman," says Malebranche, "does not accomplish by complex means that which may be performed by more simple ones."[29]

Consider the Malebranchean example of the physiological law governing the correspondence between the maternal brain and the formation of the fetus in her womb. This law-guided correspondence has the general advantage of developing a kind of social disposition in the new-born baby by producing the necessary traces and impressions in his or her brain long before birth. This physiological law can, however, cause unexpected anomalies as well, when the maternal brain undergoes a shock or an irregular passion, as in the case of the woman mentioned by Malebranche who, having attended the execution of a criminal, gave birth to a monster.[30] God could have dispensed, Malebranche insists, with the general law, and could have prevented the child from being born with disastrous consequences. However, He should not act in a miraculous way in favour of a particular creature. Similarly, "God, no doubt, could have made a world more perfect than the one we inhabit. He could for instance, have made it such that rain, which makes the earth fertile, falls more regularly on plowed lands than in the sea, where it is not necessary."[31] Nevertheless, God preferred to act according to general laws. His benevolence, by which he wishes all His creatures the best, is bound, so to speak, by his wisdom, which makes him act in a more regular manner. Sometimes, it is true, he suspends the general laws and chooses to act through a particular act of His will (*volonté particulière*) in favour of his creatures. So He really wants all His creatures to achieve the highest possible perfection, but he equally wants to keep the simplicity of his ways required by wisdom.

The outcome of these two conflicting aims is always determined by the order or inner dialectics of the relevant perfections – benevolence and wisdom in the present case. Consequently, general laws (physical or moral) that God has established from eternity are not without exception. What is without exception, is the Order or divine Reason that serves as a prescription for the divine will. It sets the scope of both general and particular volitions. "It ought here to be observed" says Malebranche, "that the essential rule of the will of God is the immutable order of justice [...]."[32] Thus, in the theory of Malebranche, the divine Order counts as a rule or a rational prescription that determines divine action.

---

29 *Traité de la nature et de la grâce* I. 1. 14, p. 29. (translated by Thomas Taylor, revised by Steven Nadler in Nicolas Malebranche, *Philosophical Selections,* ed. by Steven Nadler (Indianapolis/Cambridge: Hackett Publishing Company, 1992), 260.)
30 *Recherche de la vérité,* II. I. 7. 3., in *Œuvres de Malebranche,* 2 vols., ed. Geneviève Rodis-Lewis (Paris: Gallimard, vol. I: 1979), vol. II: 1992, I, 179–180.
31 *Traité de la nature et de la grâce,* loc. cit.
32 Ibid., p. 262.

Two aspects of this theory are worth mentioning from our point of view. First, it is evident that the Malebranchean definition of love holds both for God and for His creatures. The will of God – being the love of His own perfection – always conforms to Order. Accordingly, the true love of God – made possible by a motion impressed on the soul by God – must also be the love of Order: "wanting God as God wants Himself."[33] In Malebranche's view, this love is disinterested in the sense that it wants God to be what He is, or, to put it in a different way, it wants Him to act in conformity with His own perfection and not in accordance with some particular needs. With respect to theodicy it means that the true love of God has to want Him to act according to Order and not for the sake of our interests. That is to say, one has to accept the world with anomalies even if from a limited point of view it remains true that a better world would have been possible. The present form of the universe best expresses the perfection of the divine conduct, which is not to be measured by the fecundity of the effect alone but by the fecundity of the effect and the simplicity of the means in conjunction. Thus, the love of God means, according to a somewhat Spinozistic formulation, not to desire what seems to be evidently impossible.

Our second point is just a consequence of the first. Not to love God as He loves Himself is to fail to recognize Order. The desire, for example, that the above-mentioned fetus should not be born malformed is irregular because its realization would entail God's not acting as it is best for Him. By implication, this act of desire would only be consistent with a God who is less perfect than He really is. Indeed, in Malebranche's view, this would be an imaginary Being, an illusion created by our particular interest and idolized by our self-love. Even so, it remains true that the present world – without taking into consideration the simplicity of means – could have been better. It could have been more beautiful, for example, without monsters. Notwithstanding these affirmations, Malebranche frequently speaks of the "beauty of Order," which pleases those who love God.[34] But this rational beauty certainly cannot be identical with the Augustinian conception of the harmony displayed in the order of the visible world.

3.

Fénelon was one of the first critics of Malebranche's theodicy. The young protégé of Bossuet composed a book entited *Refutation of the system of Malebranche concerning Nature and Grace* in 1681. This early work of Fénelon, inspired by Bossuet, remained unpublished until the nineteenth century. It will be interesting to us, however, because the concept of order is one of the main targets of Fénelon's

---

33 "Vouloir Dieu comme Dieu se veut." Cf. *Traité de l'amour de Dieu,* p. 18.
34 Cf. ibid. p. 9.

criticism. Against the Malebranchean position he wished to re-establish what he took to be the original Augustinian idea.

According to Augustine, he says, the created world exists at an equal distance between the Supreme being and the Void, and "either direction the creature turns to, he perceives an infinite space."[35] The mark of divine omnipotence is the distance between the world and the Void wherefrom it was made to emerge, a distance that could only be overcome by an infinite power. When creating the universe God could choose from among an infinity of plans, none of which was simply the best. In order for the divine will to be perfectly free, we must admit, Fénelon insists, that any plan belongs to a scale, wherein all possible worlds are situated between an infinity of better and an infinity of less perfect ones, otherwise the best would infallibly determine the will of God. To save the absolute indifference of the divine will, which Fénelon takes to be the mark of liberty, the problem of divine choice should not have a single solution. "All degrees of being are good and worthy of the esteem of God, and the least degree of being exhibits the mark of the infinite perfection of the Creator."[36] Accordingly, he can choose any of them and his choice will always be perfectly good. Indeed, the real possibility of choice depends on the fact that there are equal alternatives that leave room for the indifference of the divine will. The most perfect creature is immeasurably less perfect than God but the less perfect is immeasurably more perfect than the void. "The first angel and an atom are, to be sure, quite inequal if you compare them with each other, but neither of them is farther from God or from the void than the other, for both are infinitely distant from either."[37] Fénelon's conception makes it clear that anything God choses to do is good and – an important formulation – "consistent with order." "He cannot do anything that is not good, and, consequently, everything that is possible, if it is really so... is good and conforms to Order."[38] This idea of order is obviously different from its Malebranchean counterpart. Far from being the rule divine volitions conform to, it depends on the free choice of the will. Order is consequent upon and is not presupposed by God's decisions.

According to the position of the future archbishop, true liberty consists in a superiority of the will that cannot be influenced by the inner qualities of its objects. "God is so magnificent that a creature cannot have anything in itself that would determine him to prefer one to another."[39] He adds: "This is His pure lib-

---

35 Fénelon, *Réfutation du système du père Malebranche;* in: *Fénelon, Œuvres;* ed. by Jacques Le Brun, vol. II (Paris: Gallimard, 1997), 361.
36 Ibid.
37 "Le premier des anges et un atome sont sans doute très inégaux entre eux, mais l'un n'est pas plus éloigné que l'autre de Dieu et du néant, puisqu'ils en sont tous deux infiniment distants." Ibid., p. 364.
38 "Il ne peut rien faire que de bon, par consequent tout ce qui est possible, s'il est vraiment possible... est bon et conforme à l'ordre." Ibid., p. 361.
39 Ibid., p. 366.

erty which consists in His full power to determine Himself all alone and to choose without any other cause of His decision than the sovereignty of His will, which does well all it wants to do."[40] This Fénelonian account of Order, first employed as a criticism of Malebranchean theodicy, is clearly present in his later works concerning *amour désinteressé*.

At the time of the *Maxims des saints*, when the debate about pure love was at its height, the absolute indifference of God's will and the correlative idea of order constituted an important element of Fénelon's defense of the mysticism of Madame Guyon. By that time the debate was centered on the question of the "fifth stage of love," which was completely free from any residue of self-love. Assuming that this pure and disinterested love was possible, Fénelon based his position, among others, on an argument that was slightly different from an opinion condemned as heretical by the Holy See in 1687. According to the seventh point censured in the bull *Caelestis Pastor*, the human soul engaged in the true love of God "should not think about prize and punishment, paradise and hell," since fear and anxiety about our destiny are telling marks of a selfish element in our love.[41] As was mentioned above, Madam Guyon also held that true believers should not have any other desire than that of the accomplishment of the divine will, and that their love would only be sincere if they were prepared to submit themselves to their own damnation if it happened to contribute to the glory of God and to the fulfillment of his will. We find this "false generosity" (*fausse générosité*), as Bossuet called it,[42] in the *Maximes des saints* as well. Nevertheless, in Fénelon, this scenario clearly results from a thought experiment and is not introduced as a real possibility: it is an "impossible hypothesis" (*supposition impossible*), he says.[43] The damnation of the righteous draws attention to the crucial distinction between the motive and the object of love. The person who possesses the supernatural gift of final perseverance, that is to say, who loves God at the moment of his death, cannot be excluded from salvation.[44] But even if the happiness of the righteous is *de facto* inseparable from the love of God, it must be secondary and should not be the essential motivation of love. "We cannot separate our felicity from God, whom we love," he says, "but those things that are incapable of being separated on the side of the object can be distinguished on the side of the motives."[45] So far Fénelon's position is not very far from that of

---

40 "Voilà sa pure liberté qui consiste dans le pleine puissance de se déterminer par lui seul, et de choisir sans autre cause de détermination que sa volonté suprême, qui fait bon tout ce qu'elle veut." Ibid.
41 Henri Denzinger–Karl Rahner, *Enchiridion Symbolorum, definitionum et declarationum* (Roma: Herder, 1976), 1227.
42 Bossuet, *Instruction sur les états d'oraison: ordonance et instruction pastorale,* p. 15.
43 *Maximes des Saints,* p. 1011.
44 Ibid., p. 1016.
45 Ibid.

Malebranche, who claims that the love of God is inseparable from happiness. There are two substantial differences, however. First, in Fénelon, the impossibility of the above-mentioned situation does not arise from an internal or theoretical inconsistency of the hypotheses involved, but is dependent upon the decision of the divine will which, as we have just seen, is perfectly indifferent with regard to all possibilities. "If God decided to destroy the soul of the righteous," Fénelon says, "through a case that was, due to His free promises, impossible etc.,"[46] the damnation of those who love God here is impossible on the sole ground that God has promised the opposite. Admittedly, the salvation of the righteous is an integral part of Order, though this order has been established by the sovereignty of God's will. The second difference concerns the Fénelonian distinction between the motivation of and the object of an act of love. Almost the same distinction can be found in Malebranche as well, with the notable difference that the motivation behind love, or its formal cause, is, according to him, the pleasure that endows the soul with happiness.[47] Both authors can therefore make sense of the same 'maxims of the saints': we must love God for Him alone, and ourselves only for the sake of God and inasmuch as He orders us to do so. "The saints love God," Malebranche says, "and refer everything to Him, their happiness included." (Fénelon himself could have written these words.) "They do not want to enjoy Him," Malebranche continues, "only inasmuch as He will want it... not by an arbitrary, unknown and imaginary will... but by a will that is regulated in accordance with the immutable order of justice."[48] It is apparent that only the theoretical interpretations of these last words oppose the two positions diametrically.

In conclusion, I will sum up what we have seen. The *amour-pur* affair in France triggered by Madam Guyon's activity was connected to the moral discussions about self-love and *amour-propre* in important ways. I have tried to portray the debate as an attempt to settle the problems involved in the "*souplesse de l'amour-propre*," which could cause anxiety about one's real attitude toward God and about the destiny of the soul after death. The quasi-annihilation of the self proposed by Madam Guyon was in line with a long-standing tradition but evidently lacked any theological sophistication or prudence. The original core of the *amour désintéressé* problem was, therefore, opposed or supplemented by ideas meant to respect the institutional setting, sacramental praxis, and doctrinal teaching of the Church. In the context of these conceptual requirements, we can assess the importance of the idea of order as a traditional element in the theological and philosophical articulation of Love. The concept Bossuet found wanting in the spiritual writings of Madame Guyon was, in particular, the idea of the order of providence and "the infallible traditions" (*les traditions infallibles*) that prevented

---

46 Ibid.
47 Malebranche, *Traité de l'amour de Dieu*, p. 11.
48 Ibid., p. 19.

the believer from the illusions of self-love, in the multiple forms of the sacramental praxis of the Church. Malebranche's account of Order plays an important role both in his theodicy and in his theory of love. The re-interpretation of this Augustinian term allowed him to integrate the traditional language of Christian spirituality into a rational metaphysics that resisted the imaginary order of self-love. As we have seen, almost all participants in the affair used the same language. The writings of Cardinal Bérulle, for instance, founder of the Oratory and one of the most influential agents of Catholic reform in France, contain almost all the central claims. For example, he says: "The aim of God in our creation was God Himself." We have to "leave ourselves to enter God" (*sortir soi-même pour entrer en Dieu*), and since it is only God who can act in us and in the world, man's only duty is to "offer and open himself, and to abandon himself to the will and power of his God and his Creator."[49] The very conventional but polysemous words that had been accepted in mystical or speculative theology seem to undergo different re-interpretations here and open up different perspectives in the debate. What happens is the same polarization of a polysemantic tradition that has been so clearly characterized by Robin Briggs: "A degree of equivocation had worked well enough in the past; unfortunately new standards of critical scholarship... something of a mania for legalistic definitions... were all threatening to upset the authority of tradition, less by denying it than by fragmenting it."[50]

---

49 "S'offrir, se livrer et s'abandonner au vouloir et à la puissance de son Dieu et de son Créateur." Pierre Bérulle, *Opuscules de piété*, publ. by Miklos Vetö (Grenoble: Jérôme Million, 1997), 148–151.
50 Robin Briggs, *Communities of Belief: Cultural and Social Tensions in Early Modern France* (Oxford: Clarendon Press, 1995), 343.

Love of God and Love of Creatures: The Masham-Astell Exchange*
Catherine Wilson, City University of New York

In 1694, Mary Astell (1666–1731) entered into an exchange of eleven long letters with John Norris (1657–1711), the English Platonist, over a principle expounded in his *Christian Blessedness: or Discourses Upon the Beatitudes* (1690). The principle was one upon which they both agreed though for different reasons: God alone merits our love and Creatures do not. To this exchange, published in London in 1695 under the title *Letters Concerning the Love of God, between the Author of the Proposal to the Ladies and Mr. John Norris*, Damaris Masham neé Cudworth (1659–1708), the longtime friend of John Locke (1632–1704) and an earlier correspondent of Norris, responded with a polemical anonymous attack on the Astell-Norris *Letters* as fanatical enthusiasm. Her defense of the love of Creatures was published under the somewhat misleading title of *A Discourse Concerning the Love of God* in 1696 and translated into French by Pierre Coste in 1715.[1]

The Masham-Astell controversy has been described as a reprise of the Locke-Norris controversy over Malebranche's philosophy of ideas.[2] Astell, the first woman to live respectably alone, according to her biographer,[3] is thought to represent Norris's Augustinian otherworldliness and Plotinian radical solitude, while Masham is seen to represent Lockean empiricism. Astell, on this view, aligns herself with Norris's visionary metaphysics, while Masham ridicules the flight from immanence, emphasizing the teachings of experience and the pleasures of sociability. While recent philosophical commentators have insisted on the autonomy and distinctiveness of the two female players who are more than proxies,[4] the biographers have made us aware of their complex personal relations. Norris published a moral treatise dedicated to

---

* A version of this essay was previously published in *History of Philosophy Quarterly* 21 (2004) pp. 1–23.
1 Damaris Masham, *Discours sur l'amour divin: ou l'on explique ce que c'est, &ou l'on fair voir les mauvaises consequences des explications trop subtiles que on en donne*, tr. Pierre Coste (Amsterdam, 1715).
2 Ruth Perry, *The Celebrated Mary Astell* (Chicago: University of Chicago Press, 1986), 97. Norris first criticized Locke in some remarks appended to *Christian Blessedness;* Locke followed with *Remarks on Some of Mr. Norris's Books, Wherein he asserts P. Malebranche's Opinion of our seeing all Things in God* (1692) and *An Examination of P. Malebranche's Opinion of Seeing all Things in God* (1693).
3 Perry, *Mary Astell*, p. 329.
4 Jacqueline Broad, *Women Philosophers of the Seventeenth-Century* (New York: Cambridge University Press, 2002), Chapters 4 and 5.

Lady Masham in 1690.⁵ After some years in Holland in exile, Locke moved to Masham's estate Oates in Essex in the same year and, apart from trips to the city, lived there as a rent-paying tenant until his death. Norris had criticized Locke's *Essay* on its appearance in 1690, but his later attacks on Locke in his *Essay Towards the Theory of the Ideal or Intelligible World* (1701) were fiercer. According to Maurice Cranston, Norris aroused Locke's anger when, charged with conveying a private letter from Masham to Locke in 1692, he had the impertinence to open and presumably to read it.⁶ Masham was indebted to Astell's educational treatise, *A Serious Proposal to the Ladies*, though her *Occasional Thoughts* are bitter on the subject of the socially isolating effects on women of intensive learning.

The purpose of the present paper is to describe the controversy and to examine it briefly from two different perspectives. The first perspective is that of social history: what intellectual and personal opportunities were afforded by the social position of the female philosopher of the late 17th century and what were their limitations? The second perspective is that of philosophy of mind and metaphysics: what are the philosophical obstacles in the way of a satisfactory theory of love as they are revealed in the Astell-Masham dispute. Love is an emotion that is not easy to understand with respect to its voluntary or involuntary nature, the nature of the object of the emotion, and its place within providential and retributive theologies.

1.

From the literary perspective, the Astell-Norris exchange appears to follow a somewhat conventional format. A younger woman, in a somewhat apologetic and self-effacing fashion, enters into correspondence with a well-known older man; the model for this form of exchange was Princess Elizabeth of Bohemia's exchange with Descartes in the previous century. Ostensibly, she does so with a view to requesting clarification of his opinions for her own benefit and to pointing out difficulties that he may wish to address. But the younger correspondent also appears to be seeking help with her own life's problems from a sensitive confidant and person of superior knowledge. The older correspondent appreciates the attention and the chance to expatiate before a well-disposed, unaggressive listener, whose criticisms can be more patiently heard. He is reluctant to be drawn into a discussion that is too personal.⁷

---

5 John Norris, *Reflections upon the Conduct of Human Life: with Reference to the Study of Learning and Knowledge, in a Letter to an excellent Lady* (London, 1690).
6 Maurice Cranston, *John Locke* (New York: Oxford University Press, 1985), 364–5.
7 See the opening of Descartes's "Letter to Elizabeth, May or June 1645" in *Descartes: Philosophical Letters*, tr. A Kenny (Oxford: Clarendon, 1970), 161.

These features are in plain view in the Letters, as is a certain tendency to flattery and even girlishness on the twenty-eight year old Astell's part. She contrasts the superficiality of other philosophers with Norris's depth: "[E]very Period of yours dilates my mind, calls it forth to pursue recondite Beauties in a Train of useful and delightful Thoughts."[8] Ignoring his chief metaphysical presupposition, namely, that Creatures have no efficacy, she asks, "Have you indeed been affected with my Letters? 'Tis not through any Force of theirs, but the Goodness of your own Temper, for Hearts so full of Love to GOD, like Tinder, catch at every Spark." Meanwhile, her correspondent exploits her enthusiasm. Norris's rationale for publishing the Letters, he explains in the Preface, is that Astell's letters may help to "fan and blow up that divine Fire which our Saviour came to kindle upon Earth, but which the Neglect of careless Men has let almost go out." Norris professes to be alarmed by the way in which "sensual Love is continually spreading its Victories and leading in triumph its glorious Captives" while God is neglected and he proposes to fight fire with fire. He sees a need for "warm, quickening Discourses" and Mary Astell is agreeable to supplying them.[9]

Astell agrees in principle with John Norris's claim that God is the only object that merits our love. Norris had proposed, following Malebranche, to found this claim on the principle that corporeal objects are an extended substance that does not contain real sensory qualities and that the immaterial substance God is the true cause of all effects, including our sensations of pleasure. The classic statement of the position occurs in Malebranche's *Search After Truth*, Bk I, Ch 5:

> If the mind saw in bodies only what is really in them, without being aware of what is not in them, it would neither love objects nor make use of them without great pain; thus it is necessary, as it were, that objects should appear to be pleasant by producing sensations they themselves lack. The same is not true of God. One has only to see Him as He is to be brought to love Him, and He need not avail Himself of the instinct of pleasure as a kind of stratagem to attract our love without deserving it.[10]

Hereditary sin, according to Malebranche, is poorly explained by the theory that in order to punish Adam for his disobedience, God withdrew Adam's capacity to feel pleasure in the love of God, leaving him at the mercy of his senses. Rather, Adam forfeited his capacity to arrest his natural reactions to the presentations of the senses, once he had acknowledged their advice concerning utility and danger.[11]

---

8 Mary Astell and John Norris, *Letters Concerning the Love of God, between the Author of the Proposal to the Ladies and Mr. John Norris* (London, 1695) [microform], Preface.
9 Ibid.
10 Nicolas Malebranche, *The Search After Truth*, tr. T. Lennon and P. Olscamp (Columbus: Ohio State University Press, 1980), 21.
11 Ibid., p. 22.

> Happy would he... have been... had he not voluntarily turned himself away from the presence of His God by allowing his mind's capacity to be exhausted by the beauty and anticipated sweetness of the forbidden fruit... or by his natural fondness for his wife and the inordinate fear of displeasing her.[12]

Recovery of the ability to arrest emotional reactions once their advisory function has been discharged is possible through a theologically and scientifically correct understanding of bodies and causes. "We... admit something divine in all the bodies around us when we posit forms, faculties, qualities, virtues, or real beings capable of producing certain effects through the force of their nature..."[13] and this is pagan idolatry, combated with the help of Cartesian natural philosophy.[14]

Astell at first appears to have anchored her position at the extremes of Christian piety and Platonic idealism by stating her view that "Martyrdom is the highest Pleasure a rational Creature is capable of" and that "this World is a mere show, a shadow, an emptiness."[15] But she goes on to complain that these doctrines are difficult to operationalize: "Though I often say, in your Pathetick and Divine Words, no, my fair Delight, I will never be drawn off from the Love of Thee by the Charm of any of Thy Creatures, yet alas, sensible Beauty does too often press upon my Heart, whilst intelligible is disregarded."[16] She confesses that "it is very difficult for me to love at all, without something of Desire" and she is "loath to abandon all Thought of Friendship."[17] The Charms of the Creature "perpetually press upon the outward Man." "'Tis our misfortune that we live an animal before we live a rational Life; the good we enjoy is mostly transmitted to us through Bodily Mediums." Her ardent temperament, she confesses, has often exposed her to "ungrateful Returns" and "frequent Disappointments."[18] She takes these to be divine lessons, warning her away from entanglements. Yet Astell finds Norris's distinction between seeking Creatures for our good, which Norris argues is permissible, and loving them as our good, which Norris views as idolatrous, "too nice for common Practice."

In response, Norris propounds the view, consistent with the Descartes-Malebranche view of the senses as sources of information regarding utilitarian but not objective value, that the movements of the soul should be only towards God. However, insofar as the movements of the Body "may be determined by Objects which environ it... we may unite ourselves to those things which are the natural or occasional Cause of our Pleasure." We can move towards the fire, but

---

12 Ibid., p. 22.
13 Malebranche, *Search*, VI:II:3.
14 Ibid., VI:II:2.
15 Astell-Norris, *Letters*, p. 45.
16 Ibid., p. 48.
17 Ibid.
18 Ibid., p. 50.

we must not love it.[19] This cool and somewhat rakish permission-theory hardly seems the proper response to Astell's underlying confusion, which, after all, derives from the very high cost she attaches to romantic rejection and the accordingly drastic nature of her preferred solution, which is not to move towards at all: "If we permit Desire," she lectures Norris, "we can never be secure from irregular Love, that Shame and Misery of Mankind."[20] "For Love is an insinuating Passion, and wherever it is admitted, will spread and make its way."[21]

It is apparent that Astell does not subscribe to the metaphysical principle that Creatures are inefficacious. On the contrary, she implicitly subscribes to what amounts to a doctrine of *influxus physicus* verging on pagan black magic. Creatures are such that fascination flows out of them... but not good. Only God is a steady and reliable distributor of good – and this includes hedonic benefit. Where the love of God is concerned, "Whilst our souls are inebriated with Pleasure our very Bodies partake of its Sweetness."[22] This contrasts with the "Tribute of Tears" that our friendships exact.[23] The causal powers of the lover are also considerable. She refers to the "Boundlessness of Desire" so great that no Creature "in the whole Compass of nature" can satisfy it, but only God.[24]

Eventually, Astell manages to shift the discussion to her preferred topic. Norris gives way by Letter VII, conceding the victimization of lovers by "Fears, Cares, Jealousies, unsatisfied Desires, and unprosperous Attempts, while they are breaking one another's Rests for that which when they have it will not suffer them to sleep."[25] The whole world of Creature-desiring Creatures "seems to be like a great, troubled Sea" of war and ambitious striving. He quotes St. Augustine: "I may love thee, my GOD with my whole Heart, and with all the Power of my Inward Parts, having thee in my Heart in my Mouth, and before my Eyes, always and Everywhere, [so that] there may be no Place in me open to adulterous Love."[26]

Astell does not find her confusions dissolved or her burdens lifted through the metaphysical doctrines of the Letters even though their subject – God – seems at first quite inexhaustible. "Love, as you know is talkative," she tells her correspondent, and it is not silenced even by the failure of the other to produce the desired response: "This we may observe when the Object is finite and perhaps unworthy of our Choice."[27] There are only eleven letters. The subject is not, after

---

19 Ibid., p. 76.
20 Ibid., p. 96.
21 Ibid., p. 95–6.
22 Ibid., p. 129.
23 Ibid., p. 145.
24 Ibid., p. 132.
25 Ibid., p. 236.
26 Ibid., p. 247.
27 Ibid., p. 252.

all, inexhaustible. The talkativeness of love has failed to solve the riddle of God's responsibility for this kind of undeserved suffering and both writers have stumbled into incoherence. Astell has described herself, and, by implication, all others, as creatures of boundless desire. No living being apart from God can make her happy! The amplitude of her self-description threatens and accuses God: how can there be a whole world of such creatures? Norris has as much as admitted that he is adrift in "a great troubled Sea."

The reader who found Malebranche's "explanation" for the coming of sin into the world hard to follow will doubtless be reminded of the stock objection made to theists: If God is the author of every effect, he is the author of sin and pain. These effects seem incompatible with his infinite benevolence. How can God be both the source of misery and the refuge from it; the only lovable thing and the alternative lovable thing? Creatures seem to cause in us the most powerful sensations of pleasure and pain, the sensations that a wise and benevolent Creator normally employs to guide our conduct. And, if He implanted those passions in us, how can it be true that we are supposed to ignore them? Astell wants these questions answered. Further, she wants an assurance of equivalency, the assurance that the intimacy with God can be an effective replacement for the intimacy she proposes to give up seeking. Needless to say, they are not answered.

2.

Damaris Masham declares early in her treatise that she is writing to show "the unserviceableness of an Hypothesis lately recommended to the World." The hypothesis is "that Mankind are obliged strictly, as their Duty, to love with Desire nothing but God only: Every Degree of Desire of any Creature whatsoever being Sin."[28] She defines Love as delight or pleasure in the Being of another, and she argues that desire and benevolence are different acts of the mind, as it is turned towards different loved objects of different capabilities.[29] She maintains that concupiscence is natural and intrinsic to the Creature, contrary to the Scriptural teaching that it is acquired and hereditary. (Malebranche explained the persistence of sin through his theory of *emboitement*; potential and actual mothers, in whom future generations were enclosed, were the carriers).

Astell and Norris had established to their mutual satisfaction that the scriptural injunction "Love thy neighbor" could not possibly be understood as Christ's instruction to love our neighbour with a love of desire. But this result, Masham says, is beside the point. Sociability is natural to us. "Every Man's Experience con-

---

28 Damaris Masham, *A Discourse Concerning the Love of God*, (London, 1696) [microform], p. 7.
29 Ibid., p. 18–9.

futes this Every Day – that no Creature is capable of being a Good to us."[30] It is nonsense to say that no finite thing has any worth to us. God would not merit our love unless he had given Creatures other Creatures pleasing to them, since we have "a continual Communication with and necessary Dependence upon these."

Masham's perspective invites comparison with Locke's view that "Love, to Beings capable of Happiness or Misery, is often the... Delight, which we find in our selves arising from a consideration of their very Being, or Happiness... Thus the Being and Welfare of a Man's Children or Friends, producing constantly Delight in him, he is said constantly to love them."[31] Masham contradicts the Malebranchian premise that we do not have communication with entities external to us, but only with God and therefore cannot be dependent on them. Love of Creatures, she says, no more excludes Love of God than love of cherries excludes love of friends. She attacks the rhetoric of James iv.4, who informs his audience of "Adulterers and Adulteresses... that the Friendship of the World is Enmity with God."[32] As for romantic disappointment, it is preventable by the use of sound judgment. Happiness is ours when we proportion our desire to the worth of things, not when we abandon desires. As a parting shot, she takes aim at the "Discontented, Devout people" who inhabit monasteries where pride, malevolence and faction are as widespread as they are outside, along with licentiousness. Those with the most sordid pasts behind them are often the most devout. They write more from disgust than from reason and use metaphysical reasoning to harangue people from the pulpit.[33]

Masham writes in *A Discourse Concerning the Love of God* as one situated amongst spouse, friend, siblings, and children who can take communication and sociability, the presence of and contact with others, for granted. But her other letters do not support the picture of a woman at peace with herself and at home in the world. Nor had her relations with Locke, now nearly a member of the family who enjoyed an avuncular relationship with her son, always been easy. Did she experience the sentiment of adulterous love that Norris, like St. James and St. Augustine, thought the world to be awash in? In a letter written in the year of Locke's death, Masham described Locke as "un second pere,"[34] easily explained by the age gap of twenty-six years between them. Yet whatever the arrangements at Oates, the two are known to have had a turbulent relationship for much of the period 1681–1704.

---

30 Ibid., p. 25.
31 Locke, *Essay Concerning Human Understanding*, ed., P. H. Nidditch (Oxford: Clarendon, 1975), Bk II, Ch.20 § 5.
32 Masham, *Discourse*, p. 115.
33 Ibid., p. 278.
34 Cranston, *John Locke*, p. 480. "Oddly described," Cranston remarks.

On their first acquaintance, in the early 1680s, they seem to have disagreed as to the nature of the relationship. Masham, in her early twenties and feeling herself scorned, was embittered. Locke subsequently changed his mind. This drew forth her poem, sent to him in 1682/3 in which, the spurned shepherdess Clora facing the penitent Damon shows no mercy: "His constant passion still disdains/ And laughs at all his griefs and pains.[35] Clora recites:

> Still I am the same as when
> My powers and loves you did disdain
> ...
> The friendship once I gave retain
> But think from me no more to gain
> To whom thy passion comes too late
> That scorn a passion given by fate.

The predominant emotions in her early correspondence with Locke, despite its arch teasing and self-deprecation, are anger, depression, and jealousy – hardly delight with her correspondent – or, after her marriage in 1685, enjoyment of her husband, a widower, or his eight children.[36] There is little or no philosophy in the letters and a good deal of complaining of black moods and neglect. "I am Certainlie Plac'd," she writes, "in the Wretchedest Neighborhood in the whole World and never had so Violent a Desire in my Life as now to good Companie. 'Tis in Vaine that I think... of suiting my Mind to my Condition, for Business, and the Impertienent Concernes of a Mistress of a Familie will never have Anie Place in my Heart, and I can at most do no more than submit to Them."[37] Only Locke's assurance that he still has some esteem for her, according to a letter of January 1687, "would make me think Life not Altogether Insignificant." Masham is vigilant with regard to other women with whom she suspects him of being involved, and not above making sneering remarks about "your Dutch mistress."

Locke's side of the correspondence has been lost or destroyed; we have his response to the poem ("Pray tell me Clora with what art you will/Preserve your friend and yet your lover kill?"). But the tone of a letter written in 1690, two years after his move to Oates, leaves no doubt as to strength of his later feeling for Masham. In the course of one of their frequent quarrels, he writes:

> Though I must confesse I was never lesse satisfied with any letter I ever writ to you in my life. I have some thing within me tells me that this is not the conversation I ought to have with you. The perfection and goodnesse of your inlightened and enlarged

---

35 Ibid., p. 217.
36 Damaris Masham, "Letter to John Locke, 28 October 1682," E. S. De Beer, ed., *Correspondence of John Locke*, 10 vols., (Oxford: Clarendon, 1976), II:557.
37 Damaris Masham, "Letter to John Locke, 17 January, 1687", *Correspondence*, III:105.

minde had given me the view and tast of an other kinde. Why would you without any occasion soe soon interrupt it? ...I cannot suspect your freindship though (anger) or I know not what has a little usurped the place of it. but yet I have some parts in my soule very tender and when I am in pain I can not avoid feeling it.[38]

3.

"All her life," her biographer Ruth Perry tells us, "Astell resisted male attractions with no difficulty. Not only did she never marry, but there is no evidence that she ever entertained any suitors. She explicitly disapproved of beaux as a class... and in general distrusted the intentions of men towards women."[39] She maintained her independence her entire life, preferring the company of women to an extent that, even in light of the seventeenth-century capacity for same-sex sentimental friendship, was marked. Her instincts tended, Perry argues, to the convent, though her powerful organizational energy and benevolence would have made a better abbess than nun. Her utopia is not the female educational academy, the "Convent of Pleasure," or the imaginary kingdom ruled by a bejeweled female tyrant envisioned by her genial and surpassingly ambitious predecessor, Margaret Cavendish.[40]

Mistrust and apprehension are pronounced features of Astell's discourse; her expressing this to Norris is a valiant effort to overcome it. Doubtless there are genuine differences of temperament between Masham and Astell, as well as different experiences that explain their respective positions on Love of God vs. Love of Creatures. But it is still worth asking whether Astell's pessimism or Masham's optimism was more typical. How widespread were gender-antagonism, mistrust, and resentment in the last quarter of the 17th century amongst the well-to-do classes?

This question has been the subject of considerable scholarly dispute. Edward Shorter and Lawrence Stone have tended to the view that social conditions were so unfortunate for women and their liability to exploitation so great that any self-aware and reflective female, whether of the labouring or the leisured classes, would have had to be a profound pessimist.[41] On the other side, Ferdinand Mount has argued that a surprising degree of moral and emotional equality and warmth has always characterized ordinary relations between the sexes.[42]

The case for the pessimist is supported by evidence of an expanding gulf between men and women that followed on the provision of new education and

---

38 John Locke, "Letter to Damaris Masham, 30 September, 1690," *Correspondence,* IV:141–2.
39 Perry, *Astell*, p. 145 ff.
40 Margaret, Duchess of Cavendish, *The Blazing World*, (1666).
41 Lawrence Stone, *Family, Sex and Marriage in England, 1500–1800* (New York: Harper and Row, 1977); Edward Shorter, *The Making of the Modern Family* (London: Fontana, 1976).
42 Ferdinand Mount, *The Subversive Family: An Alternative History of Love and Marriage*, (London: Unwin, 1982).

opportunities for the former but not the latter, and the resentment this generated amongst upper-class women. According to Perry, advances in education in the late 17th century produced a state of affairs in which "gender had become a more important determinant of educational status than social class."[43] This claim is supported by Stone's statement that, except for a brief period in the middle third of the 16th century during which leading Humanists advocated female education, "literacy and classical education widened the gap between the sexes."[44] While a number of aristocratic women towards the end of the 16th century had learned Latin and Greek, and were observed to read Plato and Aristotle in the original, the 17th century in England marked an end to what Stone calls the "masculine literary education" in favour of French, music, and needlework.[45] Radical minority sects of the Civil War including the Quakers had rejected Puritan doctrines and especially Original Sin and the necessary subordination of women and were supportive of female literacy and activity. But with the Restoration, egalitarian social movements lost all their impetus. "It is astonishing," Stone remarks, "how many women from knightly or even noble homes in the early and middle seventeenth-century were unable to write a literate letter."[46] Cranston notes that in the missives of Vicountess Mordaunt to Locke, "the handwriting is childish and the spelling, even by seventeenth-century standards is appalling,"[47] Women of the period grasped that they had lost ground relative to the past: "[T]he barbarous custom to breed women low is now grown among us."[48] Conditions did not markedly improve until the end of the 18th century when education in natural science as well as languages was again recommended.[49] Girls, nevertheless, persisted in trying to learn; if they had not, we would not have had so many recorded denials of permission and admonitions to keep to novels and needlework would not have been necessary.

Piety, meanwhile, is not merely a characteristic of some stricken individuals who acquire a vocation. Monastic preferences have always had economic and political significance. Piety was often less a mark of bovine conformity than of refusal, and not only because the convent had so often been used as punishment for insubordination. Christian ideology taught women that their bodies belonged to God, not to the State, with its fixed interest in military conquest and population-replenishment, setting them at odds with ordinary social expectations. Astell's piety is, moreover, intrinsically connected to the frustration of her worldly ambitions; she did not renounce them easily but in a spirit of genuine

---

43 Perry, *Astell*, p. 104.
44 Stone, *Family, Sex, and Marriage*, p. 202.
45 Ibid., p. 204.
46 Ibid.
47 Ibid., p. 307.
48 Bathsua Makin, quoted in Stone, *Family, Sex and Marriage*, p. 345.
49 Ibid., p. 354.

ressentiment, adapting her preferences to the constraints of her condition. "Mean spirited men! that bait at Honour, Praise,/A wreath of Laurel or of Baies,/How short's their Immortality" she writes in her poem "Ambition." In "Heaven," she reemphasizes her capacious desire for fame.

> [T]o its native place my Soul aspires
> And something more than Earth desires
> Heav'n only can its vast Ambition fill
> And Heav'n alone must exercise my mind and quill.

This thought has the same structure as the expression of romantic frustration voiced in the Letters: the author's aspirations – with respect to knowledge and acknowledgment as well as love – are such that there is no means by which they can be satisfied.

In summary, Astell's lifelong insistence on the cultivation of female capability and her disillusioned posture of withdrawal are understandable in view of the constraints with which her generations were faced. But in view of the claim that the 16th century afforded greater opportunities than the 17th, it should be born in mind that while Luis Vives, Erasmus, and More had pleaded for female education in the 16th century, it was women themselves who were writing treatises on this subject in the 17th century. Astell's *A Serious Proposal to the Ladies* (1694) was followed by Judith Drake's *An Essay in Defense of the Female Sex* (1696) and Damaris Masham effectively paid homage to the older Astell in her *Occasional Thoughts in Reference to a Vertuous or Christian Life* (1705). Somehow these women had found teachers and escaped assignment to drudgery, and to do so they had to enlist the co-operation of sympathetic men.

Marriage, meanwhile, was an aspiration, but here as well women's prospects were limited in the last quarter of the 17th century. Losses in domestic wars left the sex ratio at thirteen women to every ten men.[50] Not only social mobility but opportunities for the choice of a marriage partner greatly favoured men. This compounded the isolation of aristocratic women, who do not ordinarily marry into a socio-economic class beneath them. A related development bears remarking. Women's loss of relative educational status and diminished opportunities for choice of a partner were exacerbated by a change in sexual mores that followed the decline of Puritanism. The Restoration introduced a long phase of license into English social relations that culminated in the 1770s, before being succeeded by a new wave of repression. The controls of Puritan divines and civil magistrates were loosened, and every conceivable aspect of sexual chicanery, from fortune-hunting by men and women alike, to pandering by mothers, abduction (with the help of drugs and alcohol), to the seduction of teen-agers with disguised identity, was practiced. Aristocratic wives expressed frustration and helplessness over the

---

50 Ibid., p. 380–1.

predatory behavior of their male friends, the open keeping of mistresses by their husbands, and the double-standard to which they were subject.[51] While aristocratic females had affairs – the insinuating scrawls of the semi-literate Lady Mordaunt leave little doubt of this - social opprobrium for those discovered was far greater: Masham, for one, expressed herself indignantly on this subject in her *Occasional Thoughts*.[52] And where Elizabethan poetry and songs of Dowland, Wyatt, and others seems to express the emotional vulnerability of men, much Restoration verse is frankly cynical and the tears that flow are those of the female poets. Aphra Behn, writing in 1684 – roughly the period of the correspondence – portrays love as a sadistic deity and herself as victim. "Love in fantastic triumph sat,/Whilst bleeding hearts around him flowed,/For whom fresh pains he did create,/ And strange tyrannic power he showed;…"[53] Elsewhere,[54] Behn observes that the present object is of less interest than the idea:

> Since man with that inconstancy was born
> To love the absent and the present scorn,
> Why do we deck, why do we dress,
> For such a short-lived happiness?

The case for the pessimist on the question of companionship between men and women, where companionship requires the equality of education that permits the sexes to share common interests, and comparable leisure in which to cultivate those interests, is similarly undecided for the 17th century. Astell's generally segregationist writings appear to exclude the possibility. One has the impression that male attention, as many women experienced it, was not of the right sort; as observed, respect for comparably-educated women was not prevalent and predatory habits preclude the development of respect. Yet we should be cautious in accepting the complaint-literature as entirely representative of reality. Stone has been criticized for failing to acknowledge that, despite powerful pressures from governments, churches, and relatives, "ideals of affection, mutuality, and free choice in marriage and family life" have always informed male-female social relations and did so in the past five hundred years as well.[55] Mount observes that while

---

51 Lawrence Stone, *Uncertain Unions: Marriage in England 1660–1753* (Oxford: Oxford University Press, 1992), 96.
52 "[T]he aggravation of wronging another Man, and possibly a whole Family… is ordinarily talk'd as lightly of, as if it were but a Peccadillo in a Young Man." The same crime in a woman would "brand her with Perpetual Infamy," p. 154, quoted by Perry, *Astell*, p. 504, n. 56.
53 Aphra Behn (1640–1689) "Song: Love Armed", *The Oxford Book of Seventeenth-Century Verse*, ed. Alistair Fowler (Oxford: Oxford University Press, 1991), 721.
54 Behn, "To Alexis in Answer to His Poem against Fruition: Ode", op cit., p. 723.
55 Mount, *Subversive Family*, p. 130.

certain forces have ignored, or manipulated, or tried to undermine preferential companionship for their own purposes, and while the official literature is to some extent propaganda for their causes, many individuals, judging by their letters and diaries, led happy lives in association with another individual. Masham and Locke spent a good deal of time complaining to and about one another. As in all close relationships, jealousy was powerful and divisive and there were old wounds on both sides. Yet it was an association that clearly brought a good deal to them both. Locke's fundamental respect for Masham is unquestionable and there is no reason to suppose that their relationship was unique for its time.

4.

The modern reader is inclined to prefer Masham's defense of *Love of Creatures* to Astell's defense of *Love of God*. It is modern, secular, decent (without being prudish), family-oriented, and safe. Her insistence that desire and benevolence are not mutually exclusive and her point that they are consequential on delight in another's being is sound. Her implicit reproach to Astell is friendly. It takes the form, one might say, of providing reminders: In focusing on high-stakes romantic love, Astell has forgotten the continuum that exists between love of children, brothers, spouses, friends, and the high stakes kind. Delight, desire for their company, dependency, and benevolence are intermingled in a usually benign way. The reader is likely to concur with Masham's view that Astell's painful and humiliating experiences reflect her lack of moderation and poor judgment; they do not prove the lack of merit of Creatures.

Yet one cannot be completely satisfied with Masham's account. Masham writes about love as a phenomenon of presence. It is not necessary to return to the disciple-interpretation to point out that in this respect she, like Locke, is an empiricist. What affects us is what is present to us in three-dimensional space. Love of God – an insensible object, an idea we have "made" according to Locke[56] is – an abstraction and cannot be the primary phenomenon. But Masham leaves out too much that is, we would say now, a part of the concept of Love. There is no discussion of delight in the company of one who is not or who refuses to be present, of benevolence when gifts are refused, or the fears, cares, and confusions that attend love as a phenomenon of absence. Astell writes from a position of exile and her case has some merit. If one cannot love any present object, one might as well resolve to love an idea, even an idea of one's own making. The divine presence depends wholly on our will, the adversities of futile love being only, as Astell suggests, His instrument to bring us towards Him. If we have to suffer the tyranny of another, why not be certain that the tyrant is benevolent? If Astell

---

56 Locke, *Essay*, Bk II, Ch 23, § 33.

embarrasses us by dwelling on the miseries of unrequited love in what is supposed to be a metaphysical discussion of causal efficacy and objective value, Masham annoys us by papering over aspects of her subject of which she had firsthand experience.

The Astell-Masham dispute on the Love of God vs. Love of Creatures raises the following, perennially interesting questions: Is love principally a voluntary state of mind based on a rational assessment of the merits of a particular object? Or is it principally an accidental sentiment, lying outside the space of reasons, and only by strenuous application capable of being channeled towards an object of objective value, whether a Platonic virtue, or the laws of the state and its institutions, or God? Is its object an idea or a quasi-mental construction? Or is love normally directed to an embodied object and only under pathological conditions to a fictional object? And is it, like appetite and thirst, a generally trustworthy information source regarding the needs of the creature? Or is it an unhealthy, if pitiable, derangement of the well-functioning organism, as the physicians of the Renaissance held?

Each position has a good deal to be said for it. For each, a good deal has been said. Surprisingly, because he is so often considered as a representative of the ascetic tradition, it is Descartes who appears to come closest to reconciling these antinomies. The Love of God, for Descartes, is the love of God's knowledge, creation, and decrees. It comprises both acceptance of the sorrows and enjoyment of the happiness the world has to offer. "If a man meditates on [the order established by God] and understands them properly he is filled with extreme joy... He does not refuse evils and afflictions since they come to him from divine providence; still less does he refuse the permissible goods or pleasures he may enjoy in this life since they too come from God."[57] But Love of Creatures is, for Descartes, remarkably no different in principle from Love of God. Whether the object loved is judged more or less worthy than ourselves, whether it is the Prince, or merely a bird or a flower, we desire to be united with it.[58]

Tears, moreover, are inevitable, though Descartes does not say whether we can weep for any object or only for those with whom we wished to be joined in friendship, not for God, the Prince or a flower. For tears are produced when the pores of the eyes are constricted by sadness and when blood flow to the heart, produces an excess of vapour. "And there is nothing that increases it more than the blood which is sent to the heart in the passion of love. We see too that those who are sad do not shed tears continually, but only intermittently, when they

---

57 Descartes, "Letter to Chanut, 1 February 1647" in *Descartes: Philosophical Letters*, tr. A. Kenny (Oxford: Clarendon, 1970), 213.
58 Ibid., p. 215.
59 Passions of the Soul, II:131, in *Oeuvres de Descartes*, 11 volumes, edited by Charles Adam and Paul Tannery (Paris: Vrin/C.N.R.S., 1964-76) XI:425. Tr. in *The Philosophical Writings of Descartes*, 3 volumes, translated by John Cottingham, Robert Stoothoff, Dugald Murdoch and Anthony Kenny (Cambridge: Cambridge University Press, 1984–91), I:374.

reflect anew upon the object of their affection."⁵⁹ No further diagnosis of romantic melancholy – long recognized as perfectly diagnostic of love – is offered; for Descartes, 'in tears' it is simply the condition in which those people are typically to be found. Astell might have found some consolation in the thought that love, as Descartes writes in the same letter to Chanut, unlike hatred, and "however disordered it may be, gives pleasure." As evidence he adds, "[T]hough the poets often complain of it in their verses, I think that men would naturally give up loving if they did not find it more sweet than bitter."⁶⁰

---

60 Ibid., p. 216.

The Theory and Regulation of Love in 17th Century Philosophy
Catherine Wilson, City University of New York

1.

The appetite of English readers in the first half of the 17th century for sermons, devotional works, and commentaries on scripture was robust. They consumed information regarding the defects of their souls as avidly as we consume information regarding the defects of our appearances. Concern with appearances was, of course, considered a defect of the soul.

In the fallen world, the beauty of women was a reminder of Eve's temptation, Adam's fatal disobedience, and all the evil and suffering that ensued, down to the martyrdom of Christ. Pierre Du Moulin's devotional work *Théophile ou l'amour divin*[1] describes women's adornment as Satan's most deadly weapon. The faithful eye sees through their costume to the Devil's very image:

> A soldier having a sword that hath surely served him in many combats, will be carefull to scowre & polish it: and doe we marvell if the woman having served Sathan to overthrow *Adam*, bee carefully decked & embellished by him; and that women are curious in ornaments by the suggestion of the devil?[2]

Other religious writers, like Jean Senault in *Man become guilty, or, The corruption of nature by sinne, according to St. Augustines sense* translated into English in 1650, represent love of particular women as slavery, an inversion of the natural order. In his Sixth Treatise, "On the Corruption of all Creatures", Senault said:

> Love is an imperious passion, it subjects all those souls which it possesseth, it makes as many slaves as lovers, and reduceth them to a condition wherein having no longer any will, they are not Masters of their desires, they look pale, when in the presence of those that they adore, they tremble when they come neer them, and the Stars have not so much power over their bodies as those whom they love have absolute command over their souls: the object of their love is the cause of all their

---

[1] Pierre Du Moulin, *Theophilus, or Loue diuine. A treatise containing fiue degrees, fiue markes, fiue aides, of the loue of God,* translated by Richard Goring from the third French edition. Renewed, corrected, and augmented by the author M. Peter Moulin, preacher, the reformed Church of Paris (London, 1610).

[2] Ibid., p. 117.

motions, if it be absent, they consume away in desire, and languish in vain hopes... Thus these slaves take upon them their Masters livery... and betraying their own greatnesse they subject themselves to creatures which ought to obey them.[3]

Linguistic communities create numerous images of their members, many of them inconsistent with one another. Senault's and du Moulin's need to be kept in perspective. Popular drama in the early 17th century presented women very differently from the theologians. In William Shakespeare's and John Fletcher's plays, women appear kind, noble, intelligent, brave and resourceful, and as indistinguishable from men when they change their clothes. In the shepherds' romance, *L'Astrée* of Honoré d' Urfé' (1567–1625), translated into English in 1620 and again in 1658,[4] practical questions of the amorous life were discussed and debated. The inquietudes of new acquaintance, the ravages of jealousy, and all the phenomena of attachment and loss were described, and models of exemplary conduct – ideals of faithful service and renunciation – proposed.[5] The upheavals of the Civil War following the execution of the King, and the temporary collapse of censorship brought out radical egalitarian doctrines in the 1640s, and

---

3 Jean-Francois Senault, *Man become guilty, or, The corrruption of nature by sinne, according to St. Augustines sense.* Written originally in French by Iohn-Francis Senault and translated into English by Henry, Earle of Monmouth (London, 1650).
4 Honorée d'Urfé, *The history of Astrea the first part. In twelue bookes: newly translated out of French* (London, 1620). Of the pastoral, Hume later comments: "When poets form descriptions of ELYSIAN fields, where the blessed inhabitants stand in no need of each other's assistance, they yet represent them as maintaining a constant intercourse of love and friendship, and sooth our fancy with the pleasing image of these soft and gentle passions. The idea of tender tranquillity in a pastoral ARCADIA is agreeable from a like principle." From *An Enquiry Concerning the Principles of Morals*, ed. Tom Beauchamp (Oxford: Oxford University Press, 1998), Sect. 7, 136.
5 *La Princesse de Cleves* of Madame de La Fayette (1634–1693) was translated into English in 1679. Boyle, who read French fluently, had once intended to write what he called a set of "amorous controversies," dealing with the social practices of courtship and with the controversy over the worth of platonic love. Although he veered to the side of Du Moulin in several letters written to society women against "painting" and décolletage, including one that reminds his correspondent that "Some of the Primitive Fathers have fancy'd Women to have made the first Devills: the Inordinate Love of their Beauty (ev'n when unassisted & unimproved by Art), being the Fire that seduc't those now Fallen Angells & kindled those Lusts in Heau'n, for which those wretched Spirits now burne in Hell." British Museum Ms. quoted by Malcolm Oster in "Biography, Culture, and Science: The Formative Years of Robert Boyle," *History of Science* 31 (1993) pp. 177–226; p. 200. Boyle personally identified with certain dramatic heroines. He composed a lurid dramatic narrative *The Martyrdom of Theodora* after a play by Corneille, and a very passionate fictional letter from Potiphar's wife to Joseph.

questions of women's status were debated in the Interregnum. John Milton[6] wrote eloquently for freedom of choice in marriage and the right of divorce in the case of marital alienation, and radical sects and cults devoted to what J. S. Mill later called "experiments in living" flourished. One such sect, the Ranters, sang:

> Some men another world do prize
> Of which they have no measure,
> Let us make merry, sing and dance,
> There is no heaven to pleasure.
>
> Which we injoy with sweet content
> A short life, and a merry,
> Is all the heaven we expect
> Let's drink off our Canary
>
> The fellow Creature which sits next
> Is more delight to me
> Than any that I else can find
> For that she's alweaies free[7]

After the Restoration of the monarch in 1660, poets like Waller and Dryden – some of distinctly Epicurean and therefore mortalist convictions – rang changes on the theme of carpe diem.

Susan James was the first contemporary historian of philosophy to treat the theory of the emotions of 17th century philosophers systematically, revealing an unexpected depth to their reflections and a far from uncritical acceptance of the opposition between reason and passion.[8] Taking philosophy as the discipline that does not tolerate inconsistencies and aims at the truth, might we find that philosophy played a mediating role between the theological and the literary conceptions of love, curbing the excesses of both? Might we find amongst the philosophers re-conceptualizations of morality, women, and nature that contributed to the softening of theological discourse, while retaining the sobriety and critical spirit lacking in the poet? For although demonology and accounts of witchcraft remain in the theological literature in the late 17th century,[9] ordinary women are

---

6 John Milton, *The Doctrine and Discipline of Divorce* (London, 1643).

7 Quoted in John Reading, *The Ranters ranting* (London, 1650), p. 4.

8 Susan James, *Passion and Action: The Emotions in Seventeenth-Century Philosophy* (Oxford: Clarendon, 1997).

9 For example in Richard Baxter, *The certainty of the worlds of spirits and, consequently, of the immortality of souls of the malice and misery of the devils and the damned: and of the blessedness of the justified, fully evinced by the unquestionable histories of apparitions, operations, witchcrafts, voices &c. / written, as an addition to many other treatises for the conviction of Sadduces and infidels* (London, 1691).

not viewed as demonic, and beauty ceases to be denounced in such strenuous terms. In his *Characteristics of Men, Manners, Opinions, and Times*, first published in 1711, passionate attachment is conceptualized by the philosopher Shaftesbury as an unselfish and ideally moral relation. The secularization of personal ethics – including his famously utilitarian defense of female chastity – is complete in Hume, for whom love of the Creature, and not our relation to God, is the foundation of our existence. "Destroy love and friendship;" says Hume, "what remains in the world worth accepting?"[10] Love is the source, he said, "of all politeness and refinement."[11]

This paper will discuss two properly philosophical developments that were implicated in the more favourable views of love that characterize early 18th century French and English letters. These developments were the rediscovery of Platonism and the application of the theory of Platonic Love, the rise of Cartesian theodicy and the Cartesian naturalization of ethics. The view that both were implicated might seem improbable. For one thing, the value-neutral corpusculo-mechanical universe of Cartesianism seems perfectly disconnected from the Platonic world-animal, the Forms, and other terms and aspirations of Platonism. Didn't Cartesianism treat colour and beauty as illusions, arguing that the senses gave us no significant information, whereas consideration of bodies as pure extension to be treated mathematically brought results? Wasn't Plato in any case a lover of boys, not women? Bacon, the founder of experimental philosophy, famously applied metaphors of torture and unveiling to a feminine Nature, and Carolyn Merchant associated the rise of the 17th century corpuscularian philosophy with a generally negative view of women.[12]

All this can be conceded, as well as the point that philosophical texts may only reflect some images of a culture that is evolving under pressures independent of philosophical influence. Nevertheless, the decline of Augustinian *askesis* in philosophical–theological discourse stands in need of explanation, and Platonism and Cartesianism are the most likely philosophical suspects in that process. Christian Platonism is described by James Hankins as "one of those sunken Atlantises of the mind between the old world of traditional Christian society and the new world of the Enlightenment."[13] Ronald Crane has called attention to the softer, less denunciatory sermonizing style of the Cambridge Platonists, crediting them with the first steps towards the creation of the sentimental "man of feeling" in English letters.[14] While few Platonic dialogues were actually published in

---

10 David Hume, "Of Polygamy and Divorce", in *Essays Moral, Political and Literary (1741–2)*, ed. Eugene F. Miller (Indianapolis: Liberty Classics, 1987), 184.
11 Hume, "Of National Characters," in *Essays*, ed. Miller, p. 214.
12 Carolyn Merchant, *The Death of Nature* (San Francisco: Harper Collins, 1980).
13 James Hankins, *Plato in the Italian Renaissance* (Leiden: Brill, 1994), 362.
14 Ronald S. Crane, "Suggestions towards a genealogy of the man of feeling", *English Literary History* 1, 1934, 205–230; though see the comparison of Norris and Henry More below.

England, Ficinian Platonism had a significant presence in Renaissance moral theory and in literature.[15] Charles I's Queen, Henrietta Maria, is credited with introducing the cult of Platonic love into England from France. An observer wrote in 1634: "The Court affords little News at present, but that there is a love call'd Platonick Love, which much sways there of late; it is a Love abstracted from all corporeal gross impressions and sensual Appetite, but consists in Contemplations and Ideas of the Mind, not in any carnal fruition."[16] A second important stream feeding the more favourable philosophical treatment of love was Cartesian mechanism. The good world doctrine of the *Timaeus* (which even Augustine acknowledged) took on a new aspect with the theodicies of Descartes, Leibniz, and Malebranche.

2.

Augustine's theology, it might be observed, is all about love. The historical narrative of his *Confessions* describes the transition of the young Augustine from love of the Creature to love of God, and his commentary explains the role of the Platonic philosophy as he understood it in rescuing him from confusion and despair. "To Carthage I came," he tells us:

> [W]here a whole frying-pan full abominable loves crackled round me, and on every side. I was not in love as yet, yet I loved to be in love. I sought for something to love, loving still to be in love, security I hated and that way too that had no snares in it: and all because I had a famine within me, even of that inward food (thyself, O God) though that famine made me not hungry... For this cause my soul was not very well, but miserably breaking out into botches, had an extreme itch to be scratched by the touch of those sensible things... It was very pleasurable to me, both to love and to be loved; but much more, when I obtained to enjoy the person whom I loved.[17]

> I defiled therefore the spring of friendship with the filth of uncleanliness, and I besullied the purity of it with the hell of lustfulness... My God, my Mercy, with how much sourness didst thou, of thy goodness to me, besour that sweetness? For

---

15 See Jill Kraye, "Moral Philosophy" in *The Cambridge History of Renaissance Philosophy*, ed. Charles B., Schmidt, and Quentin Skinner (Cambridge: Cambridge University Press, 1988), 353ff.
16 James Howell in 1634, quoted in Lesel Dawson, "'New Sects of Love': Neoplatonism and Constructions of Gender in Davenant's *The Temple of Love* and *The Platonick Lovers*", *Early Modern Literary Studies* 8 (2002), 10.
17 Augustine, *Confessions,* Bks I–VIII, Bk III, ch. 1, tr. William Watts, (Cambridge: Harvard University Press, 1912), 99.

obtaining once to be beloved again, and secretly arriving to the bond of enjoying; I was with much joy bound with sorrow-bringing embracements, even that I might be scourged with the iron burning rods of jealousy, and suspicions, and fears, and angers, and brawls.[18]

To Augustine, the contrast between the ungrateful and perishable things of the visible world and the invisible things of God presented itself with increasing starkness. "What shall I say, whenas sitting in mine own house, a lizard catching flies, or a spider entangling them in her nets, ofttimes makes me attentive to them... One thing it is to get up quickly and another thing not to fall at all. And of such toys my life is full; and my only hope is thy wonderful great mercy."[19] Chapters 34 and 35 of Book 10 of the *Confessions* devoted to "Enticements coming in by the Eyes", and "Curiosity in knowing" treat as equivalent "delight in fair forms... in beautiful and pleasant colours," love of toys, apparel, shoes, vessels, and pictures, sadomasochistic pleasure in torn carcasses, carnal temptations in general, the theatre, experiment, the observation of nature, and the investigation of hidden powers:

> Curiosity for trial's sake pries into objects... merely out of an itch of gaining the knowledge and experience of them... Hence also men proceed to investigate some concealed powers of that nature which is not beyond our ken, which it does them no good to know, and yet men desire to know for the sake of knowing.[20]

In Book XIII of the *Confessions*, Augustine praises the creation, and describes creatures, including animals and women, as good, discounting hatred for the world as Manichaean. "We behold on all sides a moist element, teeming with fishes birds and beasts... and so there was for man, corporeally also, made a woman, who in the mind of her reasonable understanding should have a parity of nature, but in the sex of her body should be... subject to the sex of her husband... These things we behold and they are all severally Good and all together Very Good."[21] But this conclusion to Augustine's reflections, with its admiration for natural woman, did not take hold as did his implied critique of artificial woman, and his notion that curiosities, beauties, and entertainments are false corporeal goods from which we flee to the truly good and incorporeal. Amorous suffering – usually caused by artificial woman – has a purpose; like all suffering, it is chastisement and aversive therapy.

Du Moulin's *Theophilus*, as a tract of consolation and a manual for improvement, makes the same point. "God humbleth us by his affliction and pricketh the

---

18 Ibid., p. 99–100.
19 Ibid., p. 181.
20 Augustine, *Confessions,* Bk X, Ch 35, II: 177.
21 Ibid. Bk. XIII, Ch. 32; II: 465.

swelling of our pride. He cutteth and loppeth us, to the end we may bring forth the more fruit. He filleth us with bitternesse in this life to the end we might long for the life to come."[22] As one might expect, Du Moulin rejects the study of Philosophy and of the natural world. In *Heraclitus, or Meditations upon the Vanity and Misery of Humane Life*,[23] he expresses a Solomonic weariness and skepticism. "Man cannot by all his Philosophy attaine to the perfect knowledge of a small fly, or garden Lettice, much less of his own composition. We desire to traverse our spirits through all things, but remain strangers to ourselves."[24] The fallen world outside this chamber of meditation is described most vividly. There "corruption doth encrease, as a cancer or ulcer. Quarrels, vanity, superfluity in apparel, avarice, ambition and sumptuousness" are in the ascendant; Europe is overrun with brothels; in the east, churches have become mosques; the West Indies are "afflicted and tormented with evil spirits," the North with ghosts and demons, with "lying deceipts" and "strange shapes." The ordinary preoccupations of women reveal their dedication to the devil. They employ "the fourth part of their life in attiring themselves, wearing haire bought out of Tyre-women's shoppes, painting their faces, idolatrizing their own bodies... and viewing themselves in a looking glasse a thousand times in a daie."[25]

Love is classified by Du Moulin as a kind of motion, and motion not of the most pleasing sort. There is in "corporall love, an importunate itching, a furious heate, to wit, the worst of vices [...]."[26] It is "irregular agitation and endless motion." (2) Unchaste love... "kindleth in the mindes of worldly men a firebrand of filthy desires, which defile our souls with a thousand beastly thoughts, & importunate; which of our bodies dedicated to bee temples of God, make an infectious brothel [...]".[27] But that God and Nature made nothing in vain according to the philosophers proves, Du Moulin says, that our sufferings have a purpose – to make us long for peace in heaven.

3.

Du Moulin's views on woman as the devil's agent were extreme, but his brand of rhetoric was not unique, and its Augustinian credentials are impeccable. Augustine was still supplying a framework for moral reflection at mid-century. John Donne, in a sermon of 1649, states:

---

22 Du Moulin, *Theophilus*, Preface.
23 Du Moulin, *Heraclitus, or Meditations upon the Vanity and Miserie of Humane Life*, tr. R. S. (Oxford, 1609).
24 Ibid., p. 37.
25 Ibid., p. 27–8.
26 Du Moulin, *Theophilus*, p. 19.
27 Ibid., p. 108–9.

> It is one of Saint *Augustines* definitions of sinne, *Conversio ad creaturam*, that it is a turning, a withdrawing of man to the creature. And every such turning to the creature, let it be upon his side, to *her* whom he loves, let it be upwards, to *honour* that he affects, yet it is still down-ward, in respect of him, whom he was made by, and should direct himselfe to. Every inordinate love of the Creature is a descent from the dignity of our Creation, and a disavowing', a disclaiming of that Charter... There are good things in the world, which it is a sin for man to love... because though they *be good*, they are not *so good* as man; And man may not decline, and every thing, except God himself, is inferiour to man, and so, it is a *declination*, a *stooping* in man, to apply himselfe to any Creature, till he meet that Creature in God; for there, it is above him.[28]

Although Donne seems to warn against Idolatry of Creatures, he allows that we might "meet" a creature "in God," and his sermon continues in a very different vein:

> And so, as Beauty and Riches, and Honour are beames that issue from God, and glasses that represent God to us, and idea's that return us into him, in our glorifying of him, by these helpes, so we may apply our selves to them; for, in this consideration, as they assist us in our way to God, they are above us.

Beauty, in other words, as the Platonists maintained, issues from God and furnishes a pathway to God. This thought pathway – indicated by Augustine, but certainly not preferred and developed in orthodox theology – was a more hopeful view than the preceding one. For Beauty – even if its corporeal instantiation is derivative or shadowy in the Ficinian Platonic theology derived from the *Symposium* – is at least not an optical illusion produced by the devil or a diversion from the invisible things of God. Rather than starkly contrasting God with Creatures, paradise with the fallen world, and eternal life with the torments of hell, Platonism taught that the two worlds, higher and lower, were linked. Emanationist metaphysics suffused creatures with something of divinity themselves. The *Timaeus*, though it treats matter as shadowy and evanescent, leaves no doubt that the world as it is is good.

> Now why did he who framed this whole universe of becoming frame it? Let us state the reason why: He was good, and one who is good can never become jealous of anything. And so, being free of jealousy, he wanted everything to become as much like himself as was possible... The god wanted everything to be good and nothing to be bad so far as that was possible, and so he took over all that was visible – not at rest but in discordant and disorderly motion – and brought it from a state of disorder to one of order, because he believed that order was in every way better than

---

28 John Donne, "Sermon XXIII at Lincoln's Inn" in *Fifty sermons. Preached by that learned and reverend divine, John Donne* (London, 1649), 193.

disorder... He wanted to produce a piece of work that would be as excellent and supreme as its nature would allow (*Tim.* 29e–30c).

According to theological authority, says Senault:

> [T]he face of the world was changed when man altered his condition... [T]he earth lost his beauty when man lost his innocency, and... thorns were mingled with roses when concupiscence was mingled with nature. From that time forward divine Justice did fit our abode to our desert, and thought it not reasonable that guilty man should be lodged in a Palace prepared for the innocent. She punisht man in his state, after having punished him in his person, and altering the inclinations of all creatures, made them the Ministers of her vengeance.[29]

For the classical Platonist, the beauty of the creature is not the antithesis of divine beauty, and the world – never having experienced a Fall – not only was good at the creation but is still good. Though most humans have lost their synchronization with the orderly movement of the heavens, they can restore it. An ascent to the beatific vision proceeded through the terrestrial experience of love. Though originally understood to characterize love between men, Platonic love was extended to relations between the sexes. By discriminating between the love of women and the sexual use of women, it defused the anxiety attaching to the nexus *woman-beauty-evil*. Courtly love was *service*, voluntarily awarded to an object of particular merit, not *slavery* to an appetite stimulated by some arbitrary individual, and was therefore not demeaning.[30]

This new Platonizing spirit is represented in the *Amoris Effigies*[31] of Robert Waring, (1614–1658), a history professor of Oxford. This charming work, originally published in Latin, is furnished with a frontispiece illustrating a triumphant Cupid and his many victims, tumbled on the ground and fatally struck through, including a lion. The "Picture of Love Unveiled," as its English translator named it, legitimizes the pursuit of love, presents it as a model relation between equals, and excuses its excesses and troubles. It is only, the youthful translator says in his introduction, the "Mortify'd Skeletons of Old men who think women degrade and cheat."[32] The Epicureans, he says, could do without the pretense of God, but

---

29 Senault, *Man become guilty*, p. 330.
30 Hobbes mistrusted the concept. 'Women, like money are to be used, not admired', he is supposed to have said on his deathbed. Compare his comment in *Humane Nature or The Fundamental Elements of Policy* (London, 1684), Ch. 9, 58, "[T]he *Continent* have the Passion they *contain*, as *much* and more than they that *satiate* the Appetite; which maketh me suspect this *Platonick* Love for meerly sensual; but with an honourable Pretence for the Old to haunt the Company of the young and beautiful."
31 Robert Waring, *Amoris effigies, sive, Quid sit amor? efflagitanti responsum* (London 1650).
32 Robert Waring,, *Amoris effigies, The Picture of Love Unveiled*, tr. John Norris (London, 1744), 20.

not without love "in whose Religion they might more sweetly entertain themselves."³³ Our sufferings need not spur us to renounce the world; on the contrary, they are signs of the divinity within us. "The very defects of love show a disposition greedy of Divinity and the Errors of this one Passion aspire to something Immortal."³⁴ The passion of love is, in this respect, very different from the passions of greed or anger. Corporeal beauty, moreover, expresses spiritual beauty: "[S]o graphically does the Body express the lineaments of the soul, that no garment seems more distinctly to decipher those of the Body."³⁵ Love can have, literally, a divine origin in accord with the Platonic doctrine of our identity with a natal star, or through prenatal imprinting. "[I]f the stars of any mingle their Lights... in sociable and friendly Conjunctions, if the Species of any be Congenial and Innate to us from our Nativity."³⁶

The "angelical amours" described by Robert Boyle in *Seraphic Love,* the natural philosopher's most popular work in his lifetime, were, according to Ruth Perry, realized in numerous epistolary and paramarital relationships of the time – between John Locke and Lady Masham, Henry More and Anne Finch, John Donne and Mrs. Herbert, Simon Patrick and Mrs. Gauden, and between John Norris and numerous women. Perry comments:

> Both in and out of platonic circles these highly refined and sublimated friendships often became the central lifelong relationship for both parties – more important than the connection to husband or wife – and were maintained by epistolary contact. The letters express a shared passion for invisible and abstract ideals, a passion which continually reinforced the form and meaning of platonic friendship.³⁷

4.

Descartes's *Meditations* are a distinctive – one might even say aggressive – reversal of the religious *meditatio* of the sort commended by Pierre Du Moulin. "Let us withdraw some hours to give our souls unto God," says Du Moulin, "retiring our selves out of the throng and noise of this world, quietly to meditate on those things which pertaine to our salvation."³⁸ In the traditional meditation, the meditator turns his attention inward and comes to a view of himself as sinful, abject

---

33 Ibid., p. 25.
34 Ibid., p. 32.
35 Ibid., p. 47.
36 Ibid., p. 56.
37 Ruth Perry, "Radical Doubt and the Liberation of Women", *Eighteenth Century Studies* 18 (1985), 472–493, 485.
38 Du Moulin, *Theophilus*, p. 181.

and incompetent without God. He broods on the wickedness of his life, and resolves on its amendment, which involves, even when he leaves his study, a turning away from the things of the world.

The upside down Cartesian version of a meditative exercise is similar in some respects to the works it subverts. The Meditator withdraws from practical affairs in order to get to know himself better and assumes a posture of suspicion with respect to his senses. He discovers that he is utterly incompetent without God. God sustains him in existence from moment to moment and guarantees the truth of his clear and distinct perceptions.

But that is as far as it goes. The amendment of life does not proceed in the expected direction. God turns out to have no personal interest in the Meditator, and the Meditators's errors do not stem from Original Sin, but from the constitution of his will on one hand and his bodily machine on the other. Introspection and logic reveal him to himself as an excellent and capable reasoner, and he perceives that his errors proceed from his will. Equally important, the Meditator discovers that his body usually works well, and that the experiences it generates are useful. He announces in Meditation VI: There is nothing in our constitutions that does not "bear witness to the power and goodness of God".[39] Though it has been suggested that it was the influence of women – Elizabeth's criticism of dualism, Queen Christina's libertinism – that encouraged Descartes to take a benign interest in the passions, his concerns with physical health date back at least to the period of the *Discourse,* in which he praises health as the chief good and the improvement of medicine the most useful contribution of philosophy.[40] His last work, the *Passions of the Soul,* simply transfers his concern with somatic medicine – which he had not succeeded in improving on philosophical foundations – to psychosomatic medicine.[41] The passions, like the senses, are useful and necessary: "The function of all the passions consists solely in this, that they dispose our soul to want the things which nature deems useful for us, and to persist in this volition; and the same agitation of the spirits which normally causes the passions also disposes the body to make movements which help us to attain these things [...]."[42] As he says to Chanut "in examining the passions I have found almost all of them to be good, and to be so useful in this life that our soul would have no reason

---

39 Descartes, "Meditation VI" in *Oeuvres de Descartes,* 11 volumes, edited by Charles Adam and Paul Tannery (Paris, Vrin/C.N.R.S. 1964–76), AT VII: 87–8. Tr. in *The Philosophical Writings of Descartes,* 3 volumes, translated by John Cottingham, Robert Stoothoff, Dugald Murdoch and Anthony Kenny (Cambridge: Cambridge University Press), 1984–91, II: 61.
40 Descartes, *Discourse on Method,* Pt 6, AT VI: 63; CSMK I:142.
41 See Gábor Boros, "Ethics in the Age of Automata: Ambiguities in Descartes's Concept of an Ethics", *History of Philosophy Quarterly,* 18 (2001), 139–154.
42 Descartes, *Passions of the Soul,* Pt. 2 Sect. 52, AT XI: 372; CSMK 1:349.

to wish to remain joined to its body even for one minute if it could not feel them".[43]

The theory of the good world naturally raises the problems of evil and suffering, including amorous suffering. God, in Cartesian physics, is a constrained maximizer of the good. He has imposed certain laws of nature on the basic material entities, and although there are many unfortunate by-products of the laws as far as human interests are concerned, they are inevitable, are part of an overall good system, and are not specially willed by God. Amorous suffering, for Descartes, is simply a by-product of the laws of nature and tears are inevitable. They are produced when the pores of the eyes are constricted by sadness and when blood flow to the heart, produces an excess of vapour. "And there is nothing that increases it more," Descartes says, "than the blood which is sent to the heart in the passion of love. We see too that those who are sad do not shed tears continually, but only intermittently, when they reflect anew upon the object of their affection."[44] But we are advised to take adversity in stride: "If a man meditates on [the order established by God] and understands them properly he is filled with extreme joy... He does not refuse evils and afflictions since they come to him from divine providence; still less does he refuse the permissible goods or pleasures he may enjoy in this life since they too come from God."[45] Unlike hatred, Descartes insists, and "however disordered it may be, [love] gives pleasure." As evidence he adds, "[T]hough the poets often complain of it in their verses, I think that men would naturally give up loving if they did not find it more sweet than bitter."[46]

Cartesian ethics, introduced into English philosophy by Antoine Le Grand in his textbook, the *Institutio philosophiae secundum principia domini Renati Descartes*,[47] insofar as it is concerned with the amendment of life, requires an understanding of the physiology of the passions, which, like everything else in the created world, are basically good and serviceable. Pleasure is a sign of the good, to which we are spontaneously drawn (even Augustine admitted this in theory, Le Grand points out), and pain is a sign of evil. Suffering, by implication, has no

---

43 Descartes, "Letter to Chanut, 1 November 1646," CSMK III: 290. Harold J. Cook in "Body and Passions: Materialism and the Early Modern State," *Osiris*, 17 (2202) 25–48, p. 38 suggests that Descartes was undergoing an Epicurean turn as a result of his attempt to secure the patronage of Queen Christina of Sweden. His source is Susan Akerman, *Queen Christina of Sweden and Her Circle: The Transformation of a Seventeenth-Century Philosophical Libertine* (Leiden, Brill, 1991).
44 Descartes, *Passions of the Soul*, Pt. 2 Art. 131, AT XI:425; CSMK I:374.
45 Descartes, "Letter to Chanut, 1 February 1647," in *Descartes: Philosophical Letters*, tr. A. Kenny (Oxford: Clarendon, 1970), 213.
46 Ibid., p. 216.
47 Antony Le Grand, *Institutio philosophiae, secundum principia domini Renati Descartes nova methodo adornata & explicata, in usum juventutis academicae* (London, 1672).

theological meaning whatsoever, and is always undesirable. And, by implication, our errors and our sufferings are not caused by Original Sin. Where could such a trait reside? Not in the bodily machine, which is only extended matter; but not in the incorporeal human mind either. Le Grand went on to compose a treatise in defense of pleasure, *The divine Epicurus, or, The empire of pleasure over the virtues* (1676), and the same mixture of Cartesianism and Epicureanism is present in Walter Charleton's *Epicurus' morals*[48] (1670) and in his *Natural history of the passions* (1674).

Whether such favourable treatments of pleasure contributed to the warming trend I have been describing, or merely reflect it, the trend is evident. Even Richard Baxter, whose *Christian Directory or, a summe of practical theologie* devotes all of Part VIII to "Directions against the master sin: Sensuality", is content to warn against excess and Grand Idolatry. "Excessive scrupulousness", he says, "may be a greater sin and a greater hindrance in the work of God than excesses of flesh-pleasing, which are committed through ignorance or inadvertency."[49] It is a help to the work of God to "have a healthful body, and cheerful spirits," and these can be furthered by at least "the sights of prospects, and beauteous buildings, and fields, and country's or the use of gardens." Music, "your best apparel" and moderate feasting are permissible, and, by implication, other pleasures too.[50]

5.

The translator of the *Amoris Effigies* was none other than the emotional and conflicted John Norris. Though Norris's views changed over the course of his career, his early translation effort was significant, for the *Effigies* were still being reprinted thirty years after his death in 1744. With his admirably-titled work *The Theory and Regulation of Love*[51] of 1688, dedicated to Lady Masham, for whom he nursed for a time a hopeless passion, Norris ambitiously attempts to cover much of the field of ethics by categorizing various sorts of love and then describing the regulations

---

[48] Walter Charleton, *Epicurus' morals, collected partly out of his own Greek text, in Diogenes Laertius, and partly out of the rhapsodies of Marcus Antoninus, Plutarch, Cicero & Seneca; And faithfully Englished* (London, 1670).

[49] Richard Baxter, *A. Christian directory, or, A summ of practical theologie and cases of conscience directing Christians how to use their knowledge and faith, how to improve all helps and means, and to perform all duties, how to overcome temptations, and to escape or mortifie every sin* (London, 1673), 267.

[50] Ibid., p. 267.

[51] John Norris, *The theory and regulation of love a moral essay, in two parts: to which are added letters philosophical and moral between the author and Dr. Henry More* (Oxford, 1688).

necessary to each and the permissions available.[52] Though famous as the Malebranchian enthusiast scorned by Locke and Molyneux, Norris followed Epicurus and Hobbes in invoking this-world, utilitarian criteria of moral rightness, by contrast with Henry More's defense of Platonic-Stoic "eternal and intrinsic" notions of good and evil, what More terms a *"Moral Perfection* of human nature *antecedent* to all Society."

Like his predecessors, Norris characterizes love as a kind of motion, but not disorderly and futile motion. Invoking the Platonic macrocosm-microcosm analogy,[53] he identifies love with orderly, vital, and socially-reciprocal motion:

> Again as by the Continual Reciprocation of the Pulse there is caused a Circulation of the Blood, which is expell'd out of the Heart into the Arteries, out of these into the parts which are to be Nourish'd, from whence 'tis imbibed by the Capillary Veins, which lead it back to the Vena Cava and so into the Heart again; and same may in proportion be applied to Love. This is the Great Pulse of the Body Politic (27) as the other is of the Body Natural. 'Tis Love that begets and Keeps up the great Circulation and Mutual Dependence of Society, by this Men are inclined to maintain Mutual Commerce and intercourse with one another, and to distribute their Benefits and Kindnesses to all the parts of the Civil Body, till at length they return again upon themselves in the Circle and Reciprocation of Love.[54]

Every natural good is "a ray and Emanation of the universal good." But "Intellectual and Sensual" love should not be confused with the inferior "Vulgar or Epidemicall" variety:

> [Love] is a Passion that has made more slaves than the greatest Conquerors, more stir and disturbance in the world than either Ambition, Pride or Couvetousness, and has caused more Sin and Folly than the united force of all the Powers of Darkness. It has wounded almost as many as Death, and devour'd like a Contagion or the Grave... [It] is an image of the universal Conflagration.[55]

---

52 "I must further observe to the Reader, that this way of writing *Ethics* is intirely New and unblown upon. For though the reduction of all Vertue and Vice to the various Modification of Love be Obvious enough to any one that will consider, yet I do not know of any Moralist that ever drew up a Scheme of Morality upon this *Hypothesis*." Norris, *Theory and Regulation*, Preface to the Reader.
53 "I stand amazed at this wonderful Harmony and Correspondence, and... I am thereby the more Confirm'd in that Celebrated Notion of the *Platonists*, that as the Soul is the Image of God, so the Body is the Image of the Soul, and that this Visible and Material is but the *Shadow*, or (as *Plotinus* will have it) the *Echo* of the Invisible and Immaterial World." Norris, *Theory and Regulation*, p. 29.
54 Ibid., p. 28.
55 Ibid., p. 46–7.

If an angel fell in love with another angel's "refin'd vehicle", he says, that would be understandable, but "to see a man Idolize and dote upon a Masse of Flesh and Blood, that which the Apostle calls *our Vile Body*" that is at present the *Reversion* of Worms, and may the next minute be a *Carcase*" is, he suggests, astonishing.[56] Yet Norris goes on to insist that insofar as man is placed between angel and beast, he is able to love beauty in a way that mixes intellectual and sensual motives. "Original concupiscence must be far otherwise stated than usually it is. It is commonly understood to be a vicious disposition or Depravation of Nature, whereby we become inclined to *evil*."[57] But this cannot be right, he says, turning to the Cartesian theory, for the desire for pleasure is "Necessary and invincible, implanted in us by the Author of our Nature." We can "no more devest ourselves of [it], than we can of any the most essential part of our constitution."[58] "Pleasure it self," he maintains, "is a thing principally regarded and provided for by God; and consequently... is good in itself and *may* be desired by us."[59] "God has provided for the Animal as well as the Divine life. And although this is to be chiefly nourished, yet the other is not to be starv'd. For it is a tree of God's own planting."[60] As for "those severe declamations," Norris maintains, "which the Moralists of all Ages have made against sensual pleasure in general, as a low, base, brutish and dishonourabled thing, [they] must either be understood Comparatively, with respect to the higher Character of Intellectual Pleasures, or they are ill grounded and unreasonable."[61] It is love, not reason, Norris maintains, that makes men images of God:

> These are the two Noble Facultys that branche out from the Soul of man, and whereby he becomes a little *Image* of the *Trinity*. And altho' we generally value our Selves most upon the *Former*; yet I know not whether there be not an Equality in these as there is in the *Divine* Processions, and whether it be not as much the Glory of man to be an *Amorous*, as to be a *Rational* Being.[62]

That nothing is evil or sin because all things come from God was a doctrine advanced by the unpopular Ranters. This is too hasty a deduction for Norris. Having theorized love as orderly motion and motion towards the good, Norris turns to the very important subject of its regulation. He first proposes two general canons for regulation of pleasure which echo Epicurus's declarations on the sub-

---

56 Ibid., p. 48
57 Ibid., p. 109.
58 Ibid., p. 92.
59 Ibid., p. 94.
60 Ibid., p. 100.
61 Ibid., p. 108.
62 Ibid., p. 7.

ject.⁶³ "[T]hat Pleasure which has no trouble or pain annex'd, may, nay indeed cannot but be embraced; as on the contrary, that pain which has Pleasure annex'd is to be avoided. Pleasure which either hinders a greater pleasure or causes a greater pain to be is to be nill'd and avoided, as on the contrary that pain which either takes off a greater |Pain, or causes a greater pleasure is to be will'd and embraced."⁶⁴

Next, Norris moves from a criterion pertaining to the individual to one pertaining to the community. As we are creatures of God, he says, "we may desire anything that is not contrary to or Prejudiciall to the *good of Society.*" "Using rich Perfumes, drinking delicious Wines & c. are indifferent actions that are not contrary to any particular natural end and so are not forbidden."⁶⁵ Mortification as duty requires only "such a due Repression and Discipline of the Body, that our natural desire of sensual pleasure in Common may not carry us to the express willing of it in such instances as are against order, and the *good of Society.*"⁶⁶ The life and health of the social world reflect the higher harmonies of the universe, but as a result, "No particular pleasure is evil so far as Pleasure, but only by reason of some accidental Circumstances, wherein some higher Interest is opposed by it."⁶⁷

> Nay we ought to desire private good no further than as 'tis conducive to, or at least consistent with the Public Interest. For I consider Society as a Musical Instrument, consisting of variety of strings of different sizes, and strain'd up to different pitches, some of whose Sounds, though ungrateful in some junctures, are yet Musical as they stand in relation to others, and in order to a Common design. Now tho 'tis Natural to desire the grateful sound of every string singly, were this equally conducing to the harmony of the whole, yet certainly no body is so unreasonably absurd, as to desire that this or that Discord should be turned into a sound singly more grateful, to the prejudice of the general harmony, which is of infinitely greater Consequence, than the single gratefulness of one or two Particular Strings.⁶⁸

Though this view of the body politic might seem more Platonic and bio-mystical than the views of Hobbes⁶⁹ or Hume concerning the social order, the notion

---

63 "No pleasure is in itself evil, but the things which produce certain pleasures entail annoyances many times greater than the pleasures themselves." Diogenes Laertius, *Lives of the Philosophers,* Bk 10: 142ff., 2 vols, tr. R. D. Hicks (Cambridge: Harvard University Press, 1931), II: 667.
64 Norris, *Theory and Regulation,* p. 94–5.
65 Ibid., p. 101.
66 Ibid., p. 111.
67 Ibid., p. 93.
68 Ibid., p. 86.
69 Hobbes discusses virtue under the heading of Manners, which, he says, relate to "those qualities of man-kind, that concern their living together in peace and Unity." From *Leviathan,* "Of man", Pt. I, ch. 11, ed. Richard Tuck (Cambridge: Cambridge University Press, 1996), p. 69. Hobbes flatly denies that there is any such thing as a *summum bonum* (p. 70).

of the communal good draws on the political theory of Grotius and Pufendorf.[70] When orthodox writers "tax the immorality of some instances of Sensual Pleasure (suppose Adultery or Fornication)," Norris says, "they don't ground their charge wholly upon those Civil inconveniences, which either of them bring upon a Society in their respective Circumstances, but resolve part of their immorality into sensuality as such."[71] But, Norris charges, if sensuality were inherently evil, marriage could not make it good.

The contingency that makes licentious behaviour morally wrong is, according to Norris, simply that human children need the strength of fathers, not merely mothers, to subdue them. And the provision of necessities of life requires two parents, "not for a short time as in Birds, but for a considerable space of life."[72]

6.

Norris's *Theory and Regulation* led to the exchange of a series of vigorously combative letters with Henry More on the question of pleasure. Norris presents himself in the correspondence in the role of a dialectically puzzled man. He is well aware, he says, that the tradition of religion and philosophy has been to represent sensuality as evil, regardless of its social consequences. He knows that the Platonists and Stoics have declaimed against the body, and that many actions are traditionally described as filthy, brutish, and unclean. He has also noticed that many pleasurable actions are attended with shame. "From this and more that might be alledg'd," he muses, "it seems to me that there must be some Moral Turpitude in sensuality as such. But now wherein this immorality should ly, I am still to seek."[73] In his response, More insists that there is a pre-social notion of moral purity. There is intrinsically in illicit love "a foulness and uncleanness in

---

70 "For first, I find that the more Modern Masters of Morality (such as *Grotius*, Dr *Cumberland, Puffendorf* with many others) resolve the immorality of Adultery wholly into those pernicious effects it has upon Society, without bringing in the *sensuality as such* into any part of the Account," Norris, *Theory and Regulation,* p. 166.
71 Ibid., p. 96.
72 Ibid., p. 104. "Women," he notes, "are dependent upon men since the necessity of human life requires many things which cannot be supplied by one only. It is therefore convenient according to human Nature that the Man after Conjunction should abide by the Woman, and not presently depart, and take up indifferently with any body... neither will be case be alter'd by the womans being so rich as to be able to nourish her child by her self. Because the natural rectitude of Human actions is not to be measured according to those things, which happen by Accident in one Individual, but according to those things which follow the whole Species," p. 103.
73 Ibid., p. 166.

it, distinct from what it sins against *Political Society*, which by no means is the *adequate measure* of sound Morality, but there is a *Moral Perfection* of human nature *antecedent* to all Society."

> [S]uch is the nobleness of the Soul of man, that such gross enjoyments are exceedingly below her, who is designed for an *Angelical life*, where *they neither marry, nor are given in marriage*, and therefore even nature has taught her to sneak, when, she being Heaven-born, demits her noble self to such *earthly drudgery*.[74]

The practices of love outstrip their proper function. The function of appetite or pleasure in eating is simply to "engage the Animal to eat sufficiently to nourish him and to renew his strength." If, he argues, some glutton "had found some Art or Trick, to enjoy the pleasure of the Tast of Meats and Drinks all the day long in a manner, and from day to day, though he eat no more for strength and sustenance than others do, were not this man most wretchedly sensual and gluttonous?"[75] Shame does not attach to seeing, hearing, smelling, and tasting, because we will employ these senses to our delight in Paradise. The shame attaching to the pleasure of irregular loves, which we will not experience there, is a reliable indication of their absolute wrongness. But, More concedes, "if this Passion of Venereal shame be rightly interpreted, I suppose this is all it signifies, and not that there is any *intrinsick Immorality* or Turpitude in the pleasures of the *sixt sense*."[76]

The impasse reached by Norris and More, invoking mundane and angelic criteria respectively, was broken by Shaftesbury, who combined an endorsement of beauty and pleasure with a form of moral idealism. Although Shaftesbury overwhelmingly preferred the company of men to the company of women and did not hold women in great esteem,[77] he took pains to articulate a view of the compossibility and mutual harmony of the two attitudes that were divided in patristic theology: love of the Creature and objectively virtuous action. In a letter to Pierre Coste of 1706, Shaftesbury referred to "two real distinct philosophies":

> The one derived from Socrates and passing into... the Peripatetic and stoic; the other derived in reality from Democritus and passing into the Cyreniac and Epicurean... [T]he first maintained that society, right and wrong was founded in nature and that nature had a meaning and was... well-governed and administered by one

---

74 Henry More, "Letter to Norris, 13 April 1685," *Theory and Regulation*, p. 173
75 Norris, *Theory and Regulation*, p. 104–5.
76 More, "Letter to Norris," p. 173.
77 Brian Cowan, "Reasonable Ecstasies: Shaftesbury and the Languages of Libertinism," *Journal of British Studies*, 37 (1998), 111–138, 116–8.

simple and perfect intelligence. The second... denied this and made Providence and Dame Nature not so sensible as a doting old woman.[78]

Though Shaftesbury expresses a strong preference for the Platonic over the Democritean-Epicurean conception of nature and society, his opposition to the Epicureans does not reflect his rejection of hedonic motives in favour of stoic apathy, but their harshness. Conversely, he appreciates Lucretius's invocation of "Nurturing Venus, who fills with your presence the ship-bearing sea, beneath the gliding stars of heaven, and the crop-bearing lands" at the start of *De rerum natura*. Even the "cold Lucretius," he says, "makes use of inspiration when he writes against it and is forced to raise an apparition of Nature, in divine form, to animate and conduct him in his very work of degrading nature and despoiling her of all her seeming wisdom and divinity."[79]

Shaftesbury, like Norris, emphasized the connections between morality and social welfare:

> In creatures who by their particular economy are fitted to the strictest society and rule of common good, the most unnatural of all affections are those which separate from this community and the most truly natural, generous and noble are those which tend towards public service and the interest of the society at large.[80]

He finds the love of beauty conducive to virtue. "The admiration and love of order, harmony and proportion, in whatever kind, is naturally improving to the temper, advantageous to social affection, and highly assistant to virtue, which is itself no other than the love of order and beauty in society."[81] What is more, he finds in the affection between the sexes a disinterested motive of benevolence adjoined to desire that lends moral worth to their relations. The "mixture of the kind and friendly," that is found in the passion of love has a dignity to it derived from the element of sacrifice and its lack of expected recompense. Drawing as much on the literary tradition as on history, he notes:

> For the sake of the person beloved, the greatest hardships in the world have been submitted to and even death itself voluntarily embraced without any expected compensation. For where should the ground of such an expectation lie? Not in this world, surely, for death puts an end to all. Nor yet hereafter, in any other, for who

---

78 Shaftesbury, "Letter to Pierre Coste, 1 October 1706," quoted in Lawrence Klein, ed., Anthony Ashley Cooper, Third Earl of Shaftesbury, *Characteristics of Men, Manners, Opinions, Times* (Cambridge: Cambridge University Press, 1999), Introduction, p. xv.
79 Shaftesbury, "A Letter Concerning Enthusiasm" (1708) in *Characteristics*, p. 26.
80 Shaftesbury, "Miscellaneous reflections on the preceding treatises and other critical subjects: Miscellany IV" in *Characteristics*, p. 432.
81 Shaftesbury, "An Inquiry Concerning Virtue or Merit" (1699) in *Characteristics*, p. 191.

has ever thought of providing a heaven or future recompense for the suffering virtue of lovers?[82]

Amorous suffering is not, in Shaftesbury's system, an indication of demonic interference, pitiful slavery, or a motive to the love of God. Nor is it, as it is in the Cartesian system, a mere byproduct of the laws of nature to which we must be resigned. It is, rather, noble and sublime, and, in its own way, even pleasing:

> The very disturbances which belong to natural affection, though they may be thought wholly contrary to pleasure, yield still a contentment and satisfaction greater than the pleasures of indulged sense. And where a series or continued succession of the tender and kind affections can be carried on, even through fears, horrors, sorrows, griefs, the emotion of the soul is still agreeable. We continue pleased even with this melancholy aspect or sense of virtue.[83]

7.

World-renouncing motifs, it can be concluded, were in retreat by the third quarter of the 17th century as Platonic optimism and the cult of amorous worship became fashionable, and as the scientific approach to the study of nature, society, and the social emotions gained in strength and detail. Departing from both the theological tradition, which represents desire as a critical element in our individual relations with God and the Devil, and the secular Stoic tradition, which teaches that self-mastery and apathy are intrinsic goods, philosophers like Norris – and, indeed, his opponents John Locke and Damaris Masham – regarded the regulation of love and the curbing of excesses of passion in the context of the social framework and our need to live happily and harmoniously with others. The implication is that corporeal beauty is dangerous insofar as it can destabilize social relations and promote conflict amongst men, but it is not intrinsically dangerous.

This is not to say that the Calvinistic harshness of the theologians disappeared once for all. In his *Christian Blessedness: or Discourses Upon the Beatitudes* (1690), and his *Letters Concerning the Love of God, between the Author of the Proposal to the Ladies and Mr. John Norris* (1695), Norris revived the view that love of the Creature is idolatry. Perhaps as shaken and unraveled as Augustine by his amorous experiences, Norris went on, in the late 1690s, to write his own counterpart to Du Moulin's *Meditations upon the Vanity and Miserie of Humane Life*.[84]

---

82 Ibid., p. 203.
83 Ibid.
84 Norris, *An Effectual Remedy Against the Fear of Death* (London, 1733). The effectual remedy, according to Norris, is to realize that the sweetness of life is a kind of illusion and to recognize "the Successive vanity of Human life, every part of which is a Cheat, a Delusion, a Lie, and Every Man that Lives, walks in a Vain Shadow, in the Fog we were but now speaking of, till his walk is at and end," p. 77.

In response to the *Letters*, however, two treatises in defense of love of the creature appeared in 1696, one written by Lady Masham and published anonymously, the other by Daniel Whitby.[85]

Virtue theory, which rejects both divine command and the Stoic apathetic ideal, and which founds morality in moral sentiment and sympathy, was on the horizon. In Hume's formulation, it retains the emphasis on disinterest and objective merit introduced by Shaftesbury, while affording a considerable role for love and lovability.[86] Though a notable reaction sets in with Immanuel Kant – a swing of the pendulum back to other-worldliness and the devaluation of women and amorous passion – rival systems of explanation and valuation coexist in all historical eras. In this essay, I have tried to sketch the emergence and confluence of several such systems, which violate our expectation that while the poets can be expected to celebrate love, the philosophers can be expected to scorn it.

---

[85] Damaris Masham, *A discourse concerning the love of God* (London, 1696). Daniel Whitby, *Discourse of the love of God shewing that it is well consistent with some love or desire of the creature, and answering all the arguments of Mr. Norris in his sermon on Matth. 22, 37, and of the letters philosophical and divine to the contrary* (London, 1697).

[86] "When we enumerate the good qualities of any person, we always mention those parts of his character which render him a safe companion, an easy friend, a gentle master, an agreeable husband, or an indulgent father. We consider him with all his relations in society; and love or hate him according as he affects those who have any immediate intercourse with him." From Hume, *A Treatise of Human Nature*, Bk. 3, Pt. 3, Sect 3, ed. L. A. Selby-Bigge, 2nd ed. (Oxford: Clarendon, 1978), 605.

Frances Hutcheson:
From moral sense to spectatorial rights
Aaron Garrett, Boston University

This essay concerns a particular aspect of Francis Hutcheson's theory of rights – how the connection between rights and tensions in his own moral sense theory led Hutcheson to stress the importance of adventitious or acquired spectator approved rights, an idea that would be taken up in a different way by Hutcheson's student and successor Adam Smith. In order to illustrate this I will consider why Frances Hutcheson, alone among British philosophers of this generation, argued for animal rights. I am less concerned here with animal rights *per se*[1] as what his discussion of animal rights says about his view of the connection between morality and rights. Hutcheson morally justifies rights in three different ways, all of which have deep roots in his moral theory via: the moral sense, a providentialist utilitarianism, and a paternalist rational spectator theory with Shaftesburian roots. The problem of animals moves Hutcheson to stress the third of these justifications as a supplement to the first two.

In order to show this I will first present a few competing theories that Hutcheson is attempting to draw together in his own account of rights. Then, I will explore the details of Hutcheson's own theory as presented in *An Inquiry Concerning the Original of our Ideas of Virtue or Moral Good*. Next, I will consider the problem of animal rights as a problem naturally arising from Hutcheson's way of thinking about morality. In this context, I will discuss Hutcheson's System of Moral Philosophy insofar as it extends tensions and themes in the earlier work but offers a different emphasis.

1. Background

One of the greatest innovations of Scottish Enlightenment moral philosophers was rethinking the connection between morals and political and social rights. Hume, and following upon him, Adam Smith and John Millar, developed a shared account of rights and their connection to law, history, and the human sciences more broadly where rights became a cornerstone of an evolving historically negotiated system which satisfied basic human needs but was independent of the moral

---

1 A parallel and fuller account of the origin of Hutcheson's account of animal rights is the author's "Francis Hutcheson and the Origin of Animal Rights" *Journal of the History of Philosophy*, 45:2 (April 2007) 243–65. In particular, some of the contents of part 4 of this essay appear there in a modified form.

virtues or moral capacities of rulers or legislators. As developed by Adam Smith, rights follow on interests and allow for the flourishing of virtues, but they are primarily historical not metaphysical entities (I say primarily because Smith does have a very brief account of natural rights in his *Lectures on Jurisprudence*, but one that seems to do very little philosophical work as far as I can tell).[2] The scope, nature, and substance of rights change according to other changes in human needs.

Where do rights come from and what leads selfish elites to grant them? The main story of how they were acquired in late Medieval and Renaissance Europe goes like this. When a feudal baron wanted spices from the east or gleaming trinkets he was driven by his interest in possessing trinkets, spices, and so on to restrain the lords of his table from just hacking merchants to bits and stealing the spices and trinkets; instead, he granted rights of passage to local traveling merchants in hopes of even more exciting spices and trinkets in the future. When more barons saw it was in their interest to have access to a consistent stream of a large variety of goods they granted rights to free cities. These free cities in turn bred cosmopolitan virtues and equality that differed from and altered the extant feudal morality.[3] So rights follow upon interests and progressive morality follows rights. This "out of little acorns mighty oaks grow" story of the emergence of rights has obviously, and I think rightly, been enormously influential on thinkers as diverse as Max Weber, F. A. Hayek, and Amartya Sen.

This theory of rights was born of a number of different contending models, and, for our purpose, two main strands. Republican thinkers, such as James Harrington and those influenced by him (most influentially Shaftesbury), had stressed a thorough connection between civic virtues and rights or liberties.[4] For Harrington, virtues and liberties depended on the proper distribution of land, as land and the economic authority it afforded were an ultimate source of political power. Harrington understood this less as what we might think of as an economic condition than in a Roman and even Platonic sense of the regimentation of classes for the ordering of the state. Closer to Hutcheson's and Smith's home, the Scottish neo-Harringtonian, Andrew Fletcher of Saltoun provided a historical account of the devolution of virtue, rights, and civic morality in his 1698 work *A Discourse of Government with Relation to Militias* that was at antipodes with the Hume-Smith-Millar narrative. Commerce and technology, in this case, the invention of the compass, brought in Asian goods that led to impoverishment through venal desires for luxury and the ultimate mercenary enslavement of once noble barons to tyranny. On this picture, virtue and rights were sometimes synonymous but always thoroughly interconnected. Virtue was the *sine qua non* of

---

2 Cf. Knud Haakonssen, *The Science of A Legislator* (Cambridge: CUP, 1981), 101.
3 The classic statement is Book III of the *Wealth of Nations*. See particularly, WON III.iv.13.
4 See, for example, J. A. Pocock, ed., *The Political Works of James Harrington* (Cambridge: CUP, 1977), 489.

rights. As virtue was corrupted, the people slipped into tyranny and original rights were lost. When virtue flourishes, in civic militias or in Harrington's utopian and well-ordered Oceana or in the open and free bustle of the coffee houses celebrated by Shaftesbury, so too do liberties.

While living in Dublin after graduating from Glasgow and before becoming professor of moral philosophy at his alma mater, Hutcheson belonged to a circle of Shaftesbury-influenced intellectuals who pursued a post-Harringtonian virtue-centered position.

During this period in Dublin Hutcheson wrote his two early masterpieces, *An Inquiry Concerning the Original of our Ideas of Beauty and Virtue* (1725) and *Essays on the Passions and Illustrations on the Moral Sense* (1728). The second essay, on morals and virtue, in the first of these two works was dedicated to defending Shaftesbury against criticisms from Mandeville. The title of the work – 'An Inquiry Concerning the Original of our Ideas of Beauty and Virtue' – and its implicit reference to Shaftesbury's *An Inquiry Concerning Virtue and Merit* would signal to any contemporary reader that Hutcheson belonged to the tribe of Shaftesbury. Hutcheson is a virtue theorist in all of his works of moral philosophy, but particularly in these two early works. Morality, above all, concerns possessing and appraising virtues, and surprisingly little about vice,[5] although, as we shall see in a moment, in a different manner than for Harrington or Shaftesbury.

Although virtue was the common coin of many moral and political discussions in the early eighteenth century, another even more pervasive strand of argument deriving from Pufendorf took morality to be a system of rights coextensive with (and sometimes identical with) natural law, entailing moral duties and obligations in turn, and ultimately motivated by sanctions put in place by the will of a legislator or superior. Natural law theories were often mixed with other strands of moral philosophy but virtue, such as it was in these theories (and its importance was greatly diminished in most natural rights theories in comparison with Shaftesbury or Harrington), depended on the performance of duties and the meeting of obligations as warranted by rights.

For example, Gershom Carmichael, Francis Hutcheson's predecessor and the first Professor of Moral Philosophy at Glasgow, argued that the four cardinal virtues and all other virtues are coeval with justice which is "a constant and perpetual will to perform the duties which are owed to each and every one" and they arise from "that one principle from which flows all genuine obedience to law, i.e. love of God tempered with reverence, and a habitual will to show it in all one's actions."[6] In other words, the virtues were only truly virtues insofar as they were

---

5 For an example of Hutcheson's difficulty of dealing with cases like Nero, see Francis Hutcheson, *An Inquiry Concerning the Original of our Ideas of Beauty and Virtue*, Wolfgand Leidhold, ed. (Indianapolis: Liberty Fund, 2004), 230n15.

6 James Moore and Michael Silverthorne, eds. *Natural Rights on the Threshold of the Scottish Enlightenment: The Writings of Gershom Carmichael* (Indianapolis: Liberty Fund, 2002), 42.

extensions of justice and were in turn all compacted via justice into our duty to God. Duty, obligations and rights were either empirically discovered by human beings as they pursued individual happiness and interests and entered into sociable commerce with others as the means to do so, or were imposed conventionally, or were revealed by God. We have duties in and through our "offices" or roles as humans, as parents, as legislators, as Lutheran pastors, as leaders of militias, and so on. These roles or offices arise from the fact that we are sociable beings who seek and need other sociable beings, and different natural law relations follow from and give structure to conventional sociability. We have rights in order to fulfill these duties and sanctions have been attached in order to motivate us to do our duty. The ultimate existence, content, and sanction of the rights were organized in such a way as both to benefit us and make us subjects capable of moral judgment. In Pufendorf's and Carmichael's terms, they depend on a superior, they bring us to revere a superior, and they oblige us to the superior. And, as we can see from Carmichael, they were the ultimate lynchpin and force of morality in these very top-down theories. Carmichael even referred to rights as "particles" of liberty deriving from divine freedom.[7]

When Hutcheson was a student at Glasgow, Carmichael taught a Pufendorf fused with Locke through Pufendorf's great Swiss commentator Jean Barbeyrac. Hutcheson read all of the major natural law authors but Carmichael's commentary on Pufendorf's *De Officio* was the bridge between natural lawyers like Pufendorf and Barbeyrac and the post-Hutchesonian Scottish enlightenment. Hutcheson first lectured on moral philosophy using Pufendorf's *De Officio* with Carmichael's commentary, and the *De Officio* with Barbeyrac's and Carmichael's commentaries provided a skeleton for Hutcheson's later work.[8] In the 1730s, Hutcheson attempted to build his own lecture notes into a vast theory of rights called *A System of Moral Philosophy*. He ultimately decided the work was a failure and chose not to publish it,[9] although it was edited and published posthumously by one of his students. Throughout his career Hutcheson tried to draw together (in greater or lesser degrees of earnestness) the language of rights and the language of virtue into a moral philosophy that matched the needs of the emerging Scottish moderate theology.

---

7 Ibid., 78–9.
8 Ibid., xv.
9 William Robert Scott, *Francis Hutcheson: His Life, Teaching and Position in the History of Philosophy* (Cambridge: CUP, 1900), ch. XI.

2. Hutcheson's moral theory

In order to better understand the nature of this synthesis[10] we ought to look at Hutcheson's moral sense theory and how he built this theory so as to focus on a particular moral virtue: benevolence. In most of what follows I will be concentrating on Hutcheson's earliest statement of the theory in the *Inquiry*. There has been a scholarly debate about whether Hutcheson's later works should be viewed as expressing his most deeply held and considered philosophical views or as a system for teaching within a natural rights curriculum of the sort he inherited from Gershom Carmichael. Although many of his concerns were different in his later works, I think he genuinely thought them to be consistent with and outgrowths of his earlier positions – or at least until he gave up on the *System* in the 1740s.[11]

In his early works Hutcheson developed a highly original moral sense theory, ostensibly derived from Shaftesbury but far more systematic, which drew on Locke's empiricist theory of perception and particularly Locke's account of the primary/secondary quality distinction, to create a theory of moral perception. Hutcheson's basic insight was that qualities perceived by the internal senses are as authoritative and representative as qualities experienced by the external senses. Just as each external sense has its own special perceptual contents, e.g., sounds, smells, visual stimulae, so the objects of moral perception – a virtuous character or a benevolent action – are peculiar to moral perception. And insofar as we have peculiar perceptions we can individuate a sense, a power, or capacity to perceive in a distinctive manner. The moral sense is peculiar insofar as it has moral content and moral feelings as its object, just as beauty is a quality particular to aesthetic perception (although Hutcheson like Shaftesbury often refers to "moral beauty" and like him draws crucial analogies between beauty and morality). Perceptions of distinctively moral qualities give rise to distinctively moral motivations, and moral motivation to moral actions that are in turn perceived by the moral sense as morally praiseworthy or blameworthy. Moral qualities themselves supervene on non-moral, external perceptions (which is one of the differences between the external and the internal senses), but they are not reducible to them. This is the crucial idea for Hutcheson: that moral perceptions are distinctive in a way that resists any sort of reduction.[12]

The paradigm moral perception is of benevolence, and the *Inquiry Concerning Virtue or Moral Good* was meant to show, contra Mandeville and in support of Shaftesbury, that self-interest was an insufficient base for morality and that

---

10 I adopt the word and the general concept (and much else throughout this paper) from Knud Haakonssen, *Natural Law and Moral Philosophy:From Grotius to the Scottish Enlightenment* (Cambridge: CUP, 1996), ch. 2.
11 But, see James Moore, "The two systems of Francis Hutcheson: On the origins of the Scottish Enlightenment" in M. A. Stewart, ed., *Studies in the Philosophy of the Scottish Enlightenment* (Oxford: OUP, 1990), 37–59.
12 See Hutcheson, *Inquiry*, 23–24, 103–6, 115, and many other places.

benevolence was the basic moral motivation. In fact, Hutcheson's position is stronger. Not only is benevolence paradigmatic for the moral sense theory, but it is the ultimate basis for all moral approval in the moral sense theory. Hedonistic theories, insofar as they tended to eschew the idea of benevolence as constitutive failed to get at was essential about virtue for Hutcheson. Although Hutcheson openly attacked Mandeville, the sanction-based theory of motivation of the natural lawyers was also suspect on this account by extension. For these theorists the ultimate moral force of natural laws and the duties and rights they entail was the dependence on a superior. They tend to our happiness and as they are created by a superior they are moral. But, virtue and morality is not due on this theory to individual acts or perceptions or God's love, but to God's superiority – although it is good that God loves us, of course! And further, the necessity of sanctions seems to undermine the virtuous character of the act: behind the natural law theory seems to lurk just another God-sanctioned variant on Hobbist hedonism with real "moral" content sorely lacking.

Hutcheson attempted to explain how morality could be centered on benevolence with his moral sense-based account of virtue (I will discuss some other ways that Hutcheson thought about virtue in a moment as well). In the *Inquiry* he defined virtue as a quality perceived by that "superior Sense, which I call a Moral one, [by which] we perceive Pleasure in the Contemplation of such Actions in others, and are determin'd to love the Agent, (and much more do we perceive Pleasure in being conscious of having done such Actions our selves) without any View of further natural Advantage from them."[13] It is a broad definition as it includes everything morally approved of by the moral sense. On this definition, what we ultimately praise with our moral sense is the benevolent disposition of the actor, and our love for it is in turn "benevolent" in the sense that it is a morally disinterested sense of good will towards the actor. So benevolence was present both in the agent and in the perceiver, and is the necessary condition of moral approval.

One might wonder, from a natural rights perspective or more overtly from a Mandevillean one, whether as a matter of fact we are capable of the sort of disinterested acts and disinterested perception that are required by this definition. Hutcheson argued for the basic accuracy of the moral faculty of moral perception and the fact of disinterested benevolence with a great number of examples that have become subsequently familiar through Hume.[14] Hutcheson strengthened his case by pointing out that even when we incorrectly judge the actions of others, when we think that others are acting kindly and they are really scheming cruelly, or vice-versa, what we approve of is the action properly performed, i.e., from benevolent rather than interested motives. When we realize that a perception is incorrect, we correct it and disapprove just as we correct errors in our judgments of vis-

---

13 Hutcheson, *Inquiry*, 88.
14 See particularly, the *Illustrations concerning the Moral Sense*.

ual perceptions arising from illusions. But the standard of moral praiseworthiness remains the same, namely, an action pleasing to the spectator insofar as it arises from benevolent motives. This capacity to judge on the basis of standards that manifests itself in our moral perceptions must pre-exist particular moral judgments, in order that we can individuate the world morally into moral agents and moral qualities and explain how we are immediately able to feel what is right and wrong even when we fail to make rational sense of complex states of affairs.

Now, for comparison's sake, recall that Carmichael derived virtues and the four cardinal virtues from "a constant and perpetual will to perform the duties which are owed to each and every one" and they arise from "that one principle from which flows all genuine obedience to law, i.e., love of God tempered with reverence, and a habitual will to show it in all one's actions." Hutcheson remarked in a parallel passage in the *Inquiry* that "these four Qualitys, commonly call'd Cardinal Virtues, obtain that Name, because they are Dispositions universally necessary to promote publick Good, and denote Affections toward rational Agents; otherwise there would appear no virtue in them."[15] For Hutcheson, unlike Carmichael, what makes them virtues is not reverence or the attempt to show love of God in one's actions, but rather affections toward rational agents. This allows us to clearly distinguish Hutcheson from his natural lawyer predecessor on the issue of virtue.

This passage from Hutcheson may give us pause for two reasons. First, the Hutchesonian story so far seems to give no special privilege to rational agents if it is entirely based on perception, feeling, and motivation. What would be special about rational agents? Why couldn't it be the case that my approval of a St. Bernard who as far as I can tell disinterestedly rescues a snow-bound skier is a full-blown moral approval of a moral virtue? Second, Hutcheson has not just said that cardinal virtues involve good will but the "publick Good." Is there any reason to think that the public good is to be preferred as opposed to anything else we might approve of, for example the deep benevolence of a parent to a child? Or perhaps combining both problems: the love of a child for a parent?

In passages like this Hutcheson draws together two, and sometimes three, different sorts of moral justifications which he draws upon in both his earlier and later moral philosophy which draw out different senses of virtue. I am only going to discuss some of the basic evidence for the existence of these theories and not give any extensive textual support. They are not mutually exclusive but they pull his theory in quite different directions. The first is the moral sense-based virtue theory I have already discussed at some length. The second is a providentialist, utilitarian theory, which comes up tangentially in this passage insofar as it provides the warrant not only for public good but for "the more public the better." The third is a rationalist paternalist spectator theory which he seems to have ultimately derived from Stoicism and Cumberland and Shaftesbury and is built into the moral sense theory.

---

15 Hutcheson, *Inquiry*, 102.

The moral sense theory itself has been sufficiently discussed, so I will just briefly consider the other two. Hutcheson famously coined the expression "the greatest happiness for the greatest numbers" in the *Inquiry*. The entire passage reads:

> In comparing the moral Qualitys of Actions... we are led by our moral Sense of Virtue to judge thus; that in equal Degrees of Happiness, expected to proceed from the Action, the Virtue is in proportion to the Number of Persons to whom the Happiness shall extend; (and here the Dignity, or moral Importance of Persons, may compensate Numbers) and in equal Numbers, the Virtue is as the Quantity of the Happiness, or natural Good; or that the Virtue is in a compound Ratio of the Quantity of Good, and Number of Enjoyers. In the same manner, the moral Evil, or Vice, is as the Degree of Misery, and Number of Sufferers; so that, that Action is best, which procures the greatest Happiness for the greatest Numbers; and that, worst, which, in like manner, occasions Misery.[16]

In this passage the moral sense approves of what the utilitarian principle maintains, so it is the ultimate source of moral justification. But, we might ask: "Why on the basis of Hutcheson's theory of moral perception would we necessarily conclude that moral judgments like 'you are benevolent and I approve of you insofar as you are benevolent' would lead to the more happiness, the better?" For example, a benevolent act might bring no happiness at all and yet I ought to approve of benevolence as opposed to malicious acts which do make a large number of people very happy. Hutcheson's optimistic and optimific providentialism anchors his apparent disinterest in this problem. He presumes a kind of providentialist coordination between motives approved of by the moral sense and good acts – but that is certainly something that is hard to argue for.

Hutcheson also offers another more limited solution, a paternalist rational spectator theory (one important ancestor of Smith's impartial spectator in his later works). This justification differs from the other two insofar as it assigns special moral worth to a spectator or rational being with a moral sense capable of discerning the relations of a complex system (as opposed to just feeling particular actions as praiseworthy or blameworthy). The more extensive the system being judged, the more "the Dignity, or moral Importance of Persons." It further gives special moral weight to the judgment of this spectator. The spectator theory is obviously interconnected to the other two theories, it can be the basis for judgments about welfare, and it can be approved of by the moral sense, but it is independent as well. All three are drawn on in Hutcheson's account of rights, although the first two, and particularly the first, was most important in the earlier version of the theory in the *Inquiry*, and the spectator only became really crucial in the *System* although we can see its nascence in Hutcheson's discussions of the rights of children.[17]

---

16 Ibid., 125.
17 See particularly, ibid., 105.

3. Hutcheson on rights

Hutcheson first discussed rights in the final section of the *Inquiry*, "A Deduction of some Complex moral Ideas, viz. of Obligation, and Right, Perfect, Imperfect, and External, Alienable, and Unalienable, from this moral Sense." Hutcheson confronted the problem of sanctions head on by defining obligation as "[w]hen any Sanctions co-operate with our moral Sense, in exciting us to Actions which we count morally good… but when Sanctions of Rewards or Punishments oppose our moral Sense, then we say we are brib'd or constrain'd."[18] For the natural lawyers, since sanctions were the source of motivation, it was sometimes difficult to distinguish between compulsion and a free moral choice. Hutcheson responded that the sentiment of benevolence was the essential mark of moral obligation. As with virtue, moral motivation is key to moral obligation, both insofar as an appropriate sentiment is essential for the obligation to be discharged in a praiseworthy way and as the motivation reflects the virtue of the agent by which Hutcheson understands the agent's praiseworthy motivations. The sanctions are only legitimate insofar as they cooperate with the already pre-existent moral motive; in other words, they help us along with moral sentiments we already have if we are virtuous.

This brings us to Hutcheson's initial definition of right: "[w]henever it appears to us, that a Faculty of doing, demanding, or possessing any thing, universally allow'd in certain Circumstances, would in the whole tend to the general Good, we say that any Person in such Circumstances… has a Right to do, possess or demand that Thing. And according as this Tendency to the publick Good is greater or less, the Right is greater or less."[19] The definition is remarkably similar to the definition of virtue he gave in his account of Cardinal Virtue: "these four Qualitys, commonly call'd Cardinal Virtues, obtain that Name, because they are Dispositions universally necessary to promote publick Good, and denote Affections toward rational Agents; otherwise there would appear no virtue in them." When they are compared it is clear that Hutcheson is attempting to show that virtue and right coincide, that we have a right to be virtuous, which ultimately means benevolent, and sanctions are there in order to cooperate with pre-existent moral sentiments.

Those rights that all human beings have, that are "universally allow'd" for the general good are perfect, inviolable or inalienable.[20] Hutcheson did not discuss "natural rights" in the *Inquiry*. Carmichael, following Pufendorf and Barbeyrac,[21] had divided rights into natural and adventitious (or those which "arise from some human action or other event"). Hutcheson drew on this distinction in the

---

18 Ibid., 182.
19 Ibid.
20 Ibid., 185–6.
21 See Pufendorf, *Law of Nature and Nations*, I.iii.7.

Short Treatise and the *System* as I will discuss in a moment. But it is telling that in his earlier theory he did not feel a pressing need to draw such a distinction as all rights were in some sense natural and in some sense acquired by our virtue. For Carmichael, like Barbeyrac, natural rights were primary and adventitious rights that had warrant insofar as they were superadded upon natural rights and drew on "particles" of natural liberty that were derivative. In other words, adventitious rights were only rights insofar as they were derived from those natural rights placed into our human frames by God. From this schematic account of rights derived from the moral sense and a broadly utilitarian account of the 'public good' Hutcheson goes on to draw the standard natural rights distinctions between perfect rights, or those essential for the stability of society, imperfect rights, or those that increase positive goods in society, and external rights, or those rights which have no clear warrant in relation to the public good but the violation of which would lead to great "mischief."[22] I would like to mention three different problems in his discussion of rights which draw out different features of his argument: the category of external rights, the structure of paradigmatic duties, and the problem of virtue as its own reward. Then, finally, I will turn to animal rights.

Although Hutcheson could deal with rights that promote the public good and have benevolent motives by drawing on moral sense and utilitarian resources in his theory, he has a great difficulty when rights do not clearly arise from moral sense approved motives. Take the right that a wealthy miser has to recall a loan from a virtuous poor tradesman. What could possibly warrant the recall of the loan given Hutcheson's stress on the parallel between rights and virtues and the rooting of virtue in approved, benevolent sentiment? Furthermore the miser's recall in no way clearly contributes to the public good? Hutcheson answered: "But yet a violent Opposition to these Rights, would have been vastly more pernicious than all the Inhumanity in the use of them. And therefore, the external Rights cannot be opposite among themselves; yet they may be opposite to imperfect Rights, but imperfect Rights, tho violated, give no Right to Force."[23]

Hutcheson implied that although they come into conflict with imperfect rights their connection with perfect rights trumps. They cannot be imperfect rights because then there would be a conflict in imperfect rights, which would mean an internal conflict in adding to the common good, which for Hutcheson is impossible. They cannot be perfect rights *per se* because the violation of perfect rights for Hutcheson is an actively selfish desire that causes misery in others and is immediately disapprovable.[24] This does not seem to be the case here. The tradesman does not seem miserably selfish for not wanting to repay the loan at the whim of the miser. But this means that we approve of an act, the miser recalling

---

22 Hutcheson, *Inquiry*, 105.
23 Ibid., 184.
24 Ibid., 182.

the loan, which does not accrue to the public good in any obvious way but is connected with the stability of society as such. I will return to this issue in the conclusion but this is a point on which spectatorial justifications help a great deal.

Second, given that rights theories were constructed in order to explain duties, obligation and roles, how does Hutcheson deal with an actual role or duty in his virtue-centered definition of right? What would be the point otherwise? The *Inquiry* is extremely limited in its account of actual roles and duties (its purpose is different), but Hutcheson does consider a few: property, marriage, and children. In Section II of the *Inquiry* Hutcheson rejects a variety of different hedonistic accounts of the relation between children and parents and concludes:

> [T]he observing of Understanding and Affections in Children, which make them appear moral Agents, can increase Love toward them without prospect of Interest; for I hope this Increase of Love, is not from Prospect of Advantage from the Knowledge or Affections of Children, for whom Parents are still toiling, and never intend to be refunded their Expences, or recompens'd for their Labour, but in Cases of extreme Necessity. If then the observing a moral Capacity can be the occasion of increasing Love without Self-Interest, even from the Frame of our Nature; pray, may not this be a Foundation of weaker degrees of Love where there is no receding tie of Parentage, and extend it to all Mankind?[25]

Hutcheson's strategy here is to take a paradigmatic natural law duty, the duty of parents to children, show how it has at its core not sanctions or interest but, rather, love and disinterested benevolence (in Hutcheson's sense), and then to use this duty to expand it in order to structure a wide variety of other sorts of duties, for example, our love of neighbors and all of mankind. Duties trace and fuel an expanding, benevolent circle beginning with the family and moving outwards to the community of mankind. But, if many sorts of duties are grounded in expanding benevolence, this seems to make the miser's external right an even bigger problem. And can it really get you the right to war or the obligation not to commit suicide, the sort of things that Carmichael or Pufendorf had an easier time with?

A third problem is that if virtue is coextensive with rights and duty talk, would there be any virtue in and for its own sake (as opposed to for welfare or general stability)? Hutcheson attempts to recapture a sense of this by stressing that imperfect rights have a minimum of sanctions and are fully virtuous insofar as we ought to do them as much as possible in and of themselves.[26] But doesn't this put a bit of a dent in the project of full reconciliation by seeing moral sense sanctioned virtue as only a part of a natural rights theory? I will return to this point only briefly at the very end, but I think it is a deep problem for a virtue-theory

---

25 Ibid., 113.
26 Ibid., 183.

of the Harrington/Shaftesbury mold that attempts to reconcile with a natural rights theory.

4. Hutcheson on Animal Rights

There are three accounts of moral justification: the moral sense theory clearly dominant in the *Inquiry*, the providentialist utilitarianism playing an important role, and the paternalist spectator theory, tacit at most. There are three problems as well: the conflict between external rights and moral sense, the problem of expanding paradigmatic duties to explain traditional natural law duties, and the status of imperfect duties as the sole place for virtue in the rights theory.

I would finally like to turn to animal rights, which I think is, alongside the duties of parent to child, a characteristically Hutchesonian concept. I will also return to the three problems with rights and the issue of the spectator, which I mentioned but did not pursue, in terms of animal rights.

In 1728 John Balguy, a follower of the moral rationalist Samuel Clarke and a vigorous polemicist, wrote an attack on Hutcheson entitled *The Foundation of Moral Goodness: or a Further Inquiry into the Original of our Idea of Virtue*. Among his many objections Balguy noted (quite rightly) that Hutcheson's stress on sentiment seemed "to expose him to the Necessity of allowing some Degree of Virtue to Brutes... [T]here is no reason to doubt, but Brutes, as they are capable of being treated by us either mercifully, or cruelly, may be the Object either of Virtue or Vice. But the present Question is, whether according to our Author's Account of Moral Good, they are not also in some measure Subjects of Virtue."[27]

Ten years later while finishing, or shortly after finishing, the draft of the *System*, Hutcheson revised the *Inquiry*. One of the most significant changes was a lengthy response to Balguy in the final chapter of the second *Inquiry*, the chapter on rights discussed in the previous section of this essay:

> Some also object, that according to this Account, Brutes may be capable of virtue; and this is thought a great Absurdity. But 'tis manifest, that, I. Brutes are not capable of that, in which this scheme places the highest Virtue, to wit, the calm Motions of the Will toward the Good of others; if our common Accounts of Brutes are true, that they are merely led by particular Passions toward present Objects of Sense. Again, 'tis plain there is something in certain Tempers of Brutes, which engages our Liking, and some lower Good-will and Esteem, tho' we do not usually call it Virtue, nor do we call the sweeter dispositions of Children Virtue; and yet they are so very like the lower Kinds of Virtue, that I see no harm in calling them Virtues. What if they are low Virtues in Creatures void of Reflection, incapable of knowing

---

27 John Balguy, *The Foundation of Moral Goodness: or a Further Inquiry into the Original of our Idea of Virtue* (London, 1728), 14.

> Laws, or of being moved by their Sanctions, or by Example of Rewards or Punishments? Such Creatures cannot be brought to a proper Trial or Judgment: Laws, Rewards, or Punishments won't have these Effects upon them, which they may have upon rational Agents. Perhaps they are no farther rewarded or punished than by the immediate Pleasure or Pain of their Actions, or what Men immediately inflict upon them. Where is the Harm of all this, That there are lower Virtues, and lower Vices, the Rewarding or Punishing of which, in Creatures void of Reason and Reflection, can answer no wise End of Government?[28]

Hutcheson is here accepting the implication that Balguy correctly drew from the emphasis on the role of sentiment in virtue in the *Inquiry*. Animals are capable of "lower Kinds of Virtue" as are children insofar as they have particular "sweeter dispositions" which are approved of by the moral sense. If benevolence and sentiment are at the center of the moral theory, why not consider these dispositions to be moral virtues – albeit to a lesser degree – insofar as some of the basic constituents of virtue are present: benevolent sentiment and approval by the moral sense?

But there were obstacles to developing a conception of animal rights, duties, and obligations within the natural law frameworks of Pufendorf, Barbeyrac, and Carmichael. The *System* is Hutcheson's attempt at providing an extensive treatment of rights, including Hutcheson's treatments of the right to resistance, right in the state of natural liberty, and many of the other inherited topics of natural law theory. The problem Hutcheson had in addressing this range of topics was how to derive the complex structure of classical natural law theory from moral sense, benevolence, and welfare. Throughout the *System*, Hutcheson stressed the importance of benevolence and the common good and attempted to show how particular roles, duties, and obligations of classical natural law theory were "constituted for... happiness, in consistence with and subserviency to the general interest."[29] In the *System*, unlike the *Inquiry*, he defined a right independent of the moral sense and with utility in the forefront, as a claim a man has "when his acting, possessing, or obtaining from another in these circumstances tends to the good of society, or to the interest of the individual consistently with the rights of others and the general good of society, and obstructing him would have the contrary tendency."[30] The definition also clearly has a negative component as opposed to the virtue-centered definition of the *Inquiry*.

This change led Hutcheson to place far greater stress on utility and system and to derive many specific duties as demands for particular rights and duties *qua* the happiness of human beings and the systems they form. For example, Hutcheson justified the duty to prevent suicide "as we are formed by nature for the service

---

28 Hutcheson, *Inquiry*, 244.
29 Francis Hutcheson, *A System of Moral Philosophy* (London, 1755), II.iii.1.
30 Ibid., II.xvi.1.

of each other, and not each one merely for himself; each one is obliged to continue in life as long as he can be serviceable."[31] The emphases in Hutcheson's theory were altered in order to deal with a wider range of natural right duties, but animals did not even fit into this picture. Yet they needed accommodation due the older core commitment of his theory, to virtue arising from benevolence as approved of by the moral sense. Although the moral sense approved of them having rights it is not clear where they could fit. To accommodate them, Hutcheson created a niche for animals in his natural law theory between property and servants as legitimate property of a special sort: inferiors capable of feeling pleasure and pain. Second, Hutcheson restricted our duties to domestic animals in order to draw on the communalist resources of the Harringtonian and Shaftesburian theory of virtue as contribution to the public good. We do not have duties to all animals, but Hutcheson claimed that there was "provision" for the cultivation of society with animals

We can see then that in the *System* a pressure from one part of Hutcheson's theory plays itself out in an innovative idea: the good or happiness of the members of a system as having moral standing and rights independent of any cognitive capacity, independent of animals' cognitive capacities "of considering the notions of right and wrong."[32] Hutcheson viewed humans as capable of forming evolving, providentially governed moral communities with domesticated animals. In presenting this view Hutcheson presumed that we have moral affinities to animals and animals to us in order to allow for such a moral community. Of course, Shaftesbury, Cumberland, Carmichael, Locke, and many others thought that humans and animals share mental powers, but they also thought that only creatures capable of understanding laws can be held morally culpable and, by extension, can be morally praiseworthy or blameworthy. This was in turn the precondition of a moral community governed by natural law. Thus, for most of these thinkers, there are affinities between human beings and animals, but not moral affinities. For Hutcheson a being can matter morally, even if it has no moral sense and no cognitive capacities due to sentiments approved of by our moral sense and, as a further consequence of Hutcheson's utilitarianism, if it has a desire for happiness (as a desire to avoid pain) and it can contribute to the general happiness. This gives a second justification for rights:

> [B]rutes may very justly be said to have a right that no useless pain or misery should be inflicted on them. Men have intimations of this right, and of their own corresponding obligation, by their sense of pity. 'Tis plainly inhuman and immoral to create to brutes any useless torment, or to deprive them of any such natural enjoyments as do not interfere with the interests of men. 'Tis true brutes have no

---

31 Ibid.
32 Ibid.

notion of right or of moral qualities: but infants are in the same case, and yet they have their rights, which the adult are obliged to maintain.[33]

Animals have a natural right to happiness, which God wishes them to seek and, unless it must be undercut such that a being of higher standing in the system (namely, man) should be happy, animal rights should be respected. Therefore, men are obliged to not cause them pain and to not deprive them of pleasures without some other sort of moral justification. The mere thought that we might have a duty to something that was incapable of revering God would have probably led Carmichael to initiate heresy proceedings! The neo-Harrington line, and even Shaftesbury, had little use for such an idea insofar as animals were not virtuous or civic contributors in the robust sense of classical virtue, although this is precisely the element of their behavior that Hutcheson draws on to ground rights on our public life with domestic animals in communities – animals have public virtues as it were. Hutcheson's solution shows the flexibility and importance of his theory of rights insofar as he minimized the role of the individual agent's cognition as the necessary condition of making an act moral or morally relevant.

But how do we know what animals are due, given that most of them are non-rational and all of them are incapable of propagating their desires. This is where the spectatorial justification becomes important. Hutcheson stressed that our relations to domesticated animals and responsibilities to them vary with the needs of the superior members of the community: a human spectator or steward who is able to comprehend the system and guide the connections between its parts by virtue of his rational cognition of the system as a whole. Domestic animals only can and do become part of these communities in the first place because they strive for natural enjoyments, they have something in them through which a right can be acquired and anchored: their passions and sentiments susceptible to incorporation and domestication. This allows for rights to be granted and backed by local systems of beings seeking happiness, whatever their standing outside of the system. The spectator is crucial because animals do not have a moral sense, although they have moral sentiments, so they cannot make the moral sense judgments necessary to organize the system into a moral community. As these animals clearly add to happiness, augment the public good of the community, and manifest moral sentiments that we approve of, there can be no "just" warrant for taking away their happiness. They have a role in the moral system in and of themselves and through us, they have morally approved of sentiments organized for greater utility, and through the system an adventitious or acquired right anchored in the common desire for happiness.

---

33 Ibid., I/II.vi.3.

5. Conclusion

In the *System* then, driven by concerns in the *Inquiry* and the moral sense theory, we see the glimmering of a new notion of acquired right sanctioned by a spectator. A right is not just acquired through a pre-existent institution like marriage, or on the basis of a contract, as in the traditional differentiation between natural rights and adventitious rights in Protestant natural law theories, but acquired to an expanding benevolent system drawing more and more into a community approved of and guided by a spectator and secured by the moral approval of the spectator surveying the system.

It does not take much to see here that we both have a step towards the kind of theory of acquired rights in Smith and something rather different. Animals have special adventitious rights, like all domestics, insofar as they are important contributors to the happiness of a local community through their roles. If pursued, this line might lead to a theory of historically acquired rights in the spirit of Smith and Millar. For Smith acquired rights are parts of an expanding system and crucially approved of by spectators able to take account of the extent of the system for their standing as rights. The rights in Smith are, of course, historical and Smith did not believe in animal rights, in both cases due to the legacy of Hume which was quite removed from Hutcheson. However, we see something very much like a more rationalist version of Smithian history in Hutcheson's expanding spheres taking in animals through domestication.

But, for Hutcheson, quite differently from Smith and Millar, the older natural right stress on "the superior" that Hutcheson avoided for the most part in the *Inquiry* is now integrated into the theory. The system is governed by a superior: man as paternal spectator with his moral sense. The superior is guided by the moral sense, and the moral sense is the ultimate basis for moral authority, but in Hutcheson's figure of the steward or spectator with special moral standing as spectator, we see a reworking of Carmichael's Calvinist elder or patriarch into a benevolent, moderate, and kind father in a virtuous republican polity. Man is the steward of the limited part of the system that he controls, one system within the vast world system. Each man is able to be a steward because his moral sense is effective in tracking the real happiness of the system and in approving or condemning the motives of those who make it up.

We can now also see potential solutions to the problems I discussed at the end of the section on Hutcheson's account of rights before I turned to animal rights in particular. By placing special weight on the judgments of the spectator who is able to take into account the extent of system, and from whose spectatorial authority and guidance standing is at least in part derived, we can see a potential solution to the conflict between the moral sense and utility in the case of the external right of the miser. Members of the system do disapprove of the miser, but the moral sense of the steward or spectator who can take full account of the workings of the system approves of the misers access to the right *qua* system, even if *qua* individual they would not. Hutcheson's moral sense theory is not Smith's impartial spectator, but one can see again how it could tend in that direction insofar as it provides for a general rational view as ultimate warrant.

Second, as to the problem of whether all duties can be framed in terms of the moral sense as they were in the *Inquiry*, animal rights are an example of how Hutcheson attempted to retool his theory to deal with complex rights, even those not countenanced in natural right theory (although the resources were clearly there in the discussion of the parent/child relation in the *Inquiry*). Duties were new to be understood in terms of the expanding benevolent system governed by spectators. As I noted before, it had strong republican overtones but was now divested of patriotism or nationalism. It was, instead, a very general love of system and general benevolence.

Finally, we address the problem of virtue for its own sake. By stressing the difference between perfect rights and imperfect rights, while at the same time seeing them both as correlative with virtues, Hutcheson tried to address a tension between a theory that stressed that morality is rights and a theory that stressed that morality is virtue and rights follow from virtue. Insofar as our duties to animals are ultimately a reflection of our virtue, and insofar as they break down when perfect rights are threatened, animal rights are a species of adventitious imperfect rights.

Hutcheson's solution, to say that rights are part of virtue but much of what we think of as the heart of virtue and morals has minimal force of sanction (should have minimal force of sanction), is another important affinity with the Smith-Millar theory. Stability and the *sine qua non* of morality are not immediately approved of although they are essential and their violation demands severe sanctions. Most of what we ordinarily consider morality is of a different sort.[34] Of course, for Millar and Smith all of this, in particular perfect rights, is driven by interests in a way that it was not for Hutcheson. And, there is still something unsatisfactory about the way that Hutcheson sought to combine virtue talk and rights talk. But, again, we see the legacy of Hutcheson's moral tool bag in dealing with a natural law theory that in many ways contradicted his basic commitments, perhaps most productively and tensely in his account of animal right. It allowed him to synthesize disparate influences and to develop his spectator theory in a way that would be extremely fruitful for Scottish Enlightenment philosophers.

---

34 See particularly Adam Smith's discussion on justice in *Theory of Moral Sentiments*, II.ii.1. On Millar see Aaron Garrett, "Introduction" to *John Millar, The Origin of the Distinction of Ranks* (Indianapolis: Liberty Fund, 2006).

Philosophy as *medicina mentis*?
Hume and Spinoza on Emotions and Wisdom[1]
Willem Lemmens, University of Antwerp

> "While we are reasoning concerning life, life is gone; and death, though perhaps they receive them differently, yet treats alike the fool and the philosopher."
> Hume, The Sceptic

> "Beatitudo non est virtutis praemium, sed ipsa virtus..."
> Spinoza, Ethics

Spinoza and Hume each exemplify a specifically modern version of the classical idea that the practice of philosophy leads to the moderation of man's passionate nature.[2] Both integrate this conception of 'doing philosophy' as a search for wisdom, into a science which is in harmony with a modern ateleological worldview. But they diverge fundamentally when they spell out how exactly philosophy can lead to wisdom and in what this wisdom consists. In his *Ethics*, Spinoza presents the study of the relation between God and man, passion and virtue, following a geometrical method, as a form of *medicina mentis*. This method, which investigates human actions and desires as though it was concerned with "lines, planes and solids" (E 3,

---

[1] This is a modified version of the article, "The Melancholy of the Philosopher: Hume and Spinoza on Emotions and Wisdom", *Journal of Scottish Philosophy*, Vol.3.1, (2005): 47–65. I proposed my views on Hume and Spinoza at the *Third International Reid Symposium on 'Scottish Philosophy'* (University of Aberdeen, July 2004). I wish to thank the respondents of my lecture: Peter Baumann, M. A. Stewart, and other listeners for their generous comments afterwards. I received from Susan James, Jacqueline Taylor, Herman De Dijn, Ortwin de Graef, and an anonymous referee of the *JSP* invaluable suggestions for improvement of the final version of the article. Of course, I take full responsibility for any remaining flaws in my argument.

[2] In the following I avoid any discussion as to whether or not Hume actually read Spinoza. Spinoza's philosophy was without doubt *en vogue* in France when Hume was there to write his *Treatise* in the period 1734–1737 (see Wim Klever, "More about Hume's Debt to Spinoza," *Hume Studies* 19(1) (1993): 55–74). Klever argues that Hume's passion theory was directly and fundamentally influenced by reading Spinoza. I am not really convinced by this thesis, though Hume had of course knowledge of Spinoza's philosophy through Bayle's *Dictionnaire*. On the affinity between Hume's empiricist naturalism and Spinoza's rationalist naturalism, see also Annette C. Baier, "David Hume, Spinozist," *Hume Studies* 29(2), (1993): 237–252.

Intro.),³ leads to nothing less than the liberation of man from his enslavement to the emotions. True philosophy forms the way to freedom and virtue or, more precisely, Spinoza sees the unfolding of this (striving for) wisdom as identical with virtue. It may be very hard to achieve this perfection of reason in practice, but, for Spinoza, the intrinsic interwovenness of knowledge and virtue is indisputable.⁴ Insofar as wisdom merges, in its utter perfection, with the *Amor Dei intellectualis*, it even transcends human finiteness and becomes a form of salvation (*beatitudo*).

A century after Spinoza, Hume is less optimistic about this idea of philosophy understood as a *medicina mentis*. In the famous conclusion to Book I of his *Treatise*, having established the antimetaphysical framework of the science of human nature, he indicates how the desire for knowledge can lead to a deep melancholy and even a nervous breakdown. Here, reason is dethroned in the most radical way imaginable and every hope of deriving salvation from philosophical activity seems to be dissolved. Hume's biography testifies that as a youngster he suffered personally from a sort of 'disease of the learned' caused by a too excessive involvement in his 'new scene of thought'.⁵ Moreover, in his later philosophy, Hume remains

---

3 For further references to Spinoza's works I use the following abbreviations: *Ethics* (E), *Tractatus de Intellectus Emendatione* (TIE). I use the following editions of these works: Baruch de Spinoza, *Ethica*. Latin text with Dutch translation by Henri Krop (Amsterdam: Bert Bakker/Prometheus, 1677, 2002). Baruch de Spinoza, *Ethics*. English Translation by G. H. R. Parkinson (Series Oxford Philosophical Texts, Oxford: Oxford University Press, 2000). Baruch de Spinoza, "Tractatus de Intellectus Emendatione," in Herman De Dijn, *The Way to Wisdom: Commentaries and introduction to Tractatus de Intellectus Emendatione*. Latin text and English translation by Edwin Curley (West Lafayette, Indiana: Purdue University Press, 1996).

4 Cf.: "Si jam via, quam ad haec ducere ostendi perardua videatur, inveniri tamen potest. Et sanè arduum debet esse, quod adeò rarò reperitur" (E V, P42, Schol). ["If the way that I have shown to lead to this seems to be very arduous, yet it can be discovered. And indeed it must be arduous, since it is found so rarely." (translation by G. H. R. Parkinson, 2000: 316).

5 With "a new Scene of Thought" Hume refers in the famous "Letter to a Physician" (probably written March or April 1734) to his science of human nature as worked out in the *Treatise*. As a result of his philosophical enthusiasm, Hume suffered in the period 1729–30 from a crisis of emotional and physical distress, which probably lasted until his departure for France in 1734 to write the *Treatise*. For Hume's own testimony of this period in his life see the 'Letter to a Physician' in *The Letters of David Hume*, ed. J. Y. T. Greig (Oxford: Clarendon Press, 1969), Vol. 1: 12–18. Greig identifies Dr. Cheyne as intended recipient of the letter, which Hume probably never sent. Mossner claimed in 1944 that he had overwhelming evidence to conclude that only Dr. Arbuthnot could be the addressee, a thesis recently challenged by John P. Wright (John P. Wright, "Dr. George Cheyne, Chevalier Ramsay, and Hume's *Letter to a Physician*," *Hume Studies* 29 (1) (2003): 125–141). On the significance of this letter for understanding Hume's early philosophical development, see M.A. Stewart, "Hume's Intellectual development," *Impressions of Hume*, ed. Marina Frasca-Spada and Peter Kail (Oxford: Clarendon Press, 2005). For more on the emergence of the 'new scene of thought' cf. Ernest C. Mossner, *The Life of David Hume* (Oxford: Clarendon Press, 1954, 1980), Ch. 6 & 7.

sceptical about the idea that philosophy could straightforwardly turn into a sort of therapy of desire. At first sight at least, the Newtonian science of human nature does not aim at wisdom, but has a strictly theoretical goal: to understand human nature, including the role of the emotions in human life.

Recently however, some have claimed that Hume is nonetheless fundamentally in line with a more classical conception of philosophy.[6] In the tradition of Socrates, he was convinced that his philosophy, in so far as it leads to a better understanding of human nature, also contributes to the good life, which implies a life in harmony with the findings of the science of human nature (T, 3.3.6; EPM, 9.14–15).[7] Penelhum qualifies Hume's philosophical intentions as follows: "I see Hume as a philosopher who is squarely in the Socratic tradition. He is in the Socratic tradition because he sees philosophy a s a source of liberating self-knowledge".[8] And, according to Don Garrett, Hume "was concerned above all with virtue, with understanding it and cultivating it" and "of all the virtues, perhaps none concerned him more than the specifically cognitive virtue of wisdom".[9] Could one say that this intention forms a major *Leitmotiv*, not only through his strictly philosophical works, but also his more literary essays? I think so. But if this is the case, it becomes apparent that, for Hume, philosophical activity – the 'doing of philosophy'– should, in one way or another, lead to the moderation and taming of the emotions, in line with a classical conception of philosophy as the 'search for wisdom'.

---

6 See Annette C. Baier, *A Progress of Sentiments. Reflections on Hume's Treatise* (Cambridge, Mass. & London: Harvard University Press, 1991); Donald, Livingston, *Philosophical Melancholy and Delirium: Hume's Pathology of Philosophy*, (Chicago and London: University of Chicago Press, 1998); Terence Penelhum, *Themes in Hume: the Self, the Will, Religion* (Oxford: Clarendon Press, 2000). From Penelhum I derive the characterize of Hume as a Socratic thinker. For some critical notices on Penelhum's thesis, cf. Donald Ainslie, "Hume, a Scottish Socrates?" *Canadian Journal of Philosophy* 33 (1) (2003): 133–154.

7 I refer further in the text to the following editions of Hume's works with abbreviations: *A Treatise of Human Nature*, eds. David F. Norton and Mary J. Norton (Oxford/New York: Oxford University Press, 2000) [T]; *An Enquiry concerning Human Understanding*, ed. Tom Beauchamp (Oxford/New York: Clarendon/Oxford University Press, 2000) [EHU]; *An Enquiry concerning the Principles of Morals*, ed. Tom Beauchamp (Oxford/New York: Clarendon/Oxford University Press, 1998) [EPM]; *Essays, Moral, Political, Literary*, ed. By Eugene F. Miller (Indianapolis: Liberty Classics, 1985) [EMPL]; *Dialogues concerning Natural Religion*, ed. Stanley Tweyman (London/New York: Routledge, 1991) [DNR]; "Of the Passions", in *Four Dissertations*, introduction by John Immerwahr, reprint of the 1757 edition (Bristol: Thoemess Press, 1995) [OP].

8 Penelhum, 2000: vii.

9 Don Garrett, *Cognition and Commitment in Hume's* Treatise (Oxford/New York: Oxford University Press, 1997): 6.

One can hardly ignore the fact that Hume, in various places in his philosophical and essayistic works, propagates philosophy as a very special activity which yields a refined sort of happiness ("a delicate pleasure") that blesses the soul of the philosopher (T, 1.4.7.12). However, Hume considers such a salvation-through-philosophy to be a much more ambiguous good than Spinoza does. Only under proper conditions does philosophical activity yield a specific contemplative attitude and calm, which could be identified as a 'Humean' form of wisdom. In what follows, I point out what should be understood by this wisdom and how it differs from Spinoza's view on philosophical wisdom. At the same time, I try to uncover the common ground in the views of both of these major modern philosophers, on the relation between philosophy and the moderation of the passions in their search for wisdom.

1. Spinoza and the Search for Wisdom

The idea that the new philosophy should be identified with a deliberate search for wisdom had been at the center of Spinoza's thinking from an early stage. In the opening of the *Tractatus de Intellectus Emendatione*, he speaks in the voice of an imaginary philosophical everyman:

> After experience had taught me that all the things which regularly occur in ordinary life are empty and futile, and I saw that all the things which were the cause or object of my fear had nothing of good or bad in themselves, except insofar as [my] mind was moved by them, I resolved at last to try to find out whether there was anything which would be the true good, capable of communicating itself, and which alone would affect the mind, all others being rejected – whether there was something which, once found and acquired, would continuously give me the greatest joy, to eternity (TIE, 1).[10]

Spinoza further specifies the gloomy mood of the would-be philosopher. Ordinary life is 'empty and futile', because it is determined by external goods which disturb the mind and awaken the emotions. These goods are: sensual pleasure, wealth and honor. In striving for them, the vanity of the human condition finds its origin – of sensual appetite, the desire for wealth and a too self-conscious searching for recognition – which blind the mind and render it incapable of

---

[10] References are based on the Curley translation, who takes over the older reference system of paragraphs numbered in brackets. I use the Curley translation as it is integrated in De Dijn, 1996.

thinking of any further good (TIE, 3).[11] This blindness makes the self a slave to its emotions, particularly in its deep "love of those things that can perish" (TIE, 9). The striving for recognition (or honor) is particulary likely to yield sorrow, for here man makes himself the prey not only of his own emotions, but of the emotions of the other as well (TIE, 5).

Is there no other good that touches the soul and makes it possible for man to transcend this condition of blindness? In the *Tractatus*, Spinoza enigmatically identifies the highest good man can attain as "the knowledge of the union that the mind has with the whole of nature" (TIE, 13). Spinoza's philosophy can now be understood as the elucidation of the way in which this good (this 'union') can be achieved, and the exposure of philosophy's role in this process. Philosophical activity, as Spinoza points out in the *Tractatus*, is itself the 'true good' which leads (as the 'way' or 'method') to the highest good, which is a goal in itself, and should be considered as the attainment of wisdom. The striving to attain the highest good infuses the mind gradually "with a love toward the eternal and infinite" and "feeds the mind with a joy entirely exempt from sadness" (TIE, 10). The achievement of wisdom, "together with other individuals if possible," thus consists of a union with the infinite in and through the experience of a specific joy and love.

It is striking how Spinoza, already in his *Tractatus*, defines the state of blessedness in terms of a theory of the emotions (or affects), which will later be elaborated in the *Ethics*. There, 'joy exempt from sadness' is identified as an elation of the mind interwoven with the knowledge of God as infinite substance. This knowledge is in turn the achievement of a long process of transformation of the passionate self. The 'everyman' in each mortal human being becomes a truly rational self, i.e., a self that has gained adequate knowledge of its own nature and its relation as a finite mode of the infinite substance. In this process, as Spinoza points out in Parts 3 and 4 of the *Ethics*, the affects (emblematic of the immersion of human existence in its bodily and temporal condition) are transformed from passive and troublesome conceptions of the imagination into active emotions or appraisals of the thinking activity of the self. How should this process be understood? And why does it lead to such a sustained joy and love, which can only be compared with a state of blessedness?

---

11 Cf.: "Nam affectûs, quibus quotidue conlactamur, referentur plerumque ad aliquam Corporis partem, quae prae reliquis afficitur, ac proinde affectûs ut plurimum excessum habent, et Mentem in solâ unius objecti contemplatione ità detinent, ut de aliis cogiatre nequeat..." (E 4, P44, Schol). ["For the emotions by which we are harassed every day are for the most part related to some part of the body which is affected more than the rest of its parts. Accordingly, the emotions are for the most part excessive and detain the mind in the sole contemplation of one object in such a way that it cannot think of other things" (translation by G. H. R. Parkinson, 2000: 259)].

2. Conatus, Emotions, Reason

It is impossible to reconstruct Spinoza's complex conception of the emotions and his therapy of desire 'modern style' in a few paragraphs. But a rough sketch brings out the following picture.[12] For Spinoza, man is a thinking, embodied being who strives to persevere in its existence, just like any natural being. As small particles in the 'great chain of being', humans are immersed in the causal order of Nature, which infinitely transcends the power and scope of their finite mode. In what sounds like a naturalised version of man's Fall, he seems to say that human beings are moreover condemned to persevere in existence in a conscious, self-reflexive way. Man is able, in short, to see his own fragility – and the struggle to consciously overcome it becomes part of his conditon. Spinoza discerns as the principle of this simultaneously corporeal and conscious striving the *conatus* (E3, P9). In fact, *conatus*, at the level of the mind, is nothing but the consciousness of the striving of the body.[13] As far as it is conscious, Spinoza points out, the *conatus* is experienced as desire (*cupiditas*). To maintain the existence of the self as finite mode (or concrete existence) is now the underlying principle of the *conatus*, but as far as it is conscious striving, this desire yields a very specific relation of humans to the world. At this point, the importance of the emotions (or affects) for Spinozistic anthropology becomes apparent.

In a modern idiom, one could say that Spinoza defends a cognitive view of the emotions. Emotions (affects) are conceived in the *Ethics* as judgements, which express an evaluation of the specific relation of an external object (a thing, another being, a happening) to the self.[14] The mind judges through the emotions, by a conception of the imagination, whether the body is affected in its existence, in a positive or negative manner, by all sorts of changes and fluctuations in the surrounding world (E3, Def. 3, post. 1). Man's emotional life is thus fundamentally structured around the basic emotions of joy (*laetitia*) and sadness (*tristitia*), from which all other emotions are derived. Joy, as far as it signals an increase of power, is experienced as a change towards greater activity and self-reliance of the self (a "state of greater perfection," says Spinoza), whereby the self gains a certain mastery over the world and itself. Sadness, on the other hand, as a change towards greater passivity, implies a sort of consciousness of the immersion of the

---

12 For an illuminating exposition of Spinoza's theory of the emotions, see Susan James, *Passion and Action: the Emotions in Seventeenth-Century Philosophy* (Oxford: Clarendon Press, 1997).
13 For Spinoza the union of body and soul is intrinsic for the concrete existence of the self. This self is not conceivable as a mode who longs to transcend its 'low' bodily state, so as to realise a more real 'high' spiritual nature. 'High' and 'low', 'perfect' and 'imperfect' are categories which have no meaning anymore in the new, mechanistic philosophy (E IV, *Praefatio*).
14 Nico H. Frijda, "Spinoza and Current Theory of Emotion", in *Desire and Affect: Spinoza as Psychologist*, ed. Yirmiyahu Yovel (New York: Litlle Room Press, 1999).

self in the causal nexus of Nature ("a lesser perfection") (E3, P11, Sch.). When overwhelmed by sadness, its loss of power strikes the mind as painful.

The status of the emotions appears now, in the Spinozistic universe, as fundamentally ambiguous. On the one hand, emotions yield a specific knowledge of the world and turn out to have positive effects: they help to maintain the self in its existence, by increasing its active power (e.g., through joy and love) or indicating possible threats to it (e.g., through fear or hate). Spinoza at this point indicates that emotions always imply a certain active conception on the part of the self: they are not merely blind reactions, but cognitively mediated apperceptions of the surrounding world.[15] The knowledge vouchsafed by the emotions is, however, always imperfect or 'inadequate' – it is, in terms of the *Ethics*, 'knowledge of the first kind', which manifests itself as experience based on ideas of the imagination. Through the imagination, the mind forms the inadequate ideas which are the evaluative correlates of the bodily reactions of the self towards an external object or cause. Moreover, due to the particular stance of the self as a desiring mode (with its own temperament, character and life-history) the cognitive information of the emotions derived from this causal relation is always more or less distorted and biased (e.g., in the case of passionate love or jealousy).

Spinoza thus stresses that emotions are in a fundamental sense a sign, so to speak, of man's immersion in nature. In their natural *statica* and *dynamica*, they appear as a source of instability and inconstancy in human life (E4, P1–18). As the *Tractatus* has already shown, when they remain unchecked, emotions condemn humans to a state of "sickness unto death."[16] In a comment on the observation that the dynamics of the primary emotions of joy and sadness make the mind vacillate, Spinoza says in the *Ethics*: "It is evident from what I have said, that we are in many ways driven about by external causes, and that like waves of the sea driven by contrary winds we toss to and fro unwitting of the issue and of our fate" (E3, P59, Sch.). The whole of *Ethics*, Part 3 thus reads as an exposition of the mechanisms and principles which cause this stormy turbulence in man's passionate life. Spinoza especially draws attention to what one could call the infectious nature of the emotions. When in the grip of passionate love, the mind turns easily to jealousy etc., and this infection in turn has deep intersubjective roots. Spinoza also indicates at this point the often disastrous consequences of man's imitative nature and the mimetic desires caused thereby (cf. E4, App. 13): envy, disparagement, undue pride, self-abasement, and emulation exemplify the wretched condition caused by this mimetic principle (E3, P59, Sch.).

Contrary to Descartes and the Stoics, Spinoza thought man would never be able to gain through reason a strict, cognitive mastery of his own nature: "Hence

---

15 James, 1997: 149.
16 "For I saw that I was in the greatest danger... like a man suffering from a fatal illness, who, foreseeing certain death unless he employs a remedy, is forced to seek it, however uncertain, with all his strength" (TIE, 7).

it follows, that man is necessarily always a prey to his emotions, that he follows and obeys the general order of nature, and that he accommodates himself thereto, as much as the nature of things demands" (E4, P4, Corr.). On the other hand, insofar as the self consciously recognises its nature as a striving being, it is in principle able to transcend the bondage of its own nature, to a certain degree. Radical detachment from our emotions may not be achievable, but it should be possible at least to counter their destructive tendencies in a specific way. Here Spinoza's rationalistic preoccupations become apparent and the Stoic undertone of the Spinozistic 'therapy of desire' in part 4 and 5 of the *Ethics* is readily apparent. It is through reason, or more specifically, through the careful following of the 'way of the philosopher' that man can reach a state of freedom and sustained detachment of his or her immersion in his or her own passionate nature.

One should notice here the specific impact of Spinoza's a-teleological and mechanistic view on nature, especially human nature. Though he denies the intelligibility of an Aristotelian *entelecheia*, Spinoza still defends the idea that human beings live more according to their 'own nature' when they follow reason. But what can it mean to live according to human nature within the Spinozistic universe? One discerns at this level a certain tension in Spinoza's metaphysics, which encompasses the whole of his *Ethics*. On the one hand, Spinoza defines human beings as individuated *modi* which, by their specific *conatus* or particular passionate make-up, have desires, make life-plans, develop an identity and possess other typically human concerns. Through the grip of the affections and imagination, the mind unavoidably forms an anthropomorphic conception of man's existential condition. On the other hand, from the philosophical point of view, human beings are – as finite modes – manifestations of Nature 'at large', or the Substance, which has no teleological structure. Nature *qua* substance is, in part 1 of the *Ethics*, identified as *causa sui* or God and is, as such, devoid of all antropomorphic qualities and qualifications. The core of Spinoza's 'way to wisdom' consists in the idea that true freedom for man implies reaching a point of view where the anthropomorphic *Sitz-im-Leben* is substituted by a rational (i.e., adequate) understanding of oneself as part of the Divine Substance. Moreover, this very 'shift' of the mind leads, according to Spinoza, to true happiness and eternal joy – however difficult it may be to attain it (and throughout life, this shift is never totally realised). Nevertheless, it is this trust in the liberating capacities of reason which makes Spinoza a particular sort of Stoic. Hume, as will become clear, will take a position which is much more ambiguous about the force of reason and the place it can attain in human nature.

The rationalism of Spinoza – his trust in reason and in philosophy as the way to wisdom – remains, however, a peculiar one, compared with that of Descartes or Leibniz. The scientific understanding of human nature is, within the Spinozistic approach, not the end-point of the way to wisdom, but only the necessary bridge towards the *scientia intuitiva*, in which true philosophy culminates. As is well known, in the *Ethics,* Spinoza distinguishes this *scientia intuitiva* from mere reason: he calls the former the "third kind" and the latter the "second kind" of knowledge. The exploration of the way through which the finite mode 'man' transforms himself from a merely affectionate and anxiety-ridden animal, into a free and thinking part of the divine susbtance is the purpose of the Spinozistic *medicina mentis*. How should we conceive of this process? Why has philosophy such a privileged role to play in it?

For Spinoza, thinking is activity. The conscious deployment of the *conatus* as reason (or *intellectus*) deploys an increasing power of the self, insofar as the mind is able to grasp things in their true causal order and necessity. In fact, reason is the *conatus* becoming purely conscious and active, for here the mind is its own cause, not hindered or rendered passive by external causes. From this conception, Spinoza derives his view of the way philosophy or the cultivation of reason helps to master, or at least discipline, the emotions. This relative mastery consists in the integration of specific affects in the pure activity of reason, causing especially a joy which is no longer experienced as rendering the self passive. Joy thus becomes an active emotion, the affective expression, so to speak, of the successful activity of reason as such.

This fusion of affect and philosophical insight, however, asks for a careful deployment of the thinking capacities of the mind. Spinoza discerns two stages in the unfolding of the sustainable joy of the philosopher and the reaching of the *scientia intuitiva* which this joy exemplifies.

3. From knowledge to salvation

During the first stage of this process, as part 4 of the *Ethics* shows, the mind discovers how reason can become a constructive force through which the understanding gains insight into the mechanisms and principles underlying the emotions. This understanding already causes a sort of joy, for it implies a change towards perfection by which the grip of the passions and the imagination on the human mind are disentangled. The perfection of reason thus enables the self to preserve its existence as an active being by turning, so to speak, emotions on emotions (or affections on passions), in a sort of homeopathic healing process. Reason is the instrument that provides the precepts to start this process of self-transformation and modifies it as it goes along: but it is also the mode wherein the *conatus* reveals itself as conscious power (or desire to know). In other words, the mind (of the philosopher) recognises that through the perfection of reason its *conatus* perseveres in its existence in a manner which is most adapted to the human condition.[17]

---

17 For the particular significance of this transformation of the *conatus* 'merely' to the *conatus intelligendi* at E4, P26, see Yirmiyahu Yovel, "Transcending Mere Survival: from *Conatus* to *Conatus Intelligendi*," in *Desire and Affect: Spinoza as Psychologist*, ed. Yirmiyahu Yovel (New York: Little Room Press, 1999).

One of the things reason reveals to the mind of the philosopher is the way in which we achieve a certain control of our emotions through the development of a prudential ethics. In Part 4 of the *Ethics,* Spinoza defends the idea that virtue consists in the perfection of the striving for self-preservation by making reason into an instrumental guide. He says: "To act absolutely in obedience to virtue is in us the same thing as to act, to live, or to preserve one's being (these three terms are identical in meaning) in accordance with the dictates of reason on the basis of seeking what is useful to one's self" (E4, P24). At the same time, this instrumentalisation of reason implies the positive enhancement of the conscious *conatus* or desire (*cupiditas*), whereby the mind increases its power and self-reliance.

The deployment of an enlightened self-interest generates a significant shift in the self-understanding of human beings, which goes beyond the 'instrumental' control of the emotions.[18] For as far as it gains an increasingly adequate knowledge of the emotions and their workings, the mind distances itself necessarily from the 'sound and fury' caused by the external intrusions of the world. The mind thus reaches already a certain state of inner satisfaction and constancy, overcoming its passivity. Seeing the causes of its previous, deplorable condition, the philosopher becomes himself or herself an active factor in the steering of his or her desires and in the transformation of his or her passions.

In *Ethics*, part 4, Spinoza points to several aspects of this perfection of reason – which is, after all, nothing but the cultivation of virtue or the knowledge of 'good' and 'evil'. He shows, for example, how the mind can learn to calculate its long-term interest, and thus counterbalance strong but irrational emotions with more moderate and finely-tuned ones; how the mind is able to grasp specific rational precepts (*dictamina rationes*), which offer an insight in the nature and structuring principles of the emotions (E4, P19–37); and, finally, how true adequate knowledge of man's nature intrinsically depends on the knowledge of God or nature as substance.

This last aspect brings us to the heart of Spinoza's conception of philosophy as a search for wisdom, or the attainment of the *scientia intuitiva*. It appears that the conscious adaptation of the ethics of self-preservation, and the cultivation of adequate knowledge about the emotions and man's nature through reason, form a necessary, but not a sufficient, condition to actually reach the state of wisdom or blessedness at which the true philosopher aims. Why, one could ask, should the ethics of self-preservation and cognitive self-mastery (developed as far as possible) be integrated in an intuitive science of the ultimate 'things' – God, nature, the absolute?[19] Why

---

18 See De Dijn, 1996: 247–252.
19 The answer to these questions is still an object of considerable contention among specialists. I follow here in general the interpretation by De Dijn, 1996 and Theo Zweerman, *L'introduction à la philosophie selon Spinoza: une analyse structurelle de l'introduction du traité de la réforme de l'entendement, suivie d'un commentaire de ce texte* (Leuven: Presses Universitaires de Louvain, 1993).

can true wisdom or blessedness, according to Spinoza, only be achieved through a leap from merely adequate knowledge to real intuitive insight? Spinoza is firm about this, but the exact status and meaning of intuitive knowledge for his conception of wisdom remains an object of considerable contention.[20]

To elucidate this complicated matter at least a bit, one could start with Spinoza's own remark that the increased insight into human nature through abstract reasoning may foster the conditions for virtue and freedom, but that this empowering of reason also awakens all sorts of disturbances and new emotions in the mind of the philosopher. The satisfaction gained by the development of scientific knowledge is, in short, in a fundamental sense, unstable, and the alleged mastery of man's nature through reason at this stage clearly unreliable. The joy of the philosopher who stays at the level of mere abstract, scientific knowledge remains ambiguous after all. With an allusion to Ecclesiastes, Spinoza says in part 4 of the *Ethics*: "he who increases knowledge increases sorrow" (E4, P17, sch.).[21] In other words, the mind may gain strength, at least for a little while, through the cultivation of reason and can thereby experience a specific joy. However, this activity of reason may rapidly turn into sadness, when the self recognises that it remains, as before, a still 'all-too-human' part of nature. There remains, so to speak, a gap between the insight of reason – the relative control this knowledge of the second kind yields – and the concrete experience of the philosophical mind, searching for salvation as a particular thinking mind.

In *Ethics*, Part 5, Spinoza shows how the mind can reach an ultimate state of blessedness by transcending a merely abstract, general knowledge of human nature, and the place of the emotions in human existence. This ascension to a higher state of knowledge requires the activation of an idea that every human being naturally possesses, but which remains hidden to most men because of their passionate and unstable '*Sitz-im-Leben*'. Already in Part 2 of the *Ethics*, it was shown how man naturally has "an adequate knowledge of the eternal and infinite essence of God" (E3, P47). It is from the idea of the necessity and unity of the one substance that the mind derives its adequate knowledge of the whole of Nature and of the relation between Nature and its myriad modifications, among which are the concrete finite *modi* of 'human beings'. More specifically, the thinking mind reveals to itself, in the perfection of its own *conatus* as *conatus intelligendi*, how it is itself a small, fragile particle of this one substance. As a concrete, embodied being, the self contemplates itself, its emotions and its knowledge of itself in the light of the infinite knowledge and power which is God.

---

20 De Dijn 1996: 253–261; Aaron V. Garret, *Meaning in Spinoza's Method* (Cambridge: Cambridge University Press, 2003): 181–223. Cf. also: Herman De Dijn, "Theory and practice and the practice of theory," in *Ethik, Recht und Politik bei Spinoza*, ed. Marcel Senn and Manfred Walther (Zurich: Schulthess, 2001).
21 Cf. *Eccles.*: 1:18.

Ethics, Part 5, reveals how this contemplative exercise can be integrated into and become part of concrete strategies which aim at a transformation of the emotions from mere passive happenings to active states of mind. Knowledge of one's own particularity merges with knowledge of the absolute and yields a love and joy that overcomes the 'sickness unto death'. In reaching a simultaneously active and concrete state of sustained wisdom, the mind sees the profound unity between its nature, virtue and God. Or, so says Spinoza, in this pure thinking activity, the mind sees itself "accompanied by the idea of God as cause" (E5, P36, Dem.). This intuitive apprehension forms such an empowering of the *conatus*, that the self sees itself *sub specie aeternitatis*, i.e., as emanation of the formidable power and extension of God (or Nature).

It is this capacity to see the infinite in the finite *modus* of a concrete thinking being that yields the specific wisdom of the *scientia intuitiva*. This apprehension is the highest wisdom human beings can reach and should strive for.[22] The unfolding of this intuitive science illuminates, in other words, the particular mind of the philosopher in search of wisdom: it is a process which is at the same time cognitive and affective.[23] It is cognitive because this intuitive science forms the culmination of reason by yielding adequate knowledge of human nature. It is affective because through the unpacking of adequate knowledge, the thinking mind experiences its own *conatus* as sheer self-fortifying activity: an experience, which from the very structure of human nature, triggers certain affective states. However, in contrast to the haphazard fluctuations and 'tossing' of the emotions in common life, the thinking activity finds a sustainable expression of the *conatus* in such active and stable emotions as intellectual love and joy.[24]

How should this interwoveness of love and joy be understood? Because of its active, self-fortifying character, the activity of (adequate) thinking causes joy, a joy that even transcends, in a way, the finiteness of the self. In bringing the activity of thinking to perfection (through the *scientia intuitiva*), the mind of the philosopher participates in the infinite attribute of the thinking of God or the Substance, which is nothing but a formidable way of empowering of the *conatus*. This joy thus automatically fuses with the contemplation of the cause which yields this joy: God. And in participating in the Divine thinking, the mind is totally active, which makes the *Amor Dei intellectualis* into an active emotion or state of mind (E5, P32). Indeed, the overcoming of finitude by humans has a paradoxical nature and is never wholly realised. It implies a transcendence of human existence as finite mode from the point of view of the absolute (the substance or God as *causa sui*). However, infinity is here a modality of experience situated

---

22 Spinoza was influenced on this point by Maimonides in Stephen Nadler, *Spinoza. A Life* (Cambridge: Cambridge University Press, 1999).
23 Cf. for this: Herman De Dijn, *Modernité et Tradition: Essais sur l'entre-deux* (Leuven: Peeters/Vrin, 2004): 35 e.v.
24 See also: A. Garrett, 2003: 192.

within the finite life of the self, not a leap to another order of existence. But as far as it yields a pure joy, this ultimate state of wisdom means a true liberation from the bondage of the emotions and a transformation of the melancholy from which the philosopher longs to be released.

4. Hume on reason and 'the medecine of the mind'

The idea that the practice of philosophy could yield a salvation (*beatitudo*) which transcends human finitude sounds implausible and even absurd to a Humean philosopher. Even the more humble view that one could be cured from melancholy through the search for wisdom and in so doing attain virtue, remains questionable from the perspective of Hume's philosophy. The key for a better understanding of the difference between Hume and Spinoza on this point is found in their divergent views on the place of reason in human nature. Where, as we have seen, Spinoza in a certain sense sticks to the Stoic-like ideal of the life of reason as being that which is most in accordance with human nature, for Hume this ideal means ultimately that one chooses a way which is unnatural for man.

This sceptical appreciation of reason is fundamental to Hume, from his very first steps as a philosopher, as *A Treatise of Human Nature* testifies. To be sure, in the course of his youthful masterwork this scepticism becomes more moderate, or less pyrrhonic, as Hume's philosophical system 'progresses'.[25] And it is this moderate or academic scepticism that obtains pride of place in Hume's later philosophy. As becomes apparent in both the *Enquiries* and the *Dialogues concerning Natural Religion*, Hume believes that the steady cultivation of philosophy should remain in balance with common life. If philosophy becomes too detached, it will cause, rather than dissolve, melancholy and despair (D: 183–185). If salvation from melancholy by 'the philosophical act' can reasonably be expected, the philosopher will therefore have to develop a certain diffidence towards his own search for wisdom.[26] Compared to Spinoza's rationalistic naturalism, Hume's empiricist and antimetaphysical naturalism reveals a quite divergent conception of philosophy as a therapy of desire.

In the well-known essay "The Sceptic", published a year after the *Treatise*, Hume significantly remarks that "the medecine of the mind, so much boasted" remains an ambiguous issue, certainly for the bulk of mankind, but even for the philosophically minded élite.[27] The literary rhetoric and context of this essay –

---

25 Baier, 1991.
26 Hume's conception of 'doing of philosophy' is characterised by Livingston as 'the philosophical act' (Livingston, 1998).
27 It is possible that Hume had Spinoza in mind when referring to the 'medicine of the mind'. In his *Medicina mentis* Tschirnhaus was obviously influenced by Spinoza, who uses himself the medicinal metaphor for philosophy in his *Tractatus de Intellectus Emendatione*. See also De Dijn, 1996: 13.

published together with 3 others, entitled respectively, "The Epicurean", "The Stoic" and the "Platonist"– makes it somewhat unclear what Hume's own views on the role of philosophy in moderating the passions exactly are, in either in "The Sceptic" or the other essays. Obviously, however, in "The Sceptic" Hume gives voice to a certain diffidence towards the ideal of the classical philosophical sage, which is in line with the *Treatise*. Here, as in later works, he holds firm to his *scepsis* towards philosophy as a sure guide to wisdom and the liberation of the vicissitudes of common life. Most people, Hume argues in "The Sceptic", are excluded from all "pretensions to philosophy" and are unable even to wish to alter their passionate nature through the cultivation of reason (EMPL: 168–169). The emotions may be a source of suffering, but at the same time they are the flesh and bone out of which each persons particular character is made. Therefore, any "[r]easonings concerning human life and the methods of attaining happiness" are radically constrained by human nature itself, for "[a]lmost every one has a predominant inclination, to which his other desires and affections submit, and which governs him, though, perhaps, with some intervals, through the whole course of his life" (EMPL: 160). Only in vain could one think that philosophy could change substantially this inclination of the self. Therefore, one shouldn't place overly high expectations in it as a *medicina mentis*.

Hume thus takes a quite divergent stance towards the 'sickness of the mind', which is, according to Spinoza in the *Tractatus de Intellectus Emendatione*, an all too obvious consequence of the grip of the passions on human life. However, Hume admits, in line with Spinoza, that some rare minds have an inclination to philosophy. For them, the cultivation of reason seems an appropriate means to transcend their passionate nature. But even "with regard to these too", Hume adds, "the authority [of philosophy] is very weak and limited" (EMPL: 161). Even when cultivated with the utmost "art and industry", Hume contends, the search for wisdom can fall short of its ultimate goal. To be receptive to virtue, and to desire to obtain it through the cultivation of reason, is a valuable thing (EMPL: 169). But a too obsessive devotion to study and contemplation may sour the temper and yield contrary effects. This last fact Hume had already learned as a young man from personal experience, as I mentioned already.[28] Hume discerns a paradox here. On the one hand, the reflections of philosophy are usually "too subtle and distant to take place in common life, or eradicate any affection". On the other hand, when succesful, these reflections may yield an unhealthy *apatheia*. Incessant study and meditation often spreads "an universal insensibility over the mind" and plunges the self into a state of mild schizophrenia: the thinking self becomes estranged from its bodily endowment and everyday affective life (EMPL: 172-3). Remarkably, Hume, already in the essay "The Stoic", defends the idea, given voice by an imaginary Stoic sage, that "in this sullen Apathy, neither true wisdom nor true happiness can be found" (EMPL: 151).

---

28 See supra, note 5.

Nowhere did Hume point out the fatal consequences of an overly enthusiastic application of the mind to thinking with more bravura than in the closing section of the *Treatise*, Book 1. In sharp contrast with Spinoza and seventeenth century rationalism in general, Hume here shows himself to be sceptical about reason, and thus about philosophy as an autonomous, self-fortifying activity.[29] After having revealed that our most fundamental beliefs about causality, world and self are unwarranted, Hume concludes without reservation that reason is unreliable: "[T]he understanding, when it acts alone, and according to its most general principles, entirely subverts itself, and leaves not the lowest degree of evidence in any proposition, either in philosophy or in common life" (T, 1.4.7.7). The nexus of beliefs on which human understanding is built appears to be ill-structured and even contradictory in its very nature.

The subversive consequences of Hume's anti-metaphysical epistemology are clear. Any reliance on a fixed, absolute point of view (a 'view from nowhere') as the ground of science (Descartes' *cogito*, Spinoza's *Deus sive substantia*) is dismissed as illusory.[30] Hume explains his doubt about the philosophical enterprise conceived along these foundationalist lines in a sharp tone:

> For with what confidence can I venture upon such bold enterprizes, when beside those numberless infirmities peculiar to myself, I find so many which are common to human nature? Can I be sure, that in leaving all establish'd opinion I am following truth; and by what criterion shall I distinguish her, even if fortune shou'd at last guide me on her foot-steps? After the most accurate and exact of my reasonings, I can give no reason why I shou'd assent to it... (T, 1.4.7.3).

The confidence of Spinoza's everyman is here turned upside-down.

The empire of philosophy becomes, at this stage of Humean scepticism, an extremely inhospitable place. In what sounds like an inversion of Spinoza's image of man tossed back and forth on the sea of passions, Hume pities himself for having followed reason too enthusiastically: "Methinks I am like a man, who having struck on many shoals, and having narrowly escap'd shipwreck in passing a small frith, has yet the temerity to put out to sea in the same leaky weather-

---

29 According to Donald Livingston, this conception of philosophy as an 'autonomous' activity is for Hume a characteristic of 'false' philosophy. See Livingston, 1998, Ch. 6.
30 According to De Dijn, the dismissal of the idea of a Cartesian *scientia* forms for Hume the background for his antifoundational and nonreductionistic 'philosophical anthropology' (Herman De Dijn, "Hume's nonreductionist Philosophical Anthropology," *The Review of Metaphysics* 56 (2003): 587–603). Also, in the interpretation by Annette Baier, Hume's 'broad' conception of philosophy is presented as anti-foundationalist in character. However, Baier sees in Hume's science of human nature (as given shape in the *Treatise*) more an anticipation of Marx, Darwin, Freud and Foucault (Baier 1991: 25).

beaten vessel" (T, 1.4.7.1). Further on, the collapse of reason is openly identified as the cause of a sort of emotional breakdown:

> The intense view of these manifold contradictions and imperfections in human reason has so wrought upon me, and heated my brain, that I am ready to reject all belief and reasoning, and can look upon no opinion even as more probable or likely than another. Where am I, or what? From what causes do I derive my existence, and to what condition shall I return? What beings surround me? ...I am confounded with all these questions, and begin to fancy myself in the most deplorable condition imaginable, inviron'd with the deepest darkness (T, 1.4.7.8).

Even by his friends, the philosopher is considered a strange 'monster', cut of from all normal human interaction.

However, as is well known, Hume never gives a sustained scepticism the last word. At the moment of the deepest vertigo, a remarkable shift of mind cures it of this "philosophical melancholy and delirium" (T, 1.4.7.9). Through a sort of over-saturation, the obsessive desire for intellectual certainty is suddenly silenced, and the philosopher is chased from his closet and forced to return to the world. The catharsis sketched in the closing section of the *Treatise*, Book 1, is remarkable. The philosopher leaves his room, he dines, he plays back-gammon with his friends and will only return to his study when he finds himself in a more detached and relaxed mood. In the shift from Book 1 to Book 2 and 3 of the *Treatise*, the reader sees Hume not so much abandon the practice of philosophy, as modify the expectations one can reasonably gain from the satisfaction of one's philosophical curiosity. When one accepts the limits of human understanding and the lack of foundations for reason as such, radical scepticism is freed from its fatal character and appears even 'futile'.[31] The philosophical mind finds a renewed energy to apply itself to the study of the very sphere which saves human beings from a radical scepticism: common life itself.[32]

Hume turns to the study of this common life in the rest of his *Treatise*, and in all of his later works. The skillful exploration of human nature, as it emerges "in men's behaviour in company, in affairs, and in their pleasures" becomes now his chief object of study (T, Intro, 10). And when the philoso-

---

31 For this characterization of Hume's scepticism as 'futile', see Patricia De Martelaere, "Hume over kennis: van scepticisme tot naturalisme", in *David Hume. Filosoof van de menselijke natuur*, ed. P. De Martelaere and W. Lemmens (Kapellen/Kampen: Pelckmans/Agora, 2001).

32 The 'return' to a *sensus communis* as emblematic of Hume's philosophy of 'common life' is analysed in an original manner by Donald Livingston (see: Livingston, 1998: 383–407).

pher returns to the investigation of the understanding as such, as happens in the first sections of the first *Enquiry*, it will be in a more relaxed state of mind. From this perspective, it also becomes apparent that the 'inclination to philosophy' that we find in some rare minds has its merits. More specifically, in line with the classical view and with Spinoza's contention, Hume admits that the search for philosophical wisdom fosters virtue and moulds the emotions. This is how it sounds in "The Sceptic": "[A] serious attention to the sciences and liberal arts softens and humanizes the temper, and cherish those fine emotions, in which true virtue and honour consists" (EMPL: 170). Hume seems here to approach, to a certain degree, the ideal of the stoic sage, who manifests in the eponymous essay a more classical conception of wisdom: "the true philosopher" is called here the "man of virtue" who "governs his appetites, subdues his passions, and has learned, from reason, to set a just value on every pursuit and enjoyment" (EMPL: 148). How exactly to understand this merging of scepticism and stoicism is a problem all its own. However, if we take it as a sign of Hume's admission that the 'doing of philosophy' can have, under the proper conditions, a healing and liberating capacity, it is equally clear that in what the true philosophy reveals about human nature (and in particular about the emotions), as in what sort of wisdom it helps to establish, Humean wisdom diverges substantially from that of Spinoza's sage.

5. From Passions to Reason

The return to common life as the proper object of study for the new science of man reveals Hume's intellectual and philosophical commitment. This decision implies the acknowledgment by the philosopher of his own 'bent of mind' as a special source of pleasure – and thus worth pursuing. Here also, as with Spinoza, we see a sort of homeopathic principle at work. In other words, the philosophical attitude, which was in its initial enthusiastic outburst a cause of melancholy, transforms itself into a medium of healing, into a medicine of the mind. Part of this process of self-transformation relies precisely on the acceptance of a dimension in human nature which reason cannot wholly control, but which is, at the same time, constitutive of human nature as such: the passions or emotions.

But what does this acceptance imply exactly? Does its significance lie in the fortification of adequate knowledge of human nature, which necessarily yields the transformation of the passions into affections (or active forces of joy and love)? Or does Hume have another conception of the sort of wisdom philosophy should and could aim for, given his particular outlook of human nature? Let me first give a brief overview of the positive findings of Hume's anatomy of the passions. I will then take a closer look at the Humean conception of wisdom and how it is related to his way of 'doing philosophy'.

Hume delivers, in line with forerunners such as Hobbes and Spinoza, an account of the passions and affections that corroborates the new deterministic-mechanistic world view.[33] He identifies passions as reflective impressions, which should be distinguished from thoughts (beliefs) and purely bodily movements and thus have, as perceptions of the mind, a *sui generis* status. He also discerns a homeostatic principle at work in the affective realm of the human mind: the avoidance of pain and the continuation of pleasure, without which we would be incapable of "passion or action, of desire or volition" (T, 3.3.1.2). Hume offers no direct equivalent of Spinoza's *conatus* or Hobbes's 'endeavour' for self-preservation as an all-encompassing basic principle of the passionate life. Rather, he distinguishes more primitive passions and drives, which are innate and almost instinctive, from more complex passions or affections, which depend on previous experiences of pain and pleasure (T, 2.1.1 & 2).[34] Generally speaking, what Hume calls 'passions', would nowadays be called 'emotions'– although he uses this latter term as well, without distinguishing the two terms in a very consistent way.

Exemplary of the first sort of passions or drives are, according to Hume, bodily appetites as well as passions such as benevolence and the love of children. Among these primary passions, Hume reckons some additional ones with a specific phenomenological colour: the desire that enemies should be punished and friends should be happy, next to the love of life. The second sort of passions are instinctive only in a very general sense: they all derive from the principle of pain and pleasure. For their concrete manifestation, however, these passions depend on the affective and volitional structure of the self and on the way this self is situated in a world of natural, social and existential relations.[35] Within this last class of passions, Hume distinguishes the 'direct passions' such as grief and joy, fear and hope, from what he calls the 'indirect passions' of pride and humility, love and hate. Each of these passions forms a reflective evaluation of information yielded by the senses and the imagination. This reflective perception can rise up directly, as when a fearful object is felt to be

---

33 Whether Hume is defending a purely mechanistic view on the passions, or a more proto-Darwinian account, is still an object of contention. For a nuanced view on Hume's alleged Newtonianism cf: Jane McIntyre, "Hume: Second Newton of the Moral Sciences," *Hume Studies* 20(2)(1994): 3–18 and John P. Wright, *The Sceptical Realism of David Hume* (Manchester: Manchester University Press, 1983).

34 For an interesting account of the moral significance of this distinction between more instinctive and other passions in the *Treatise* cf. Jacqueline Taylor, "Justice and the Foundations of Social Morality in Hume's *Treatise*," *Hume Studies* 24 (1) (1998): 5–30 (esp. sections II & III).

35 For the importance of 'existential relations' in Hume's passion theory cf. Donald Ainslie, "Scepticism about Persons in Book II of Hume's *Treatise*," *Journal of the History of Philosophy* 37(3), (1999): 69–492.

threatening and the mind forms an idea of it, or more indirectly, as when a beautiful object (say a house) is seen as 'mine': then the passion of pride rises up as a complex association of ideas (of house and self) and impressions (of pleasure because of the beauty of the house and pride properly speaking). According to Hume, closely related to these latter passions are the moral sentiments, which also have a specific phenomenology, but cannot be conceived of as arising independently of pride and humility, love and hate.

In general, Hume introduces some observations in his passion theory which sound familiar to contemporary scholars of emotion theory, but also reveal some specific interpretative difficulties. Passions, understood as reflective perceptions of the mind, form an evaluative reaction to changes in body and mind, caused by some external cause (object, happening, another human being), which is experienced as painful or pleasurable (OP: 121). Mental occurences like grief or joy, fear or hope, for example, reflect information about the outer world yielded by the senses and by (ideas of) the imagination or understanding (T, 2.3.9). In collaboration with the more direct drives and desires, these passions thus structure the interaction of a bodily incarnated and conscious self within the world. Hume has largely been interpreted as the defender of a feeling-theory of passions (or emotions). In the *Treatise*, Book 2, he stresses the primitive character of the passions as reflective impressions and declares that they reveal their phenomenological colour by direct introspection. Pride, for example, is initially characterised as "a simple and uniform impression" of which it is impossible to give a definition "by a multitude of words." However, Hume admits, that to have a proper insight in this emotion, among others, it is necessary to reconstruct the circumstances which attend it (T, 2.1.2.1).

A careful reading of his theory of the passions (as developed in the *Treatise* and later in the dissertation "Of the Passions"), reveals how Hume can be interpreted as defending a view of the passions as complex and dynamic realities, which need to be understood from a functional perspective. Rather than blind mental occurences or self-contained feelings, the passions appear (in this charitable reconstruction of Humes *Treatise*, Book 2) as evaluative attitudes, which structure the relation of the self to the world in a unifying manner. Is Hume here in line with contemporary cognitivism in emotion theory, as defended by Robert Solomon, Robert de Sousa, and Martha Nussbaum, among others?[36] Many Hume scholars are perhaps unconvinced by this interpretation, but there are exceptions. Sympathising with the minority, I would say that Hume exemplifies the idea that emotions have a more or less appro-

---

36 Cf. Robert C. Solomon, *The Passions: Emotions and the Meaning of Life* (Indianapolis: Hackett, 1993), Martha Nussbaum, *Upheavals of Thought: The Intelligence of Emotions* (Cambridge: Cambridge University Press, 2001) and Ronald De Sousa, *The Rationality of Emotion* (Cambridge, Mass.: MIT Press, 1987).

priate judgemental content and intentionality, which can be more or less reasonable or appropriate to the circumstances.[37]

Hume's view of the role of the passions and emotions in human life is at first sight not at all tragic and pessimistic. Especially in the *Treatise* and "The Sceptic" he seems eager to point out how the self relies on the passions as constructive and necessary realities to empower its struggle to sustain its existence. Without the impulses of pride and love, for example, the self would not identify with things, meanings and persons it considers valuable, and would therefore not be driven by the "propense and averse motions of the mind", which derive from this evaluative involvement in the world (T, 2.2.4.4; 3.3.1.2). Hume stresses the 'contagious' character of the emotions and passions, and considers the mechanism of sympathy to be one of the chief regulating principles of human nature. However, where forebears like Hobbes and Spinoza see in this tendency of comparison (or *affectuum imitatio*, as Spinoza calls it), a sign of the dependence of the self on what it doesn't control, Hume welcomes the fact that minds are "like mirrors for each other", sympathetically responding to one another's emotions.[38]

Sympathy – the spontaneous tendency of the human mind to reflect the passions of others – is for Hume directly constitutive for the identity of the self, and the intercourse of sentiments and opinions in common life. However, one should not give a one-sided account of Hume's view on man's passionate and social nature. In line with more traditional philosophical conceptions of the passions, Hume is not blind to the destructive forces of selfishness and pride, jealousy and hate, avarice and ambition, fear and uncertainty, which are all, in general, the result of the principle of comparison (as a sort of inversion of sympathy) (T, 2.2.8.7–20; 3.3.2.5).

---

[37] Baier defends the view that Hume distinguishes between passions as complexes (or attitudes) and 'mere' emotions, which should be identified then as mental occurences with a strongly episodic character (Baier 1991: 160–170, 180–181). This distinction between attitude and feeling allows for a much richer interpretation of Hume's theory of the passions (esp. what I call here the evaluative passions), but I am not so sure whether one can so neatly identify and distinguish concepts like 'feeling', 'affection', 'emotion' and 'passion' from each other in Hume's account: he uses them all in a not very coherent way. I therefore abstract from Baier's distinction, though I follow in general her mild 'cognitive' view of Hume's account of the passions. Baier's view had before been defended by, among others, Alasdair MacIntyre, *Whose Justice? Which Rationality?* (Notre Dame: University of Notre Dame Press, 1988) and Donald Davidson, "Hume's Cognitive theory of Pride," in *Essays on Actions and Events* (Oxford: Oxford University Press, 1980).

[38] Cf. Spinoza, *Ethica*, III, Propositio 27, Scholium. For an example of Hobbes's view on the destructive character of 'comparison' in social life, cf. his observations on 'honour' throughout the *Leviathan*, esp. Part I.

Hume admits, as becomes apparent throughout the *Treatise*, that there is a constitutive role of reason in moderating the passions, especially by the establishment of morals and politics. This rehabilitation of reason throughout Hume's *Treatise* is often underestimated in the literature, but can hardly be ignored.[39] Of course, reason, this "wonderful instinct" which makes man "an inventive species" and remarkably superior to beasts (T, 3.3.4.5), is not the source of an absolutely adequate knowledge that makes us love the Good or God, or helps us to radically transcend our finite nature. Reason, as a naturalised instance of the relation between mind and world, should be considered rather, in Hume's empiricism, as a constructive force which has no sovereign authority.

At the most basic level, Humean reason is a function of the imagination and the passions, and is in the first instance an instrumental slave which yields information about the world and means-end relations to obtain specific goals and desires (T, 1.4.1.3; 2.3.3.2; 3.1.1). On a more structural level, Hume defends the idea that the moulding of the passions and emotions, through education and custom, creates a stability of character in the self which is generally interpreted in common life as a 'determination of reason' (T, 2.3.3.9–10). From a philosophical point of view, this general calmness of the passions and emotions cannot be identified as reason in the strict sense of the term. But the observation confirms that, in common life, passions can be more or less integrated into the character of the self, and thus be considered more or less reasonable. In short, the calmness of the passions should be identified as a sign of the reasonableness of the virtuous self.

One could also discern a socio-historical dimension of reason in Hume's exposition of morals in the *Treatise*, Book 3. 'Reason' emerges here as a capacity for judgment and contrivance, at work in the general rules and precepts of the conventions through which society is given shape and is sustained.[40] Here, Hume's account of artificial morality (justice, promises, and government) appears as the background for a more institutional taming and moulding of the passions, which contributes to the flourishing of virtue and happiness. Through civil society, passions and affections are made calm and moderate: the violent passions (such as hate and revenge or jealousy) are, through custom and habit, disciplined and put to a certain degree under the guidance of the moral sentiments.

Thanks to the philosopher, this complex process of the moulding of the passions can thus, according to Hume, be understood in its origins and appreciated for its public utility. Also in this sense, philosophy can foster the taste of Hume's famous 'judicious spectator', whose ability to judge properly about vice and virtue, irrespective of his or her particular interests and desires, is identified as a specific form of reasonableness: "This language will be easily understood, if we consider what we formerly said concerning that reason, which is able to oppose our passion; and

---

39 Baier: 1991, Ch. 12.
40 For the social dimension of Hume's account of reason and the role of conventions as a type of general rules, cf. Baier 1991, ch. 10-12 and Taylor 1998: 220–24.

which we have found to be nothing but a general calm determination of the passions, founded on some distant view or reflection" (T, 3.3.1.18).

6. Humean Wisdom and Diffidence

But how does this gradual rehabilitation of reason throughout the science of human nature relate to a Humean conception of wisdom? As Hume himself admits, his science of human nature is the work of an 'anatomist' rather than a 'painter' (T, 3.3.6.6). Responding to Hutcheson, who thought the *Treatise* lacked "a certain warmth for the cause of virtue", Hume seems to distance himself from any normative intention or practical perspective in his philosophy. The philosopher aims only to explain in a cold, detached manner. His task is not to depict virtue in lively colours with the purpose of instructing his readers. In this perspective, the skilfull anatomy of the role of the emotions in human life can only indirectly function as a way to wisdom or a therapy of desire. But maybe it is exactly this indirect 'anatomising' attitude which can provide, for those rare minds with an inclination to philosophy, and in the appropriate circumstances, a certain salvation and blessedness Humean style.

But how is this salvation reached, according to Hume? In what sense does it make Hume into a philosopher with a coherent and recurrent conception of philosopher as a specific way to wisdom? In addition, how does the medicine of the mind Humean style differ then from the Spinozistic one?

At the end of Book 2 of the *Treatise*, Hume draws attention to a peculiar passion, the love of truth, which lies at the origin of philosophical activity. Hume here admits that this passion has a remarkable, but also somewhat ambiguous outlook (T, 2.3.10.4). First of all, this passion mobilises human reason, but not in the instrumental manner ascribed to it in the previous sections of Book 1 and especially Book 2 of the *Treatise*. In the famous metaphor of Book 2 of the *Treatise* (T, 2.3.3), reason is considered "the slave of the passions", which detects the means-end relations in function of the satisfaction of all sorts of passions and desires. But now Hume recognises that under proper circumstances the search for truth and knowledge can become, in human life, a goal on its own.

Hume does not connect this appreciation of the search for knowledge, as Spinoza does, with a sort of ideal of self-mastery: but he here distances himself in a significant way from his diffidence towards a overly enthusiastic application of oneself to philosophy, as typified in the closing sections of Book I. Not spleen and melancholy, but joy and 'a delicate pleasure', have become the result of an appropriate commitment to this love of truth. In his typical, mildly ironic style, Hume even compares the delight of 'doing philosophy' with this other most honourable activity of the eighteenth-century gentleman: hunting. Both hunting and philosophy mobilise some specific attitudes and virtues in men (and perhaps also in women? – one would like to ask Hume), which makes one more or less successful in these activities.

For the philosopher, it is clear, Hume asserts, that the very application of the mind to study or the search for truth almost spontaneously awakens specific qualities of the understanding or intellectual virtues. More precisely, the importance of the object of study, the genius and extraordinary capacity with which it is studied, the peculiar pleasure this activity yields, and the successful outcome of the investigation, all cause the mind to apply itself, often with extraordinary energy, to study and contemplation. As a result, the curiosity or love of truth captivates the mind and becomes the source of a specific joy and satisfaction. As Hume admits in the conclusion of the *Treatise*, Book 1, he would feel himself "a loser in the point of pleasure" if he did not here follow his inclination. The origin of his philosophy thus lies in the delicate pleasure vouchsafed by following his philosophical curiosity (T, 1.4.7.12). Furthermore, this satisfaction has an enduring character: it not only relaxes the mind of the philosopher, but causes a sort of calm, steady self-acceptance and quietude.

Could one say that this inner satisfaction and quietude of the mind, caused by the practice of philosophy, is as important in Hume as joy and blessedness are in Spinoza? Despite Hume's lightness of tone, one should not underestimate the positive effects of the application of the mind to philosophy in 'this careless manner' (T, 1.4.7.14). The successful philosopher will experience a significant change in his temperament and affections when he devotes his mind to study and science in the right manner. As Hume remarks in "The Sceptic":

> It rarely, very rarely happens, that a man of taste and learning is not, at least, an honest man, whatever frailties may attend him. The bent of his mind to speculative studies must mortify in him the passions of interest and ambition, and must, at the same time, give him a greater sensibility of all the decencies and duties of life. He feels more fully a moral distinction in characters and manners; nor is his sense of this kind diminished, but, on the contrary, it is much encreased by speculation (EMPL: 170).[41]

Moreover, the cultivation of what Hume calls at the beginning of the first *Enquiry* his 'true metaphysics', offers not only a harmless pleasure to the 'mere philosopher', but will also change morals and manners.[42] "The genius of philosophy, if carefully cultivated by several", so he specifies, "must gradually diffuse itself throughout the whole society, and bestow a similar correctness on every art and calling" (EHU, 1.9). For the cultivation of true metaphysics implies the grad-

---

41 The idea that through philosophy the mind can become more calm and discerning, thus cultivating a taste for wise judgment which goes beyond the aesthetic sphere, cf. also the essays "Of the Delicacy of Taste and Passions" and "Of the Standard of Taste" (EMPL: 3–8, 226–249).

42 For the characterization of Hume's philosophy as a form of 'true metaphysics' cf. EHU, 1.12.

ual dissolution of the 'false' philosophy as well as the specific forms of religious enthusiasm and superstition which form the background thereof. As far as religion has its origin in an unhealthy proliferation of the emotions [especially of fear and hope (DNR: 183)], the cultivation of true philosophy will help to restore reasonableness and moderation in society.

Yet, at the same time, Hume never forgets to warn his readers of an excessive estimation of the role that philosophy or the search for wisdom could play in the transformation of human nature. After all, human understanding is limited in its scope and force, and the passion for knowledge or love of truth becomes vain and powerless when the mind of the philosopher loses all contact with common life. In sharp contrast with Spinoza, Hume again and again voices a certain diffidence towards the very pretensions of philosophy, and even towards the outcome of his own 'true metaphysics'.[43] As he says in "The Sceptic" again:

> Philosophical devotion... like the enthusiasm of the poet, is the transitory effect of high spirits, great leisure, a fine genius, and a habit of study and contemplation: But notwithstanding all these circumstances, an abstract, invisible object, like that which natural religion alone presents to us, cannot long actuate the mind, or be of any moment in life (EMPL: 167).

As the sceptical catharsis at the end of the *Treatise* of Book 1 reveals, the philosopher will in due time leave his closet and return to his friends, to dine, converse and have a game of back-gammon. Only when he thus keeps his emotional life in tune with "a share of this gross earthy mixture" can he return safely to his study to follow his philosophical "bent of mind" (T, 1.4.7.14). Humean wisdom consists, one might conclude, in accepting that it is impossible to transform one's own finitude and in the immersion in common life through reason and philosophy.

---

[43] In the last section of *An Enquiry concerning the Principles of Morals*, Hume makes from this perspective a remarkable observation: "Yet, I must confess, (...), that I cannot, *at present,* be more assured of any truth, which I learn from reasoning and argument, than that personal merit consists entirely in the usefulness or agreeableness of qualities to the person himself possessed of them, or to others, who have any intercourse with him. But when I reflect that, though the bulk and figure of the earth have been measured and delineated, though the motions of the tides have been accounted for, the order and economy of the heavenly bodies subjected to their proper laws, and Infinite itself reduced to calculation; yet men still dispute concerning the foundation of their moral duties. When I reflect on this, I say, I fall back into diffidence and scepticism, and suspect that an hypothesis, so obvious, had it been a true one, would, long ere now, have been received by the unanimous suffrage and consent of mankind" (EPM, 9.13).

The Depth of the Heart – "even if a bit tumultuous". On Compassion and Erotic Love in Diderot's Ethics[1]

Miklós Vassányi, Catholic University of Leuven

1.

In the present paper, we propose the thesis that Diderot's pivotal ethical concept of the "bottom of the heart," "*le fond du coeur*," belongs in the field of a problematic philosophy of the soul conceived as the (relatively) free determining ground and canon of moral action. We shall argue, then, that this ethical conception of the soul, which admits a degree of the freedom of the will, seems, philosophically, rather incompatible with Diderot's mechanical-deterministic, materialistic natural scientific theory of the soul. While this incompatibility or incoherence emerges in the domain of the philosophy of the soul, there appears a related antagonism in the field of the ontology of the Self in so far as Diderot, first, carries out a Cartesian isolation of the Self from the Other in epistemological terms (in respect of metaphysical-religious information, the Other is seen as an unreliable source of knowledge, and whatever is considered to be true knowledge has to be verified by the rational faculty of the individual mind).[2] Second,

---

[1] All translations in the present paper are by the author.
[2] Cf. e.g., Diderot's citation of Cicero (*De divinatione*, book II, chapter xi) in point 47 of the *Pensées philosophiques* ('Philosophical thoughts', 1745): "*I do not think that it is compatible with the philosopher's vocation to recur to the testimony of others, who may bear witness to something true by chance, or to something untrue and fictitious, if they are so disposed by their ill will.*" Printed in eds. H. Dieckmann and J. Varloot (hereafter cited DV), *Diderot: Oeuvres complètes*. Édition critique et annotée (Paris: Hermann, 1975–1986), vol. I, 43: "*Hoc ego philosophi non arbitror testibus uti, qui aut casu veri, aut malitiâ falsi fictique esse possunt.*" See also points 53–54 of the *Pensées philosophiques*. Cf. further point 19 of the *Addition aux pensées philosophiques* ('Addition to the Philosophical Thoughts', 1764): "*Such facts which only a few people could witness are insufficient proofs of a religion that is to be believed equally by everyone.*" (DV, vol. IX, 362: "*Les faits dont quelques hommes seulement peuvent avoir été témoins, sont insuffisants pour démontrer une religion qui doit être également crue par tout le monde.*") The tendency of Enlightenment scientific methodology to conceive of the rational faculty of the individual as the ultimate criterion of truth is in a tense logical relationship with the then widely shared presupposition that reason

whereas knowledge as such thus has an outright 'first person singular' character for Diderot, he still advocates the return of the Self toward the Other in moral philosophical respect. An implicit theory of the return of the Self toward the Other (or better, of the *offer of the Self* in favour of the Other) appears in Diderot's more literary works, together with such central normative concepts as the *act of compassion* (*acte de commisération*), and *conversion*. These crowning ethical terms denote spontaneous, critical, and climactic manifestations of sympathy with a fellow human, which the soul, according to Diderot, experiences in the 'depth of the heart'. Hence, the specific differentia of man as against lower animals seems to be man's capacity of empathy as manifested by the act of vicarious suffering, or substitutive sacrifice, of the Self. Since, however, the depth of the heart is also the part of the soul where the emotions and passions (first and foremost *erotic love* and jealousy) are localized, it appears that they as sources of temperamental disorder will disturb the regulative functioning of the determining ground and canon of moral feeling and action. In other words, this canon will not be able to remain an objective source of the moral law.

Therefore, Diderot's ethical theory seems trapped between the two following difficulties. On the one hand, it conceives the soul simultaneously as active (free) to some degree *as well as* passive (mechanically determined). This antagonism in Diderot's thought might be called the *conflict of natural philosophy with moral philosophy around the concept of soul*.

On the other hand, Diderot's ethical theory localizes the passions as well as the moral law in the absolute psychological and moral centre of the human person, which is the 'depth of the heart' or the 'heart of hearts'. This more complex problem is manifested by the conflict there is in Diderot's *oeuvre* between erotic love and the traditional system of virtue, and again, between self-love and humanitarian love, in the depth of the heart. In general terms, then, the problem may be designated as the antagonism between emotions and passions conceived as spontaneous and autonomous actions of the soul on the one hand, and compassion as a regulative principle of the soul on the other.

2.

To put our considerations of Diderot's key ethical concepts in a systematic historical framework, we will first offer a brief periodization of the evolution of his

---

is at the same time a universally, i.e., supra-individually, valid logical instrument, which is structurally, though not numerically, identical in every rational being. Thus, reason was trusted to be a veracious faculty only when operating as part of an individualized and personalized structure (i.e., in the frame of the psychological unity of an individual mind), though one guarantee for the veracity of reason was precisely its absolute universality, i.e., supra-individual logical validity.

philosophical thought. This periodization imposes itself somewhat evidently. As a matter of historical fact, Diderot's philosophical thinking went through at least the following three major stages of development. The young Diderot first embraced physico-theology and natural religion in a version that appeared just compatible with a restricted creed of Roman Catholicism, despite the really explicit criticism of existing religion that he simultaneously voiced. An incisive summary of this state of mind is *Pensée 58* of Diderot's anonymously published *Pensées philosophiques* ('*Philosophical thoughts*', 1745):

> I was born in the Roman Catholic and apostolic Church, and I submit myself with all my force to all its decisions. I want to persist, until I die, in the religion of my forefathers, and I believe that religion to be good as much as it is possible for whoever has never had any immediate commerce with the Deity, and has never witnessed any miracle. This is my creed...[3]

We will find this creed less surprising coming from the mouth of someone who later passed for an established atheist, when we put it in the light of the full text of *Les pensées philosophiques*, from which we learn that, to believe Diderot, the occurrence of miracles is hardly conceivable at all; and that it is not reasonable either to suppose that God should ever communicate Himself directly with any of those believing in Him. So when the young Diderot here says, "*I believe the Catholic religion to be good, as much as this is possible for whoever has never had any immediate commerce with the Deity*" etc., he means 'I believe it to be good to a very little degree indeed – but still, I do not find it totally incompatible with my principles of rational theology and deism'.

Next, Diderot passes through a short phase of sceptically tinged dualistic pantheism in the years preceding the publication of the *Lettre sur les aveugles* (1749). Some chief philosophical as well as literary documents of this period are Diderot's then unpublished, imaginary philosophical dialogue entitled *La promenade du sceptique* ('*The Sceptic's Promenade*', 1747), and his 1749 letter to Voltaire. Here, Diderot is already a step farther down the road of his evolving metaphysical views: he is in an 'in-between' state of mind concerning the existence of God and the soul. Namely, he is in between deism and a pantheism combined with the doctrine of the duality of substance. He is nevertheless apparently more inclined to accept the second option, proposing "*that the intelligent being and the corporeal being are eternal, that these two substances constitute the universe, and that the universe is God*" – a statement made by the ultimately victorious, imaginary interlocutor of

---

3 Cf. DV, vol. II, 49: "*Je suis né dans l'Église catholique, apostolique et romaine, et je me soumets de toute ma force à ses décisions. Je veux mourir dans la religion de mes pères, et je la crois bonne autant qu'il est possible à quiconque n'a jamais eu aucun contact immédiat avec la Divinité, et qui n'a jamais été témoin d'aucun miracle. Voilà ma profession de foi...*"

the debate, Oribaze.⁴ Again, it is here that the concept of *plaisir* (pleasure) first appears as an alternative to facing the practically insoluble question of the existence of God;⁵ and it is also around this time that Diderot, married since 1743, has his first *maîtresse* (Mme de Puisieux).

Finally, the middle-aged and elderly Diderot gradually turns toward a hypothetically deterministic hylozoism in his physiology and philosophy of soul, and toward atheism in his metaphysics. We call Diderot 'middle-aged' after his imprisonment in the fortress of Vincennes in 1749 (which is a major watershed in his life, and probably a serious impulse for him for a radicalisation in philosophical thought, though also for caution in respect of publishing) until his writing of *Le Rêve de D'Alembert* (1769). We use the term 'elderly' to refer to Diderot after 1769 until the end of his life (1784). In this long period after Vincennes, he is, as is known, first editor-in-chief of the grand *Encyclopédie ou Dictionnaire raisonné des arts, des sciences et des métiers* for a good twenty years, and writes, while he is editor, and later, when he is not, outstanding literary works, destined either for manuscript distribution (as supplements to F. M. Grimm's *Correspondance littéraire*) or for posthumous publication.⁶ At the same time, he expounds his most important ideas concerning free erotic love and utilitarian ethics in the famous *Supplément au voyage de Bougainville* ('Supplement to Bougainville's voyage around the world', 1772). His materialistic philosophy of soul is put forward in a dialogue form in *Le rêve de D'Alembert* (written 1769, publ. 1782). In this dialogue the two metaphysical principles, matter and spirit, are definitively reduced to one: material substance (*"il n'y a plus qu'une substance dans l'univers"*),⁷ which is affirmed to

---

4 DV, vol. II, 138: *"que l'être intelligent et l'être corporel sont éternels, que ces deux substances composent l'univers, et que l'univers est Dieu."* When metaphysically interpreting *La promenade du sceptique*, it has to be kept in mind, however, that it is a 'polyphonic' philosophical text composed in the form of a dialogue. This means that no one interlocutor in the debate concerning the existence of God, etc. may be considered to voice Diderot's views exclusively, although there are some (e.g., the Pyrrhonists, solipsists, and religious fanatics) who certainly do not represent his metaphysical thought. At the end of part two (*L'Allée des Marroniers*), the philosophical discussion stops abruptly at a point where Oribaze has had the last word, but has not systematically demonstrated his position. All considered, however, it seems reasonable to identify Oribaze as the nearest representative of Diderot's probabilisitic metaphysics at the time of writing *La promenade du sceptique*.
5 Cf. part three, *L'Allée des Fleurs*.
6 Such works include *Le Neveu de Rameau* ('Rameau's Nephew', written 1760–61, publ. posthum. in Goethe's German transl. 1805, in the French original 1821), *Jacques le Fataliste* ('James the Fatalist', first elaboration 1771, publ. in the *Correspondance littéraire* 1778–80), and Diderot's masterpiece, *La Religieuse* ('The Nun', 1780, publ. in the *Correspondance littéraire* 1780–83).
7 DV, vol. XVII, 107 (underlining added).

have the attributes of *sensibility, motion,* and *life* by itself, though sometimes in an active or live form (*actu*), sometimes in an inert or dormant form (*potentiâ*). This theory, also called '*néo-spinozisme*' in French technical literature, is hence rightly termed '*hylozoism*' – a theory which suffers from the major problem that it is unable to specify the efficient cause of the systematically coordinated changes that (organic and inorganic) matter constantly undergoes, while it explicitly denies that there are final causes operating in the natural universe.

In what follows, we shall suggest that Diderot is a philosopher whose moral thought (in which the idea of the 'depth of the heart' is the central regulative concept) is on a different level from his natural scientific thought, which, in turn, is the general criterion of truth for his evolving theological convictions. Unwilling to carry through a strict biological determinism (unlike his friend D'Holbach), Diderot remains first and foremost a moralist, whose main interest is precisely in the ethical overcoming of the determinism of nature, in the climactic moment of renouncement, or offer, of the Self in favour of the Other – which is, with Diderot's term, the "*acte de commisération*," the act of compassion towards a fellow human being.

3.

Before going further, it seems appropriate to point out here that in the terminology of Diderot's problematic philosophy of soul, the term 'heart' ("*coeur*") may not be substituted plainly for the term 'soul' ("*âme*") in his texts, though as a rule, this seems to be the case. To put it more precisely, the expression "*au fond du coeur*" ('*in the depth of one's heart*') carries, in most contexts, the same meaning as "*au fond de l'âme*" ('*in the depth of one's soul*'); but there are passages in Diderot's *oeuvre* in which the term 'heart' is taken in a strict physiological sense, denoting the organ responsible for the circulation of blood in our bodies. In such passages, Diderot sometimes raises the question as to whether or not the soul may be physically localized in the heart as a material organ. This is the case, for example, in the chapter *Métaphysique de Mirzoza. Les Ames* ('*Mirzoza's metaphysics. The Souls*')[8]

---

8 First part, chapter XXVI, a dialogue containing hypothetically formulated theories about the soul (note that several popular editions have a different chapter numbering). Diderot, in this relatively early work, still seems to hypothetically accept (on the testimony of the interior sense rather than by virtue of philosophical demonstration) that the soul is an ontologically different substance from matter. Cf. in this respect the statement of protagonist Mangogul, the sultan: "*...without an interior feeling which seems to suggest to me that it* <scil. the soul> *is a substance different from matter, I would either have denied that it exists, or would have confused it with the body.*" (DV, vol. III, 119: "*...sans un sentiment intérieur qui semble me suggérer que c'est une substance différente de la matière, ou j'en aurais nié l'existence, ou je l'aurais confondue avec le corps.*") Mirzoza, the sultan's

of Diderot's early libertine novel *Les bijoux indiscrets* ('*The tell-tale trinkets*', 1748),[9] where it is proposed that the soul may occupy different organs in persons of different mentality or temperament.[10]

Another interesting case of such usage is that of *les vapeurs*, 'the mists', a concept that regards the physiology and the psychology of the human soul. As we learn from novels like *Les bijoux indiscrets*, *Le Neveu de Rameau* and *La Religieuse*, certain 'mists' or internal exhalations in the body can cause melancholy, which is typical of ladies. These 'mists', for Diderot, come from the heart as a corporeal organ and are able to wrap into obscurity the mind and thought. We say they come from the heart 'for Diderot' because, curiously, the *Dictionnaire de l'Académie Française* (edition of 1762, "of the philosophers") and J.-F. Féraud's *Dictionnaire critique de la langue française*, of 1787–88, differ from Diderot on the origin of *les vapeurs*: they attribute them to the stomach or the underbelly. Whichever party may be right, it is certain that in this case, Diderot implicitly accepted an interaction between the heart as an organ of the body and the mind, the possibility of which is denied in his article on the Soul in the *Encylopédie*.

Despite the existence of these physiological denotations of the term 'heart', we will go on using this word as a synonym for 'soul', i.e., in its usual denotation in Diderot's non-physiological texts, keeping the equivocity of the term in mind.

4.

After these preliminary historical and terminological considerations, we address the central issue of our paper, which is, in a first instance, the conflict of natural philosophy with moral philosophy around the concept of soul in Diderot's thought. First, we investigate the evolution of Diderot's deterministic natural philosophical doctrine, which is in a striking contradiction with his moral philosophy concerning the existence and attributes of the soul or the individual spiritual substance.

---

favourite, reinforces Mangogul's statement as she says that "*...the only difference there is between them* <scil. the philosophers> *and me is that I only suppose the existence of a substance different from matter, whereas they take it for demonstrated existence.*" (ibid.: "*...la seule différence qu'il y ait entre eux et moi, c'est que je suppose l'existence d'une substance différente de la matière, et qu'ils la tiennent pour démontrée.*")

9 Written in late 1747, published anonymously in early 1748. The word '*bijou*' or 'trinket' notoriously refers to the female *genitalia* throughout the novel.
10 Cf. e.g. Mirzoza's definition of the flirtatious lady: "*The flirtatious lady* <is> *the one whose soul is now in the 'trinket', now in the eyes.*" (DV, vol. III, 124: "*La femme galante,* <c'est> *celle dont l'âme est tantôt dans le bijou, et tantôt dans les yeux.*" The virtuous lady, then, is defined by her as follows: "*The virtuous lady* <is> *the one whose soul is now in the head, now in the heart, but never elsewhere.*" (ibid.: "*La femme vertueuse,* <c'est> *celle dont l'âme est tantôt dans la tête, tantôt dans le coeur, mais jamais ailleurs.*").

It is intriguing to find that the earliest Diderot admits not only the existence of soul as an ontologically self-sufficient substance, but even the immortality of the soul (together with the existence of God, which he accepts on the ground of the physico-theological argument). In the above-mentioned *Pensées philosophiques* (the *'Philosophical thoughts'* of 1745, a text that begins with the paradoxical statement, *"I am writing about God; hence, I do not count on many readers..."*),[11] Diderot outlines in paragraph 23 his own creed of natural religion (deism) in the following terms: *"The deist affirms the existence of God, the immortality of the soul, and its consequences..."*[12] Natural religion as a coherent system of self-evident principles and rationally demonstrable theses about the traditional subjects of religious belief thus incorporates the Christian doctrine of the immortality of the soul in the thought of the young Diderot.

Two years later, in the persuasive dialogue *La promenade du sceptique*, the ultimately victorious interlocutor, as we have seen, posits spiritual substance as well as material substance, but, further, seems to advocate the ancient theory, later revived by the Romantics, that there is a universal soul subordinate to the supreme deity. Oribaze specifies the relation between individual souls on the one hand, and the unitary spiritual substance of the world soul on the other, with the familiar image of the swarm of bees: *"...the bees have received, as their share, a ray of the Deity, and they are parts of the Great Spirit."*[13] In this proposition, Diderot seems to conceive of God as the composite of the two substances (respectively, material and spiritual), i.e., as the universe as a whole, while the 'Great Spirit' is probably spiritual substance considered apart, as the sum total of all individual souls.[14] On this non-Platonic interpretation of the world soul hypothesis, however, the world soul has no principle of identity on its own, as it is a distributive unity of the individual souls, which are, in turn, considered real substances.

Next, the middle-aged philosopher, in his contribution to the article on *Âme* (Soul) in the first volume (published in 1751) of the *Encyclopédie*, already emphasizes our complete ignorance of the soul, and theorizes about the union of the body with the soul (*"l'union du corps avec l'âme"*) only in a hypothetical register, with reference to the authority of Scripture: we may rest assured that this was a bow to the authorities. However, Diderot was not so respectful of established dogma in the article of the *Encyclopaedia* he wrote about 'Birth' (*"Naître"*, vol. XI, published in 1766). One is tempted to think that the temporary suppression of the *Encyclopedia* in 1759 may have further radicalized

---

11 DV, vol. II, 17: *"J'écris de Dieu; je compte sur peu de lecteurs..."*
12 DV, vol. II, 30: *"Le déiste assure l'existence de Dieu, l'immortalité de l'âme et ses suites..."*
13 DV, vol. II, 136: *"...les abeilles <scil. the individual souls> ont reçu en partage un rayon de la Divinité, et... elles font partie du Grand-Esprit."* (part *L'Allée des Marroniers*, point 47; a reference to Virgil's Aeneid, VI/706 sqq.)
14 Cf. our preceding citation from this text under point II.

Diderot's thought.[15] In any case, life is attributed, in this article, forthwith to matter, seen as alive down to the minutest atom, whereby a separate, substantially independent principle of life is implicitly dropped. This new doctrine is developed in dialogue form in *Le Rêve de D'Alembert*, in which as a novelty Diderot explicitly raises theoretical difficulties about the concept of soul, putting the accent of his argument on the impossibility of interaction between two essentially different kinds of substance. Finally, we know the last, radical stage of Diderot's natural scientific thought concerning the concept of soul from his manuscript entitled *Physiologie* (1780),[16] which systematically propounds the materialistic position that life is an essential attribute of matter; that consequently, there is no separate independent principle of life (soul); and that all phenomena traditionally ascribed to the soul as a free principle are therefore, in reality, mechanically determined, insofar as matter is so.

With this, the natural scientific investigation seems to have said the last word on the existence of the soul, and this judgment is in the negative: there is no soul, even if this implies, *ad absurdum*, that a mind like that of D'Alembert (as we are explicitly told in *Le Rêve*) came to be only by eating: "<D'Alembert> *was suckled, and grew up to be a great man both in respect of body and spirit, he became a man of letters, a mechanic, a geometer; and how did all this happen? By eating, and by other operations of a purely mechanical nature.*"[17] We have thus seen the first, natural scientific constituent of what we have called the conflict of natural philosophy with moral philosophy around the concept of soul. Yet before proceeding to find out about the moral philosophical reversal, we should briefly situate Diderot's natural scientific concept of the soul in the context of Enlightenment (British and French) theories of the same, in order to see that despite its sometimes superficial philosophical argumentation, it was conceived to offer a perfectly serious scientific alternative to the Cartesian doctrine of the duality of substance, and that in an historical respect, it derived precisely from the insufficiency or breakdown of that Cartesian scheme. Thus Diderot's natural scientific concept of the soul depends on the metaphysical theory of the unicity of substance. In order to support that theory, then, he could turn, first and foremost, to some of the greatest authorities of the early modern empiricist tradition.

---

15 The 1759 suppression of the *Encyclopaedia* was the most violent of the three major crises that this undertaking had to hold out, and which also brought about the desertion of D'Alembert, in a year which, to top it all off, definitively alienated Diderot from Rousseau as well.

16 Published in DV, vol. XVII, 295–516.

17 DV, vol. XVII, 96: "*allaité, devenu grand de corps et d'esprit, littérateur, mécanicien, géomètre; comment cela s'est-il fait? En mangeant, et par d'autres opérations purement mécaniques.*"

5.

Historically, the doctrine of the duality of substance became problematic when Descartes asserted (cf. e.g. Sixth Meditation, 1641) that the two, respectively material and spiritual substances have no essential attributes in common, whereby their commerce (*commercium mentis cum corpore*, actual mutual influx) seems unthinkable. In Cartesian metaphysics, soul is conceived as pure unextended and uninterrupted cogitation, which cannot be localized in physical space so it cannot experience locomotion either. Matter, on the other hand, is conceived to be ontologically really or essentially different (*differentia realis*), to wit, to be extended and to undergo locomotion in physical space. The unthinkability of the cooperation between the two substances, deriving from the incompatibility of their essential attributes then elicited a tendency of hypothetical ontological reduction in the thought of Locke, who, in book IV, ch. iii, §6 of *An Essay Concerning Human Understanding* (1690), advanced the idea of 'thinking matter' as an example supporting the thesis that our actual knowledge is more restricted than the scope of the ideas we effectively have. For Locke, it logically follows from the concept of divine omnipotence that God was able first to create unthinking matter, and then to superadd to it the capacity of thought. On this hypothesis, matter as an extended substance may have cogitation as an essential attribute, so there is no need to posit a second (spiritual) substance. While Locke did not put forward his hypothesis assertively, Voltaire, in *Élémens de la philosophie de Neuton* ('Elements of Newtonian philosophy', 1741) and in letter XIII of his *Lettres philosophiques* (1734), popularized in France, without much philosophical originality, the idea of thinking matter or *matière pensante*. In the meantime, John Toland, for a time a Lockean, wished to demonstrate in the fifth epistle of his *Letters to Serena* (1704)[18] the related materialistic thesis that *"Action is essential to Matter."*[19] A synthesis of several of these ideas appears in Maupertuis's *Essai sur la formation des corps organizés* (1754),[20] where Maupertuis tries to explain, by the hypothesis of

---

18 Diderot's friend, the baron d'Holbach, translated Toland's *Letters to Serena* into French in 1768 (i.e., in a period critical for the formation of Diderot's definitive position on the soul) under the title *Lettres philosophiques sur l'origine des Préjugés... et sur l'origine du mouvement dans la matiere.*
19 § 21 of Letter V in John Toland, *Letters to Serena*, ed. G. Gawlick (Faksimile-Neudruck der Ausgabe London 1704; Frommann: Stuttgart-Bad Cannstatt, 1964), 202.
20 First version (Erlangen 1751) in Latin under the misleading title *Dissertatio inauguralis metaphysica de universali naturae systemate*, published under the pseudonym Dr. Baumann. In France, this edition was frequently referred to as the *'dissertation d'Erlangen'*, while the original Latin title was also translated into French as *Système de la nature*, and later used as a designation of the work. Our detailed bibliographical research has made it very likely that this Latin original is no longer extant in any public library in Western Europe.

spontaneous creative degeneration (transformationalism), the evolution of all species of plants and animals from a single prototype, a kind of universal animal. Though Maupertuis maintains that in man the unity of apperception as well as the moral principle have a separate (external or adventitious) origin, he contends that as far as the biological principles of life are concerned, the foetus by itself has the capacity spontaneously to alter its original organic structure. As the material particles composing the foetus have desire, aversion, and memory, says Maupertuis, they can form a new internal organic constitution of the animal freely, and by their inherent power.[21] They are thus creative by themselves (while, we may add, the originating theological principle, the concept of a creator God who made the universal prototype may hypothetically be dropped or neglected). This fundamental idea of transformationalism, so important for the theory of evolution, was further developed in Jean-Baptiste Robinet's *De la nature* (1761). While Robinet is a deist with agnostic tendencies in theology, he carries on Maupertuis's idea of the universal prototype of the living being, and combines it with his own version of hylozoism (in which even minerals are considered to be alive), and with the idea of a continuous transition in the spectrum or hierarchy of living beings. This latter doctrine implies that there is no breach in the hierarchically ordered scale of the species, but transitions from the mineral kingdom to the vegetal kingdom, and from there to the animal kingdom, are imperceptible. This doctrine of imperceptible transitions among the phenomenal forms of universal nature was most systematically elaborated by the great Buffon in his *Histoire naturelle générale et particulière* (1749–1789), an intellectual undertaking comparable, in the 18th century, only to the *Encyclopédie* in scope, precision, and scientific value.[22] Buffon is a theist, but his somewhat agnostic explanations of the respective concepts of 'plant' and 'animal' (precisely in the *Encyclopédie*, article *Animal*) contributed quite a lot to the formation of Diderot's theory that the emergence and full evolution of life in its endless manifestations on earth, could be explained by a continuous transition, from the spontaneous apparition of the primordial molecule to the highest-ranking animal: man.

In this theory, then, as we hope to have shown, Diderot had drawn on the very best of contemporary systematic natural science, which put forward several different hypotheses on the spontaneous organization and 'animalization' of matter. As Maupertuis, Buffon, and Robinet refrained from attributing the higher soul, or mind, to matter, Diderot seems to have gone back to Locke and Voltaire

---

21 Cf. especially paragraphs xxxiii–xxxiv, and xlv of the *Système de la nature*, in P. L. M. Maupertuis: *Oeuvres*, ed. G. Tonelli (Hildesheim: Olms, 1965–1974), vol. II, 158–159 and 164–165. (Note that the title '*Système de la nature*' refers to the same text as the title '*Essai sur la formation des corps organizés*'; cf. preceding footnote.)

22 For a general presentation of Buffon's theory of life, cf. in especial the cardinal volumes *De la nature* (vol. I of the *Histoire naturelle*) and *Des époques de la nature* (vol. IX of the *Histoire naturelle*).

for the idea of thinking matter (he received as a personal gift from Voltaire the substantially revised 1748 edition of the *Élémens de la philosophie de Neuton*).[23] Hence, when we consider the antagonism there is between Diderot's natural philosophical and moral philosophical concepts of the soul, we have to keep in mind that his natural scientific concept of the soul is representative of a systematic, critically conceived, and well-considered empiricist-materialist position, which in historical respects ultimately derives from the unthinkability of the Cartesian dualistic ontological scheme. A latent contradiction in Diderot's natural scientific position is, however, that it accounts for the emergence of life by the *spontaneous* organization of matter, while it considers the phenomenal forms (the species) of organic life, and among them man, to be *mechanically determined* by their internal nature and by external forces. But since the examination of this problem would require a strictly natural philosophical inquiry, we proceed to an analysis of the moral philosophical counterpart of Diderot's dilemma around the concept of soul.

6.

If matter is, as we have seen, a concept that is overcharged with metaphysical attributes and significance in Diderot's philosophy, then, conversely, the concept of '*le fond du coeur*', 'the heart of hearts' occupies the corresponding, pivotal position in Diderot's moral philosophy, where it is regarded as the ultimate fundament and canon of ethical choice, and consequently, also as the factor that determines the moral quality of a person, i.e., as the criterion of moral personhood.

In historical terms, it seems more or less safe to maintain that on this point, Diderot was decisively influenced by a disciple of John Locke: Lord Ashley, the third Earl of Shaftesbury, as Diderot translated (1745)[24] Shaftesbury's *Inquiry concerning Virtue or Merit* (1711) into French. Shaftesbury exercised a general as well as particular influence on Diderot's ethics. By Shaftesbury's general influence on Diderot's moral philosophy we mean that Diderot, throughout his career as a moralist, essentially realized the main philosophical programme of Shaftesbury's *Inquiry*, which is the liberation of individual, intrinsic moral judgment from

---

23 Cf. Voltaire's letter to Diderot, 9 June 1749, in Denis Diderot, *Correspondance*, ed. G. Roth (Paris: Éditions de Minuit, 1955), vol. I, 74–75. When Voltaire revised the first authorized edition (1741) of the *Élémens de la philosophie de Neuton*, he elaborated more on the Lockean theory of thinking matter than before. There had been an unauthorized (pirated) edition of the book in 1738.

24 *Principes de la philosophie morale ou Essai de M. S.*** sur le Mérite et la Vertu. Avec Réflexions* (Amsterdam 1745; DV vol. I, 289–428). Diderot's version is on many points more a paraphrase than a translation, and it carries very extensive reflexions in the footnotes.

under the externally imposed prescriptions and regulations of religion.[25] As virtue itself is the only real good (and vice itself the only real ill) of the individual, says Shaftesbury, morality will be able to acquire a status of autonomy, and will be, to a large extent, exempt from the regulative use of the concept of divine reward and retribution. Now Diderot (although he gives up a great part of that autonomy because of the mechanical determinism deriving from his natural philosophy) follows Shaftesbury's main tendency, as Diderot also weans morality off religion, and grounds it in the depth of the heart. And here we may move on to a discussion of Shaftesbury's particular philosophical influence on Diderot.

We refer to the circumstance that many of the more specific crucial terms of Diderot's ethics seem to derive from Shaftesbury's *Inquiry*. For a start, Shaftesbury localizes the '*natural sense of right and wrong*', just like Diderot, in the heart understood as the moral instrument of the human soul. The heart, as the internal court of moral judgment, as a canon of morality, emotionally relates to, and naturally and instinctively censures, the quality of the characters and actions inevitably perceived by the mind, while the mind has a more rational-calculative understanding of what is good or ill for the community:

> In these vagrant characters or pictures of manners, which the mind of necessity figures to itself and carries still about with it, the heart cannot possibly remain neutral but constantly takes part one way or other. However false or corrupt it be within itself, it finds the difference, as to beauty and comeliness, between one heart and another, one turn of affection, one behaviour, one sentiment and another and, accordingly, in all disinterested cases, must approve in some measure of what is natural and honest and disapprove what is dishonest and corrupt.
>
> Thus the several motions, inclinations, passions, dispositions and consequent carriage and behaviour of creatures in the various parts of life, being in several views or perspectives represented to the mind, which readily discerns the good and ill towards the species or public, there arises a new trial or exercise of the heart, which must either rightly and soundly affect what is just and right and disaffect what is contrary or corruptly affect what is ill and disaffect what is worthy and good.[26]

---

25 Shaftesbury's main argument should not be seen as destructive in respect of religion. In fact, it is directed not against religion as such, but against such forms of religiosity that contradict the evangelical doctrine of charity, like superstition, fanatic devotion, exaggerated zeal, which take it as a religious duty to eliminate (or enforce the conversion of) believers belonging to other denominations. Thus, Shaftesbury's moral philosophy is to be understood as a reaction to the late 17th century political context of religious intolerance, and it has to be considered that for him, the perfect moral disposition may be achieved only when unbiassed religious belief supports the virtue of honesty.

26 Book I, part 2, section 3 of A. A. Cooper, Third Earl of Shaftesbury, *Characteristics of Men, Manners, Opinions, Times*, ed. L. E. Klein (Cambridge: CUP, 1999), 173. In Diderot's translation and paraphrase, this passage reads as follows:

In more specific terms, Shaftesbury conceives of the sense of right and wrong as an affective faculty, an original affection in the soul, *"a first principle in our constitution and make,"*[27] whereby the heart as the seat or ground of this emotionally normative-directive faculty obtains primordial importance in morality. This affective capacity, *"implanted in the heart"*[28] will 'affect', i.e., desire, even the excellent moral habit or disposition of honesty itself, in which case only the soul may properly be called 'virtuous'.[29] This ethical theory, which combines in a coherent conceptual scheme the respective notions of 'heart', 'natural sense of right and wrong', 'honesty' and 'virtue', contains, as we shall see, much of the kernel of Diderot's ethics.

7.

In the wake of this review of some of Shaftesbury's seminal moral ideas, it is now possible to reconstruct the principles that contribute to Diderot's ethical conception of the soul so that we may have a better understanding of the conflict of natural philosophy with moral philosophy around the concept of soul in his thought. First, we shall try to offer a formal definition of Diderot's crucial ethical

---

> *"Mais le coeur regarde-t-il avec indifférence les esquisses des moeurs que l'esprit est forcé de tracer, et qui lui sont presque toujours présentes? Je m'en rapporte au sentiment intérieur. Il me dit qu'aussi nécessité dans ses jugements, que l'esprit dans ses opérations, sa corruption ne va jamais jusqu'à lui dérober totalement la différence du beau et du laid, et qu'il ne manquera pas d'approuver le naturel et l'honnête, et de rejeter le déshonnête et le dépravé, surtout dans les moments désintéressés: c'est alors un connaisseur équitable qui se promène dans une galerie de peintures, qui s'émerveille de la hardiesse de ce trait, qui sourit à la douceur de ce sentiment, qui se prête au tour de cette affection, et qui passe dédaigneusement sur tout ce qui blesse la belle nature.*
>
> *Les sentiments, les inclinations, les affections, les penchants, les dispositions, et conséquemment toute la conduite des créatures dans les différents états de la vie sont les sujets d'une infinité de tableaux exécutés par l'esprit qui saisit avec promptitude et rend avec vivacité et le bien et le mal. Nouvelle épreuve, nouvel exercice pour le coeur qui dans son état naturel et sain est affecté du raisonnable et du beau; mais qui dans la dépravation renonce à ses lumières pour embrasser le monstrueux et le laid."* (DV, vol. I, 325).

27 Book I, part 3, section 1 in ed. Klein, 179.
28 Ibid., 185.
29 Cf. Book I, part 2, section 3 in ed. Klein, 173: *"So that if a creature be generous, kind, constant, compassionate, yet if he cannot reflect on what he himself does or sees others do, so as to take notice of what is worthy or honest and make that notice or conception of worth and honesty to be an object of his affection, he has not the character of being virtuous."* In other words, the concept of virtue implies the momentum of conscious reflection on moral excellence, which the properly virtuous soul desires (loves) for itself.

concept of '*le fond du coeur*' as the determining ground of considered choice, and of the ideal moral habit which is its effect: the virtue of honesty.

The first thing that we have to point out with respect to Diderot's use of the idea of the 'depth of the heart' or 'heart of hearts' is its omnipresence in his production, with a preponderance, however, in the more literary genres like the novels. To be sure, these novels (in chronological order, *Les bijoux indiscrets, Le Neveu de Rameau, Jacques le Fataliste, La Religieuse*)[30] are far from being exempt from philosophical reflections, and have the enormous advantage over Diderot's more purely philosophical works, of showing the human being as he or she really acts and reacts within the bounds of society, exposed to the vicissitudes of life, and confronted with the most tantalizing ethical choices. At the same time, we encounter the concept of the 'heart of hearts' (or some analogous concept) in several philosophical texts of Diderot as well, at least in the early period.

The first formal specification of this concept is that Diderot regards it as the foundation of human personhood: '*le fond du coeur*' is essentially the determining ground of a person's moral choice. A person is morally good if they tend to act in accordance with the naturally good inclination of '*le fond du coeur*', in which case the excellence of the moral disposition they have developed in themselves is called '*honnêteté*'. This is, for Diderot, essentially the moral virtue of sincerity, candidness, straightforwardness, and is constituted in a first formal approach by the *identity of appearance and fundament*, surface and ground, exterior and inmost core, of the soul.

If, however, we habitually act in a different manner in order to obtain some material advantage, then we dissimulate what is inside our souls. This is seen by Diderot as vice, for it aims at deceiving our fellow human by concealing the real intention of our actions (by hiding the depth of our heart). In Diderot's texts, this kind of behaviour is very often, almost invariably, associated with religious zeal and devotion: *jouer le dévot/la dévote* ('to play the devout') is one of the most common swear words in his writings. For him, religiosity is something that should appear only in a concrete act of commiseration. Religiosity may otherwise also be a matter of the 'bottom of the heart' (see below in X) but should not be manifested as pure religious faith or creed in an externally conspicuous manner.

Before proceeding to the essential definition of the concept of the depth of the heart we have to point out a semantic equivocity in Diderot's use of the technical terms *vertu* (virtue) and *moeurs* (*mores*) here. Strange as it may seem, our author often, but not always, regards *vertu* and *moeurs* as 'vice' when he refers to actions he conceives to be contrary to nature. Hence, *vertu* or *moeurs*, in contradistinction to *honnêteté*, are the general terms which describe artificial or specious behaviour related to religious zeal – or even to monogamy.

---

[30] See respective dates of composition and publication above, under paragraph II.

8.

It is here that we have to make a peculiar qualification concerning the concept of the moral virtue, *honnêteté*, achieved by the proper use of the voice of conscience or the ground of moral choice, '*le fond du coeur*'. This qualification is that for Diderot, quite evidently, a moderate degree of sexual licentiousness is compatible with the positive disposition or hexis of honesty. A man can be considered honest, says Diderot, and therefore, morally sound, while being married and keeping a *maîtresse* or mistress. Diderot is convinced of this partly because he considers that the erotic instinct is deeply related with the fundament of human personality, with the 'bottom of the heart'. As Mirzoza, the sultan's favourite in *Les bijoux indiscrets* puts it, "<t>he tender lady," which is the morally, or even absolutely, best kind of woman, "<is> the one who has her soul habitually in the heart; but sometimes also in her '*trinket*'."[31] The discourse of Orou, in the *Supplement to Bougainville's Voyage*, about the alleged custom of free love in Tahiti (an utterly naïve account even in the mirror of Bougainville's own description),[32] makes it equally clear that Diderot found contrary to nature the ethical restrictions posed on the erotic instinct by, in particular, the institution of marriage. The concept of the omnipresent but invisible Creator is also criticized. Orou says:

> I find these peculiar rules opposed to nature, contrary to reason, apt to propagate sin and to disturb at all times the ancient craftsman, who made the universe without a head, without hands and without tools; who is omnipresent but cannot be seen anywhere; who persists in existence today and tomorrow, but is not one day older thereby; who commands and is not obeyed; who is able to check crime but does not do so. I find these rules contrary to nature, inasmuch as they suppose that a sentient, thinking and free being may be the possession of another being similar to him or her. ...I find these rules contrary to the general law of beings; because in fact, does anything seem more foolish to you than a precept which forbids the change that is in us, which commands a constancy that cannot be, which violates the nature and the liberty of the male and of the female as it chains them together forever; is there any-

---

31 First part, chapter XXVI, "*Métaphysique de Mirzoza. Les Ames*" in DV, vol. III, 124: "*La femme tendre, <est> celle dont l'âme est habituellement dans le coeur; mais quelquefois aussi dans le bijou.*"
32 A modern popular edition of Bougainville's account (1771) of his journey around the world (1766–69) is L.-A. Bougainville, *Voyage de la frégate La Boudeuse et de la flute L'Étoile autour du monde*, ed. L. Constant (Paris: Maspero, 1980). Bougainville recounts the episode in Tahiti (certainly the most interesting one in the whole book) chiefly in chapters IX–X, 133–170. What appears to be the established custom of 'free love' in Diderot's interpretation of Bougainville, seems more a case of sexual exploitation of women by men, in Bougainville's own account (cf. also the footnote commentary to Orou's discourse in DV, vol. XII, 605).

thing more foolish than a fidelity which restricts the enjoyment of the most capricious of all delights to the person of a single individual; than an oath of immutability taken by two creatures of flesh, under a sky that is not a second the same...?[33]

Thus honesty, the chief virtue in Diderot's system of moral values, does not exclude matrimonial infidelity: it allows a married person to keep a lover so long as they honestly acknowledge it. The virtue of honesty is, then, in a way, complementary to the other chief moral virtue in Diderot, namely, tenderness (which usually appears in the texts in adjectival form, e.g., *la femme tendre, l'homme tendre*). While honesty is essentially the identity of surface and fundament in (or the transparency of) the soul, 'tenderness' denotes the exclusive character of erotic love, i.e., it does not allow a married man to keep a *second* mistress (in addition to his first one). Erotic love must be exclusive, marriage is indifferent, insists Diderot, who, in fact, lived up to this norm: while he was married, he had three consecutive mistresses, two of them married.

But, as the virtue of honesty is merely the formal transparency of the soul and not an essential manifestation of the excellence of the moral disposition, we shall now consider a description of how Diderot conceives the normative functioning of the depth of the heart, of what the ideal effect of the proper operation of the ground and canon of morality should be. The following account from *Le Neveu de Rameau* reveals the undeniable greatness of Diderot, and leads us on towards our next point, the essential definition of the concept of '*le fond du coeur*'. Diderot himself has the final word, talking to the nephew (involved in the discrediting campaign of 1758 against the *Encyclopédie*) of the famous composer Rameau:

> I do not despise the sensual delights. I also have a palate, and it is pleased by a tasty meal, or by a delicious wine. I have a heart and eyes; and I like seeing a beautiful lady. I like feeling under my hand the firmness of her bosom; pressing her lips with mine; getting pleasure from her glances, and breathing it out in her arms. Every now and then, a drinking party with my friends, even if a little bit tumultuous, is not against

---

33 Part III (*L'entretien de l'aumonier et d'Orou*) of the *Supplément au voyage de Bougainville* (DV, vol. XII, 604–605): "*Ces préceptes singuliers, je les trouves opposés à la nature, contraires à la raison, faits pour multiplier les crimes, et fâcher à tout moment le vieil ouvrier qui a tout fait sans tête, sans mains et sans outils; qui est partout et qu'on ne voit nulle part; qui dure aujourd'hui et demain et qui n'a pas un jour de plus; qui commande et qui n'est pas obéi; qui peut empêcher et n'empêche pas. Contraires à la nature, parce qu'ils supposent qu'un être sentant, pensant et libre peut être la propriété d'un être semblable à lui. ...Contraires à la loi générale des êtres; rien en effet te paraît-il plus insensé qu'un précepte qui proscrit le changement qui est en nous, qui commande une constance qui n'y peut être, et qui viole la nature et la liberté du mâle et de la femelle en les enchaînant pour jamais l'un à l'autre; qu'une fidélité qui borne la plus capricieuse des jouissances à un même individu; qu'un serment d'immutabilité de deux êtres de chair, à la face d'un ciel qui n'est pas un instant le même...?*"

my will. But I will not dissimulate before you that it is endlessly sweeter to me to have helped the unfortunate, settled an embarrassing affair, given helpful advice; to have read an agreeable passage, taken a walk with a man or woman who is dear to my heart; to have passed a couple of instructive hours with my children, written a good page, fulfilled the duties of my standing; to have said to my beloved one tender and gentle things, which make her throw her arms around my neck.[34]

In this passage (perhaps the artistic and philosophical culmination of *Le Neveu de Rameau*) we find a transition from the acknowledgment of a degree of erotic and sensual licentiousness, which qualifies the disposition of honesty, toward the supreme ethical concept of the act of compassion with a fellow human. Erotic licentiousness, in Diderot's scale of moral values, is thus not considered a flaw but, perhaps, part and parcel of the virtue of honesty and is, in an ethical respect, dwarfed by the overwhelming importance of the act of compassion, *l'acte de commisération*.

9.

So we may formulate the effect-oriented or essential definition of Diderot's idea of the '*fond du coeur*' or '*fond de l'âme*', 'heart of hearts' or 'interior voice', by the concept of the act of compassion, in the following manner. We use the canon of moral choice properly (i.e., our moral disposition is excellent) only if we habitually carry out the morally highest-ranking action, which is the '*acte de commisération*', the act of compassion. '*C'est d'avoir secouru le malheureux*' – it is to have helped the unfortunate even at our own expense, as Diderot's 'real life' examples in *Le Neveu de Rameau* and *Jacques le Fataliste* reveal,[35] and as Shaftes-

---

34 DV, vol. XII, 116–117: "*Je ne méprise pas les plaisirs des sens. J'ai un palais aussi, et il est flatté d'un mets délicat, ou d'un vin délicieux. J'ai un coeur et des yeux; et j'aime à voir une jolie femme. J'aime à sentir sous ma main la fermeté et la rondeur de sa gorge; à presser ses lèvres des miennes; à puiser la volupté dans ses regards, et à en expirer entre ses bras. Quelquefois avec mes amis, une partie de débauche, même un peu tumultueuse, ne me déplaît pas. Mais je ne vous dissimulerai pas, il m'est infiniment plus doux encore d'avoir secouru le malheureux, d'avoir terminé une affaire épineuse, donné un conseil salutaire, fait une lecture agréable; une promenade avec un homme ou une femme chère à mon coeur; passé quelques heures instructives avec mes enfants, écrit une bonne page, rempli les devoirs de mon état; dit à celle que j'aime quelques choses, tendres et douces qui amènent ses bras autour de mon col.*"
35 In *Le Neveu de Rameau*, cf. the story of the *cadet de famille* ("younger son") in the same paragraph as the one we have cited above (DV, vol. XII, 117), as an example of self-sacrifice. In *Jacques le Fataliste*, several actions of the protagonist may illustrate the concept of the altruistic turn of the Self toward the Other – see e.g. – the story of the broken oil vessel, where Jacques's master comments on Jacques's selfless act with the following words: "*...c'est l'oubli de ton propre besoin qui fait le principal mérite de ton action*" (DV, vol. XXIII, 98).

bury also suggests to some extent when talking about *"the exercise of benignity and goodness,"* which is accompanied by *"the most delightful affection of the soul."*[36] The essence of Diderot's moral doctrine is thus expressed by the central normative precept of the offer, or substitutive sacrifice, of the Self, to the good of the Other, even at the expense of the Self. When, in an extraordinary, climactic moment, a moment of truth, the Self, by a complete change of its constant moral disposition, renounces the social and material advantages it is otherwise entitled to enjoy, in order to help a person in utter destitution, the supreme event of *conversion* sets in. In this, the Self is confronted with the Other, and thereby with absolute truth, in a manner that pervasively alters its moral disposition for good, and shakes its existence. At this point, then, the thorough change in the morality of the Self influences the ontology of the Self, revealing to the Self that the ontological ground of the Other is radically independent from that of the Self.[37] Thus, the moral development of the Self, when the depth of the heart optimally fulfills its regulative function, counterbalances, in a way, the fundamental epistemological tendency of Diderot's philosophy, which is a suspicion towards what the Other may offer to the Self, at least in respect of metaphysical-religious information. It is in this manner that Diderot's 'lop-sided' ontology of the Self is re-established and poised.

10.

Furthermore, for Diderot, the 'heart of hearts' might be the place of true religiosity also; the inmost recess of the human person may hide a religious receptivity as well. Even in a novel as late as *Jacques le Fataliste*, we find examples of such receptivity. Consider the episode of Mr. Le Pelletier: a positive figure, *le capitaine* (by no means a devout), defends Mr. Le Pelletier who is unjustly insulted when collecting alms for the poor. The captain, as a soldier, prepares to punish the offender of the generous soul with his sword; but he is rebuked by an onlooker for ignoring what the Gospel teaches on love of the enemy. He retorts with the unforgettable phrase that *"[t]he Gospel is in my heart and in my sheath and I do not know of any other..."*[38] Then, in the early *Bijoux indiscrets*, we learn about the sar-

---

36 Book II, part II, section 1 of the *Inquiry*, ed. Klein, 203.
37 An example of such a conversion is to be found in *Jacques le Fataliste*, in the episode of Mme de la Pommeraye. As the (philologically very problematic) text of *Jacques le fataliste* is not divided into chapters, we can only say that the story of Mme de la Pommeraye is to be found around the halfway point of the book, and we refer the interested reader to the page numbering of the critical edition: DV, vol. XXIII, 122–173.
38 Cf. the episode of M. Le Pelletier in DV, vol. XXIII, 75: *"L'Évangile est dans mon coeur et dans mon fourreau et je n'en connais pas d'autre..."*

castic sultan that even he *"he had some religion at the bottom of his soul..."*[39] Again, *La religieuse* contains a small number of passages in which the protagonist, a nun brutally forced by her mother and stepfather to take the monastic vows, gives evidence of honest religious feeling coming 'from the bottom of her heart'. When questioned by the visiting vicar about where she takes her prayer from, she responds saying *"[<f>]rom the bottom of my heart, these are my own thoughts and my feelings. I call God to witness of this, who can hear us everywhere, and who is present on this altar."*[40] In brief, Diderot does allow that a shadow of religion or even serious religious feeling may be present in the fundament of the soul, in certain *honest* people at least. Although, evidently, the mature Diderot himself did not entertain such feelings in his own heart, he does seem to have allowed for them in the hearts of others.[41]

11.

Returning to our initial presentation of the difficulties Diderot's ethical theory seems laden with, we can propose now, in respect of the first antagonism we identified as the conflict of natural philosophy with moral philosophy around the concept of soul, the following summary. Diderot demonstrates with the full weight of contemporary cutting-edge natural science that there is no soul, while at the same time he implicitly postulates that there is a soul in moral philosophical terms. The concept of soul is to be abandoned in natural philosophy, but it is impossible to abandon it in moral philosophy. This is what may be proposed as a sum total of his complex ideas concerning the problematic existence of the soul. Though materialistic natural science inevitably concludes that the soul does not exist and that all natural events (among them, on Diderot's physiological theory, the phenomena traditionally dogmatically ascribed to the soul) are fully determined, it seems that the concept of the 'man-machine' is *not* Diderot's last word in moral theory, as it was for his friend Helvétius. Diderot's last word is apparently formulated by *Jacques*, admittedly a fatalist. For *Jacques*, this *philosophe*, as his master classifies him,[42] concludes at the end of the novel that *"...we <scil. Jacques and his master> were, in truth, two living and thinking machines...*

---

39 Part I, chapter XXIII in DV, vol. III, 106: *"...le sultan... avait de la religion dans le fond de l'âme..."*

40 The visit of the grand vicar in DV, vol. XI, 176: *"Du fond de mon coeur, ce sont mes pensées et mes sentiments. J'en atteste Dieu qui nous écoute partout et qui est présent sur cet autel."*

41 On this point, we contradict the conclusions of R. Pomeau's study "Sur la religion de La Religieuse", *Travaux de Linguistique et de Littérature*, XIII/2 (1975), 557–567.

42 Cf. DV, vol. XXIII, 91: *"Jacques, mon ami, vous êtes un philosophe..."*

Master, we spend three quarters of our lives wanting, without doing... And doing without wanting... Is it not evidently demonstrated that we act, most of the time, without wanting?"[43]

Well, *les trois quarts de notre vie*, yes; *la plupart du temps*, yes. But, still, not always. It seems reasonable to suppose that to Diderot's mind, the remaining one quarter of our lives is attributable to the principle of freedom in the human being: to the soul, which is the only principle that can account for the climactic moments in which man may overcome ethically the deterministic mechanism of nature. And this principle is, in actual fact, implicitly postulated by Diderot wherever he describes how the heart of hearts operates in us, directing our moral choice toward the act of compassion, *'la bonne oeuvre'*,[44] the good deed, and, ultimately, toward conversion.

This is, we suggest, Diderot's true and ultimate answer to the first dilemma and we hope this claim has been substantiated by our showing the primordial ethical importance Diderot attributed to the concept of an autonomous and spontaneous *'fond du coeur'*, depth of the heart, the canon of moral choice and instrument of moral action.

12.

We have already discussed a part (the conflict between erotic love and the traditional system of virtue) of the second, compound problem we have identified in Diderot's moral philosophy. In respect of that conflict, Diderot seems to have considered that a degree of erotic licentiousness derives precisely from the fundament of the heart and that it is compatible with the virtue of honesty. But, we have argued that in more general terms, the second problem is that the 'bottom of the soul' is the seat of sovereignly, i.e., autonomously, arising emotions and passions *as well as* of compassion as a regulative principle. Is it conceivable that the emotions of the soul are the moral action *and* the norm of that action alike;

---

43 DV, vol. XXIII, 270, 271, 286: "...*nous étions deux vraies machines vivantes et pensantes. ...Mon maître, on passe les trois quarts de sa vie à vouloir, sans faire. ...Et à faire sans vouloir. ...N'est-il pas évidemment démontré que nous agissons la plupart du temps sans vouloir?*" These statements are parts of a relatively long discussion of the free will-problem between Jacques and his master toward the end of *Jacques le Fataliste*.

44 Cf. Jacques's account of how the maidservant he had selflessly helped reported on his compassion for her. In this account, Diderot uses two clue terms ("*acte de commisération*" and "*bonne oeuvre*") of his moral philosophy one after the other: "*Jeanne praised in the castle the act of compassion I had committed to her benefit; the master of the castle heard of my good deed...*" ("*Jeanne avait prôné dans le château l'acte de commisération que j'avais exercé envers elle; ma bonne oeuvre était parvenue aux oreilles du maître...*" DV, vol. XXIII, 177).

that they are autonomous and heteronomous at the same time? If the depth of the heart is the determining ground or canon of right action, the seat of the sense of Right and Wrong, then it seems likely that the more violent passions like erotic love, jealousy, revengefulness, or extreme depression will easily vanquish the painfully acquired good disposition of the heart, regarded as a regulative-normative principle. Hence, the ultimate question of Diderot's moral philosophy is whether one can entrust both the emotions *and* moral judgment to the same, central part of the soul. Though Diderot has a utilitarian subsidiary theory, taken from Shaftesbury, that in a final analysis, personal interest coincides with the public good,[45] he probably had his doubts about the efficiency of his implicit moral theory. So do we. For it appears that the localization of the emotions and passions into the ultimate ground of moral choice will only strengthen the moral determinism which has already emerged as a result of Diderot's mechanistic-deterministic natural scientific idea of the soul.

The depth of the heart, conceived as the spiritual organ where passion and compassion are identified, thus appears 'a little bit tumultuous' given that the canon of morality is fully interiorized within the individual soul. While Diderot certainly considered this re-foundation of morality as the *liberation* of morality from external, i.e., heterogeneous, constraint, it could seem to us that on this theory, the autonomy of the moral sentiment as an objective and absolute judge will be jeopardized from another direction by the passions. Diderot's moral doctrine as it is implicitly or latently proposed in the great novels is, at the same time, beyond any possible doubt, a highest peak in late Enlightenment moral philosophy despite its unsystematic, literary means of exposition. It is the position of a thinker who *defended* morality effectively, even from his own natural scientific convictions, let alone from the uninhibited egoism and systematic immorality of the party *anti-philosophe*, represented by, for example, Rameau's nephew.

---

[45] Cf. the *Supplément au voyage de Bougainville*, Part IV (a continuation of *L'entretien de l'aumonier et d'Orou*), where Orou says to the priest that "...*you will not accuse the European mores on the basis of those of Tahiti, nor, by consequence, the Tahitian mores on the basis of those of Europe. We need a more dependable rule; and what will be that rule? Do you know any better than that of public good and individual utility?*" ("...*tu n'accuseras pas les moeurs d'Europe par celles d'Otaïti, ni par conséquent les moeurs d'Otaïti par celles de ton pays. Il nous faut une règle plus sûre; et quelle sera cette règle? En connais-tu une autre que le bien général et l'utilité particulière?*"; DV, vol. XII, 619).

Motivational Internalism: A Kantian Perspective on Moral Motives and Reasons[1]

Heiner F. Klemme, Bergische Universität Wuppertal

Introduction

The modern debate about moral motivation concerns two alternative conceptions of motivation. On the one side, there is an internalist account of moral motivation. This account says that practical reasons are internal to our desires, interests, or dispositions. Because desires, interests or dispositions are empirical and causal powers, to know a moral reason means at the same time to be motivated in a certain way. Typically, students of David Hume are internalists.[2] On the other hand, there are externalist accounts of moral motivation. Externalists claim that moral reasons are not – or not exclusively – founded on desires and interests, but on the faculty of reason. Since the faculty of reason is practical in itself, so the externalists argue, moral reasons are at the same time motivating reasons. Generally speaking, Kant and the Kantians are externalists.[3]

In this paper, I will discuss the concept of moral motivation from a Kantian point of view. I call this a Kantian conception of moral motivation because of its similarities with the account of moral motivation found in Kant's writings on

---

1 Revised version of "Internalismo motivazionale. Profilo di un punto di vista kantiano," in V*erifiche* (Padova), vol. 33 (2004): 179–205. See also H. F. Klemme, "Praktische Gründe und moralische Motivation. Eine deontologische Perspektive" in *Moralische Motivation. Kant und die Alternativen*, ed. H. F. Klemme, M. Kühn, and D. Schönecker (Hamburg: Felix Meiner, 2006).
2 See Bernard Williams, "Internal and External Reasons," in *Moral Luck. Philosophical Papers 1973–1980* (New York: Cambridge, 1981).
3 However, according to an alternative way of understanding the meaning of "internalism" and "externalism", Kant and the Kantians are internalists because they claim that practical reasons and motives are internal to our reason, and Aristotelians and Humeans are externalists because they argue that reason can neither be the source of practical reasons nor can she motivate us in any specific way. See W. D. Falk, "'Ought' and Motivation" (1947–48), in *Ought, Reasons, and Morality. The Collected Papers of W. D. Falk* (Ithaca and London: Cornell, 1986), 21–41, and William K. Frankena, "Obligation and Motivation in Recent Moral Philosophy," in *Essays in Moral Philosophy*, ed. A. I. Melden (Seattle and London: University of Washington Press, 1958), 40–81.

moral philosophy. But because it neglects some other important aspects of Kant's conception of moral reasons, it is Kantian in spirit, but not Kant's own position. My paper has four parts. In the first part, I discuss some aspects of the debate about moral motivation in British philosophy at the beginning of the eighteenth century. This debate seems to me to be of vital interest for understanding our discussions today. In the second part, I outline the main idea of Kant's conception of moral motivation. In the third part of my paper, I argue that moral motivation should be understood as a complex phenomenon comprising a formal, an emotive and an autonomous dimension. For the sake of brevity, however, I will concentrate on the formal aspect of moral motivation. Finally, in part four, I summarize my argument.

1. Reason or feeling? The British Debate concerning moral motives

Starting in the seventeenth and early eighteenth century, modern ethics was shaped by two different disputes. This becomes particularly obvious from the discussions in Britain.[4] The first dispute regards the function of reason and feeling (or sentiments) in morals.[5] Moral rationalists like Ralph Cudworth, Samuel Clark, and John Balguy argued that reason is the foundation of morals. To their minds, we not only know our moral obligations through our reason, but reason also sets us in motion. We take her commands seriously, because she leads us to our happiness.

Criticising the rationalist account of moral reasons and motives, empiricists like Thomas Hobbes, Francis Hutcheson, and David Hume were of the opinion that a sober analysis of human nature shows that reason is neither the source of

---

4 For literature and further details see Stephen Darwall, *The British Moralists and the Internal 'Ought', 1640–1740* (Cambridge: Cambridge University Press, 1995), and J. B. Schneewind, *The Invention of Autonomy: A History of Modern Moral Philosophy* (Cambridge: Cambridge University Press, 1998).

5 This dispute is put into words by Hume in his *Enquiry Concerning the Principles of Morals*: "There has been a controversy started of late, much better worth examination, concerning the general foundation of *Morals*; whether they be derived from *Reason*, or from *Sentiment*; whether we attain the knowledge of them by a chain of argument and induction, or by an immediate feeling and finer internal sense; whether, like all sound judgment of truth and falsehood, they should be the same to every rational intelligent being; or whether, like the perception of beauty and deformity, they be founded entirely on the particular fabric and constitution of the human species." David Hume, *Enquiry Concerning the Principles of Morals*, ed. Tom L. Beauchamp (Oxford: Oxford University Press, 1998), 3–4.

our moral obligations nor of our moral motives. Instead, human beings are motivated exclusively by their affections, desires and passions. They not only set us into motion, but they also give us reasons to act. They do so by giving us empirical purposes and aims.[6]

The second dispute concerns the question as to what kinds of desires or interests human beings actually have. One can find this dispute within both the rationalist and the empiricist camps. Within in the empiricist camp, the position of the Scottish moral philosophers is most noteworthy. Philosophers like Hutcheson and Adam Smith argued against the egoistic picture of human nature, advanced by Thomas Hobbes and Bernard de Mandeville, that people not only have the desire to promote their own well-being, they also have the desire to promote the well-being of other people. A particularly striking passage can be found at the very beginning of Smith's *Theory of Moral Sentiments*:

> How selfish soever man may be supposed, there are evidently some principles in his nature, which interest him in the fortune of the others, and render their happiness necessary to him, though he derives nothing from it except the pleasure of seeing it. Of this kind is pity or compassion, the emotion which we feel for the misery of others, when we either see it, or are made to conceive it in a very lively manner.[7]

Before Smith, Hutcheson argued that although it seems hard to imagine, human beings might not only have egoistic and benevolent desires, they also might have the original desire to promote the harm of other people, even if they harm themselves in doing so.

> Human Nature seems scarce capable of malicious disinterested Hatred, or a sedate Delight in the Misery of others, when we imagine them no way pernicious to us, or opposite to our Interests: And for that Hatred which makes us oppose those whose Interests are opposite to ours, it is only the Effect of Self-Love, and not of disinterested Malice.[8]

Looking at the complex structure of our desires and motives, Hutcheson comes to the conclusion that our actions can be called 'good' in two different senses,

---

6 Hume most famously asserts: "Reason is, and ought only to be the slave of the passions, and can never pretend to any other office than to serve and obey them." David Hume, *A Treatise of Human Nature*, ed. L. A. Selby-Bigge, second edition, ed. P. H. Nidditch (Oxford: Clarendon Press, 1978), I, iii, 3, p. 415.
7 Adam Smith, *The Theory of Moral Sentiments* , ed. D. D. Raphael and A. L. Macfie (Oxford: Clarendon Press, 1976), 9.
8 Francis Hutcheson, *An Inquiry into the Original of our Ideas of Beauty and Virtue* (London, 1725; reprint Hildesheim, 1971), Treatise II, Sect. 2, IV, 132.

because my own natural and private good (self-love) and the moral and public good (benevolence) are the two final purposes of my actions:

> But it must be observ'd, That as all Men have Self-Love, as well as Benevolence, these two Principles may jointly excite a Man to the same Action; and then they are to be consider'd as two Forces impelling the same Body to Motion; sometimes they conspire, sometimes are indifferent to each other, and sometimes are in some degree opposite.[9]

This amounts to saying that an action which promotes my own well-being and the well-being of another person at the same time is, morally speaking, better than an action which only promotes the well-being of another person. In cases where my action promotes my well-being but harms another person, my action is of course morally bad.

Considered from the standpoint of the two disputes I just outlined, the choice between reason and feeling on the one side, and egoism and altruism on the other is fundamental to moral debates even today. Although claims similar to those of Hutcheson or Hume could already be found in the writings of ancient philosophers, Scottish philosophers framed the modern debate like nobody else did before. To give just two examples: First, Hutcheson's thesis that an action can be called morally good in two different ways is a forerunner of W. D. Ross' theory of "complex motives"[10] and of the concept of "overdetermined actions" to be found in the writings of Barbara Herman[11] and others.

Second, Hutcheson pointed out that ethics had to answer two questions. The first question is: What are our "exciting reasons"? And the second question is: What are our "justifying reasons"?[12] With his distinction between exciting and justifying reasons, Hutcheson shaped discussions in the field of moral philosophy not least because this distinction leads to two further questions. The first question concerns the distinction itself. If it were true that our motives and reasons are both founded either on reason or on feeling, then it seems senseless to draw a distinction between a motive and a reason at all. In this case, to argue that something is a reason amounts to saying that we have a motive to do something and vice versa. However, Hutcheson argues that the distinction indeed makes sense. And this is because it is, conceptually speaking, possible that a person has a motive to act in a certain way, but has no moral reason to do so. To have moral reasons, Hutcheson argues, is to have a moral sense by which we judge whether

---

9 Hutcheson, *Inquiry*, Treatise II, Sect. 2, III, p. 129–130; cf. Introduction, p. 102.
10 William D. Ross, *The Right and the Good* (Oxford: Oxford University Press, 1930).
11 Barbara Herman, "On the Value of Acting from the Motive of Duty," in *The Practice of Moral Judgment* (Cambridge: Harvard University Press, 1993), 1–22.
12 Francis Hutcheson, *Illustrations on the Moral Sense*, ed. Bernard Peach (Cambridge: Harvard University Press, 1971), 21.

a motive is morally good or bad.[13] Although he seems to believe that all adult human beings have a moral sense, it could be, as a matter of fact, that someone does not have one. At least Hutcheson is of the opinion that the source of moral reasoning is totally distinct from the source of our motives, even if both sources are situated in our affective nature.

As is well known, Hutcheson's concept of the moral sense was given up, by Hume, among others, who did not subscribe to the view that human beings do have a special moral sense at all. For Hume, it makes no sense to distinguish any longer between moral motives and moral reasons. He replaces Hutcheson's dualistic conception with a monistic conception of motives and reasons. To have a reason for actions just means for Hume that a specific desire is, causally speaking, stronger than an alternative desire. To say it in Hutcheson's terminology, for Hume exciting reasons are justifying reasons, and there are no justifying reasons that are not exciting reasons. This monistic conception has an enormous influence on our understanding of moral motivation. It is the founding doctrine of modern Humean internalism.

This becomes particularly obvious in Williams's article "Internal and External reasons." Internal reasons are reasons a person has to act in a certain way. External reasons are reasons that exist for a person even if this person does not have the desire to act accordingly. Williams rejects external reasons because he thinks that a person can only have practical reasons that are elements in what he calls the agent's "subjective motivational set."[14] According to Williams, there are no practical reasons at all that do not exist as elements in the subjective motivational set of an agent. If an agent has a motive, then an agent has the desire to act in a certain way. As Williams sees it, Kant and the Kantians are externalists. Their theory, therefore, is obviously wrong, because a reason that cannot be a motive for a person cannot be a reason at all.

Williams uses the word "desire" in a very broad sense. At least the sense is much broader than it was in eighteenth century Scottish moral philosophy. To Williams, "desire" is a term for everything that can be a motive for a person, for instance dispositions, feelings, personal loyalties or aims. Unlike Hutcheson, Hume or Smith, therefore, Williams does not restrict moral motives and reasons to feelings. The subjective motivational set "can contain such things as dispositions of evaluation, patterns of emotional reaction, personal loyalties, and various projects, as they may abstractly be called, embodying commitments of the agent."[15]

The second question connected with Hutcheson's distinction between motivating and justifying reasons regards the order in which motives and reasons

---

13 The title of Sect. I of the *Inquiry concerning Moral Good and Evil* reads "Of the Moral Sense by which we perceive Virtue and Vice, and approve or disapprove them in others," 107.
14 Williams, "Internal and external reasons," 104–105.
15 Williams, "Internal and external reasons," 105.

should be discussed. Naturally enough, for Hume, since there is no reason without a motive and no motive without a reason, this question does not make sense. Among those philosophers who believed that there is a difference between them, however, belonged Kant. Kant famously started his moral philosophy with a theory of practical reasons.

2. Kant's conception of moral motivation

In his model of moral motivation, Kant tries to do justice to both the rationalist and the empiricist tradition. He believes that the complex phenomenon of moral motivation must be explained by reason and by feeling. To Kant's mind, however, there is a very deep gulf between reason and feeling. But before he explains how this gulf can be bridged in terms of moral motivation, Kant starts with a theory of practical reasons. This theory prepares the ground for his conception of moral motivation. Before we can discuss Kant's conception of moral motivation in more detail, therefore, we should have a quick look at his theory of practical and moral reasons. In doing so, we should look at three questions in particular, namely: Why do persons ask normative questions at all? What is the nature of these questions? And how do persons answer them?

As is generally acknowledged, Kant's conception of moral obligations is closely connected with his dualistic (or dichotomous) conception of practical reasons. According to Kant, human beings have two different final ends. One final end is empirical, and the other is rational in nature. In the *Critique of Practical Reason*, Kant refers to these ends in distinguishing between the physical good (*das Wohl*) and the moral good (*das Gute*);[16] in the *Groundwork to the Metaphysics of Morals*, he calls these final ends the "matter"[17] or the object of our willing. The empirical and subjective end of my acting consists in my own happiness here on earth, i.e. the fulfilment of my inclinations. I ask normative questions because I have to decide what to do to fulfil these inclinations. My desire to be happy, i.e., to fulfil my desires, therefore, is the ground for what Kant calls hypothetical imperatives. This desire to be happy is a clear proof to Kant that Hobbes and Mandeville are

---

16 "The German Language has the good fortune to possess expressions which do not allow this difference to be overlooked. For that which the Latins denominate with a single word, *bonum*, it has two very different concepts and equally different expressions as well: for *bonum* it has *das Gute* and *das Wohl*, for malum is has *das Böse* und *das Übel*." Immanuel Kant, *Critique of Practical Reason*, in *Practical Philosophy*, trans. and ed. Mary Gregor (Cambridge, 1996), V 59. All references to Kant's works are to the pagination of Akademie-Edition of Kant's *Gesammelte Werke*, Berlin 1900ff.

17 IV 436; cf. 431, 438. The translation cited is Immanuel Kant, *Groundwork of the Metaphysics of Morals*, ed. and trans. Allen W. Wood (New Haven and London: Cambridge, 2002).

right and Hutcheson and Hume are wrong. As sensible beings, all our acting is motivated by egoistic reasons.

On the other hand, Kant believes that persons also have an interest in pure reason. And having an interest in rationality means to him, that people respect the existence of persons as rational beings as the final rational end of their willing. As pure rational beings, the existence of rational beings as final ends is the rational matter of our willing. Kant expresses this aspect of his theory most clearly in the second special formulation of the categorical imperative in the *Groundwork*: "Act so that you use humanity, as much in your own person as in the person of every other, always at the same time as end and never merely as means" (IV 429). Later on, Kant writes that all maxims, besides having a form also have "a matter, namely an end, and then the formula says: 'That the rational being, as an end in accordance with its nature, hence as an end in itself, must serve for every maxim as a limiting condition of all merely relative and arbitrary ends'" (IV 436).

As a rational being, therefore, persons are willing to restrict their desire to be happy to those actions by which they do not oppose the existence of persons as ends in themselves. But because persons are at the same time both sensible and rational beings, their rational willing is transformed into a moral ought, famously expressed in the general formula of the categorical imperative: "Act only in accordance with that maxim through which you can at the same time will that it become a universal law" (IV 421).

With their status as pure rational beings, the sphere of normativity provides new meaning to human beings. We do not only ask normative questions because we are asking ourselves what to do to fulfil our (selfish) desires. We also ask normative questions because we must decide whether or not we want to respect persons as ends in themselves. We must decide if we want to do our duty – or if we want to live egoistic lives. To Kant, therefore, the very idea of moral obligation presupposes that we, as human beings, take seriously our moral reasons at the same time as we weigh the subjective and arbitrary ends given by our sensible nature. In this sense, pure reason is practical from the very start. Otherwise we would not care about our rationality and its reasons at all.

Moral obligation presupposes that the rational end of our action is of more value than the empirical end. How can this axiological primacy of persons existing as rational and free subjects be proven? Why should I respect rational beings as ends in themselves? Why shouldn't I use them as mere means wherever and whenever it seems appropriate to do so? In the *Groundwork*, Kant gives two arguments for the axiological primacy of persons as ends in themselves. The first argument is objective and metaphysical in nature. It says that we should respect persons as ends in themselves because persons exist as citizens of the *mundus intelligibilis* and have, therefore, "absolute worth".[18]

---

18 IV 428, cf. V 448–49 Fn.

To this objective and metaphysical argument corresponds a subjective and reflexive argument, which says that persons understand themselves inevitably as subjects that must decide for themselves if their empirical or their rational reasons should be decisive for their actions. Whatever persons think and do and wherever they may live, as persons they must choose whether morality or egoism should be the object of their lives. In Kant's own words:

> The foundation of this principle is: rational nature exists as an end in itself. Man necessarily conceives his own existence as being so; so far then this is a subjective principle of human actions. But every other rational being regards its existence similarly, just on the same rational principle that holds for me: so that it is at the same time an objective principle, from which as a supreme practical law all laws of the will must be capable of being deduced (IV 429).

But why should every single human being regard its own existence as an end in itself? Kant's answer is: Because human beings inevitably act under the "idea of freedom". In the third part of the *Groundwork*, Kant writes:

> Now I say every being that cannot act except under the idea of freedom is just for that reason in a practical point of view really free, that is to say, all laws which are inseparably connected with freedom have the same force for him as if his will had been shown to be free in itself by a proof theoretically conclusive. Now I affirm that we must attribute to every rational being which has a will that it has also the idea of freedom and acts entirely under this idea. For in such a being we conceive a reason that is practical, that is, has causality in reference to its objects. Now we cannot possibly conceive a reason consciously receiving a bias from any other quarter with respect to its judgements, for then the subject would ascribe the determination of its judgement not to its own reason, but to an impulse. It must regard itself as the author of its principles independent of foreign influences. Consequently, as practical reason or as the will of a rational being it must regard itself as free, that is to say, the will of such a being cannot be a will of its own except under the idea of freedom. This idea must therefore from a practical point of view be ascribed to every rational being (IV 448).

At this point in the argument it becomes clear that freedom is the key to our understanding of the concept of normativity in Kant. Freedom of will is not only the reason why human beings have moral problems, it is also the ground on which we can solve our moral problems. Because freedom is the reason why persons have axiological priority, it is also the answer to the question as to what to do in order to respect persons as ends in themselves. This is because the moral law is the law of freedom. From the moral law, we understand how to make use of our freedom in order to respect persons as ends in themselves. To put it differently: The moral law is the form of our moral willing. Whatever content or matter fits into this form, we are allowed to make it the object or aim of our willing.

To Kant, freedom of the will has at least three aspects. First of all, without freedom of the will persons wouldn't have the opportunity to judge their desires and empirical interests from a perspective external to these desires and interest. Kant calls this the "negative" (IV 446) concept of freedom. Second, without freedom of the will, man could not be an autonomous being acting out of respect for the moral law. This is what the "positive" (IV 446) concept of freedom is all about: I am a self-legislating being if I act on the moral law out of respect for it. Third, freedom of the will includes our freedom to choose on our own whether we want to be autonomous or heteronomous agents. Kant doesn't discuss this third meaning of the freedom of the will explicitly in his *Groundwork*, but his concept of obligation clearly implies that human beings have the choice between acting on moral or on non-moral maxims. In a striking passage of Section III of the *Groundwork*, Kant argues: "All human beings think of themselves, regarding the will, as free. Hence all judgments about actions come as if they ought to have happened even if they have not happened."[19]

With these considerations, I have arrived at the topic of moral motivation in a way that fits with Kant's theory of normativity. As we have found two different dimensions of normativity in Kant, we have to distinguish between two different kinds of motives in his moral writings. According to Kant, we are first of all motivated by our inclinations, passions and feelings, that is to say, by the sensible side of our nature. But we are also motivated by pure reason. In the *Critique of Practical Reason*, Kant expresses this twofold structure of motivation by distinguishing between our "empirical" and our "moral interests."[20] On the basis of this twofold structure of moral motivation, Kant argues, on the one hand, against the empiricist tradition in ethics that reason can cause an interest for herself in us. On the other hand, he argues against traditional rationalist ethics that our knowledge of moral reasons does not determine our willing. To be sure: Kant does not question the ancient principle that we will always strives for a good.[21] But with his dualistic conception of reasons and motives, Kant is eager to show that human beings have to decide whether the moral or the sensible good will be the actual aim of their actions. In his second *Critique*, Kant uses, as we have seen, the concepts of the 'physical' and the 'moral good' to explain his position. It is with this conception of the good that Kant breaks with both the empiricist and the rationalist traditions in moral philosophy at the same time.

What does Kant mean by his statement that pure reason can cause a moral interest for itself in us? How does pure reason become practical? These questions

---

[19] IV 455. On Kant's concept of the freedom of the will see H. F. Klemme, "Moralisches Sollen, Autonomie und Achtung. Kants Konzeption der "ibertas indifferentiae" zwischen Wolff und Crusius", in *Akten des X. Internationalen Kant-Kongresses* (Berlin: Walter de Gruyter, 2008) (forthcoming).

[20] V 152, cf. 80, 90, 119–120.

[21] See V 59 and Klemme, "Moralisches Sollen, Autonomie und Achtung".

have three aspects. First of all, we can ask whether pure reason becomes practical at all. Second, we can ask why it becomes practical, if it becomes practical at all. And, third, we can ask how it becomes practical. In his *Critique of Practical Reason*, Kant answers the first question with his doctrine of the "fact of reason" (V 31). According to this doctrine, all human beings are conscious of their moral obligations. Even the greatest villain perceives within himself the voice of pure reason. He or she knows the difference between moral good and evil. As far as the second question is concerned, Kant thinks that it cannot be answered. We will never know why pure reason becomes practical (cf. IV 455 ff.). The only thing we can do is to accept it as a fact of our being persons.

We are left with the third question. Kant takes this question very seriously. It is central to his theory of moral motivation. Pure reason is objectively practical. This we know for sure. But how, Kant asks, does it occur that human beings take her commands seriously? Why do human beings bother about the commands of pure reason at all? Why don't they just take their own happiness into account? In other words, how does pure reason become subjectively real? It is Kant's conviction that there is only one way for pure reason to cause an interest in us for it. Pure reason must cause in us a certain feeling which binds us to its commands. In Kant's view, this feeling is caused in us by humbling ourselves as sensible beings (cf. V 79). In humbling ourselves as sensible creatures, pure reason at the same time causes in us a feeling of respect for itself. We realize that there is something in us, which humbles us as sensible creatures, but is at the same time an object of self-esteem, namely the moral law as the law of rational and free persons. In Kant's own words:

> What I immediately recognize as a law for me, I recognize with respect, which signifies merely the consciousness of the subjection of my will to a law without any mediation of other influences on my sense. The immediate determination of the will through the law and the consciousness of it is called respect, so that the latter is to be regarded as the effect of the law on the subject and not as its cause. Authentically, respect is the representation of a worth that infringes on my self-love (IV 401).

With his concept of respect for the moral law, Kant makes sure that we take the voice of pure reason seriously. To some extent, empiricist philosophers are right: pure reason does not demand that we neglect or suppress our feelings and desires. Without them, our willing would be without content. But empiricist philosophers do not see that reason is a source of moral rightness and of moral motivation on its own.

Kant agreed with his rationalist predecessors that reason is practical. But he rejected their idea that to know one's duties means at the same time being determined to act accordingly. Respect for the moral law, Kant argues, does not include the idea of being causally determined to will in a certain way. If this were true, then the moral 'ought' expressed in the categorical imperative would not make sense. Unlike the rationalist, Kant did not believe that morally good behaviour is just a matter of right moral reasoning. Instead, acting against our moral obligations presupposes, to Kant's mind, that we know what our moral obligations are. It is his conviction that it is up to every single person whether she wants to act from duty or not.

Looking at Kant's concept of moral motivation from a general perspective, we can distinguish between a formal, an emotive and an autonomous dimension: The formal dimension means that pure reason itself is practical. Pure reason is not only the source of moral reasons and obligations. These reasons would also be determining reasons for any purely rational being.

> If reason determines the will without exception, then the actions of such a being, which are recognized as objectively necessary, are also subjectively necessary, i.e. the will is a faculty of choosing only that which reason, independently of inclination, recognizes as practically necessary, i.e., as good (IV 412).

Because human beings are sensible and rational beings, moral reasons are moral obligations for them.

The emotive dimension of moral motivation means that pure reason is subjectively practical in human beings, because pure reason causes a feeling of respect for itself in them. Because human beings are both rational and sensible beings at the same time, pure reason must also reach our sensibility, our hearts and emotions, in order to become subjectively practical. Without the feeling of respect for the moral law, we wouldn't take seriously our moral obligations.

The autonomous dimension[22] means that we can know our moral obligations in the full sense of the word, without being determined to act on moral maxims. To Kant, human beings are free to decide whether or not they want to be egoists or moral beings. This freedom is, as Kant makes clear in the *Religion Within the Limits of Reason Alone*, indispensable and unexplainable.[23]

---

22 This meaning of "autonomy" should not be equated with Kant's use of the term "autonomy" in the *Groundwork*, where autonomy means that a person acts on maxims which qualify as moral laws; cf. IV 433.
23 On this see H. F. Klemme, "Die Freiheit der Willkür und die Herrschaft des Bösen. Kants Lehre vom radikalen Bösen zwischen Moral, Religion und Recht," in *Aufklärung und Interpretation. Studien zur Philosophie Kants und ihrem Umkreis*, ed. H. F. Klemme, B. Ludwig, M. Pauen, and W. Stark (Würzburg: Königshausen & Neumann, 1999), 125–151.

3. The formal, emotive and autonomous dimensions of moral motivation

As we have seen in the first section, Kant is regarded by Williams and other philosophers as an externalist regarding moral motivation, because Kant is of the opinion that there are practical reasons that are not part of our subjective motivational set. Indeed, there can be no doubt that the Kantian theory has an externalist element, because Kant argues, as we have seen in the second section, for the distinction between two different types of practical reasons. Since moral reasons are based on reason, and not on our sensible nature, they are reasons external to our "desires". However, as we have already seen, Williams himself uses the term "subjective motivational set" in a very broad sense, which seems to be open to practical reasons not based on feelings or sentiments. If we understand "subjective motivational set" in this very broad sense, then, we might argue that even Kant advanced an internalist account of moral motivation.

In what follows, I would like to explore this line of thought. However, it is not my intention to show that Kant himself is an internalist regarding moral motivation. Although I am actually of the opinion that he is an internalist insofar as he believes that reason itself is practical from the very beginning, this will not be the goal of my argument. Instead, I will take up the philosophical question of what it means today to argue for a Kantian conception of moral motivation, which is not founded on Kant's problematic Transcendental Idealism (i.e., the distinction between the thing-in-itself and appearance). Looking at Kant's own theory of moral motivation, a theory that claims to be Kantian in nature must fulfil three conditions: First, it must show how pure reason can be practical. Second, it must have a plausible theory of moral emotions, because moral motivation without an emotive dimension seems to be defective. Morality concerns the whole person, not just her rationality.[24] Third, such a theory should explain the concept of autonomy. It should explain how moral reasons can be moral motives without determining our willing.

For brevity's sake, I will concentrate on the first condition: How can pure reason be practical? Formulated in this straightforward manner, it seems impossible to give a meaningful answer to this question. This is because before we can discuss the formal aspect of moral motivation, we need to know what it means to have moral reasons. Therefore, if we want to advance a Kantian theory of moral motivation, we first need to have a Kantian theory of moral reasons. And to have a Kantian theory of moral reasons means, among other things, to explain the concept of persons existing as final ends of our willing. How, then, can a Kantian

---

[24] There is still no comprehensive account of Kant's concept of moral emotions. Among other things, such an account should comprise discussions of his concepts of respect, sympathy, compassion, and practical love.

explain that persons exist as final ends? Why should I limit my freedom to promote my subjective ends, which are founded on my own desires and inclinations, by means of moral reasons at all? As we have seen in the *Groundwork*, Kant argues that persons exist as ends in themselves because they are rational. As rational creatures they have absolute worth and dignity, because as rational creatures, they are free and self-legislating subjects. However, although Kant argues that human beings are obliged to act morally because persons have absolute worth, he does not try to prove formally that rational beings have absolute worth.[25] Rather, he claims that they, as a matter of fact, regard themselves inevitably as freely acting creatures. In other words: it is not up to human beings not to regard themselves as acting under the idea of freedom. And because they cannot do so, they are, so to speak, practically free. This idea of freedom, at least, is enough to be the foundation of moral obligation. There is no need to prove theoretically that we are, practically speaking, free.

It might be regarded as an irony that what is probably the most ambitious theory of moral obligation in modern times, namely Kant's theory, seems to rest on such a weak ground. But to Kant, it is all we have and it is enough to explain why human beings feel themselves obliged to do what pure practical reasons commands. With the concept of pure practical reason, we have reached, Kant argues in 1785, the "uttermost boundary" of practical philosophy: "All human beings think of themselves, regarding the will, as free. Hence all judgments about actions come if they ought to have happened even if they have not happened" (IV 455).

Following up Kant's argument from the *Groundwork*, I would like to claim that we do not regard ourselves only as freely acting beings. Arguing from the moral point of view, we also presuppose that every human being has insight into two fundamental practical assumptions. The first proposition regards the content of our personal desires, interests and value judgements. A moral liberalist, as I would like to call a modern Kantian, is convinced that a person cannot lead a good and happy life without taking certain things very seriously, even if these things change over time. But this does not mean that the things a persons takes very seriously have, considered in themselves, more value than what another person takes very seriously for his or her life. At least we do not have any insight into

---

25 Christine M. Korsgaard thinks that Kant provides such a proof by arguing that *any* particular normative identity presupposes respect for our humanity. "If we do not treat our humanity as a normative identity, none of our other identities can be normative, and then we can have no reasons to act at all. Moral identity is therefore inescapable." Christine M. Korsgaard, *The Sources of Normativity* (Cambridge and New York: Cambridge University Press, 1996), 29–130; cf. 125. I do not think that Kant argues in this way. If he did do so then practical egoism would not be a choice for human beings. But this is exactly what Kant claims with his concept of radical evil in *Religion within the Limits of Reason Alone*.

a procedure by which we could decide, once and for all, which things have more value than other things.

The second insight regards the axiological status of the person itself. According to the moral liberalist, we have no reason at all to believe that one person has more value than another person. If there are, as such, no subjective ends that do have more value than other ends, then the person striving for her subjective ends does not become more valuable than any other person. We do not have insight into anything that would make our lives or our persons more important than the life or existence of another person. Persons have value, but they do not have this value because of their subjective ends. Rather, they have value because they are human beings who must lead there own lives.

This insight into the equality of persons as freely acting beings explains in both epistemological and anthropological respects why human beings have moral problems in the first place. If we did not identify ourselves with other persons as a matter of fact, we would not ask moral questions. We ask these questions because we have respect for other persons as free and equal subjects of their own lives. At the same time, the freedom and equality of persons is the key to answering these questions. They are answered through a procedure that guarantees that the freedom of one person matches with the freedom of others, without improperly limiting the interest of a person in leading a self-determined life. It is only on the basis of these considerations that we can distinguish between morally good and morally bad persons.

If we did not regard ourselves as free and equal beings, therefore, there could be no moral obligations. But because we actually do so, there are moral obligations that are indispensable to our rational self-understanding. The moral point of view is something that we do not get rid of, except by destroying our humanity, i.e., our capacity to identify ourselves with other people and with their subjective ends, as if they were our subjective ends.[26]

However we might describe the procedure (by which we can distinguish between moral and non-moral reasons) in detail, it should have become clear by now that Kantians are, in one sense of the term, normative externalists. They believe that moral reasons are reasons by which we judge our personal desires, inclinations and empirical interests from a moral point of view. As human

---

[26] In this respect, there is a strong affinity with Adam Smith's concept of an impartial spectator. Christian Garve argued that the "sympathetic spectator of Smith... is in fact the lawgiver of Kant"; see Garve, *Uebersicht der vornehmsten Principien der Sittenlehre, von dem Zeitalter des Aristoteles an bis auf unsre Zeiten* (Breslau, 1798), 166 (= *Gesammelte Werke*, vol. 8). This thesis was later brought forward again by August Oncken, *Adam Smith und Immanuel Kant. Der Einklang und das Wechselverhältnis ihrer Lehre über Sitte, Staat und Wirtschaft* (Leipzig: Duncken and Humblot, 1877). Arthur Schopenhauer argued in a similar way; see Schopenhauer, *Der handschriftliche Nachlaß*, vol. 5: Randschriften zu Büchern, ed. Arthur Hübscher (Munich, 1985), 166.

beings, we not only want to lead a happy life, we are also willing to respect other persons as beings who have the moral right to decide on their own which life they want to live.

Although Kantians are normative externalists, they are also motivational internalists. They believe that persons are not only motivated to lead a happy life, they are also willing to lead a morally good life. They are willing to respect persons as ends in themselves. In which sense are they motivational internalists?

Let us start to answer this question with Bernard Williams's distinction between internal and external reasons. According to Williams, Kantians are externalists with regard to moral reasons because they believe that there can be a reason for a person that is not an element in the person's subjective motivational set. The whole point of a Kantian theory of practical reasons, Williams argues, is that there can be moral reasons without moral motives. But Williams regards this as wrong, because a reason must fit the motivational requirement. It must be possible for a reason to motivate us. If we follow Williams's argument, then Kantians advance a very strange theory of moral reasons indeed. If it is true that all reasons have to be an element in the subjective motivational set of a person in order to be a motive for us, then Kantians claim that there are reasons that cannot be motives at all. If they cannot be motives, then the whole Kantian concept of morality goes wrong from the very start.

Fortunately, Kantians do not claim that moral reasons cannot be moral motives. They do not claim that moral reasons stand outside the subjective motivational set of a person.[27] Instead, practical reasons do motivate us in the sense that there are two different types of practical reasons corresponding to two different elements in our subjective motivational set. Both moral and non-moral reasons are part of this set. To the Kantian, we have moral dispositions and non-moral dispositions. The difference between Williams's account of moral reasons and the Kantian account of moral reason is not that the Kantians claim that moral reasons are not an element in the subjective motivational set. Rather, the difference is that Kantians claim that there are some reasons that qualify as criteria of the moral worth of other reasons. In a nutshell, Kantians think that we should be normative externalists and motivational internalists. We should judge our non-moral reasons from the perspective of our moral reasons. Both types of reasons, however, are part of our subjective motivational set. It is only because moral reasons are part of this set that human beings have moral problems. They not only care about their own freedom and well-being, they also care about the freedom and well-being of other people.

---

27 On this point see Korsgaard's very influential essay, "Skepticism About Practical Reason," in *Creating the Kingdom of Ends* (Cambridge: Cambridge University Press, 1996), 311–334. Korsgaard writes: "Practical-reason claims, if they are really to present us with reasons for action, must be capable of motivating rational persons. I will call this the *internalism requirement*", 317.

The dispute between the Kantians and Williams is not, I think, about the relationship that exists between our subjective motivational set and our moral reasons. Instead, it is about the nature of these reasons.[28] Kantians must show that moral reasons have a different origin and standing than instrumental or non-moral reasons. And in showing this, they refer to the concepts of freedom and of persons existing as ends in themselves.

But what exactly do I mean by saying that persons have a disposition to act according to their moral insights? Leaving the question of how we can justify moral reasons on a Kantian basis aside, I think that the best explanation of this formal sense of moral motivation can still be found in H. A. Prichard's famous essay, "Does Moral Philosophy Rest on a Mistake?"[29] Prichard argues in this essay that a person who knows her moral obligation does not rationally ask the moral question why she should act morally. There is no need to prove our moral obligation, nor is it possible to do so, because the "sense of obligation to do, or of the rightness of, an action of a particular kind is absolutely underivative or immediate."[30]

Taking up Prichard's argument, we could say: A person who knows her moral obligations does not morally ask why she should be moral, just because she knows what her obligations are. But this person can still ask the non-moral question of why she should be moral. A person can ask this because she not only can judge her non-moral reasons from the point of view of her moral reasons, she can also judge her moral reasons from the point of view of her non-moral reasons. And that is exactly the way we think about the nature of our moral reasoning. We are not only asking what we are morally obliged to do, we are also asking whether or not we are willing to carry the 'burden' of being moral, if we will be losers in terms of satisfying our personal desires. The formal sense of moral motivation, then, means that we take seriously our moral obligations and our non-moral interests at the same time. Moral persons have the will to be moral, and therefore they take moral reasons into account. But persons are not determined by their moral reasons. They have the freedom to decide against their moral obligations if they want to do so.

---

28 See Korsgaard, "Skepticism about practical reason," 331: "If a philosopher can show us that something that is recognizably a law of reason has bearing on conduct, there is no special reason to doubt that human beings might be motivated by that consideration. The fact that the law might not govern conduct, even when someone understood it, is no reason for skepticism: the necessity is in the law, and not in us."

29 H. A. Prichard, "Does Moral Philosophy rest on a Mistake?" in *Mind* 21, (1912), 21–37; reprinted in Prichard, *Moral Obligation. Essays and Lectures* (Oxford: Clarendon Press, 1949).

30 Prichard, "Does Moral Philosophy rest on a Mistake," 27.

Conclusion

As we have seen, the eighteenth century debate over the nature of moral reasons and motives was about the primacy of feeling or reason. Although this debate is not finished even today, it has changed in appearance considerably, if judged on the basis of Williams's distinction between internal and external reasons. I have argued that Williams's critique of the Kantian concept of moral reasons is misleading. Kantians do not claim that moral reasons are not part of the subjective motivational set of a person. Rather, they argue that moral reasons are elements of this set, and because they are, they are at the same time moral motives. The modern debate, therefore, over the nature of moral motives is actually a debate concerning the nature of moral reasons. Now, we do not have a 'free-standing' theory of moral motivation. Every concept of moral motivation rests on a theory of moral reasons and on a particular conception of moral reasoning. Kantians at least believe that there are moral reasons not resting on desires, empirical interest, or inclinations.[31] Instead, moral reasons are reasons based on elements of our subjective motivational set, namely on reason itself.

However, to argue that there are two different types of practical reasons, namely moral and non-moral reasons, requires us to argue at the same time for a concept of freedom of the will that is foreign to Hume or Williams. In other words: if we are arguing for a conception of normative externalism comprising moral and non-moral reasons at the same time, we need to presuppose that persons have the freedom to decide whether or not they want to act on their moral or on their non-moral reasons. To the empiricist tradition in philosophy, this concept of freedom is totally unwarranted, because it is a clear sign of irrationality: we cannot have two contradictory practical reasons at the same time, without being irrational or practically paralysed. But to a Kantian, freedom of the will, first and foremost, means our freedom to decide whether we want to be egoists or moral persons respecting other persons for being equal to ourselves. Seen from a practical point of view, we all consider ourselves as "acting under the idea of freedom."

In the end, we are left with the insight that a Kantian moral theory does not, as Williams suggests, fail because of its unwarranted theory of moral motives. On the contrary, Williams's concept of a 'subjective motivational set' might be acceptable to a Kantian moral philosopher too.[32] But this does not mean, of course, that because Williams's critique is unwarranted, that the Kantian conception of morality is without serious problems. Kantians need to start their argument with a plausible theory of practical reasons, but I do not claim to pro-

---

31 This statement would be rejected by persons advancing a naturalistic interpretation of Kant's moral theory.
32 This point is stressed by Korsgaard: "The internalism requirement is correct, but there is probably no moral theory that it excludes," "Skepticism about practical reason," 329.

vide such a theory of normative externalism and freedom of the will in this essay. Nor do I claim that Kantians agree on what a moral reason might be. Actually, the fruitful debates within the field of Kantian moral philosophy are debates about the nature of practical reasons in general and moral reasons in particular. The main debate within the Kantian camp is between a naturalistic and a non-naturalistic account of practical reasons.[33] I believe that we should try to find a plausible, non-naturalistic account of moral reasons, obligations and motives. If we do not find such an account, Hume and the Humeans might be right in the end.

---

33 A naturalistic account of moral obligation is given by Korsgaard in *The Sources of Normativity* . She writes: "In one sense, the account of obligation which I have given in these lectures is naturalistic. It grounds normativity in certain natural – that is, psychological and biological – facts," 160.

Kant on: "Love God above all, and your neighbour as yourself"[1]
Martin Moors, Catholic University of Leuven

Hegel's criticisms of Kant's practical philosophy are based on, first, "the emptiness of the categorical imperative,"[2] and, second, Kant's doctrine of the postulates, especially the postulation of the existence of God.[3]

In the 'Analytic' of the *Critique of Practical Reason*, Kant establishes the moral principle of the higher faculty of desire with regard to both its subjective and objective determination. There, Kant states in allegedly 'empty' terms the well-known objective law of the universalizability of maxims and the subjective law of respect for this law. Furthermore, in the 'Dialectic' of the same work, Kant is puzzled, within his formal theory on morality, by the difficulty of reconciling the unconditioned object of all moral willing insofar as it must be formally subsumed under the categorical constraint of the moral law with the material conditions under which, for human beings, its completed (consummated) realization is possible in the actual world of nature. The antinomy between the pure will's moral virtuousness and man's natural desire for happiness is solved, by a transcendental deduction,[4] on the basis of the idea that "there must be some *onto-*

---

1 *Critique of Practical Reason* (hereafter *CrPrR*) in Immanuel Kant, *Practical Philosophy*, translated and edited by Mary J. Gregor, (*The Cambridge Edition of the Works of Immanuel Kant*) (Cambridge: Cambridge University Press, 1996), 207 (*Ak*. V, 83). Also in *Religion within the Boundaries of Mere Reason*, (hereafter referred to as *Religion*) translated and edited by Allen Wood and George di Giovanni (*Cambridge Texts in the History of Philosophy*) (Cambridge: Cambridge University Press, 1998), 158 (*Ak*. VI, 160–161). References to Kant's works edited in the *Akademie-Ausgabe* (*Ak*.) are given parenthetically (volume number, pagination).
2 Hegel, *Faith and Knowledge*, translated by Walter Cerf and H.S. Harris, (Albany: State University of New York Press, 1977), 81: "As freedom, Reason is supposed to be absolute, yet the essence of this freedom consists in being solely through an opposite. This contradiction, which remains insuperable in the system and destroys it, becomes a real inconsistency (*reale Inconsequenz*) when this absolute emptiness is supposed to give itself content as practical Reason and to expand itself in the form of duties."
3 *Id.*, p. 67: "[i]n the final stage of its development, Kant's philosophy establishes the highest Idea as a postulate which is supposed to have a necessary subjectivity, but not that absolute objectivity which would get it recognized as the only starting point of philosophy and its sole content instead of being the point where philosophy terminates in faith."
4 "[B]ecause the possibility of the highest good does not rest on any empirical principles, it follows that the *deduction* of this concept must be *transcendental*" (*CrPrR*, 231) (*Ak*. V, 113).

logical provision for such realization".⁵ A mere empty formalism, on the one hand, and, a mere postulated 'ontological provision' as an object of faith, on the other hand, seem to Hegel to be major reasons for retreating from the standpoint of Kant's *Critique of Practical Reason*.

Without entering into the philosophical details of Hegel's arguments, or into the historical details of Fichte's role in the development of Hegel's understanding of Kant, I want to discuss in this paper two issues intrinsically related to the two objections raised by Hegel's criticism. In the first part, I will criticize Hegel's criticism of the so-called formalism and emptiness of the Kantian moral principle. The upshot of this criticism will provide the stimulant for my inquiry in the second part into the multi-faced, key-issue of love, both in its religious and ethical dimension, and to a critical assessment of Kant's delineation of it. Finally, I will formulate some remarks concerning the metaphysical role of the 'ontological (say *theological*) provision' to which Kant appeals twice in his ethics of autonomy.

1. Love As The Content Of Kant's Ethics Of Virtue

The *nervus demonstrationis* that runs through the opening part of our investigation can most appropriately be brought to the fore by examining the important concept of *love*. In Kant's moral philosophy the concept of love is a concept that does not, presumably, give an accidental content on a non-essential (merely anthropological) basis to the in-itself empty rational concept of duty.⁶ On the contrary, for humans, love is, so to say, *materially* or *objectively* acknowledged by

---

5 Quoted from Kenneth L. Schmitz, *Hegel on Kant*, in *The Philosophy of Immanuel Kant*. Ed. By Richard Kennington, (*Studies in Philosophy and the History of Philosophy*, Volume 12) (Washington, D.C.: The Catholic University of America Press, 1985), 231 [who quotes J. Robinson's, "Hegel's Criticism of the Postulates of Practical Reason," in *Le Congrès d'Ottouais de Kant* (Ottawa, 1974), 245].

6 An accidental, "empirical" content would be that content which would be taken into consideration if one concentrates on "the condition[s]" wherein human beings relate toward one another: "differences of the *subjects* to whom the principle of virtue (in terms of what is formal) is *applied* in cases that come up in experience (the material)". See *The Metaphysics of Morals*, "Doctrine of the Elements of Ethics," (hereafter *M. M./Virtue*), "Part II: Duties of Virtue to Others," Chapter II: § 45 "On ethical duties of human beings toward one another with regard to their **condition**" (in Immanuel Kant, *Practical Philosophy*, translated and edited by Mary J. Gregor (*The Cambridge Edition of the works of Immanuel Kant*) (Cambridge: Cambridge University Press, 1996), 584 (*Ak*. V, 468 ff).

Kant to be a moral duty in and by itself.[7] Stated the other way around: what the a priori concept of duty essentially means to humans – its objective meaning, its material content – is, in this sense, objectively identified with, among other things, "the duty of love" (*Liebespflicht*).[8] In a while, we will enter into the general problem of how, for Kant, love to other human beings[9] can *überhaupt* be called a duty. For now, it suffices to see that the objection of emptiness and mere formalism with regard to the moral law has tailored itself to such an objection *merely abstractly*. On the sheer abstracting moment, namely, when one narrows down the meaning of the principle of morality to 'pure rational beings', one closes one's eyes to what this principle in its constraining presentation as duty objectively entails *for humans*.[10]

In discussions on the emptiness of the moral law in Kant and the mere formalism of his ethics, it is amazing that commentators are generally silent about Kant's *Metaphysics of Morals*, especially the second part: 'Metaphysical Principles of the Doctrine of Virtue'. In what Kant here[11] calls "metaphysical principles", he displays what the moral law, being in itself the expression of pure reason's deter-

---

7 In Schopenhauer's criticism, it is precisely this aspect of Kant's ethics – "duty (of love) for duty's sake" – that elicits him to assess Kant's ethics as being "the apotheosis of want of love" [*Apotheose der Lieblosigkeit*] in *Preisschrift über die Grundlage der Moral*. Mit einer Einleitung, Bibliografie und Registern herausgegeben von Hans Ebeling (Hamburg, Meiner, 1979), 31.

8 *M.M/Virtue*, § 26, 569 (*Ak*. VI, 450).

9 *M.M./Virtue*, Part II: "Duties of Virtue to Others," § 23, 568 ff (*Ak*. VI, 448 ff).

10 The emphasis put here on "for humans" is essential as it points to a necessary presupposition for every sound understanding and interpretation of Kant's duty of love. In accordance with Kant's general idea of a metaphysics of morals (see *M. M., Introduction* I, 370 (*Ak*. VI, 214)), every interpretation of the duty of love must take into account the following general regulative remark: "just as there must be principles in a metaphysics of nature for applying those highest universal principles of a nature in general to objects of experience, a metaphysics of morals cannot dispense with principles of application, and we shall often have to take as our object the particular *nature* of human beings, which is cognised only by experience, in order to show in it what can be inferred from universal moral principles. But this will in no way detract from the purity of these principles or cast doubt on their a priori source" (*id.*, 372, *Ak*. VI, 216–217).

11 As he already did sixteen years earlier in his *Critique of Pure Reason* (1781): "Metaphysics is divided into the metaphysics of the **speculative** and the **practical** use of pure reason, and is therefore either **metaphysics of nature** or **metaphysics of morals**... [T]he latter [contains] the principles which determine **action and omission** a priori and make them necessary" (B 869). Even when Kant in 1797 had a definition of the term *metaphysics* in mind differing from transcendental philosophy, what he says in the last part of the former statement about metaphysical principles remains the same.

mination of the will, objectively entails a priori for human beings. Contrary to the suspected emptiness of his ethics, Kant himself proposes explicitly: "[E]thics... provides a *matter* (an object of free choice), an **end** of pure reason which it represents as an end that is also objectively necessary, that is, an end that, as far as human beings are concerned, it is a duty to have."[12] Actually, what this ethics does entail for human beings – hence: the principle of morality disclosed in its content – deals, to a great extent,[13] with "the duty of love to other human beings." As such, Kant lets this ethical law of perfection come together with the two components of the well-known biblical command: "Love your neighbour as yourself"[14] or, expressed more fully, "Love your neighbour as you have to love the humanity in your own person."[15]

Thus far, it is clear that in Kant's doctrine of virtue the concept of love becomes a most essential moral concept. Just like the moral law itself, the 'duty of love' presents itself to human beings in a proper a priori status. Indeed, Kant qualifies practical love[16] as a *metaphysical* concept, which in his metaphysics of virtue discloses in an a priori manner for humans the real objective practical content of the moral law. Let us say then that, on the one hand, the abstract moral principle of the universalizability of maxims is pure reason's practical expression of what it means, in general, to be a person; nevertheless, on the other hand, and in their concrete actualisation – e.g., when account is taken of human nature – these universal maxims are materially identified with the duty of love (*Liebespflicht*).

2. How must the Duty of Love be seen as a Divine Command?

Let me now, in the second part of my expository notes on Kant's concept of love, dwell upon the puzzling theme of 'love for God' (*Liebe zu Gott*).[17] Nowhere in his metaphysical doctrine of virtue where Kant explores, as we said, the objective content of the law of duty (*Pflichtgesetz*), does he propose a duty of love (*Liebespflicht*) to God. His doctrine on *Liebespflicht* is restricted to "duties to

---

12 *M.M./V*, "Introduction I," 513 (*Ak*. VI, 380).
13 Section I of Part II: "On duties to others merely as human beings" in *M. M./Virtue*, 568 (*Ak*. VI, 448).
14 Cf. "In accordance with the ethical law of perfection "love your neighbour as yourself," the maxim of benevolence (practical love of human beings) is a duty of all human beings toward one another" (*M.M./Virtue*, § 27, 570 (*Ak*. VI, 450).
15 Cf. *infra* "§ 3, A. Love to others: feeling and benevolence."
16 "Love... must be thought as the maxim of benevolence (practical love), which results in beneficence." (*M. M./Virtue*, § 25, 569 (*Ak*. VI, 449)).
17 *CrPrR*, 207 (*Ak*. V, 83).

others merely as human beings."[18] However, in his moral investigations, Kant affirmatively introduces two 'religious' duties. First, he introduces the "duty of religion" (*Religionspflicht*), which he defines as "the duty, namely, 'of recognizing all our duties *as (instar)* divine commands'."[19] I will henceforth call this first 'religious' *momentum* in Kant's moral theory *the momentum of recognition*. Second, in the *Critique of Practical Reason*, Kant posits as "a kernel of all laws"[20] the rule of practical love (*praktische Liebe*) as a command to love God (and to love one's neighbour): "To love God means, in this sense [i.e., practical] to do what He commands *gladly*; to love one's neighbour means to practice all duties towards him *gladly*."[21] Whereas the duty of religion, firstly, commands one to link, for some reason,[22] all duties to the idea of God, and by this means to transform laws of virtue semantically into (*"seen as"*) divine commands, the constraining principle of gladness, secondly, empowers the practice of these (now religious) commands with a disposition of love. Recognizing all our duties as divine commands, united with the gladness in practising them, constitutes, in Kant, the principle of (practical) love for God.

In order to do justice to Kant's criticism in this religious matter, and, consequently, to arrive at a proper understanding of what he is proposing here in terms of love, one has to take account of the following critical restrictions with regard to the two 'religious' *momenta* that have come to the fore in my investigation: the epistemic *momentum* of recognition and the aesthetic *momentum* of gladness. Constituting in a structural way the concept of 'love for God', both *momenta* are presented by Kant as genuine duties. Yet, the dogmatic naiveté in the understanding of these duties, especially with respect to their object (God), is strongly attacked. The impact of Kant's criticism of religion ("within the limits of reason alone") attacks, twice, the role of the representation of God in moral endeavours. This representation is attacked a first time in his critical evaluation of how the representation of God can play any role whatsoever in a systematically established ethics of autonomy. The significance of the same representation is critically restricted a second time when Kant examines its possible energizing role in the aesthetic domain of moral incentives and inner moral dispositions.

---

18 *M. M./Virtue*, § 23 ff, 568 (*Ak*. VI, 448).
19 *M. M./Virtue*, § 18, 564 (*Ak*. VI, 443), see also the very important "Conclusion" of the *M. M./Virtue* entitled, "Religion as the doctrine of duties to God lies beyond the bounds of pure moral philosophy", 598 (*Ak*. VI, 486). Without linking it to a concept of duty, Kant entertains this definition of religion also in his *Religion within the Boundaries of mere Reason*, Part Four, First Part: "Concerning the service of God in a religion in general", 153 ff (*Ak*.VI, 153 ff.).
20 *CrPrR*, 207 (*Ak*. V, 83).
21 *Ibid.*
22 See *infra* "§ 2, A.1. The recognition of all our duties as divine commands".

In his scientific shaping of a system of pure moral philosophy, Kant is using Ockham's razor, as it were, especially in confrontation with religion as the doctrine of duties to God. The way in which Kant uses this razor, specifically in determining the command of 'love for God', has a troubling impact on the concept of love itself. This will become clear after the following analytical explorations.

A. The Duty Of Religion As A Duty Of A Human Being To Himself

1. The recognition of all our duties as divine commands

First, in Kant's doctrine of duties (in his *Metaphysics of Morals*[23]), let us concentrate on the 'religious' *momentum* of recognition ("the recognition of all our duties as divine commands"). He deals with this issue, first, in the Episodic Section:[24] 'On an **amphiboly** in **Moral Concepts of Reflection**, taking what is a human being's duty to himself for a duty to other beings'.[25] This theme is again addressed in the "Conclusion" of the *Metaphysics of Morals*: 'Religion as the doctrine of duties to God lies beyond the bounds of pure moral philosophy'.[26]

In his first presentation[27] of the meaning of this duty of religion (*Religionspflicht*), Kant inserts a highly critical "but":

> But [– he states –] this [duty of religion][*scil.* recognition] is not consciousness of a duty *to* God. For this idea [of God] proceeds entirely from our own reason and we ourselves make it, whether for the theoretical purpose of explaining to ourselves the purposiveness in the universe as a whole or also for the purpose of serving as the incentive in our conduct. Hence, we do not have before us, in this idea, a given being to whom we would be under obligation... Rather, it is a duty of a human being to himself to apply this idea, which presents itself unavoidably to reason, to the moral law in him, where it is of the greatest moral fruitfulness. In this (**practi-**

---

23 Attached to this work, we made fruitful use of the *Notes on the Lectures of Mr. Kant on the Metaphysics of Morals* (begun October 14, 1793), notes taken by J. Fr. Vigilantius [in Immanuel Kant, *Lectures on Ethics*, edited by Peter Heath and J. B. Schneewind, translated by Peter Heath (*The Cambridge Edition of the works of Immanuel Kant*) (Cambridge University Press, 2001), Part IV, 249–452 (Ak. XXVII, 479–732)] (referred to hereafter as *Lectures on Ethics*-Vigilantius).
24 Belonging to *M. M./Virtue*, Book I, Chapter II: "On a Human Being's Duties to Himself Merely as a *Moral* Being", 552 ff (*Ak.* VI, 428 ff).
25 *M. M./Virtue*, 563 ff (*Ak*.VI, 442 ff).
26 *M. M./Virtue*, "Conclusion", 598 ff (*Ak*. VI, 486).
27 *M. M./Virtue*, § 18, 564 (*Ak*. VI, 443–444).

cal) sense it can therefore be said that to have religion is a duty of the human being to himself.[28]

Kant repeats this in the 'Conclusion' of his *Metaphysics of Morals, Doctrine of Virtue*: "Admitting that *religion* is an integral part of the general *doctrine of duties*, the problem now is to determine the boundaries of the *science* to which it belongs. Is it to be considered a part of ethics... or must it be regarded as lying entirely beyond the bounds of a purely philosophical morals?"[29] The criticism in his answer to this scholarly,[30] philosophical question regarding systematicity and religion in the doctrine of duties is clearly expressed in the term "only" (as a restricting conjunction) in the following passage:

> The *formal aspect* of all religion, if religion is defined as "the sum of all duties as (*instar*) divine commands," belongs to philosophical morals, since this definition expresses **only** the relation of reason to the *idea* of God which reason makes for itself; and this does not yet make a duty of religion into a duty to (*erga*) God, as a being existing outside our idea, since we still abstract from his existence".[31]

Using Okham's razor, Kant cuts off, twice, "duties to (*erga*) God" from "duties with regard to (*instar*) God." What is critically cut off as being unnecessary in the conception of "duty of religion" (as duty of love) is the representation of "God, as a being existing outside our idea"[32] to whom (*erga*) we would have "an obligation to perform certain services".[33]

Yet, what remains after this critical removal of God's existence and, by this, the *material* aspect of religion,[34] amounts to what seems to be practically necessary

---

28 *M. M./Virtue* § 18, 564 (*Ak*. VI, 443–444).
29 *M. M./Virtue*, "Conclusion," 598–599 (*Ak*. VI, 487).
30 I am referring here to Kant's concept of (practical) philosophy *in sensu scholastico* (differing from *in sensu cosmico*), "namely that of a system of cognition that is sought only as a science without having as its end anything more than the systematic unity of this knowledge" (*CrpR*, B 866). See also *Lectures on Logic*, (translated and edited by J. Michael Young (*The Cambridge Edition of the Works of Immanuel Kant*) (Cambridge University Press, 1992) Part IV, "The Jäsche Logic, Introduction III," 537 (*Ak*. IX, 23–24).
31 *M. M./Virtue*, "Conclusion", 599 (*Ak*. VI, 487) (bold emphasis mine).
32 *M. M./Virtue*, "Conclusion", 598 (*Ak*. VI, 487).
33 *Ibid.*; see also Kant on courtly service (*Hofdienste*) in *Religion*, Part four, 151 ff (*Ak*. VI, 151 ff): "Concerning service and counterfeit service under the dominion of the good principle, or, Of Religion and priestcraft".
34 Cf. *M. M./Virtue*, "Conclusion," 599 (*Ak*. VI, 487): "the sum of duties *to* (*erga*) God, that is, the service to be performed for him (*ad praestandum*)... which do not proceed only from reason giving universal laws".

"for the sake – namely – of strengthening the moral incentive in our own lawgiving reason."[35] The practical necessity by which Kant critically identifies a duty of religion formally as a moral duty is a necessity based exclusively on a "subjectively logical ground."[36] Kant's explanation of this specific mode of necessity reveals how he takes a fictitious[37] (although rational) idea of God to be at the service of putting additional constraining power on moral duties. His explanation rests on the following argument: "we cannot very well make obligation (moral constraint) intuitive for ourselves, without thereby thinking of *another's* will, namely God's (of which reason in giving universal laws is only the spokesman)."[38] The ground on which we must think of all our duties in relation to a divine will given a priori – hence, the ground of our duty of religion – lies, objectively speaking, in the absolute character of the constraint of a categorical imperative. Subjectively speaking, however, this ground must be sought in our imagination (the power of making things "intuitive for ourselves"). Furthermore, imagination's representation of a divine Obligator is subjectively – as we stated above already – required, as Kant stated, only "for the sake of strengthening the moral incentive." Since Kant assesses the latter to be only the feeling of *respect* (for the moral law),[39] he makes it a duty to let this moral feeling become practically strengthened by religion. The mere imaginary representation of a divine Obligator, according to him, effectively empowers, *in subsidium*, the feeling of

---

35 M. M./Virtue, "Conclusion," 599 (*Ak*. VI, 447).
36 *Ibid*.
37 Ulrich Barth, in his *Gott als Projekt der Vernunft* (Tübingen, Mohr Siebeck, 2005), 303–305, has examined the epistemic meaning of Kant's 'as' in the formula 'as divine commands' in confrontation with Vaihinger's theory of religious fictions in his *Die Philosophie des Als Ob. System der theoretischen, praktischen und religiösen Fiktionen der Menschheit aufgrund eines idealistischen Positivismus*, (Leipzig, 1922). As a result of this inquiry, the author (rightly) states that in Kant's religious 'as' there is no (as Vaihinger thinks) heuristic function involved which would operate within the epistemic domain of thinking a non-objective reality. On the contrary, the meaning of Kant's 'as' is grounded on a notion of reality that is repeatedly said to be practically objective. The semantic transformation that takes place in virtue of the operator 'as' can rightly be understood in the (Wittgensteinian) sense of 'seeing as'. U. Barth states: "Wenn der Begriff des Fiktionalen überhaupt auf Kants Religionstheorie Anwendung finden soll, wird man am ehesten an die dort begegnenden intentionalen Begriffe wie 'Ansehen als', 'Vorstellen als', 'Denken als' und die durch sie eingeführten theologischen Quasiprädikationen zu denken haben" (*o.c.*, 305). A monographical work on this topic is written by H. Scholz, *Die Religionsphilosophy des Als-Ob: Eine Nachprüfung Kants und des idealistischen Positivismus* (Leipzig: F. Meiner, 1921).
38 *Ibid*.
39 See *Groundwork of the Metaphysics of Morals*, 55 (*Ak*. IV, 400), 85 (*Ak*. IV, 435); *CrPrR*, Book One, Ch. III: "On the incentives of pure practical reason", 198 ff (Ak.IV, 71 ff).

respect due to the moral law, and does so even though the feeling itself is, still, produced only by the law. It is itself a duty (of religion) to have religion (according to the *momentum* of recognition) that renders the moral incentive at the service of increasing it power (*Zuwachs*[40]), and *vice versa*: the moral law in its holiness becomes a more empowered object of respect by the intensifying power yielded by the entertainment of the idea of a divine Obligator. What Kant calls "the **practical** sense" of (the duty of) religion [*scil.* recognition] as a duty of a human being to himself, requires us, as already said, "to apply this idea [of God]... to the moral law in him, where it is of the greatest moral fruitfulness."[41]

This short examination of the idea of subjective necessity upon which Kant bases the 'duty of religion' has revealed the following elements according to which we can better understand the religious *momentum* of recognition in relation to love: first, it entertains a mere *idea* of God; further, it makes sense only in the mode of application to the moral law in us; finally, it practically functions solely for the sake of strengthening the moral incentive of respect.

2. God, a fiction strengthening the moral feeling of respect

Given all this, one might rightly conclude that the religious *momentum* of recognition that establishes the (*instar-*)relation of the moral human being to God (as Obligator) can, in itself, hardly be called a *momentum* of *love*. Reason's adherence to a mere self-made idea of God, which, on subjectively logical grounds, is needed in order to give the categorical imperative its required unconditional strength, does not, in any way, agree with the meaning of *love* for God.[42] Furthermore, from the moment that the feeling of *respect* comes exclusively to the fore, adher-

---

40 Already in the *Groundwork*, 88 (*Ak.* IV, 439), Kant acknowledges: "Even if the kingdom of nature as well as the kingdom of ends were thought as united under one sovereign, so that the latter would no longer remain a mere idea but would obtain true reality, it would no doubt *gain the increment of a strong incentive*" (italics mine).

41 *M. M./Virtue*, § 18, 564 (*Ak.* VI, 444).

42 Contrary to *M. M./Virtue* § 18 and the "Conclusion" where Kant presents the epistemic momentum of recognition in the form of a duty (of religion) without any reference to the concept of love, he does refer to this latter concept in the "Preface" to the first edition of the *Religion* where he argues: "Morality inevitably leads to Religion" (35) (*Ak.* VI, 6). Whereas in the former work, religion, presented as a duty, is grounded on the unconditional character of the constraint of a categorical imperative (for the sake of giving this constraint on the level of the moral incentive additional strength), Kant in the latter work will ground the religious momentum in morality on the human being's concern with the result (end) of its moral endeavors: "Now, in this end human beings seek something that they can *love*, even though it is being proposed to them through reason alone" [*o.c.* footnote, p. 36 (*Ak.* VI, 7n)].

ence becomes dominated not by attraction but by a repulsive "keeping oneself at a distance."[43] Moreover, in the given religious situation (duties *instar* God), the feeling of respect takes the form of guilt-inspired awe (*schuldige Ehrfurcht*)[44] about which Kant states: "Should we want to transform our guilt-inspired awe before him [God] into a particular duty, we would forget that such an awe is not a particular act of religion but the religious disposition which universally accompanies all our actions done in conformity to duty."[45] The recognition of all our duties as divine commands (the duty of religion), based on the recognition of God as Obligator or holy law-giver, is itself not at all fit for being called a duty of love. As the necessity of the recognition does not itself originate from a necessity induced by an incentive of love, the duty of religion is consequently put at a principal distance from an ethics of love.

Although this first *momentum* of recognition, based rather on guilt-inspired awe, does not in itself contain a sufficient ground for *love* in relation to God, it nevertheless represents a necessary precondition for this love. At the moment of a necessary fictitious[46] recognition, one first brings all moral duties in relation to God, by *seeing* them *as if* they all depend on a divine Obligator, in order, in a second moment, to empower this relation with a disposition of love. Within this structural framework, let us inquire now into how Kant provides this second, supplementary basis for establishing his concept of duty of practical love for God.

B. The Command 'To Love God' and The Disposition of Gladness

1. Gladness and holiness

As already indicated, Kant locates the practical love for God on the aesthetic[47] *momentum* of gladness (*gerne*) in the fulfilling of one's moral duties: "to do what He commands *gladly.*"[48] The aesthetics of this concept of gladness defined as love for God fully coincides in Kant's moral theory with the aesthetics of the single moral incentive (*elater animi*) (respect for the moral law) as elaborated in Chapter

---

43 Cfr. *M. M./V*, § 24, 568 (*Ak.* VI, 449).
44 Cf. *Religion*, 153 n (*Ak.* VI, 154 n).
45 *Ibid.*
46 See *supra* footnote 34.
47 The practical meaning of the term *aesthetics* parallels with the theoretical in the sense that in both cases reference is made to the subject's senses and sensibility [cfr. *CrPrR*, "Introduction," 149 (*Ak.* V, 16)].
48 *CrPrR*, 207 (*Ak.* V, 83).

III of the "Analytic of practical reason."[49] In this work, Kant does not bring the feeling of respect to the fore as if it should be taken as *a possible* incentive to morality. Rather, in the feeling of respect, morality itself is represented subjectively as an incentive.[50] Hence, the concept of gladness coincides fully with the concept of morality and thus shares the imperative's weight of authentically being a duty.

The principal question that remains is how this duty of gladness can be conceived of as a duty of love for God. In this regard, Kant creates again a puzzling situation because, as a matter of fact, the concept of gladness is essentially the aesthetic flipside of what he calls "a human being's duty to himself to increase his moral perfection."[51] According to this "merely human" (not religious) understanding, the disposition of gladness equals the obligated striving for inner moral perfection. The latter consists, subjectively considered, in the striving for purity (*puritas moralis*) in one's inner disposition to duty.[52] Expressed in the form of a command, gladness means: "Be holy".[53] In the Vigilantius *Lecture notes on Ethics* § 143, Kant repeatedly identifies "the highest stage of morality" with the command "to acquire a love for the law, and respect for it, and likewise a transplanted moral love and respect for the professor thereof".[54] Emphasizing the aesthetic location of the practical love for God, Kant states: "the so-called categorical: *Love God* tells us no more than to base our observance of laws, not merely on obedience, which produces the coercion and necessitation of the law, but on an inclination in conformity with what the law prescribes".[55] It is on the aesthetic level of inclination or inner disposition that love of God gets its moral imperative definition as an uninterrupted striving to gladness understood as holiness.[56] Thus, Kant states: "Love towards God is the foundation of all inner religion".[57] In his book *Religion*, Kant presents this ideal of holiness in a more religious semantics

---

49 See *CrPrR*, 198 ff (*Ak.* V, 71 ff).
50 Cfr. *CrPrR,* 201 (*Ak.* V, 76): "And so respect for the law is not the incentive to morality; instead it is morality itself subjectively considered as an incentive inasmuch as pure practical reason, by rejecting all the claims of self-love in opposition with its own, supplies authority to the law, which now alone has influence."
51 See *M. M./Virtue* §§ 21–22, 566–567 (*Ak.* VI, 446–447).
52 See *ibid*.
53 *M. M./Virtue* § 21, 566 (*Ak.* VI, 446); see also *Religion*, 158 (*Ak*.VI, 161).
54 *Lectures on Ethics*-Vigilantius § 143, 442 (*Ak.* XXVII, 720).
55 *Id*., p. 443 (*Ak.* XXVII, 721).
56 Cfr. *CrPrR*, 207 (*Ak.* V, 83) where the command to love God is presented as follows: "That law of all laws (...) like all the moral precepts of the Gospel, presents the moral disposition in its complete perfection, in such a way that as an ideal of holiness it is not attainable by any creature but is yet the archetype which we should strive to approach and resemble in an uninterrupted but endless progress."
57 *Lectures on Ethics*-Vigilantius § 143, 442 (*Ak.* XXVII, 720).

when he contextualizes it by referring to the process of conversion from evil, the supernatural cooperation herewith, the doctrine of grace, the idea of moral religion,[58] and, finally, to his Christology ("the prototype of moral disposition in its entire purity").[59]

2. Inner religion as rational self-love

Given all of this textual evidence regarding Kant's moral concept of "inner religion," one might critically ask what such a so-called religion effectively has to do with love for God. If, for Kant, 'to love God' means, by definition, what is expressed in the moral command of gladness, then should we not conclude that this love as striving is led away from a *theo*-centric adherence? Rather, is this striving not topologically diverted towards the aesthetics of a human being's inner moral disposition where it should aim at holiness? Is not the concept of love of God structurally distorted as soon as it becomes transformed into the love (as an imperative concern) one has to have for one's own purified heart? In Kant's definition, the love of God equals what he in his *Religion* and in some *Reflections*[60] calls: rational self-love (*Vernunftliebe seiner selbst*) or moral self-love (*moralische Selbstliebe*). What he specifically means by this comes to light after the following conceptual analysis: "Like *love* in general, *self-love* too can be divided into love of *good will* [*Wohlwollens*] and love of *good pleasure* [*Wohlgefallens*] (*benevolentiae et complacentiae*), and both (as is self-evident) must be rational."[61] While excluding from the moral perspective the first, namely, *empirically conditioned* rational self-love,[62] Kant opts for a rational love of *good pleasure in oneself*. Then, excluding empirical conditions a second time, now with regard to this *complacentia*, Kant arrives at the following definition: "the maxim of self-love, of *unconditional good pleasure* in oneself (independent of gain or loss resulting from action), is... the inner principle of a contentment only possible for us on condition that our maxims are subordinated to the moral law... We could call this love a *rational love* of oneself [*Vernunftliebe* seiner selbst] [...]."[63] By this conceptual analysis, it is most

---

58 *Religion*, 65–73 (*Ak*. V, 44–53).
59 *id*., p. 79-81 (*Ak*. V, 60–62).
60 *Reflexions* 7199, 7249 in *Notes and Fragments*, Part 4: "Notes on Moral Philosophy", 462–463 (*Ak*. XIX 272–273), 474 (*Ak*. XIX, 294).
61 *Religion*, p. 66n (*Ak*. VI, 45n).
62 Kant does not do so in the *CrPrR*, 199 (*Ak*. V, 73) where he excludes the *Wohlgefallen an sich selbst* (*arrogantia*) (self-conceit) (*Eigendünkel*) and entertains instead the *Wohlwollen gegen sich selbst* (*philautia*) (self-love) (*Eigenliebe*) which he subordinates to the moral law and thus arrives at the concept of rational self-love (*vernünftige Selbstliebe*). See also *infra* § 3, B., the interpretation of the 'as yourself'.
63 *Id*., p. 66n (*Ak*. VI, 46n).

clearly shown that Kant's concept of love of God is indeed nothing but this *ego*-centric, rationally sublimated variation of *amor complacentiae* (a morally sublimated *Liebe des Wohlgefallens an sich selbst*).[64]

Looking back on Kant's construction of the concept of love of God based on the moral ideal of an imperatively constraining gladness, one will notice how he has managed a twofold transformation:

1. the 'holiness of the law' is transformed into 'law of holiness' ("be holy");
2. the 'love of the law' (gladness) is transformed into 'law of love'.

The first transformation initiates in Kant a replacement of the 'law of holiness' by a law of love for the holy law-giver. The second transformation initiates a similar replacement: the 'law of love' ascents into a law of love "for the professor thereof."[65]

Both replacements actually concern a leap which leads from an imperative egocentric rational/moral self-love to a fictitiously entertained so-called *theo*-centric love. In the end, this leap does not seem to be more than the imagination's projection of the abysmal depth of obligated moral self-love into an indefinite myth-like religious fiction about the origin of this obligation.

We conclude this part of our investigation by stating that the way in which Kant construed the concepts of moral obligation and the ideal aesthetic aim of gladness, both related to the idea of a divine Obligator, cannot possibly be taken to be an adequate basis for the introduction of any concept of love. Put differently, the obligated respect for the moral law in its holiness and, in virtue of a fictitious extension, for the holy law-giver, cannot possibly transfigure itself into the affective appeal of an inclination called love.

C. A Theological Principle Of The Duty Of Love Of God: God's Love For Us

1. Love deduced from God's goodness

Surprisingly, around the time of the publication of his *Metaphysics of Morals*, Kant proposed, simultaneously, a quite different basis for the introduction of the concept/duty of love (of God and, consequently, of neighbour) into his ethical theory.

---

64 It could be interesting to compare this concept of rational self-love as good pleasure in oneself (*complacentia*) with the idea of contentment with oneself (*Selbstzufriedenheit*) from the Second *Critique*: "a word that does not denote enjoyment, as the word happiness does, but that nevertheless indicates a satisfaction with one's own existence, an analogue of happiness that must necessarily accompany consciousness of virtue" (*CrPrR*, 234 (*Ak*. V, 117).
65 As expressed in *Lectures on Ethics*-Vigilantius § 143, 442 (*Ak*. XXVII, 720).

As extensively evidenced in the Vigilantius-*Lectures on Ethics* § 143, in his attempt to ground the duty of love of God (until now understood as *genitivus objectivus*), Kant switches to a theological basis: God's love for us (*genitivus subjectivus*).[66] He brings this new basis to the fore by successively exploring, first, the theological concepts of the 'end of creation' and providence, revealing thereafter the moral presupposition of these theological concepts. Then, from this moral presupposition, he finally 'deduces' the imperative meaning of the duty of love. The following passage is quite clear:

> If we are to think, morally, that we love God, then it is necessary for us to presuppose His love for us, and His will for our well-being, or His loving-kindness. For no return of love can be elicited there, if the command to that effect does not itself arise from moral love. This is also, however, explicable, if we were able to view religion, objectively considered, as the divine legislation of our duties, and to reduce the whole of religion to that; from which it again follows that religion is rooted in the love of God. Now every *potestas legislatoria* presupposes that the law-giver be well disposed towards his subjects, and hence that in virtue of this he intends their well-being; for only through such an intention is he in a position to bind us.[67]

Instead of basing (unsuccessfully) the meaning of love on the mere concept of duty as a practical category of modality, the duty of love is now grounded – more successfully in our provisional opinion – on a theologico-metaphysical idea of goodness (divine *amor benevolentiae*). Actually, with regard to this last foundational idea, Kant presupposes implicitly his doctrine of the postulate of God's existence (*bonum originarium*), which, in turn, is deduced as a condition of possibility from the practical idea of *summum bonum*. Essential to this deduction is the idea of God's benevolence: "[T]herefore, the highest good in the world is possible only insofar as a supreme cause of nature *having a causality in keeping with the moral disposition* is assumed."[68] The foundational character of the idea of divine beneficence is reaffirmed in the following: "[O]nly from a will that is morally perfect (holy and beneficent) and at the same time all-powerful, and so through harmony with this will, can we hope to attain the highest good, which the moral law makes it our duty to take as the object of our endeavors."[69]

---

66 Kant also touches on this succinctly in *M.M./Virtue,* 600 (*Ak.* VI, 488), see also *Religion,* 80 (*Ak.* VI, 60–61) where he comments on, in the frame of his philosophical christology, the sayings: *"For God so loved the world," "In this was manifested the love of God towards us"* (from John 3, 14 and 1 John 4, 9–10).
67 *Lectures on Ethics*-Vigilantius § 143, 442–443 (*Ak.* XXVII, 720).
68 *CrPrR*, 240 (*Ak.* V, 125) (italics mine).
69 *CrPrR*, 244 (*Ak.* V, 129). Contrary to his argument in the *M.M./Virtue,* § 38 and "Conclusion," establishing the *momentum* of recognition as 'duty of religion', Kant in the Second *Critique* establishes this recognition on the postulatory basis of God's exist-

With respect to the duty of love, both components – duty and love – get by this idea of God's benevolence an original and, at the same time, originating theologico-metaphysical basis. The concept of duty, namely, is in this regard transformed into the representation of a binding obligation derived from the awareness of divine goodness: "from the notion of the sum of all our duties, we ascend to the source of laws, and persuade ourselves that He has given them to us out of His goodness."[70] Moreover, "[H]is kindly will [is seen] as *the basis of the force that binds us* to follow His laws for the sake of our own welfare."[71] The concept of love in turn undergoes a similar transformation; it becomes 'love in return': "God's love for us (also expressed by the words: *God is love*) is thus the divine benevolence and kindness toward us, which constitutes the foundation of the *potestas legislatoria divina*. Now to return that love is the corresponding duty of all His subjects, and constitutes the prime source of any disposition to religion."[72]

In sum, in this presentation (in the *Lectures on Ethics*), it is the postulated *theological* idea of God's goodness that figures as the only adequate basis for eliciting in us the affective (compulsory) appeal of love of God.

2. God's goodness limited by justice

With regard to this concept of God's goodness, Kant significantly makes a very important and far-reaching critical remark. As he states in the "Concluding Remark" of the "Conclusion" in the *Metaphysics of Morals*:

> The divine end with regard to the human race (in creating and guiding it) can be thought only as proceeding from love, that is, as the *happiness* of human beings. But the principle of God's will with regard to the respect (awe) due him, **which limits the effects of love,** that is, the principle of God's right, can be none other

---

ence and His benevolence (see 243–244, *Ak*. V, 129). Therefore, it appears rather strange (or is it an anticipation?) why in this book he already referred to 'God's commands' in the chapter on the moral incentives (207, *Ak*. V, 83) before he has construed the meaning of the moral idea of God in general. This anticipatory reference to a religious idea becomes for Schopenhauer, in his critique of the *Critique of Practical Reason*, clear evidence "dass Kant *die imperative Form* der Ethik, also den Begriff des Sollens, des Gesetzes und der Pflicht, ohne weiteres aus der theologischen Moral herübergenommen, während er Das, was diesen Begriffen dort allein Kraft und Bedeutung verleiht, doch zurücklassen musste" [*Preisschrift über die Grundlage der Moral*, § 6: *Vom Fundament der Kantischen Ethik*. Mit e. Einl., Bibliogr. u. Reg. hrsg. von Hans Ebeling, (Hamburg: Felix Meiner Verlag, 1979), 31].

70 *Lectures on Ethics*-Vigilantius, 444 (*Ak*. XXVII, 721–722).
71 *id*., p. 443 (*Ak*. XXVII, 720) (italics mine).
72 *id*., p. 443 (*Ak*. XXVII, 720–721).

than that of justice. To express this in human terms, God has created rational beings from the need, as it were, to have something outside himself which he could love or by which he could also be loved.[73]

Kant here subordinates the principle of God's will as beneficence (His *benignitas*) to the principle of God's will as justice. Justice is stated as "the limiting principle"[74] with which accords, in a conditioning manner, God's love and beneficence with human happiness as *praemium* or *remuneratio gratuita*. From this, a most important conclusion must be drawn: in Kant, an ethics of justice rules simultaneously, both in his moral religion (which is a religion of love (for the moral law) by which I make myself worthy of happiness) and his moral theology (which is a theology of a God of love as kindly sustainer and ruler of nature). The repeatedly affirmed predominance of the idea of justice in these religious and theological matters ultimately yields a religion of godly fear as well as a theology of a God as righteous judge.

In the final section of our investigation, we will interpret this conclusion in combination with the results of our former analyses and finally arrive at a more encompassing critical judgment regarding Kant's moral philosophy and theology of love.

3. The Second Commandment: Menschenliebe in its Universality

A. Love to others: feeling and benevolence

How does Kant interpret the second commandment, "Love thy neighbour as thyself"? In this matter, Kant, as he did in the former religious part, entertains a twofold style of argumentation. His understanding of *Menschenliebe* as a duty in the *Metaphysics of Morals,* "Part II: Metaphysical first principles of the doctrine of virtue" differs significantly from how he grounds *Menschenliebe* in the *Lectures on Ethics* (Vigilantius).

Attempting to give the concept of love of human beings (*Menschenliebe*) a position in relation to the concept of duty, Kant, in the "Introduction" to the first work, balances between counting it as one of the "*Concepts of what is presupposed on the part of sensibility by the mind's receptivity to concepts of duty as such*"[75] and

---

73 *M.M./Virtue*, 600 (*Ak.* VI, 488)(bold emphasis mine).
74 *M.M./Virtue*, 600 (*Ak.* VI, 489).
75 *M.M./Virtue,* "Introduction XII," 528 (*Ak.* VI, 399)(my translation) (the title in the German original is as follows: *Ästhetische Vorbegriffe der Empfänglichkeit des Gemüts für Pflichtbegriffe überhaupt*). My translation of the German *Ästhetisch* into sensibility avoids an ambivalent understanding of the term feeling, used by the translator Mary Gregor, because (moral) feeling is counted as one of the concepts under discussion.

counting it as a love that must be posited as an authentic duty. In accordance with the former, Kant states that love of one's neighbour is one of the four moral endowments[76] (*Beschaffenheiten*) that are "*subjective* conditions of receptiveness to the concept of duty."[77] In this aesthetic understanding, "there is no obligation to have these" [*scil.* love of one's neighbour].[78] Conversely, in his "Doctrine of the elements of ethics," among the "Duties of virtue to others,"[79] Kant brings the (imperfect) duty of love to other human beings (philanthropy) to the fore as the duty on which he puts the full imperative weight of maxim of moral comportment, namely, active benevolence.[80]

This variation between "*aesthetischer Vorbegriff*" and "*moralischer Pflichtbegriff*" concerning love, is Kant's philosophical attempt to deal with love both as a feeling and as a moral obligation. As a feeling (*amor complacentiae*), love cannot be considered as a duty; however, considered as a duty (*amor benevolentiae*), love cannot be reduced to a feeling. As a feeling, "that is, as pleasure in the perfection of others,"[81] love is presupposed (*Vorbegriff*) in making the mind susceptible to concepts of duty as such. As a concept of duty, love is the determination of the will's maxim "to make other's ends my own (provided only that these are not immoral)".[82]

Amor benevolentiae is indirect (as it is mediated by the determination of the law of duty: "For benevolence always remains a duty"[83]), whereas *amor complacentiae* is direct, which means that it is a pleasure (delight) yielded immediately by the mere representation and reflection of some philanthropic beneficence.

Treated as a feeling, love that is delight (*Wohlgefallen*) belongs to the aesthetic domain of pleasure and pain (*amor complacentiae*). In this aesthetic sense, love as delight is either non-practical (mere *complacentia*) or it is, as an effect, originated by benevolence (*amor benevolentiae*; *Wohlwollen*). It sounds very Aristotelian to hear Kant saying in this last (practical) respect: "[D]*o good* to your fellow human beings, and your beneficence will produce love of them in you (as an aptitude of the inclination to beneficence in general)."[84]

---

76 "*Moral feeling, conscience, love* of one's neighbor, and *respect* for oneself (*self-esteem*)" (*ibid.*)
77 *Ibid.*
78 *Ibid.*
79 *M. M./Virtue,* Part II, 568ff (*Ak.* VI, 448ff).
80 Expressed in its negative form, Kant states "Failure to fulfill mere duties of love is *lack of virtue* (*Untugend*) (*peccatum*)." in *M. M./Virtue,* § 41 581 (*Ak.* VI, 464).
81 *M. M./Virtue,* § 25, 569 (*Ak.* VI, 449).
82 *M. M./Virtue,* § 25, 569 (*Ak.* VI, 450).
83 *M. M./Virtue,* Introduction XIIc, 530 (*Ak.* VI, 402).
84 *M. M./Virtue,* Introduction XIIc, 531 (*Ak.* VI, 402) (translation modified).

B. "As myself"

Kant's proposition that *amor benevolentiae* also includes myself (*cfr.* "Love your neighbour *as yourself*") is based on a perfect duty's inner qualification, namely, that the maxim carries in itself the universality of a law. Kant writes: "[t]he law making benevolence a duty will include myself, as an object of benevolence, in the command of practical reason... [L]awgiving reason, which includes the whole species (and so myself as well) in its idea of humanity as such, includes me as giving universal law along with all others in the duty of mutual benevolence, in accordance with the principle of equality."[85]

In Kant's ethics of virtue, we are here confronted with a quite peculiar issue. In this case ("myself as an object of benevolence"), what can be morally defined (by practical reason) as the *bonum* at which *benevolentia* is intentionally aiming? Which end can be denoted, materially speaking, to be a duty of virtue, i.e., a duty of love towards myself, taking into account the condition of universality? It amounts to the question of which self as an end is involved in this moral willing? In chapter VIII and in the diagram designed in chapter XI of the "Introduction to the doctrine of virtue," Kant proposes in this regard: "My own *perfection*" as "*My own end* which is also my duty."[86] The content of this ideal of perfection related to the self, or the perfected moral aim of self-love consists of two parts: first, *natural* perfection, and second, the *cultivation of morality* in us.

Natural perfection is presented as "the duty, to make ourselves worthy of humanity by culture in general, by procuring or promoting the capacity to realize all sorts of possible ends, so far as this is to be found in the human being himself."[87] In this regard, Kant proposes the following law for maxims of actions: "Cultivate your powers of mind and body so that they are fit to realize any ends you might encounter."[88] Myself as object of *amor benevolentiae*, i.e., the self that is submitted to this law of natural self-perfection equals myself *quoad* subject of culture and happiness[89] (in permitting[90] me to strive for good fortune). On the other hand, the *cultivation of morality* in us – "[t]he greatest perfection of a human

---

85 *M. M./Virtue*, § 27, 570 (*Ak.* VI, 451).
86 *M. M./Virtue*, Introduction XI, 527 (*Ak.* VI, 398) and. *id.*, VIII, 522–523 (*Ak.* VI, 391–393).
87 *M. M./Virtue,* Introduction VIII, 522–523 (*Ak.* VI, 392).
88 *Id.*, p. 523 (*Ak.* VI, 392).
89 This is Kant's moral version of his presentation of happiness and culture in his *Critique of Judgment* § 83: "On the Ultimate Purpose That Nature Has as a Teleological System," translated with an introduction by Werner S. Pluhar (Indianapolis: Hackett Publishing Company, 1987) [hereafter *CrJ*], 317–321 (*Ak.* V, 429–434).
90 Here we have one of the special cases in his ethical theory (see also Kant on sexual love, in *M. M./Virtue*, § 7, 548–550 (*Ak.* VI, 424–426)) in which he brings a *permissive* law (*Erlaubnisgesetz*) of morally practical reason to the fore: "lawgiving reason... *permits* you to be benevolent to yourself on the condition of your being benevolent to every other as well" [*M. M./Virtue*, 570 (*Ak.* VI, 451)].

being is to do his duty *from duty* (for the law to be not only the rule but also the incentive of his actions)"[91] – is an engagement of the noumenal self (*homo noumenon*), myself being with all other members of a moral (intelligible) world.[92] As already explored above, this noumenal self equals myself *quoad* subject of virtuousness that is submitted to the law of moral self-love.[93]

In sum, obeying the principal requirement of universality, Kant perfectly parallels or unites the duty of self-love ('as yourself') with the duty of 'love your neighbour' as follows:

1. in respect of *natural* perfection, Kant states as a duty "to make other's [my neighbour's] ends [of culture and happiness] my own" *as* I have to assume for myself as an end (that is also a duty) the cultivation of my capacities for furthering ends [of culture and happiness].
2. in respect of *moral* perfection, Kant expresses the unity of both in his well-known principle from the *Groundwork*: "*So act that you use humanity, whether in* **your own** *person or in the person of* **any other**, *always at the same time as an end, never merely as a means.*"[94]

C. A Theological Principle For The Second Commandment

Reviewing the overall structure of the argumentation Kant used concerning the commandment "love your neighbour as yourself" in his *Doctrine of Virtue*, it is obvious that he grounded both components of it (one's own perfection and the happiness of others) exclusively on "principles given a priori in pure practical reason."[95] Yet, in the *Lectures on the Metaphysics of Morals*,[96] he grounds the second commandment on an explicit *theological* basis. He states: "[F]rom the love for God, the second commandment, to love thy neighbour as thyself, is known by inference."[97] As we explained above, the human being's love for God was in its turn deduced ('love in return') from God's goodness. Hence, "the source of all love is the commandments given to us out of God's goodness."[98] What in Kant's

---

91 *M. M./Virtue*, Introduction VIII, 523 (*Ak.* VI, 392).
92 See *Groundwork of the Metaphysics of Morals*, 83, 87 (*Ak.* IV, 433–434, 438).
93 Cfr. *supra*, "§ 2, B.2. Inner religion as rational self-love." This law holds evidently as a moral law on its own, irrespective of the religious meaning that Kant confers on it, cfr. *supra* the examination of the concept of gladness, "§ 2, B.1. Gladness and holiness."
94 *G. M. M.*, 80 (*Ak.* IV, 429) (bold emphasis mine).
95 *M. M./Virtue*, "Introduction III: On the basis for thinking of an end that is also a duty", 517 (*Ak.* VI, 385).
96 Notes taken by J.F. Vigilantius in *Lectures on Ethics*, Part IV, 249–452 (*Ak.* XXVII, 479–732).
97 *Id.*, p. 444 (*Ak.* XXVII, 722).
98 *Ibid.*

published *Metaphysics of Morals/Doctrine of Virtue* is called "the obligatory making of my neighbour's ends my own" ("love thy neighbour") is now deduced from the following theological premise: "God loves all men, i.e., He makes their welfare His end; now in that we make this end of His into our own, we love all men, and since this consists in observing all our duties, and thus primarily the duties to oneself, we love ourselves for the sake of other men, or others as oneself."[99] If we combine this with a previous conclusion that we formulated concerning love for God,[100] we are now able to complete this by stating that Kant entertains the same postulated idea of God's goodness which is likewise to be the only adequate source from which is elicited in us the affective (compulsory) appeal of love for others as ourselves. Divine goodness is taken as a postulate twice, i.e., it serves both horizontally and vertically as the ultimate ground of the duty of love, recognized in both cases as a divine commandment.

4. Struggling with the Noumenal Freedom in Practical Love: Emotions and Passions

As a last investigation, let us look into Kant's anthropological study, *Anthropology from a pragmatic point of view*,[101] and into how he treats in this work the concept of love in the chapters on emotions (*Affekten*) and passions (*Leidenschaften*). As this book of 1798 is specifically conceived of "from a pragmatic point of view," Kant constantly focuses on "observed human characteristics ["in the Interior as well the Exterior of man"[102]] which are of practical consequence."[103] This opens the following perspective regarding our theme. Kant, in this work, examines the anthropological phenomena of emotions and passions specifically in relation to his already established practical philosophy (*scil.* of love). Hence, whereas in the moral domain proper Kant treated the topic of practical love fundamentally as being "a morally practical relation to human beings... that is, a relation of free actions in accordance with maxims that qualify for a giving of universal law,"[104] here, in an anthropological domain, he confronts emotions and passions with the proposition of moral freedom in matters of practical love. On this *topos* of con-

---

99 *Ibid.*
100 See *supra* "§ 2, C.1. Love deduced from God's goodness".
101 Translated by Victor Lyle Dowdell, with an Introduction by Frederick P. Van de Pitte (Carbondale & Edwardsville, Southern Illinois University Press, 1978) (hereafter *Anthropology*).
102 Inserted from *Anthropology*, Part One: "Anthropological Didactic. On the Art of knowing the Interior as well as the Exterior of Man", 7 (*Ak.* VII, 125).
103 *Id.* p. 6 (*Ak.* VII, 121).
104 *M. M./Virtue*, § 27, 570 (*Ak.* VI, 451).

frontation – emotions and passions confronted with moral freedom in man – the phlegmatic philosopher of Königsberg sees no possibility at all of bestowing on emotions and passions any positive energetic *momentum* in the fulfilment of one's duties. Rather, quite the reverse is the case: "One can easily see that passions do the greatest harm to freedom; and if emotion is a delirium, then passion is an illness which abhors all medication. Therefore, passion is by far worse than all those transitory emotions which stir themselves at least to the good intention of improvement; instead, passion is an enchantment which also rejects improvement."[105] In the same emotional style of abhorrence, Kant continues: "Emotion produces a momentary loss of freedom and self-control. Passion surrenders both, and finds pleasure and satisfaction in a servile disposition [*Sklavensinn*]. But because reason does not desist from its summons to inner freedom, the unfortunate victim is suffering under the chains from which he cannot free himself because they have already grown into his limbs, so to speak."[106] In the following quote, Kant illustrates his moral condemnation of the passions with an example that refers to love:

> [P]assions are not, like emotions, merely *unfortunate* moods teeming with many evils, but they are without exception *bad* (*böse*). Even the most well-intended desire if it aims (according to matter) at what belongs to virtue, for instance, to beneficence [*Wohltätigkeit*], is nevertheless (according to form), as soon as it changes to passion, not merely *pragmatically* pernicious, but also *morally* reprehensible.[107]

What makes passions morally reprehensible is their impact on the form in which maxims of the will should be synthesized with pure practical reason. If in the faculty of desire's formatting of maxims, reason is hindered in legislating by its law because of an overpowering inclination, the upshot will be a reversal of the moral order as regards the incentives of a *free* power of choice.[108] Curing oneself of these passions, i.e., from this "cancerous harm for pure practical reason",[109] can only consist in re-establishing "the sovereignty of reason"[110] and eliminating (regarding emotions) "the want of reflection"[111] [*Unbesonnenheit*]. Agreeing with the Stoics, Kant brings *the principle of apathy* to the fore: "in cases of moral apathy feelings arising from sensible impressions lose their influence on moral feeling only because respect for the law is more powerful than all such feel-

---

105 *Anthropology* § 80, 172 (*Ak*. VII, 265–266).
106 *Id*. § 81, 174 (*Ak*. VII, 267).
107 *Ibid*. (translation corrected).
108 See *Religion*, Part One, Chapter II: "Concerning the propensity to evil in human nature", 54 (*Ak*. VI, 30).
109 *Anthropology* § 81, 173 (*Ak*. VII, 266) (translation corrected)
110 *Id*., § 73, 155 (*Ak*. VII, 251).
111 *Id*., § 75, 158–159 (*Ak*. VII, 254).

ings together."[112] Making this principle of apathy efficient requires an *ethical gymnastics* which "consists only in combating natural impulses sufficiently to be able to master them when a situation comes up in which they threaten morality; hence it makes one valiant and cheerful in the consciousness of one's restored freedom."[113] Under the regulation of the "the happy self-possession [*das glückliche Pflegma*] (in the moral sense),"[114] practical love is, in Kant's ethics of virtue, completely disempowered from every affective drive. In a frame of mind that is both valiant and cheerful,[115] practical love is finally reduced to a reflection-based, tranquil-minded and virtuous disposition of the will directed at letting the law of duty be its only incentive.

5. Recapitulation and Assessment: Love Languishing in Awe, Guilt and Justice

I will now, by way of conclusion, formulate a general evaluation of Kant's philosophy of love by bringing together in summary fashion all of the remarks that I have made in the previous sections.

The main framework in which Kant's philosophy on love is presented is his already established ethics of duty (*Groundwork of the Metaphysics of Morals* and *Critique of Practical Reason*) and, in the wake of this, his ethics of virtue (*Metaphysical first principles of the doctrine of virtue*).[116] At a crucial moment in the elaboration of this ethics based on the principle of autonomy of pure practical reason, Kant states: "the kernel of all [ethical] laws"[117] is an issue of love and this is primarily of a *religious* nature. Immediately rejecting every *pathological* interpretation (love as sensible inclination) with regard to this, Kant defines his religiously contoured concept of love in a *practical* sense as follows: the command "to love God above all" by definition means "to do what He commands *gladly*." On the basis of our previous analysis of this principal and multi-faced proposition, we come to the following pattern of assessments with regard to Kant's practical concept of love:

1. Love in Kant's *religious* understanding of it, i.e., understood as a virtuousness practising duties seen as God's commandments, on the level of incentives,

---

112 *M. M./Virtue, Introduction* XVI, 536 (*Ak*. VI, 408); cfr. *Anthropology* § 75, 158ff (*Ak*. VII, 253 ff).
113 *M. M./Virtue*, § 53, 598 (*Ak*. VI, 485).
114 *Anthropology* § 75, 158 (*Ak*. VII, 254).
115 Cfr. *M. M./Virtue*, §53, 597 (*Ak*. VI, 484).
116 Methodologically spoken, we should take account of the distinction between the ethical part in this philosophy and the anthropological part. However, as the latter is conceived of "from a pragmatic point of view", we integrate this into the former.
117 *CrPrR*, 207 (*Ak*. V, 83).

undergoes an *ethical reduction*; its essence boils down to a purified disposition of the heart called gladness.
2. Love in Kant's *theological* understanding of it, i.e., understood as a relation (*instar*) with regard to God, undergoes a *fictionalizing reduction*; the relation of love to God is essentially one with regard to a fictitious Obligator ("of which reason in giving universal laws is only the spokesman"[118]).
3. Love in Kant's *theonomical* understanding of it, i.e., understood as a relation inaugurated by God in His goodness, undergoes an *economical reduction*; this love is in its effects measured "within the limits of justice alone."
4. Love in Kant's *ethical* understanding of it, i.e., understood as a duty to others as to oneself, undergoes an *ego-centric reduction*; its essence is brought back to rational self-love.
5. Love in Kant's *voluntaristic* understanding of it, i.e., understood as *amor benevolentiae* effectuating beneficence, undergoes an *eudaimonistic reduction*; the love that aims at the end of well-being is directed to an inner noumenal awareness of self-contentment and delight (a sublimated *amor complacentiae*).
6. Love in Kant's *anthropological* understanding of it, i.e., understood as an emotional spring and passionate drive, undergoes a *naturalistic reduction*; it is devaluated to a pathological and slavish impulsion stripped of any personalistic significance.

In my opinion, Kant compromises the consistency of his concept of love – which typifies the kernel of all moral laws! – when he argues for the necessary transfer of morality to religion, expressed in the famous saying: "morality leads inevitably to religion."[119] As explained above, Kant actually acknowledges a double motive for this *inevitable* transfer. The necessity, namely, in virtue of which this transfer must be carried out is, in one case, a *subjective* necessity, and in the other it is an *objective* necessity. The former concerns the understanding of the *modality* of the constraint proper to the absolutely imperative moral law; the latter relies on the objective *content* (the perfected highest good) at which the autonomous lawgiving of pure practical reason aims. *Love* now, taken first, as to its modality, in its moral qualification as duty, evaporates completely as soon as it – necessarily! –must be seen as coming from a fictitious Obligator which inspires us to myth-like awe and guilt rather than to love. When taken, secondly, in relation to the objective content of imperative lawgiving reason (the highest good of which God's goodness is a necessary condition of possibility), love is substituted by justice. Once it is interpreted in its necessary relation with regard to God, moral self-love as the kernel of all virtuousness becomes solely the economical moral pre-condition to make myself *worthy* of Gods *praemia remunerantia*.[120] Through the concept of worthiness, a religion of love thus becomes a religion of justice. In this

---

118 *M. M./Virtue*, "Conclusion", 599 (*Ak*. VI, 487).
119 *Religion*, "Preface to the first edition", 36n (*Ak*. VI, 8n).
120 See Kant's *Lectures on Ethics* (–Menzer) on "Reward and Punishment," p. 53: "Actions which result solely from good disposition and pure morality are qualified for *praemia remunerantia*".

regard, Kant still amplifies the economics of justice while letting God, in addition to His rewarding us with *praemia* for our good moral disposition, pay a debt (*merces*) to be yielded from our good deeds towards others.[121]

6. A metaphysics of love beyond the Kantian limits of reason alone

A final critical remark that overarches all my previous assessments concerns the issue of *ontological provision*. Twice, Kant calls upon a theology in order to sustain his moral system of autonomy. Firstly, he postulates God's existence and goodness and by this sustains the possibility of the objective end-goal of all moral endeavours. Secondly, he calls upon a divine Obligator in order to sustain the categorical modality of all moral imperatives. Thus, in Kant's hands, theology is put at the service of an immanent metaphysics of freedom. Consequently, the idea of God, either as existent or merely fictitious, is thought of in a merely functional relevance. As this idea belongs to the noumenal realm of transcendent thought, it renders the service of providing a transcendent provision for morality's sake. Consequently, a metaphysical conflict arises when we take account of Kant's often repeated statement that "the reality of the intelligible world is given to us, and indeed as *determined* from a practical perspective, and [that] this determination, which for theoretical purposes would be *transcendent* (extravagant), is for practical purposes **immanent**."[122] The following metaphysical query is hereby opened, namely, whether a transcendence, thought to be at the immanent service of what is made up by pure reason's absolute autonomy, can be qualified to be called an authenticated transcendence. Can the transcendent help that is needed from within the immanent projects of an autonomous pure practical reason, be called the authentic transcendence of a living God Who appeals to us by His Word to be loved (in the love of others)? Any philosopher, whose audacity brings him to elucidate the biblical command of love, has to take account of the *hetero-allocutional origin* by which this Word originally reached mankind.[123] Does not

---

121 Cfr. *Id.*, p. 54: "[H]e may be regarded as one who pays men's debts. For services to others... place those others under a debt to us which they can in no way discharge and which God discharges for them... Thus we earn payment from others, but it is God who recompenses us."
122 *CrPrR*, "Critical Elucidation of the Analytic of pure practical Reason," 224 (*Ak.* V, 105) (bold italics mine).
123 In his work *Traces bibliques dans la loi morale chez Kant* (Paris, Beauchesne, 1986), Henri d'Aviau de Ternay criticizes Kant correctly for not having liberated "the spirit" of the law of holiness from its imperative character and hence not having grasped it as a law of freedom (*o.c.* p. 104–112). Unfortunately, in his criticism de Ternay remained blind to the major 'biblical trace' characteristic of the [biblical] law of love, namely, its hetero-allocutionary offspring.

the philosopher, in his sincere search for enlightenment lose his way towards discovering the original *topos* of this Word if he is not ready to assume the heterogonous character of this Word and its authority? Is Kant's enlightened concept of pure reason's autonomy together with this reason's attachment to immanence not critically discarding the mind's receptivity for a living Word which by itself reveals, on its own authority, a "God Who speaks"? In Kant, it is the representation of autonomy that regulates our understanding of God. Whereas in Schelling[124] (1809), for example, it is the representation of God that regulates our understanding of autonomy. Given Kant's statements, "to love God is to love one-self; to love one-self is to love God," the *ordo amoris* is, in his philosophy, enclosed within the circular structure enjoined by a self-authenticating autonomy. In Schelling's philosophy on human freedom, in contrast, the *ordo amoris* discloses itself from within a theology of creation.[125]

The upshot of this metaphysical remark might be the following query (suggested by Heidegger[126]): Which is the best philosophy (on love)? One is obviously right in expecting from the best philosophy – *love of wisdom* – that she must awaken a love that can lead man eventually "beyond himself"[127] into the profoundest wisdom. Personally, I have no feeling that Kant's love has seduced me in this way.

---

124 F. W. J. Schelling, *Philosophische Untersuchungen über das Wesen der menschlichen Freiheit und die damit zusammenhängenden Gegenstände*, Herausgegeben von Thomas Buchheim, (Philosophische Bibliothek Band 503) (Hamburg, Meiner, 1997). [English translation used: Schelling, *Of Human Freedom*, by James Gutman (Chicago: The Open Court, 1936)].

125 Cfr. in Schelling's theology of creation the following passage: "This Spirit, moved by that Love which it itself is, utters the Word which then becomes creative and omnipotent Will combining reason [*Verstand*] and longing [*Sehnsucht*]" (*Of Human Freedom*, 36).

126 In the "Introductory Remarks" to his commentary (1936) on Schelling's work on human freedom, Martin Heidegger, *Schelling's Treatise on the Essence of Human Freedom*, Translated by Joan Stambaugh (Ohio/Athens/London, Ohio University Press, 1985). After having praised Schelling's work as "one of the most profound works of German, thus of Western, philosophy" (*o.c.* pg. 2), Heidegger justifies his assessment stating that: "[Schelling] is questioning beyond man to that which is more essential and powerful than he himself: freedom, not as an addition and attribute of the human will, but rather as the nature of true Being, as the nature of the ground for beings as a whole" (*id.* pg. 9). What Heidegger in this quote so positively assesses with regard to Schelling's philosophy of freedom, holds intrinsically also for his philosophy of love.

127 As Heidegger states on the final page of his commentary on Schelling's *Freiheitsschrift*: "God is not debased to the level of man, but on the contrary, man is experienced in what drives him beyond himself" (*o.c.*, p. 164).

www.ingramcontent.com/pod-product-compliance
Lightning Source LLC
Chambersburg PA
CBHW051518230426
43668CB00012B/1654